AMERICAN COUNTY GOVERNMENT

with an annotated bibliography

JOHN C. BOLLENS

in association with

JOHN R. BAYES KATHRYN L. UTTER

Department of Political Science
University of California, Los Angeles

SAGE PUBLICATIONS, INC./BEVERLY HILLS, CALIFORNIA

This project was supported by Grant OER-042-G-66-5 from the U.S. Department of Commerce pursuant to the provisions (Sec. 301 [c]) of the Public Works and Economic Development Act of 1965.

For information address:

SAGE PUBLICATIONS, INC.
275 South Beverly Drive
Beverly Hills, California 90212

First Printing

Printed in the United States of America

Standard Book Number 8039-0011-2

Library of Congress Catalog Card No. 69-20118

TABLE OF CONTENTS

PART TWO

AN INQUIRY INTO THE COUNTY'S POLITICAL VITALITY:

A Research Design and Supporting Evidence

PART THREE

A BIBLIOGRAPHICAL COMMENTARY

Preface

American county government is a significant but little understood and often maligned unit. The conflicting appellations applied to counties, such as "the dark continent," "the dead Indian," "the headless wonder," "a government of rising importance," and "the local government of the future," stand as strong evidence of the lack of sufficient information and analysis about them. This book attempts to determine the current state of knowledge about counties and suggests research in this field that seemingly would be highly productive.

Part One is a review essay on the literature of county government. Starting with a summary portrayal of counties, it then makes a general appraisal of existing county research and presents an agenda of needed investigations. Part Two is concerned first with new approaches that might be useful in inquiries about counties and second—and largely—with a design for testing the political vitality of these units and evidence in support of the design. Part Three is a bibliographical commentary which describes and analyzes in text form the contents of a large number of books, monographs, articles, and public documents. Unusual among bibliographies, it is a full discussion of materials and not simply a group of listings or brief annotations. The focus is on items published since 1945, although certain earlier works are included that continue to be valuable or have not been superseded. Further details about the commentary appear on the page preceding its first entry.

Much of the work for this book was financed by a grant from the U.S. Department of Commerce pursuant to the provisions (Sec.

301(c)) of the Public Works and Economic Development Act of 1965, and acknowledgment of that support is gladly given here.

It is a pleasure to express appreciation to many people who contributed to the progress of this book. Kathryn Utter and John Bayes, who served as research assistants in the Department of Political Science, University of California, Los Angeles, were associated with me in this massive project. In recognition of their untiring efforts over many months, their names are included on the title page of this publication. I am also grateful to Virginia Franklin, Joan Messenger, Roger Durand, Terrell Manyak, and Orrie Wilner, who participated at various stages. Four faculty associates—Henry J. Schmandt, University of Wisconsin-Milwaukee, and John C. Ries, Harry M. Scoble, and Marvin Hoffenberg, University of California, Los Angeles—graciously commented on the research design concerning the county's political vitality during its development.

Numerous individuals were receptive to questions and requests during my cross-country field activity; although there are too many to name here, they certainly have my gratitude. Bernard Hillenbrand and Allen Moore of the National Association of Counties were very helpful. Lastly, but only in terms of listing, I want to extend my thanks to several librarians and their staffs—without their cooperation no book would have been produced: Barbara Hudson, Institute of Governmental Studies, University of California, Berkeley; Mary Ryan, Government Publication Service, and Dorothy Wells, Government and Public Affairs Reading Room, both of the University of California, Los Angeles; and Loretta Taylor, National Association of Counties.

Los Angeles —J. C. B.

PART ONE

THE LITERATURE

and

RESEARCH NEEDS:

An Analysis

AN OVERVIEW OF COUNTY GOVERNMENT

County governments are long-existing and well-established American political institutions that demonstrate great durability. In brief, they are units that over a span of many years were and still are there, and much of their present significance is tied to this fact. They are also virtually universal; they are present in practically all states, where almost without exception they encompass the entire area. Thus, most of what occurs in the United States, regardless of who has primary responsibility, takes place in counties, and county governments often affect and are affected by such developments.

There are 3,049 county governments, a total but little altered in recent years. In fact, during the first two-thirds of the current century, only slight, if any, change in the number of county governments has generally developed in individual states, which have from no counties at all to 254 of them. Occasionally two counties have been consolidated, a new county carved from an existing one, or county governments eliminated, as in various portions of Virginia which became independent cities (not within county boundaries), or throughout the state of Connecticut. These practices are the exceptions, however. In most states, county boundaries, laid out before the advent of modern technological improvements in transportation and communication, have long remained completely or largely static.

Vast variations are present in the areal size of counties. Some contain less than a hundred square miles (the smallest having twenty-four), many embrace several hundred, many others several thousand, and a few have tens of thousands of square miles. As a rule, the earlier-settled states have counties of smaller average area than the later-populated states. Tremendous territorial differences are also sometimes present in a single state. In New Mexico, for example, the range goes from 108 to 6,897 square miles.

Because a relatively small number of heavily populated counties contains a near majority of the nation's people (in 1967, 107 counties had almost 44 per cent of the total), the image of counties is often one of large population. In reality, however, the typical county has a small number of residents. More than three-fifths have fewer than 25,000 inhabitants, and almost one of every ten has less than 5,000. Yet, while some counties have only several hundred residents, Los Angeles County has in excess of seven million.

In a time of continuing population growth in the United States, many counties are experiencing increases but many others are facing losses. This mixed trend has a long-time history. In the decade of the 1930's, about one-third of the counties lost population; this proportion rose to about one-half in the following decade, and it maintained that level from 1950 to 1960. In this most recent decade, the less populous counties suffered most of the losses. Almost 85 per cent of the counties that decreased in population had fewer than 25,000 people, and about one-half of the declining counties were entirely rural. In comparison, less than 10 per cent of the counties with at least 50,000 people had a population decline.

Huge intercounty differences exist in expenditures, personnel, and services. Some counties spend as little as a couple of hundred thousand dollars yearly, have as few as two dozen employees, and provide simply a very limited number of services as an aid to the state government (for instance, election administration, recording, and assistance to state courts) and as a rural local government (for example, rudimentary law enforcement in unincorporated portions). At the other extreme, certain counties expend hundreds of thousands of dollars each year (in one instance, more than one billion), carry a personnel complement in the tens of thousands, and furnish an extremely wide variety of services and facilities.

The growth of county functions, which in turn has prompted increases in expenditures and personnel, is a prominent characteristic of American counties. Such functional expansion, however, has not generally resulted from the design and implementation of comprehensive plans to endow counties with extensive new responsibilities. Instead, it has almost always come about because counties were existing institutions to which additional tasks could be given on an individual, accretionary basis. In other words, counties were and still are there.

Two facts of life about counties have made them the natural center of many intergovernmental relations, thus contributing further to their significance. The first is that one of the original and continuing primary roles of counties has been to serve as the administrative functionary of the state government in carrying out certain statewide programs. This responsibility, which has broadened over the years, immediately cast counties into the midst of important intergovernmental affairs. The second fact is that counties straddle the boundaries of most other local governments, which gives them an areawide jurisdiction unmatched by other local units in general. A single jurisdiction of large territorial scope almost automatically must have relations with the few or many local units of smaller areal size located within its legal limits (such as in the case of municipalities, practically all of which lie inside counties). Such a jurisdiction, moreover, is often viewed by the national or state government as being attractive as an intergovernmental partner, since the nation or state may then deal with a single large unit rather than with a number of small jurisdictions in an area.

Many counties have two major formal deficiencies—often not of their own making. These are the drastic restrictions on their powers and the ramshackle nature of their organization and processes. As to powers, many counties are saddled with severe state constitutional and legislative limitations on their taxing and debt authority as well as on the substantive areas in which they may engage. Frequently states prescribe in great detail what counties may do and may not do, and the prescriptions are made without consideration of the usefulness of counties as local units.

As for organization and processes, many counties have obviously carried them down in basic outline from an ancient age, and they are insufficient for modern times. A lengthy list of elected officials (many handling administrative and routine jobs), a governing body (if it warrants such a title) with a mixture of legislative and executive and sometimes judicial functions, and, most important of all, the absence of a general executive, are characteristics of outmoded county organization. The lack of a general merit system and of up-to-date financial procedures and controls are frequent shortcomings in processes.

Many times defects in county organization and processes are rooted in state limitations. In these instances, by not providing either a grant of county home rule or permissive state legislation to give the counties latitude to reform, the state in actuality requires counties to have ramshackle structural and procedural arrangements. However, the blame for these county weaknesses does not always rest with the state. Sometimes the authority to reform has been conferred upon counties and has been used poorly or not at all.

In total, the significance of county governments is unquestionable. They spend approximately $10.8 billion annually, which is about one-fifth of the total for all local governments. They employ the full-time equivalent of approximately 950,000 people, which is about one-sixth of the local total. Collectively they provide a broad array of services and facilities, with a heavy concentration in the fields of welfare, highway, education, and hosptitals. The county is the primary general local government for many people; some do not live within city limits but in county unincorporated territory, and others reside in small cities and receive more local services from the county government than from the municipal government.

Overall, county governments are a mixed bag: they show signs of adaptability and inflexibility, of innovativeness and sluggishness, of being the most important local government of the future and of becoming practically lifeless. These contrasting characterizations are true of certain American counties, but one statement seems appropriate to all of them: As members of the late twentieth-century system of American government, they are in transition to increased or decreased political vitality. The question now appropriate to consider is whether research on the county up to the present time provides the knowledge required to make sound decisions about its future.

THE STATUS OF RESEARCH

The literature on county government may be delineated in various ways. It is structural, descriptive, and legalistic. It is prescriptive and pragmatic. Conversely, it is not systematic, behavioral, or theoretical. These adjectives do not apply to all written material about counties, but they are general characteristics. In sum, the literature is incomplete.

Writings on county government are scattered throughout a wide range of publications. Many are contained in so-called fugitive materials, which are issued in small quantities. These include monographs, research reports, and newsletters produced by university research bureaus and institutes, privately-financed governmental research organizations, national and state associations of counties and county officials (both of general membership and specialized activity), and legislative research and other government agencies. County-related materials are similarly found in a variety of periodicals, including those of the National Association of Counties and of a number of comparable state groups. Many general books on state and local government (commonly written as college texts), both those concerned with individual states and the nation in general, usually contain information about counties in a chapter devoted exclusively to them and in sections of other chapters. Other scattered references to county government appear in publications—mostly books—on elections, politics, and party organization. A few general volumes, usually written many years ago, are devoted entirely to counties.

The topics pertaining to county government in the literature are variegated. Discussions of practically everything about the county are presented—the use of television in maintaining sewer systems, the duties of the clerk, the county's relations with the state and national governments in administering public welfare programs, organizational features, its role in the governmental system of a particular state, and many others. Yet despite the variety, county government research is incomplete and generally lacks systematic, theoretical analysis.

Evaluations of Municipal Research

Until recently, all literature on local government suffered from the same deficiencies that currently are found in most writings on counties. More than a decade ago, Lawrence J. R. Herson (1957a) first attacked these failings by sharply criticizing municipal government textbooks, which, in his judgment, had the same weaknesses as municipal research in general. Professor Herson asserted that such research fell short of the "minimum requirements of systematic political science." He further claimed that it was largely an array of facts gathered with little concern for the construction of general theories, and that statements were often presented without regard for empirical data.

According to Herson, the authors of these texts considered municipal government from the viewpoint of the political reformers and classical public administration theorists of the early decades of this century. Accordingly, the study of municipal government had been based upon the doctrine of the separation of politics from administration, the gospel of efficiency, and other now-discredited principles of public administration. Furthermore, it had ignored the latent functions of municipal government, such as furnishing its citizens first-hand experience with the governmental process, and had instead emphasized structure and administration, thereby implying that the provision of services was the only function of city government. The authors were also charged with having elitist tendencies, since they assumed that the electorate was fogged, confused, and incapable of rendering an intelligent judgment on important questions. These writers also lauded the short ballot, council-manager government, and related reforms. An ideal or prototype government thus emerged from the textbooks. It consisted of a broad civil service system, single directors instead of boards, a chief administrator with the power to prepare the annual budget, and a city structure conforming to principles of administrative management. These principles included separation of policy and administration, at-large election, small legislative body, and strong mayor or manager.

The authors were further charged with employing imprecise methodologies. Herson held that they failed to integrate their materials with the general body of political science writing, such as the works of Key, Truman, Riesman, and others. They did not weigh and evaluate the evidence used to support their assertions and did not pursue their statements and commitments to their logical ends. They were committed to one-dimensional analysis since they failed to appreciate the complexities of any important political activity. In general, the textbooks made value judgments and prescribed the methods by which to attain these values without justifying them, specifying what other value judgments might be made, or taking into account values that might conflict with those selected.[1]

Some contemporary observers believe that Herson's views still have validity for municipal research. They maintain that such research, with some exceptions, continues to cling to the social engineering tradition, treating the post-war urban problems as difficulties to be dealt with largely by adjusting the legal and governmental machinery. For example, Norton Long (1967:243) has asserted that political science

> . . . has shown only fitful concern with making explicit the hypotheses underlying its prescriptions and submitting them to empirical test. . . . Herson's strictures . . . seem still applicable . . . . The prescriptions of political science for the city (and for local government generally) are still a piece with classical organization theory.

A number of others are more optimistic about the progress in municipal research. Wallace Sayre and Nelson Polsby (1965:123) have observed that ". . . the present decade has witnessed significant efforts to examine the city as a political system rather than a subject of reform." Henry Schmandt (1966:9-10) further points out that because of the growth of the behavioral movement within political science and the influence upon the field by sociology and social psychology, there ". . . has been a substantial upgrading of the quality of urban political research, so much so that earlier strictures against it are no longer valid."

Appraisal of County Research

Despite the probable decreasing validity of Herson's criticisms of municipal research, they still apply generally to research on county government. County research customarily employs a structural, legalistic, and descriptive approach and does not attempt to undertake systematic analysis within a theoretical framework. The literature often accepts state laws, constitutional provisions, ad-

1. William Anderson (1957:776-783) and Herson (1957b:783-784) engaged in a not-so-polite argument over the validity of Herson's criticisms of the municipal textbooks. Although Anderson was able to substantiate a few minor points of attack on the latter's methodology, with the exception of his criticism of the narrowness of Herson's definition of efficiency, Anderson was unable to attack any of his arguments directly.

ministrative orders, court decisions, organizational charts, and other official pieces of paper as descriptive of reality. For example, a publication may examine county finances mainly, if not solely, in terms of the legal limitations on the property tax and the prescribed duties of county financial officers, such as the assessor, auditor, and treasurer. On the other hand, the adequacy of county financial resources and the purposes for which revenues are expended may receive scant, if any, attention. Legal descriptions do not reveal actual practice. In a sense, the legal research determines what social goals have been enacted into law; however, much county research denies this purpose by interpreting laws to be descriptions of actual behavior rather than norms for government (Richards, 1954:273).

The emphasis in the literature upon the description of structure is directly related to the reformist orientation of much of the writing on county government. Undoubtedly, county organization and many processes (budgeting, personnel selection and administration, planning, purchasing, and others) frequently are archaic and in need of reform. Many who write about county government are concerned with showing the obsolescence of structure and processes in order to demonstrate the need for reform, but the changes they offer are those that reformers have been prescribing for at least a half century—county manager government, the short ballot, single appointed department heads, the merit system, and the like. They are the reforms which classical public administration theory dictates in the name of efficiency. However, virtually no empirical research has been done into the effects of these reforms on county governments that have adopted them. Many researchers on counties have become preoccupied with governmental form, rather than with community needs, desires, and resources. As Alan Richards (1954: 274) has pointed out, organizational changes may save money,

> . . . but they may also disrupt social structure, threaten the existence of groups, and even affect the community's mental health. Changes in forms of government may well be evaluated by criteria other than "economy and efficiency." Indeed, from the point of view of the total well-being of a community, a change in governmental form may prove detrimental even in the economic sense.

Another example of the lack of empirical analysis in the literature on counties is the paucity of behavioral research. Although behavioral methods have become widely-used and important research tools in the discipline of political science generally, only a very small, though significant, group of behavioral studies have been made of county government, politics, and elections.

Meaningful empirical investigation requires a systematic conceptual framework within which theories may be developed and hypotheses confirming or disproving them may be tested. Such a framework is needed so that empirical findings, both narrow and broad in scope, may be interrelated, research encouraged in unexplored areas, and present conclusions reevaluated in the future. The absence of an adequate structure for analysis in the literature of county government may largely account for the dearth of empirical analysis and theorizing in county government research.

A factor which helps to account for the structural, descriptive nature of county literature is that much of it is of a pragmatic and not academic origin. Many published materials on county government have been written as practical, informational guides for state legislatures, county charter commissions, county officials, and voters generally. Such documents stress legislation, procedures, organizational structure, and other formal matters. A large number of these guides have been issued by organizations not affiliated with institutions of higher education. Aside from some work being done in university governmental research bureaus and institutes, few political scientists or other scholars have done continuing research on county government. Much of the research related to counties has been incidental to the main purpose of the inquiry, which might be the study of intergovernmental relations, some aspect of political behavior, nonpartisan elections, or local public finance. With some major exceptions, little comprehensive research centering on county government has been done.

The preceding characterization of the existing literature seems to paint a dismal picture. However, all is not as dark as it might seem; there are some analytical, systematic, empirical studies which involve various aspects of county government. Among the scholars who have made such contributions are Boles and Cook (1959), Cape (1967), Fenton (1957), Hanson (1965), Jones (1962), Key (1962), Kitsos (1968), Spencer (1965), Stoner (1967), and Weidner (1960). Also, comprehensive descriptive studies may be of value in providing a framework and background information. Duncombe (1966) has completed the most recent general study of this type.

A RESEARCH AGENDA

The foregoing assessment of the status of written materials on county government indicates that much more research, especially of an analytical, theoretical nature, is required in the study of counties. A discussion of some of these pressing research needs follows.

Reform Movements

Several writers have probed into the history of counties from their origins as shires in Anglo-Saxon England to their evolution as subdivisions of modern American states. These historical treatments have stressed changes in structure, officers, powers, functions, number, and size of counties. However, little attention has been given to the sources of support of reform measures such as nonpartisan elections, the short ballot, manager government, and taxation and debt limitations. A better understanding of their historical origins and rationale might provide insights into their contemporary validity.

Actual Operations and Decision-Making

A great deal has been written about the structure of county government, particularly from a legal-formal standpoint. Many authors have set forth lengthy descriptions of the duties and responsibilities of the county governing body and various other county officials and boards, but few have looked at actual operations. Research is needed to determine the activities of county officials other than their legally specified duties; the patterns of relations among the county governing board, appointed officials, and elected officials; and the formulation of policy when formal decision-making power is fragmented. Inquiries should also be made into the type of control which the county governing board and chief executive, when the latter exists, actually exercise over county administrative agencies; what kinds of budgetary processes and financial planning are employed by counties; and other matters which cannot be determined simply by examining laws, court cases, and organizational charts. Moreover, research should also include case studies of the county decision-making process and behavioral (including attitudinal) studies of county governing bodies and other county officials and boards. Once such information is produced, county decision-making processes may be analyzed in the light of current organizational decision-making theories, such as those propounded by Herbert Simon, Charles Lindblom, and James March.

Integration and Disintegration

The literature contains much discussion of the need for modernized forms of county government that feature one of the several varieties of chief executives, either appointed or elected. Usually these forms also include the reduction in number of elective officers and the centralization of the budgetary process. However, little research has been undertaken to determine the actual administrative, political, economic, and social effects of these organizations in the limited number of counties where they have been adopted.

Although much emphasis has been placed in county research upon the slowness of organizational integration, a substantial countertendency has gone almost unobserved. A disintegration of county government has taken place through proliferation of independent and semi-independent boards, agencies, authorities, corporations, and dependent special districts (the last named, although responsible to the county governing body, have their own personnel, as distinguished from special assessment areas which operate within the regular county bureaucracy). The extent, nature, and effects of this trend in many county governments deserve examination.

New Services

County activities may be divided into those administered by departments that are under the direction of the traditional county officers (the assessor, clerk, auditor, sheriff, superintendent of schools, treasurer, and others) and those carried out by the newer departments that are managed by appointed heads. The latter departments are responsible for most of the service functions of county government, for example, public works, health, parks, recreation, and planning. Despite the greater importance of the new units, the traditional ones have received more research attention.

Service Performance and Composition

The most common approach to the study of county activities is to describe the legal duties of the officers responsible for them and the legal specifications for handling them. Some researchers have made admirable but incomplete descriptions of the nature of county functions in actual practice, but few have analyzed the level and effectiveness of their performance. A number of writers have sought to make informed judgments of level and effectiveness through interviews and limited field research. Some have presented certain data to support their judgments of county performances of selected activities. However, the literature does not contain any systematic attempts to account for intercounty variations in the level and effectiveness of performance of activities in general; here is a definite research need. In addition, much investigation is required to determine more clearly their nature; that is, what each activity involves and how its composition varies from state to state and county to county and differs according to social, economic, demographic, governmental, and other factors. Examples of such factors are economic base, per capita personal income, educational level of the population, proportion of white to nonwhite inhabitants, rate of population change, population density, governmental structure, and financial capability.

Trends in Activities

Aside from definite evidence that counties are generally rendering more services at higher levels of performance than in the past, almost no information is available in the literature on the trends in county activities. In fact, little is known even about which types of counties are increasing urban services. Perhaps only counties which have relatively large urban populations or are fast growing are increasing urban services and their experience is being generalized to all. Possibly rural counties or those with declining or relatively stable populations are not enlarging all kinds of services and may even be retrenching some of them. However, research evidence is insufficient to justify any generalization.

All sorts of information about trends in county activities would be useful. In addition to inquiries about absolute level of activities, research is needed to determine changes in their number and composition and how the relative importance of each varies with changes in economic, social, demographic, and governmental factors. In a similar vein, county activities may be classified into urban and non-urban and into those which do or do not contribute to economic development. Correlations might be made between the proportions of urban activities and economic development activities (the latter including education and conservation) and the above mentioned variables. Data needed for this kind of research are not readily available in published form, at least not on a national basis; the functional breakdown of county activities in the *Census of Governments* by the Bureau of the Census is too gross to make its employment and expenditure data adequate for such research.

Professionalization and Expertness

The increase in professionalization and the use of technical expertness are bringing vast changes to governmental services and administration, but very little research has been undertaken into the nature and effects of such changes at the local level and almost none concerning county government. Efforts should be made to discover the role of professionals and expertise in functional areas and what effects they have upon county government, notably in decision-making.

Finance

The literature contains much legalistic, descriptive material on county finances and much discussion of the problems associated with the heavy dependence of the county upon the property tax. However, more intensive examination of the sources of county revenues would be valuable. In particular, research should delve into trends in county revenues, including the emergence of new sources and the changing importance of traditional ones. Moreover, an examination might be made of revenue sources as they vary with economic, social, demographic, and governmental factors.

Of special importance would be a detailed consideration of intergovernmental revenues. At present, the amount of financial aid which counties receive from the national government is unknown for most states, since most of it is channeled through the states and is listed in census reports as state aid. As a consequence, the degree to which most states assist counties from their own sources is also unknown. Close comparative examination of state and national financial reports might shed light on the nature of national-state-county fiscal relations.

Another largely unexplored area of county finances is the amount of discretion counties possess in using their financial resources. A large proportion of county funds is earmarked, that is, dedicated for particular expenditure purposes. Earmarked revenues frequently include: state and federal grants-in-aid and their local matching funds; revenues, such as the gasoline tax, shared with the states; fees and charges for services rendered; portions of the general fund assigned to pay off bonded indebtedness; and property tax revenues from special assessments. When such revenues comprise a large part of county funds, flexibility in county budgeting is seriously hampered. Research is needed to determine the extent and effects of the earmarking of revenues and how they differ from county to county according to economic characteristics, such as assessed valuation and per capita personal income. Finally, since the literature gives little indication of the extent to which counties utilize their financial capacity, useful studies could be made of this subject.

Politics and Elections

Exploration of county politics and elections has been highly fragmentary. Much of the literature does not differentiate counties from other local governments and makes vague references to "local" politics and elections. Also, when many writers refer to local politics and elections, they appear to be drawing solely on the the experience of municipalities. This indefiniteness is, in fact, in itself a problem in much of the total literature of county government.

One of the most important topics in need of investigation is the relationship between county governmental and political leadership. A number of authors have mentioned that particularly in southern and border states a county official, for example, the sheriff or clerk, is often the head of the local political organization or machine or is the county boss. On the other hand, such an official may sometimes be merely a pawn for a county political machine, party organization, or political leader or boss.

Patronage or the spoils system is another often mentioned link between county political and governmental leaders. The traditional county government is reputed to be a major source of patronage jobs and spoils for loyal party or machine workers. Some writers have also discussed the use of county patronage to buy the votes of marginally-attached partisans. Merit systems have made at least some inroads into patronage in practically every county, and some counties (the exact number is not known, but it is probably 300 or 400) have adopted merit systems for nearly all county employees. Work should be done on the extent of use of merit systems and the effects of the decline of patronage on counties, especially on their political machines and party organizations.

In general, the literature gives a good but incomplete picture of the extensiveness and characteristics of county political machines. Information about them has limited comparability, however, since it is based on different approaches to the subject. To obtain more adequate knowledge of the role of the county machine, comparative study and analysis are required. Little has been done to assess the strength of county political machines or to determine whether they are really declining in importance.

Some interesting and significant research has been completed on the operations of political parties at the county level. However, most of the literature ignores actual operations in favor of a recital of state laws covering the party structure. These writings contain little information on how county party machinery is really organized and managed and about its role in county politics and elections.

Few investigations have been made to discover the basis of support for county political parties, particularly the inducements, other than patronage, they offer potential workers and supporters. Evidence is limited concerning the effects of nonpartisan local elections on campaigns for county offices and the part played by county party organizations in such elections. Further studies into all these matters would constitute significant contributions to the literature.

An area in which very little research has been done but which might prove fruitful is that of state-county political ties. A worthwhile inquiry is whether the position of the county as an administrative arm of the state is paralleled by political dominance of the state party in power over its county counterpart. In some states, notably in the border region, a representative—called either the statehouse or administration man—of the dominant state party organization or machine keeps watch over the activities of the county organization or machine of that party and seeks to keep it in line with state party interests. Also, fragmentary evidence can be found that county party organizations are oriented toward the state. In particular, county political organizations are frequently involved in campaigns for seats in the state legislature and less often for statewide offices. Party interest in the races for county and other local offices often suffers as a result of this involvement at the state level. Whether this identification with the state is increasing, particularly with the incursions being made by the merit system into county patronage, should be determined, and the nature and magnitude of such a trend, if it exists, should be ascertained. Furthermore, investigations into the roles of elected and appointed county officials in state politics and political parties and of state legislators in county politics and party organizations should be carried out.

Power and Influence

Various writers have mentioned some of the individuals and groups which influence the county decision-making process. Together, these influentials are often irreverently referred to as the "courthouse gang." This gang, the exact composition of which differs from county to county, is said to be the most powerful political force in county government. Lancaster (1952:57) has well described such a clique as ". . . a more or less permanent group of elective and appointive officeholders together with private individuals whose business normally brings them in contact with public officials."

Some researchers have found that county governing board members are very powerful in matters affecting the districts from which they are elected. They can be particularly jealous of their power to control road and highway work in their districts and use this authority as a source of personal influence. Often county officials gain power beyond the prerogatives of their offices as a result of being entrenched in their positions so long that they gain extensive knowledge of county affairs and widespread contacts with people who affect county government.

Although the literature presents some valuable leads about the characteristics of county power and influence, it is still incomplete. Much more information about what groups are important and how they operate within the county power structure is required, as is knowledge about the roles of both elected and appointed county officials in such a system. Only a limited number of case studies on county government have analyzed the county power structure, and they have used such diverse methods of data collection and analysis as to make comparison practically impossible. Case studies of county power structure should be undertaken with the use of a uniform research method so that comparative analysis would be possible. Only after the various forms of county power structure are differentiated is it possible to find the underlying social, demographic, economic, legal, institutional, and cultural patterns lying behind these variations.

Accountability

Any democratic government must be accountable to the electorate, and an equitably apportioned governing board is a requisite of accountability. The U. S. Supreme Court in the Midland County decision of 1968 applied the "one man, one vote" principle to county governing boards by requiring that their members who are elected by districts must represent approximately equal numbers of people. Much speculation abounds, but only beginning research has been presented concerning the effects on county boards. In the case of state legislative reapportionment, more effective representation of urban interests was predicted. However, experience thus far has not borne this out to the extent assumed. Whether county experience will parallel that of a number of state legislatures is a moot point, and only further research will give an answer.

Another requirement for public accountability is the availability of adequate public information, through accounts of activities in the communication media and formal governmental reports. Most writers have agreed that, judged by these criteria, county government is not very accountable; they often term the situation as one of very low visibility. However, more research is necessary to determine the characteristics of counties that have relatively high or low visibility. In addition, the kinds of public information that would make a county more visible should be determined.

Office Competition and Voting

Closely connected with accountability, but broader in scope, are the questions of competition for office and voting in county elections. Several researchers have reported that the lack of competition for many county offices has produced numerous entrenched officeholders. Very skimpy competition has often been present for offices whose duties are primarily administrative, technical, or clerical, such as the assessor, auditor, surveyor, and treasurer. These officers have often held their positions for many years without facing effective electoral challenge. Such a lack of opposition may lead to insufficient accountability and mediocre performance of duties. Some writers have declared that many entrenched county officers resist reform of county organizational structure, since they fear that renovation might destroy the little provinces of power which they have been able to demarcate for themselves. Great in-depth inquiry into the extent of lack of competition and comparative research into its effects on the effectiveness of county government would be of immense value.

Voting is closely related to both competition for office and accountability. Many writers have noted the relatively low turnout of voters for county elections, though a few have reported the opposite under special conditions. Low turnout may reflect lack of competition and is probably also closely related to the low visibility of county government. Moreover, although the point is debatable, such a turnout is a likely cause of low accountability. Low voter turnout thus may be both a cause and an effect of the generally low level of accountability of county government. However, without further research on the extent of voting in county elections, these generalizations cannot be substantiated. Behavioral research into a number of other topics related to elections and voting at the county level would also be useful. Among the topics which should be considered are the effects of nonpartisanship (where it exists) on voting, the degree of party loyalty in voting, and the relationship between economic, social, demographic, and governmental characteristics of counties and voter turnout.

Intergovernmental Relations

To gain a fuller knowledge about county government, its role in the system of federal-state-local relations—which Daniel J. Elazar calls "the American partnership"—must be studied. Much has been written about county intergovernmental relations, largely in terms of formal relations. Particular attention has been given to the description, and somewhat less to the analysis, of the legal formal relationships between county and state governments. The status of the county as a legal subdivision of the state has been the focus of most of this writing. Much investigation into the nature of state financial aid, technical assistance, and administrative regulation of county activities remains to be done. The states exercise supervision over certain county activities, including public health, welfare, and financial administration. Research is needed to determine the extent of such supervision and its effects on the county's ability to exercise discretion.

Federal-Aid Programs

A considerable amount of legal, descriptive material has been produced on federal-aid programs that are important to county government, especially the long established ones in public health, welfare, and highways. The impacts of these programs on local government generally have been analyzed, but little has been done to assess their effects on county government specifically. In fact, many commentators disagree on the nature of this impact. Some believe the strictness with which the national government limits the purposes for which federal grants may be used and the tightness of federal supervision over local administration of federally-aided programs severely restrict local innovation and initiative and the flexibility necessary to adjust to local needs. On the other hand, other observers stress that federal grant-in-aid programs have allowed local governments to undertake activities which they could not otherwise afford and that local administration has brought greater flexibility into the administration of national policy than if the programs were carried out by a national bureaucracy.

This dispute demonstrates the need for further research on the nature of the impact of federal-aid programs on county government, especially since the states act as intermediaries in many important county programs receiving federal aid. Little is known about the role of the states in these programs, even in terms of the amount of financial support they add to federal money. As previously mentioned, federal and state financial reports do not separate state from federal aid when reporting financial statistics on programs in which the states act as intermediaries. However, comparative study of these reports might yield these data. Little is also known about federal technical and nontechnical assistance to county government; this, too, is a fruitful field for study.

Interlocal Relations

Another realm of county intergovernmental relations centers around its interactions with other local units. One form of such interlocal relations are contract services provided by the county to municipalities within its boundaries. This has greatest use in Los Angeles County, where, under the Lakewood Plan, a number of cities contract for most of their services from the county government. Although much discussion has been held about the use of contract services to provide economies of scale, while preserving local governmental autonomy, little general information is at hand about the extent and nature of their use. Studies have been made of the device in a few counties, but they are the exceptions. The contract idea has been mentioned frequently as a means for expanding the volume and scope of county activities and as a means for coordinating local government services, thereby providing a partial substitute for metropolitan government. Thus, it seems necessary to study on a nationwide basis the provision by counties of contract services. Somewhat less written material, mostly legal and descriptive, is devoted to enterprises and services provided jointly by counties with one another or other local units. Since these are mechanisms which are believed to enhance quality and efficiency of local services, they also deserve more study.

County relations with special districts represent another case of county-local relations. First, counties often have representatives on metropolitan district governing boards. Second, county governing boards often serve *ex officio* as the directors of dependent special districts, which range in size from countywide to less than a few square miles. Because of these close associations between counties and some special districts, the nature of their relationships is of great interest. A few studies dealing with special districts contain valuable, but far from complete, investigation of county-district relations. More research, notably on county relations with metropolitan and dependent districts, would be worthwhile.

Research into informal intergovernmental relations scarcely exists. Informal relations largely consisting of contacts between county officials and those of other governments are different from formal agreements, contracts, and methods of financial assistance. Many of the informal contacts are made for the purpose of obtaining information or coordinating activities. However, at least one study contains some information about informal county intergovernmental relations (Weidner, 1960). Further research in this area could contribute importantly to a fuller understanding of county government.

Few behavioral studies have been made of county intergovernmental relations. Three studies have examined, through survey questionnaires, the views of public officials from all levels of government on intergovernmental relations (Weidner, 1960; U. S. Senate Committee on Government Operations, 1965a; U. S. Senate Committee on Government Operations, 1965b) and have provided some very interesting and useful data relating to county intergovernmental relations. More studies along the same lines would provide further insights into the behavior and attitudes of officials of counties and other governments toward one another. Such studies might also provide revealing data on informal relationships involving counties.

The major argument for the use of counties as metropolitan governments has been that approximately half of the Standard Metropolitan Statistical Areas (SMSA's) are within the boundaries of single counties, and thus they are existing general governments with adequate geographical size to provide areawide services. However, most of the largest metropolitan areas are multicounty, and the most likely candidates for metropolitan governmental status in these areas may be regional councils of governments, which are associations of elected officials from many local units. These councils of governments (COG's) have sprung up in metropolises of all sizes at the urging of the national government, and they may develop into major arenas for many important intergovernmental contacts in such areas. They may become a regular channel for contact between federal and local officials.

Even in single-county metropolitan areas, COG's may emerge as competitors of the county in the exercise of leadership in the metropolis. Little research has been done on the role of counties in councils of governments. Comparative studies of councils of governments should determine exactly what parts counties are playing in these new theaters for intergovernmental relations in both single-county and multicounty metropolitan areas. Are counties active participants, passive members, or obstructionists in COG's? Have cities used these new organizations to solidify their position at the expense of counties?

Linkages and Systems

A general deficiency of research on county intergovernmental relations is the failure to view them within a systematic framework. One approach might be to consider the county as a local political system which has linkages with other external political forces, including the state legislature, the governor, the state bureaucracy, municipalities, other counties, special districts, the national bureaucracy, and Congress. Research would then seek to determine the character of these linkages. An alternative approach would be to consider the county as a local political subsystem which exists together with others in a larger state subsystem. These entities are then contained within an even larger national political system. Research would determine what strategies and resources the county subsystems use in dealing with other subsystems and the national system and their component parts in various decision-making arenas and with different issues.

Urban and Metropolitan Government

The literature discusses at length the increasing role of the county as a metropolitan or urban government. However, it tells us little about the extensiveness of or variations in this trend according to county characteristics. Case studies have been made of the use of the county as a general metropolitan government in Dade County, Florida; Davidson County, Tennessee; and East Baton Rouge Parish, Louisiana. However, no current publications provide comparative studies of its use in this manner, although Daniel R. Grant is undertaking a comparative investigation of Dade and Davidson counties and Metropolitan Toronto, Canada. Likewise, no comparisons have been made of the evolution of certain counties into metropolitan units of government, such as is taking place in Los Angeles County, California, and, to a lesser extent, in Cuyahoga County, Ohio, Milwaukee County, Wisconsin, and various places elsewhere. Without more comparative research in this area, neither a true assessment of the role of the county as an urban or metropolitan unit nor an evaluation of the ability of counties to perform such a role is possible.

The Need to Study Relationships

Basically, most research into county government has suffered from a lack of concern about relationships. The county literature largely ignores the study of relationships between legal norms and governmental practices, between forms of government and voter participation, between community structure and governmental policies, between the strength and practices of political parties and government organizations, between community growth and changes in governmental policy, and between many other socioeconomic and governmental-political phenomena. In addition, the study of county government has made only slight use of sociological, economic, psychological, and other approaches, and few studies have been based on substantial amounts of field work. The use of mathematical and statistical methods in county research has not yet begun to be explored extensively, particularly in the realm of psychosocial space, as discussed by many urban sociologists, as contrasted with geographic space. To discover the nature of the above relationships, the research methods of modern social science must be used to make a comparative study of county government within a systematic framework.

REFERENCES

ANDERSON, WILLIAM (1957) "Municipal government: no lost world." American Political Science Review, LI (September): 776-783.

BOLES, DONALD E. and HERBERT C. COOK (1959) An Evaluation of Iowa State Government. Ames: Community Research Center, Iowa State College.

CAPE, WILLIAM H. (1967) The Emerging Patterns of County Executives, Governmental Research Series No. 35. Lawrence: Governmental Research Center, University of Kansas.

DUNCOMBE, HERBERT S. (1966) County Government in America. Washington: National Association of Counties Research Foundation.

FENTON, JOHN H. (1957) Politics in the Border States. New Orleans: The Hauser Press.

HANSON, BERTIL L. (1965) "County commissioners of Oklahoma." Midwest Journal of Political Science, IX (November): 388-400.

HERSON, LAWRENCE J. R. (1957a) "The lost world of municipal government." American Political Science Review, LI (June): 330-345.

______, (1957b) "A reply to William Anderson." American Political Science Review, LI (September): 783-784.

JONES, VICTOR (1962) "Urban and metropolitan counties." Pp. 57-87 in The Municipal Year Book: 1962. Chicago: The International City Managers' Association.

KEY, V. O., JR. (1962) Southern Politics in State and Nation. New York: Random House.

KITSOS, THOMAS (1968) The 1966 County Elections. Illinois Government [Published by the Institute of Government and Public Affairs, University of Illinois] (April): 1-4.

LANCASTER, LANE W. (1952) Government in Rural America, 2nd ed. New York: D. Van Nostrand Company.

LONG, NORTON (1967) "Political science and the city." Pp. 243-262 in Leo F. Schnore and Henry Fagin (eds.) Urban Research and Policy Planning. Beverly Hills: Sage Publications.

RICHARDS, ALAN R. (1954) "Local government research: a partial evaluation." Public Adminstration Review, XIV (Autumn): 271-277.

SAYRE, WALLACE S. and NELSON POLSBY (1965) "American political science and the study of urbanization." Pp. 115-156 in Philip M. Hauser and Leo F. Schnore (eds.), The Study of Urbanization. New York: John Wiley and Sons.

SCHMANDT, HENRY J. (1966) "Toward comparability in urban research." Pp. 6-40 in Thomas R. Dye (ed.), Comparative Research in Community Politics. Athens: University of Georgia.

SPENCER, JEAN E. (1965) Contemporary Local Government in Maryland. College Park: Bureau of Governmental Research, University of Maryland.

STONER, JOHN E. (1967) Interlocal Governmental Cooperation: A Study of Five States. Washington: U. S. Department of Agriculture.

U.S. Senate Committee on Government Operations, Subcommittee on Intergovernmental Relations (1965a) The Federal System as Seen by Federal Aid Officials. Washington, D.C.: Government Printing Office.

______, (1965b) The Federal System as Seen by State and Local Officials. Washington, D.C.: Government Printing Office.

WEIDNER, EDWARD W. (1960) Intergovernmental Relations as Seen by Public Officials: Intergovernmental Relations in the United States as Observed in the State of Minnesota. Minneapolis: University of Minnesota Press.

PART TWO

AN INQUIRY into the COUNTY'S POLITICAL VITALITY: A Research Design and Supporting Evidence

NEW RESEARCH APPROACHES

The evaluation of completed research and the suggestions for further investigation, which were presented in Part One, raise the difficult question of how the study of county government might best proceed. Fortunately, scholars have been grappling with this dilemma and related problems of methodology in their research on state and municipal governments. Thus, a brief review of the literature they have produced should be helpful in providing possible aids for county research.[1]

The reshaping of research direction in state and municipal governments was given impetus by V. O. Key, Jr. (1949) who pointed to the possible influence of such political variables as party competition and factionalism on the public welfare policies adopted by southern states. This line of investigation was extended to other areas of the nation and applied by Lockard (1959) and Fenton (1966) to other policies. Interest in explaining variations among governmental units of the same type has increasingly become a continuing research theme among writers in the field, particularly in the 1960's. Although little agreement has been reached as to the prime determinants of public policy, the general approach has been to investigate the various relations among socioeconomic inputs, the political system, and policy outputs.

A typical and extensive study of this sort was made by Thomas R. Dye (1966) who attempted to analyze policy differences among the fifty states. He divided inputs into the four environmental variables of industrialization, urbanization, wealth, and education. To represent the political system characteristics, he used measures of partisanship, party competition, voter participation, and malapportionment. He then employed simple, partial, and multiple correlation analysis to determine which of these variables appeared

1. The studies cited in the discussion are meant to be representative samples, rather than inclusive of all the work in the field.

to be most important in explaining more than ninety different policy outcomes. From this investigation, Dye concluded that economic factors were the primary force in shaping political systems and public policy. Similar techniques were applied by Dawson and Robinson (1965) to state welfare policies and again by Dye (1967) to educational policies in large cities. The results of these studies showed once more the prevailing influence of economic factors.

Sharkansky (1967a), however, has disputed the sweeping nature of these findings. By using a similar technique, but employing different measures of state political and economic characteristics, he concluded that the political system played a much more important role in determining policy outputs than the proponents of the socioeconomic explanation found to be so. Thus, he has provided evidence underlining the idea raised earlier by Key and his followers that political characteristics are influential.

A second area of research centers on governmental structure. The Banfield and Wilson (1963) hypothesis that reformed city government is the product of the "middle-class ethos" has stimulated a large quantity of research on the determinants of governmental form. Schnore and Alford (1963) supported this hypothesis by showing that reformed cities appear to be the natural habitat of the middle class. In addition, Alford and Scoble (1965) amply documented the fact that cities of extensive growth and mobility are highly likely to be council-manager communities.

Lineberry and Fowler (1967), although interested in elucidating the ethos theory, were less concerned with the determinants of structure than with the effects that either a reformed or unreformed government would have on the translation of environmental inputs into policy outputs. They concluded that unreformed municipalities are more responsive than their reformed counterparts to the socioeconomic cleavages existing within their environments. However, Wolfinger and Field (1966) found in their investigation that the ethos theory needed modification. They proposed that it should be altered to account for the effect of geographic region on both government forms and policy outputs.

Additional articles appearing recently have dealt with other aspects which deserve consideration in the investigation of how state and municipal governments function. Of particular importance is the work of Sharkansky (1967b) which refuted the assumption made in many policy studies that expenditures are indicative of the actual services provided. He suggested that such variables as differing market costs and levels of private spending may account for much of the apparent variation in service levels. Penniman (1965) proposed that tradition and previous decisions constitute major factors in determining effort and burden in present tax policy decisions. Sharkansky (1967a) has also pointed to the incremental nature of policy decisions, explaining that past decisions have a great effect on present ones. Crittenden (1967), drawing on the work of Daniel Elazar (1966), concentrated on the possible impact of the cultural context within which governments operate.

Eulau and Eyestone (1968) focused their analysis on the individual and examined the connection between the personal predilections, preferences, orientations, and expectations of city councilmen and the development of policy. They concluded that policy development is affected not only by forces in the environment but also is mediated by the orientations of the policy-makers to possible courses of action.

Many of the research interests and approaches that now abound in the study of state and municipal governments have recently been collected in texts by Jacob and Vines (1965) and Wilson (1968). Also, Jacob and Lipsky (1968) have provided a very interesting commentary on the strengths and weaknesses of research in this area. Despite the multiplicity and inconsistency of the findings, the material surveyed above is stimulating and provocative. The concepts and ideas that have occupied the attention of these scholars certainly should have an impact on county research.

AN INDEX OF POLITICAL VITALITY

In our present attempt to develop an analytical framework for the comparative study of county government, we will focus on the political vitality of the county. As we know from our synthesis of the relatively few general studies and the many statewide and specialized ones made by individuals and organizations, various counties have been exhibiting certain kinds of vitality.[2] These findings are useful, but they represent merely an important initial step toward gaining a thorough understanding of county governments. They tell us something about counties, but not all we would like to know.

To be able to analyze counties individually and with a degree of precision, it is necessary to develop an index that permits us to determine intercounty variations within a significant dimension. We believe that the most basic index warranting formulation and application is that of political vitality. This must be a characteristic of a local governmental unit if it is to deserve continued life and financial aid from federal and state agencies. Without such a characteristic, either existing or potential, a local unit is a meaningless relic and a poor investment. Thus, we will develop a research design for the study of political vitality and present findings from numerous studies that are relevant to this design. The development of a design represents an important first stage in our quest to assess the political vitality of county government. In future research we will determine index scores for a sample of counties throughout the nation.

We propose to discuss first the components that may be validly included in an index of political vitality and, in turn, to consider the elements making up each component. Then, we will lay out various categories of demographic, economic, governmental, and social factors that are the independent variables in a series of key hypotheses in which the index of political vitality is the dependent variable. In sum, this analytical model should reveal that variations in the political vitality of counties apparently are a function of a number of factors. We might also consider political vitality to be an intervening variable between these independent factors and various performance measures of county activity, such as percentage of county expenditures devoted to amenities or proportion of families with annual incomes under $3,000 that receive welfare assistance. This latter type of analysis is a matter for future investigation and will not be explored here.

2. These studies are identified and discussed in Part Three of this book.

The decisions to place the factors in our analysis in either the independent variable or index category have been made on the basis of our scrutiny of the literature. However, certain factors might logically be placed in either category. The multiple correlation analysis to be undertaken will reveal whether the directions of the relationships we hypothesize are correct.

A uniform procedure is used in presenting each component of the index. A general analysis is first given, followed by summaries of selected findings from various studies that commonly indicate variations among counties within that component. The importance of variations is that they allow us to score counties according to some statistical measure of that component. Components may then be weighted and the scores added together to determine the relative levels of political vitality of specific counties.

There are five components of the index of political vitality: (1) resource utilization; (2) volume of intergovernmental linkages; (3) changes in organization and processes; (4) adequacy of public accountability; and (5) extent of voting and competition in elections. In total, the components tell us a great deal about the capability of counties to decide upon and carry out policies and to respond quickly, responsibly, and efficiently to problems and demands.

RESOURCE UTILIZATION

General Analysis

Resource utilization, the first component of the index, is a measure of the extent to which the county uses its capacity to generate revenue. By "capacity" we mean the total money that the county should be able to derive from its resource base, given the tax structure of the state in which it is located. Counties depend on the property tax for almost all their locally collected revenue, as other county sources generally yield very little. State aid and shared revenues also contribute importantly to county income; however, counties have little control over the amount and uses of most of these funds since they are allocated according to precise formulas and for designated purposes such as welfare payments and road construction. Accordingly, county financial capacity and tax yield must be defined in terms of the property tax.

The measurement of resource utilization, which has been adapted from a study by the Advisory Commission on Intergovernmental Relations (1962a), is a three-stage process composed of the calculation of capacity, the determination of tax yield, and the fixing of a ratio between the two. Financial capacity may be ascertained as follows: the equalized property valuations of counties are summed; the property tax revenues of all counties in the state are also added together; the latter total is divided into the former to obtain a statewide county property tax rate; and this rate is applied to (multiplied by) the equalized assessed valuation of each county to arrive at its financial capacity. The tax yield of a county is its actual revenue from the property tax. The ratio of tax yield to capacity is an indicator of resource utilization, often referred to as tax effort: the higher the ratio, the greater the utilization.

State restrictions on the use by counties of non-property tax sources—retail sales and individual and corporate income, for example—have largely limited their ability to mobilize other local resources which might be available to them. Also, statutory and constitutional restrictions on the level of property taxation and debt limitations stated in terms of property valuation have seriously circumscribed their ability to employ the property tax to the fullest extent to finance current and capital expenditures.

RESOURCE UTILIZATION

Selected Findings

In 1962 about three-fourths of the states limited the property taxing power of counties for general governmental purposes. Such provisions tend to restrict the extent of county services. The property tax itself has not produced revenue sufficient to keep pace with increases in population, price levels, and costs of government. In addition, county officials have been subjected to political pressure to keep property assessments low, while at the same time exemptions have reduced the revenue base and the taxes on many categories of personal property. Meanwhile, other sources of revenue have not met county needs. In 1964 county sales taxes were imposed by only about 150 counties, and the income tax was utilized by only one. A large number of counties employ selective sales taxes, licenses, and fees, but none of these sources produces sufficient revenue to substitute for property taxes. County use of nonproperty tax sources is greatly restricted by state constitutions and statutes (Duncombe, 1966: 112-113, 125).

Although the overall ceiling on county property tax rates imposed by the Arkansas constitution is 20 mills, the average levied by counties in 1959 equaled only about one-half this limit. A few counties have voluntarily imposed additional taxes on property, which are either in excess of the constitutional ceilings for particular purposes or for purposes not specifically authorized by state law (Alexander, 1959: 195).

Expanded county services and costs have recently placed a great strain on the sources of revenue available to Georgia counties. The county financial squeeze also results from a greater proportion of the tax dollar going to the state government and from increasing restrictions on the revenue sources available to counties. To meet increased costs and to provide more services, the revenues of counties and the per capita payments to them by the state have both been growing. In addition, grants-in-aid from the national and state governments have become a vital source of county revenues in an effort to keep up with service demands (Gosnell and Anderson, 1956: 345).

Some Idaho counties are in good financial condition, while others that contain only small amounts of taxable land and scattered populations find it difficult to raise the revenues necessary to provide minimum governmental services. Throughout the state as a whole, however, counties have built up a surplus of over $10 million (Idaho Governmental Cost and Tax Structure Committee, 1954: 9).

A county governing board in Illinois may seek to raise the statutory property tax rate limit by submitting a proposal to increase the existing tax rate to the voters; majority approval is required for passage. County officials, however, have been reluctant to employ this method because of the unpopularity of making the existing rate limits higher (Howards and Richey, 1959:36-37).

Fifty percent of county revenues in Kansas comes from property taxes. Many problems are presented by heavy reliance on this source. Widespread sentiment that the property tax is financing as much of governmental costs as can be reasonably expected has produced strong pressures to keep down county property tax rates. Inflationary pressures have lessened the capacity of this type of tax, as presently administered, to yield sufficient revenue. While total assessed property valuation has gone up, it has not grown as rapidly as the purchasing power of the dollar has declined. Accordingly, counties have had to ask the state legislature for two types of relief: increases in the amount of the levy which the county can make for particular functions or which it can make in the aggregate outside such specified purposes (Drury, 1961: 349-350).

In South Carolina total county revenues grew 306.5 percent from 1940 to 1957. Surprisingly, however, these gains were greatest for farm counties and lowest for urban counties – 357.5 percent as compared to 293 percent. During this period dependence on the property tax declined from 43 percent to 29 percent of all revenues. Again contrary to expectations, urban counties rely much more on the property tax than farm counties. Likewise, increases in per capita revenue from property taxes were greatest for urban counties and smallest for farm counties. The relative decline of property taxes has generally resulted from increases in state aid to counties (Favor et al., 1960: 33-36).

In West Virginia county property tax levies expanded by 148 percent between 1945 and 1959. Despite this growth, the actual income of some counties is so low that it is amazing they operate at all. In 1959 the productivity of the levies ranged from about $2.5 million to less than $25,000, with nineteen at less than $100,000. Actual income from property taxes is even further reduced because the full collection of taxes is never realized (Davis et al., 1963: 459-460).

VOLUME OF INTER-GOVERNMENTAL LINKAGES

General Analysis

Volume of intergovernmental linkages, the second component of the index of political vitality, involves a variety of interrelations. Some are of a horizontal nature; they may concern relationships between a county and one or more other counties or those between a county and a second type of local unit. This second type may be a city, a school district, a non-school special district, or, in some parts of the United States, a township or a town. Other interrelations are of a vertical nature; they concern relationships between a county and a government at a different level, either state or nation. Still others are of a mixed vertical-horizontal nature because they pertain to a county and a second county or another type of local unit and to either or both a state government and the national government.

Interrelations may further be either formal or informal. Examples of the former are the execution of written contracts and the granting of money under certain specified conditions. An illustration of the latter is a verbal understanding between administrators about the exchange of particular information.

There has been a considerable growth in both the number and types of county intergovernmental linkages, particularly in the post-World War II years, but the increase has varied measurably on a county-by-county basis. Counties always have had important and fundamental relations with the state government; this is so because one of their original sets of responsibilities was to serve as an agent of the state in performing certain functions of statewide importance. The administration of national, state, and some local elections exemplifies this role. Subsequently, while this original set of responsibilities increased in volume, other types of county-state linkages emerged. One such is state supervision of particular county affairs, especially those relating to finance, which grew very noticeably in the depression years of the 1930's. Another is state financial aid and staff assistance (planning advice is an example of the latter) in support of an increasing number of county programs.

County-national relations represent another major phase of county intergovernmental linkages, and they, too, have been expanding. These relations have developed chiefly through the granting and administering of federal aid, which is sometimes routed to counties through the state government and other times is transmitted directly to them.

The number of national programs of financial assistance have been increasing rapidly, with a large share of them having been established since 1950. By 1966 there were 162 major federal assistance programs, and in many instances a program had several grant authorizations. In that year the number of authorizations was 399. Almost all grant authorizations are available to local governments, and in practically all cases counties are eligible.

The proliferation of federal grants and of local requests for them has prompted the national government to foster the establishment of a locally-based organization in heavily populated centers. Often this organization, charged by the Model Cities and Metropolitan Development Act of 1966 with reviewing applications by local governments for a broad variety of federal grants, is a regional council of governments. Such a council is a voluntary association of local units that select representatives who study and attempt to decide upon solutions to problems of mutual concern. Counties may be members of most councils. Many counties have joined councils of governments, pay dues or assessments, and participate in their activities. Some of them are leaders in the organization. On the other hand, a number of counties have refused to become affiliated with these councils or have withdrawn from membership. In sum, councils of governments constitute an institutional mechanism both for increasing national-county and county-local relations and for bringing them into sharper focus.

Interlocal county linkages have become numerous. This development is very evident in urban areas containing many local units which frequently develop common needs and problems. The trend is also apparent, however, in a number of rural areas, where the resources of individual governments are sometimes severely limited.

Of the various forms of interlocal county linkages, county-city relations are unusually plentiful. A common type of such relations is for a county and a city to furnish aid to one another in emergencies, such as a major fire or a riot. For instance, if a large fire breaks out in a city which has a mutual aid agreement with a county and the city's personnel and equipment cannot cope with the emergency, the county government will supply assistance. Mutual aid pacts are therefore standby arrangements.

Another type of county-city relationship involves the performance of a service by a county for a city (or by a city for a county). This is usually done under a contract stipulating the amount of money to be paid to the supplying government for rendering a specified amount of service and for the period of time during which the arrangement is to be in effect, subject to renewal by consent of the participating parties. Service contracts constitute a transfer of functions on an individual basis and a designated time, although in practice many appear to be permanent. They pertain to a wide variety of activities, including fire and police protection, libraries, planning, refuse and sewage disposal, and tax assessment and collection. The general direction of such transfers has been from cities to counties.

The growing use of the county as a provider of contractual services to cities has been stimulated by a number of factors, two of which are relevant here. The first is the expansion of county activities; such expansion has widened the range of services for which contracts may be made. The second is increased confidence in the competence of various counties; if this confidence, which often has been attained only in recent years, were not present, cities would not sign service agreements.

County-county relations represent an additional phase of interlocal linkages. Agreements have been reached between counties about a number of services. Often the arrangement is a joint effort involving financing and policy participation by both governments. (This same practice is present in county-city relations and may concern a facility, such as construction of a public building, instead of a service.) Sometimes it consists of one county performing a service for another; the performance may be reciprocal when emergencies develop. In particular, intercounty agreements have materialized in various counties of small population and resources;

this procedure constitutes a method of pooling some of their limited wealth to establish a service or to increase the level of an existing one. Such agreements are not unknown, however, in certain heavily populated counties that view specific needs as intercounty or regional. They exist in fire protection, library service, planning, public health, public welfare, and other functions.

A further type of county-county relations is exemplified by membership in statewide associations of county officials (or counties) and a national association of county governments. There are forty-five state organizations of this kind operating in forty-three states. They usually have the official name of the county governing body in their designations (for example, County Supervisors Association of California and Florida State Association of County Commissioners). However, other major county officials are also active in a number of these statewide associations. In contrast, the national organization stresses county governments in its title, which reflects a change of recent years. It is called the National Association of Counties (NACO), formerly the National Association of County Officials. All forty-five of the state groups are affiliated with NACO.

Although the staff size and particular activities of the state and national groups vary, all provide information about county organization and practices and legislative developments affecting counties. This service is designed to keep members up to date and to equip them better to deal with today's problems. According to the NACO by-laws, for instance, "the objects and purposes of this Association are to stimulate and contribute to the continuing improvement of county government throughout the United States through increased efficiency and higher standards of public service." Membership in these groups is voluntary and depends upon the payment of annual dues, which are often scaled to the different population sizes of counties. Organizational membership is an important manifestation of county-county relations, but not all eligible county officials and counties belong to these state and national associations.

An additional form of interlocal county linkages concerns relations between counties and school districts, which are the most prevalent kind of special district. We are here concerned with school districts that are independent governmental units and not with other public school systems that are dependent agencies of state and local governments. In most states, school districts are the exclusive providers of public education below the collegiate level, and in a significant number of other states they are the most frequent supplier. The office of county superintendent of schools, an agency of county government, is involved in the most important continuing county-school district relations. The responsibilities of the office differ considerably among the states. In addition to assisting the state educational agencies to carry out their assignment, this county department undertakes other activities prescribed by state law. In brief, it is active in supervision, enforcement, record-keeping, specialized services (audio-visual aids, services to the handicapped, and so on), and leadership.

Counties also have relations with non-school special district governments (providing water, sewage disposal, fire protection, and many other services), which are fast growing in number. Some of these relations are of a fundamental nature, at times occurring at the inception of a district. The county governing body often is the legal recipient of petitions to form a district. In some instances the governing board is limited to determining the adequacy and legal correctness of the petition, but in others it may change the proposed boundaries, usually by contracting them, and in still others it may decide whether the proposed district should be formed. Moreover, when the governing board of a district is an appointed group, the county governing body frequently selects the appointees. On occasion, the county governing body may choose one of its own members or another county official to serve on a district board. In addition, a number of counties and districts have entered into mutual aid agreements, notably in firefighting.

Finally, in discussing the second component of the index of political vitality, a still unusual but potentially highly significant form of interlocal and state-local county linkage deserves consideration. It has developed recently in a limited number of western and midwestern states through the creation of boundary review agencies composed in part of county officials or representatives. The review authority of these agencies differs, but it most often relates to proposals for municipal incorporation and annexation and non-school special district formation and annexation. Agency disapproval usually stops the progress of the proposition, while approbation customarily allows it to move on to a popular vote.

Each county in a state may have such a commission, or only particular ones may be permitted to do so.

The activation of this kind of institution is important to intergovernmental county linkages not only because it places counties in a crucial position in deciding various boundary questions but also because it brings them together regularly with other participating governments. Such regular convening has prompted the members of some of these agencies to try to formulate guidelines for attaining a pattern of preferred future governmental development in an area.

VOLUME OF INTER-GOVERNMENTAL LINKAGES

Selected Findings

Professionalization and bureaucratization in local government can enhance its position vis-a-vis the professionals and bureaucrats of both the state and national governments. The more energetic states, which run the best interference, also tend to exert the most control over local use of federal aids, while the least energetic states actually jeopardize their local units' chances to get federal assistance, since the federal system is so constructed as to make state action almost mandatory before all but the largest localities can get a proper hearing. The great increase in county governmental activity in the last generation has resulted directly from the expansion of state and state-federal programs that must be administered locally. Also, the dependence of counties upon state aid, which is usually greater than that of any other general local government's, tends to cement the position of the county as an arm of the state (Elazar, 1966: 173-176).

Metropolitan grants-in-aid are currently more likely to be administered at the county level than are other urban assistance programs, and grant programs may be more susceptible to county administration than federal aid programs generally (U. S. Senate Committee on Government Operations, 1965:80).

County governing board members and functional officials in Minnesota are involved in intergovernmental relations more than are their counterparts in any other local unit. In fact, county functional officials in Minnesota are so involved in intergovernmental affairs that some observers feel that no county has a real government but exists instead as a mere agency or outpost of the state government. A very decisive majority of county functional officials in this state feels that their power in decision-making has not been lessened as the result of contacts with the state, while a slight majority of county governing board members feels that their power has been reduced. County school superintendents are strongly of the belief that localities should deal with the national government only through the state government, while other county functional officials are less markedly of this opinion, and county governing-board members even less so (Weidner, 1960:62, 78, 91).

The range and amount of state administrative supervision over local governments in Kansas have been increasing. This development has been particularly noticeable in agriculture, public health, highways, and social welfare. The county is the local unit most involved in state supervisory activities (Drury, 1961:365).

Various methods of interlocal cooperation are in use. One method is parallel action, which involves cooperation of two or more governments on a common project or in a common service area, such as 116 communities in the six-county Southeast Michigan region being members of reciprocal licensing councils for television, electrical, and other trades. A second method is joint-agency performance, whereby a board or agency is formed by two or more governments to carry out a common service project, such as the joint city-county health department in Emporia, Kansas, which is administered by representatives from the city and county governments and the county medical society. A third method is single-agency performance, whereby the participating governments name one of the units as the administrative agency, such as the Butler-Greenwood bi-county health board in Kansas which provides public health services for the two counties and for two cities.

A fourth method is the service contract, whereby one unit supplies a service to one or more other units, such as the county government of Ramsey County, Minnesota, offering a service contract to municipalities in the county which permits them to choose the type of police service desired. A fifth method is the conference, whereby local governments are called together for discussion sessions, such as in the Pittsburgh area where the Allegheny Seminar has been organized (Colman, 1965:22-25).

CHANGES IN ORGANIZATION AND PROCESSES

General Analysis

Changes in organization and processes constitute the third component of the index of political vitality. The changes have not all been in the same direction: some have produced a more unified structure and a stronger means of productivity, while others have caused a further atomization of organization and procedures. Among the alterations of greatest consequence that have effected increased unification has been the establishment of some type of general executive officer in a number of counties. He may be an appointed executive, called usually either manager or chief administrative officer. He may be an elected executive, identified as mayor or county executive. Or he may be a long-established department head, such as a county clerk, to whom increased general responsibilities have gravitated, often gradually and informally. The powers of a general executive officer may range from a vast array including the appointment and removal of most department heads and the preparation and execution of the budget to simply the coordination of county activities, through his ability to persuade various department heads by tactfully showing them the wisdom of and benefits to accrue from his recommendations. A general executive officer thus often represents changes in both organization and processes.

Another indicator of change is the reduction in the number of elected officials who have administrative duties. For many years all counties had a long list of elected department heads, often including the assessor, auditor, clerk, coroner, district attorney, recorder, sheriff, superintendent of schools, surveyor, tax collector, and treasurer. In the present century, particularly in recent decades, some counties have reduced the quantity of elective offices by either converting certain posts to appointive status or consolidating two or more elective positions. Reduction in the number of elected administrative officials is generally accompanied by the establishment of a general executive officer, but the reverse is much less often the case. There is little doubt that the creation of a general executive position usually has more profound effects on county operations than a numerical decrease in elected department heads.

A further indicator of change is the allocation of new or more specialized county functions. Such functions may be assigned to already- or newly-established independently elected department heads or to new independent boards, thus causing more atomization of organization and procedures. Or they may be allotted to newly authorized department heads, who are professionally-trained functional specialists, appointed by and made accountable either to the general executive officer or the county governing body, thereby bringing about greater unification of structure and operations.

The status of a merit system is still another important indicator of change. For many years counties in general were the happy hunting grounds of the spoils system: when new officials were elected to office they removed many employees from their jobs and replaced them with campaign supporters and relatives. Gradually the spoils arrangement has given way in some counties to either a comprehensive or limited use of the merit principle: it calls for the appointment, promotion, and retention of employees on the basis of their qualifications, which includes performance on the job for advancement and tenure. However, it is open to question as to whether governmental reforms such as the merit system increase the political vitality of counties. Possibly unreformed governments can mobilize greater extractive and distributive capabilities. Hopefully this question may be resolved by our future research.

Counties utilizing the merit principle either have their own civil-service (personnel) commission (board) or personnel officer or are served by a state personnel agency. The proportion of county employees appointed and functioning on a merit basis determines whether particular counties have a comprehensive or limited merit system. A county may have limited merit coverage because large numbers of positions are exempted from the jurisdiction of the personnel agency or officer or because many positions are filled by "temporary" appointments which are renewed again and again. In addition, a third class of counties, which is numerically the largest, makes no use of the merit standard at all beyond what is required in specific federal-aid programs.

A final measure of change to be presented is the degree of planning capability demonstrated by counties. Some counties have an organized planning effort while others do not. Some with organized planning programs rely entirely on a lay planning commission, possibly aided by a part-time consultant. Others with programs have a professional staff; it may be large or small in relation to the population served. Some planning organizations devote all their time to zoning matters in unincorporated areas (a number of counties do not even possess zoning authority, however). Others spend much of their time on the development and periodic revision of comprehensive general plans and other long-range planning items such as economic development. The range of activities and financial support of county planning operations extends from the nonexistent to the very broad indeed.

CHANGES IN ORGANIZATION AND PROCESSES

Selected Findings

Since 1950, with the assumption of increased program roles by counties in Maryland, a pronounced trend has developed toward the creation of county offices whose relationship to the county governing body is one of direct and full responsibility. A modification of the traditional offices has also occurred, although this trend is less well marked.

Two of Maryland's four charter counties (Baltimore and Anne Arundel) have an elected executive-council form of government, while the other two (Montgomery and Wicomico) have a county manager form. In Prince George's County, by governing board decision, each member serves as a liaison agent between the board and a major county activity, and the board chairman may be assigned broad executive and administrative powers beyond those he would ordinarily exercise as presiding officer and board member. Some other counties have also utilized the chairman as the full-time officer and have employed administrative staffs to assist him. In a number of counties, the clerk to the board, traditionally a clerical and recordkeeping office, has become the equivalent of an administrative assistant to the board (Spencer, 1965:58, 50-51, 53).

Boards and commissions possessing specific administrative functions exist in varying numbers in many county governments. Hundreds of state laws provide for mandatory or optional creation of these special-function boards, which are numerous in such fields as agriculture, airports, health, highways, libraries, planning, schools, and welfare. Although some of these boards are entirely or partially integrated into the general county structure through appointment of their members by the county governing body or by fiscal control or administrative supervision being exercised by the general county authority, many have a substantial degree of autonomy. Independent special-function boards represent a major form of administrative disintegration. (Snider, 1957:147).

More than 450 counties in the United States have some sort of chief administrator of whom about half are appointed officials and the other half are elected. Three of the principal executive systems are county manager, chief administrative officer, and elected chief executive (the last named comparable to a city mayor and directly elected to the post). In all three systems the executive officer exercises control over budgeting and purchasing procedures, some control over personnel, and certain supervisory responsibilities. In general, however, the chief administrative officer has less legal authority than either of the other two executive types. Another alternative is the administrative assistant, who often has only that authority which is delegated to him by the county governing body.

In other instances, a certain degree of general executive authority is conferred upon the chairman of the county governing board or the elected county clerk or auditor. The development of executive systems is a major change from the traditional headless county organization (Cape, 1967:26-29).

In his own local area, the farmer has consciously felt that the retention of the long ballot has increased his control over county officials. In practice, it has meant lower efficiency and often has had the effect of turning over the government to the "courthouse gang." However, the introduction of the short ballot and the merit system would take nothing short of a revolution in rural political mores (Lancaster, 1952:94).

By and large, the county is the last unchallenged stronghold of the spoils system in Texas. Employees are not hired primarily on the basis of merit but as a political favor. Job insecurity, poor pay, and "government by crony" take their toll in the public service. Speakers at a meeting pointed out two formidable sources of opposition to county reform: the County Judges and Commissioners Association and the companies selling road machinery and other supplies to counties (McCleskey, 1963:265-68).

According to William Brussat of the United States Bureau of the Budget, there is a need for a unit of general local government to serve both as building block and bridge in planning for the development of a region. The county is the only such unit with the potential to fill this need; but, unfortunately, in many states it is only a potential, and many obstacles stand in the way. Brussat, who made his statements in a panel discussion, believes the county may serve both as a bridge between the geographically smaller governmental units comprising the county and as a building block in developing cooperative action on broader regional problems, extending beyond the county ("Bridges and Building Blocks," 1966:55).

County planning in Pennsylvania is a vital part of governmental planning, but in Delaware and New Jersey it has been closely connected with the county engineering functions. The latter orientation has caused planning agencies in these two states to view planning more as a matter of drainage, street grades, and center lines than as a continuous comprehensive process. By the time some agencies in Delaware and New Jersey had looked beyond engineering concerns, many cities had already established their own planning programs and felt no need for assistance from counties. On the other hand, Pennsylvania county planning commissions have used their operations to build constituencies for planning. They have employed subdivision control as a key to demonstrate their usefulness and ability. By being able to achieve community acceptance fairly rapidly, they have been able to expand their programs. However, in Delaware and New Jersey, due to the weak constituencies of county planning, the prospect of comprehensive county planning exerting a significant impact on public policy is remote (Coke and Anton, 1962:16).

A survey of 1,667 counties in 1964 indicated that 23 per cent had industrial development programs and 4 per cent worked cooperatively with other local governments in such programs. Industrial development has become a county function because many new industries have been locating in unincorporated areas outside cities, and county governments are providing services for these areas. Industrial development has become a function both of rural and urban counties (Duncombe, 1966:95).

Not many county governing boards and administrators have legislative or administrative authority over all matters within the scope of comprehensive physical planning. Nevertheless, the number of county planning agencies and of regional planning organizations in which counties participate is increasing (Jones, 1962:66).

ADEQUACY OF PUBLIC ACCOUNTABILITY

General Analysis

Adequacy of public accountability is the fourth component of the index of political vitality. An important measure of accountability is the degree of equitability employed in apportioning seats on the county governing body when all or most of its members are elected from districts or are elected at large but must reside within specified local areas. This measure is applicable to about 80 per cent of the counties which utilize one of these two types of local requirements; it could not be applied to any county in a few states, including Massachusetts, Ohio, Pennsylvania, and Utah, where all county governing board members are elected at large and no local area residence rule exists.

The apportionment of governing-body seats determines the nature of the system of representation and the ability of the county electorate to hold its elected officials accountable. If the electoral or residence districts contain substantially unequal populations, some persons have much less voting power and legal competence to hold elected officials accountable than other individuals possess. That equitable apportionment leads to responsive and responsible government is an assumption found in the state and local literature and court decisions. If political vitality indeed proves to be an intervening variable, we can then test the validity of this proposition.

Until recent years, county governing boards generally had the authority to reapportion their seats with few, if any, valuable guidelines provided by the state constitution, state laws, or court decisions. In fact, in many instances the exercise of such authority was viewed as being at the discretion of the governing board members, and very often an extraordinary majority vote by them was necessary to realize a change. The frequent result was that many counties were not reapportioned over long stretches of time, chiefly because some incumbent governing body members felt their chances of being defeated for reelection would be greater in reapportioned districts.

As population redistribution took place within many counties—some sections making rapid gains and others registering losses—the disparity of population in various electoral districts used in selecting county board members widened increasingly. County apportionment became more and more of an issue, particularly in counties where a small percentage of the people elected a majority of the governing board or where a large proportion of the people, sometimes a substantial majority, resided in a single district. Some counties reacted positively to the pressure of population change or extensive complaints, but many took no action.

The big stimulus to county reapportionment developed in the 1960's. First, the United States Supreme Court stated that it could assume jurisdiction in cases pertaining to state legislative reapportionment (*Baker v. Carr,* 1962), and then it declared that "as nearly as is practicable one man's vote in a congressional election is to be worth as much as another's" (*Wesberry v. Sanders,* 1964) and that both houses of state legislatures are to be apportioned on the basis of population (*Reynolds v. Sims,* 1964). Generally, around the time of these Supreme Court decisions, the courts and legislatures of a few states developed more exacting standards for county apportionment, sometimes requiring reapportionment to be undertaken periodically. Finally, in 1968 (*Avery v. Midland County*) the Supreme Court applied the one-man, one-vote principle to counties and other general local governments by declaring that the national constitution permits no substantial variation from equal population in drawing districts for such units. In the same decision, the Court also touched on the relationship of equitable apportionment and adequate public accountability, when it said, ". . . institutions of local government have always been a major aspect of our system, and their responsible and responsive operation is today of increasing importance to the quality of life of more and more of our citizens."

In view of the *Midland County* decision, it may now be said that a sufficent degree of equitability in apportioning county governing board seats is present when single-member districts are of substantially equal population. Counties will continue to vary in meeting this standard for some time to come; accordingly, this element of the index component of public accountability will remain useful. For one thing, some counties met the standard even before its enunciation by the Court and others will be prompt in complying, but still others will likely proceed very slowly. In the second place, some counties that respond will probably respond inadequately: the formulas they devise will not satisfy the standard of substantially equal population.

Apportionment is not the only measure of the adequacy of public accountability. The benefits of equitable apportionment may be severely diluted if the county governing body is dominated by committees or elite groups within it. Thus, another indicator of the adequacy of accountability is whether such dominance exists and, if so, its extent—a very difficult condition to determine, let alone measure.

An additional test of adequate accountability centers on information and control. The basic mechanisms are accounting, auditing, public information, and formal reports. Consequently, a further measure of accountability is the sufficiency of these informational and control devices, including the quantity and caliber of the coverage of county affairs by the mass media.

ADEQUACY OF PUBLIC ACCOUNTABILITY

Selected Findings

The first court decision directly applying the one-man, one-vote dictate of *Reynolds v. Sims* (1964) to a county governing body was handed down eight days later by the State Circuit Court of Kent County, Michigan, in *Brouwer v. Bronkema.* At the time of the case there were seventy-three supervisors on the county board, and both city and township representation were very unequal on a per capita basis. The court decided that the county board, like its parent body, the state legislature, must be apportioned on a population basis (Ward, 1965:1).

In 1965 the Wisconsin Supreme Court declared unconstitutional the existing state law providing for the apportionment of county governing boards. The possession by county governing boards of many solely administrative functions and limited legislative powers, the court said, does not destroy the fact that the county is a unit of government with vital powers over the lives of its residents. Therefore, it continued, the principle of equal representation applies to a county board of supervisors when that board is given legislative power and is composed of elective members (Wollenzien, 1965: 44-45).

The New York State Court of Appeals has ruled that legislative bodies of local government must be apportioned in accordance with the one-man, one-vote requirement. The state's courts have said that elections at large, elections from relatively equal population districts, and elections from single-member or multi-member districts can satisfy the equal population requirement. There has been considerable supportive and opposing discussion of weighted voting and fractional voting: some courts have ordered weighted voting as an interim, temporary remedy in local government cases (New York Office for Local Government, 1966:2-4).

Many counties in Michigan have large governing boards. In any county of less than 500,000 population, the board of supervisors is authorized by state law to provide for a finance committee of three to five members that audits claims, examines accounts, and performs other designated duties. Members of the finance committee are appointed for one-year terms by the board chairman, subject to approval by a majority of the board. Finance committees of those counties in excess of 75,000 people have more extensive duties and, in addition, may include persons who are not members of the board of supervisors. Besides auditing claims against the county and examining county accounts, the finance committee in these larger counties may examine the methods of operations in all county offices and departments, has immediate charge and control of the county courthouse and jail, and controls and supervises the use of most county-owned vehicles. It reports annually to the board on various personnel matters, including recommendations on salaries, departmental reorganization, and increases or decreases in personnel. All requests for appropriations must be submitted to the committee, which then submits a report with recommendations to the board. The committee also prepares an annual county budget, along with an estimate of receipts other than from taxation. It further recommends the amount of money to be raised by taxation to finance proposed county expenditures (Michigan State University, 1959:10-13).

Because of the large size of the county board of supervisors (usually composed of township supervisors, serving *ex officio*, and city representatives) in a number of counties, much of its actual work is carried out through committees. This procedure contributes to making county government obscure to its citizens, since they are personally acquainted with few of the committee members and even fewer members of the entire board. It also facilitates "buckpassing" because large numbers make inaction safer (Blair, 1964:181).

Of forty-four states surveyed, thirty-one publish some types of financial data about counties. The most frequent kinds are tax rates, bonded debt, general county expenditures, general county receipts, and tax levies. Less common are gross debt, selected county expenditures, and selected county receipts. Financial reporting need not involve strict state control; in fact, in various states, comprehensive financial reporting is accompanied by minimum state supervision. However, county financial records are audited by a state agency in most of these states, and about three-fourths prescribe mandatory budgetary procedures (Illinois County Study and Survey Commission, 1961:18-20, 28).

Citizens cannot be expected to develop a major interest in a government whose activities are tucked away in the form of legal notices in an obscure section of the newspapers—when they do appear at all. Also, counties generate very little information about their operations. This problem is particularly acute in Iowa where the statutory law dealing with reporting county governmental activities permits large areas where no specific information needs to be placed in written records at the county level. Moreover, in Iowa, there are relatively few state offices to which the activities of the various county departments are reported with any thoroughness, or even on an annual basis. For instance, the secretary of state maintains no records of county election returns throughout the state (Boles and Cook, 1959:1).

EXTENT OF VOTING AND COMPETITION IN ELECTIONS

General Analysis

Extent of voting and competition in elections is the fifth component of the index of political vitality. The extent of voting may be found by determining the percentage of registered voters who participate in the electoral process. Another test, to be derived from reasonable estimates based on demographic data, is to ascertain the percentage of potential voters who take part. The potential electorate would be computed by determining the number of people who are of voting age and satisfy residence requirements, irrespective of whether they are registered. Participation in both general and special elections would be of value, the latter being important since they pertain to issues of a controversial or emergency nature which it is believed cannot be delayed for decision until the next regular election. Where possible, general elections involving only the county government should be employed; consolidated elections (state-county or national-state-county) tend to get a larger voter turnout and are therefore less useful in isolating the extent of voter participation in county electoral affairs. In some states, county voters may use the initiative, referendum, and recall procedures; this may be a factor in voter participation. Finally, primary elections have to be analyzed to determine the extent of voting for party nominations in both competitive and one-party areas and also as one measure of participation in non-partisan counties.

We believe that the extent of voting in elections is an indicator of political vitality in counties. It is argued by some scholars (and denied by others) that low voter turnout in suburban communities reflects public satisfaction with incumbent elected officials and with the government of which they are a part. Regardless of the merits of this judgment, we doubt its applicability to counties, which generally are significantly more heterogeneous than suburbs.

Competition for public office is another element of the fifth component of the index. In some counties, spirited and vigorous contests are held for elective offices, especially for positions on the county governing board. In others, no competition at all, or at least no major competition, takes place for elective posts. In a number of the latter counties, moreover, many incumbents were originally appointed to the offices because of the death or resignation of the previous officeholders before the expiration of their terms and subsequently have had few, if any, opposing candidates at election time. In addition, the presence of turnover in office should be an indicator of the effectiveness of competition by showing whether an out party or group has the ability to challenge incumbents successfully or whether the electoral process is dominated by an unchanging majority.

EXTENT OF VOTING AND COMPETITION IN ELECTIONS

Selected Findings

Many county offices in New Mexico are elective and almost every citizen may qualify to run for them. Competition for these offices is often lively and frequently generates more interest locally than candidacies for state and national positions (Donnelly, 1947: 277).

The allocation of authority for enforcement of prohibition against liquor sales makes the sheriff's post in Mississippi extremely important and the campaign for this office one of the hardest fought in county politics. In some counties the legitimate fees of the office mount up, and outside the genuinely dry counties supplementary revenues are available. In some counties local bootleggers support a candidate for sheriff. If factions of bootleggers are in competition, each may back a different candidate. The candidate of the bootleggers is not always the winner on election day (Key, 1962:235).

The conditions of government in rural America are less hospitable to the development of a favorable climate of democracy than those of other environments. Small government lacks the substance to support a system which is or can be really democratic. Rural government has little magic to stir people's minds. It is too picayune, narrow in outlook, limited in horizon, and self-centered in interests to enlist the support of the voter (Martin, 1957:91-92).

Of the 289 winning Republican candidates for the county offices of clerk, sheriff, treasurer, and superintendent of schools in the county partisan elections throughout Illinois in 1966, 123 (42.6 per cent) faced effective competition in neither the primary nor general election. (Effective competition is defined as no one candidate receiving more than 75 per cent of the vote in the primary or more than 60 per cent in the general election.) Thirty-five of the

119 winning Democratic candidates (29.4 per cent) faced effective competition in neither election. Overall, 38.7 per cent of all these elected county officers faced effective competition in neither the primary nor general election. Almost one-half (46.7 per cent) of the winning Republicans and slightly more than one-half (52.9 per cent) of the winning Democrats faced effective competition in either the primary or general election. Therefore, just under one-half (48.5 per cent) of all the victors were confronted by effective competition in either election.

In total, only 52 victorious candidates (12.7 per cent) had effective competition in both the county primary and general elections in Illinois in 1966: 31 Republicans and 21 Democrats. Because so many counties in the state are strong one-party political units, the emerging picture of county elections seemingly is one of electoral inertia rather than effective competitiveness (Kitsos, 1968: 3-4).

In more than one-third of the counties in Iowa, there was no contest for any county office in either the primary or general election in 1944. Moreover, in more than half of the counties, no contest was present in the primary for any county office. In many of the remaining offices, contests were present in only one or two of the available offices (Porter, 1945:734-735).

Fifteen counties in Kentucky operate with a four-member governing board composed of the county judge and three commissioners, each of the latter a resident of a district but elected at large. The remaining counties have governing boards composed of the judge and three to eight justices of the peace, each justice elected from a district. A problem of the justice form of county organization is that well-qualified persons are often deterred from seeking membership on the county board because as justices of the peace they might be expected to serve in a judicial capacity (Vanlandingham, 1964:16).

County political party organizations in Wyoming must frequently petition for nomination of candidates in order to fill out the ticket. This practice is most widespread when a county is basically one-party. Even in a bipartisan county, certain local offices become the entrenched domains of particular individuals, a situation that discourages prospective candidates from filing. Some county offices are so unattractive both politically and remuneratively that no one in either party wants to file. In the past two elections of state and county officials, both Democrats and Republicans in Albany County have been unable to get candidates to file for county coroner. As the deadline for filing approached in 1954, there were no Democratic candidates in Albany County for two county commissioner positions, two state legislative posts, county clerk, clerk of the court, or coroner. In long arduous sessions the party's county central committee obtained candidates for the county commission, legislature, and coroner. The failure to file was not due to the hopelessness of the Democratic position; all the Democratic candidates won in contested elections. Only the unopposed Republican clerk and clerk of the court were reelected (Beall, 1961:342).

THE INDEPENDENT VARIABLES

We now turn to a number of major demographic, social, economic, and governmental factors, each of which is an independent variable. In other words, the level of political vitality is believed to be a function of each of these independent variables. Thus, stated as a hypothesis and using the first independent variable to be listed, the higher the rate of population increase, the higher the level of political vitality. This is not to posit that the relationship will be direct. Once we have established a correlation between an independent variable and the dependent variable (political vitality), we would subsequently investigate whether this relationship is direct or due to the intervention of another variable. Such intervention would create a spurious rather than direct relationship between the original independent variable and political vitality. Also, to determine the relationship between a particular independent variable and the index, it might be profitable at times to develop correlations between this independent variable (for instance, the rate of population increase) and an element of a component of the index, such as the volume of county contacts with other local units.

The independent variables may be usefully grouped into four categories. They are (1) demographic, (2) economic, (3) governmental, and (4) social. We will enumerate the factors within each of these classifications and make comments about one in each group. Following each of these illustrations are summaries of selected findings from various studies pertaining to the relation between most independent variables in a specific category and the index of political vitality or one of its components. In most instances the authors of these studies were not seeking to test the relationships between the independent variables and political vitality of counties. As a consequence, their findings indicate, sometimes roughly, the direction of relationships rather than their exact nature; the latter would be revealed by the analysis proposed in our research design.

DEMOGRAPHIC VARIABLES

Comments

The variables included within the demographic category are:

A. rate of population change (1940 or 1950 to 1960 and preferably later)

B. population density

C. proportion of county population that is urban

D. proportion of county population which is farm and living in unincorporated areas

E. proportion of county population which is non-farm and living in unincorporated areas

F. regional location (nationally and within a state)

G. size of population

H. population mobility (gross migration)

We may take Variable E as an example of the way in which demographic factors may be related to the index of political vitality. The proportion of county population that is non-farm and living in unincorporated areas should tell us something about the responsibilities cast upon the county government to provide urban-type services in localized sections of the county. Although granting that other local governments, such as towns, townships, and special districts, may be operative in unincorporated areas and may supply certain services to non-farm, non-city dwellers (which is a variable under the governmental category), it seems likely that Variable E affects some components of the index of political vitality. Resource utilization is the most likely candidate; changes in organization and processes is a second possibility.

DEMOGRAPHIC VARIABLES

Selected Findings

Demographic Variable A: Rate of Population Change

Many California counties continue to undergo major population growth. Los Angeles County increased by almost one-half between 1950 and 1960 and has since been growing at an average yearly rate of about 170,000 residents. Nine other counties had at least 200,000 more residents in 1965 than fifteen years earlier. In a time of general county population expansion in California, the loss of people by some counties has been largely unnoticed. Since 1950, four counties, all predominantly rural, plus San Francisco, have declined in population. Rising and decreasing populations both produce a need for changes in county government. The former results in the need to expand county public services and facilities. The latter, if sizable, may indicate a serious dislocation in the local economy and the desirability of curtailing services and combining certain county departments (Crouch et al., 1967:233).

Between 1950 and 1960, forty-five of South Dakota's sixty-seven counties lost population. This decline is clearly reflected in increased per capita governmental costs, which have a particularly severe impact on counties of low population. It is evident that the larger the county population, the lower the per capita cost of maintaining departments headed by elected county officials. The essential problem of county government is how to decrease per capita costs while retaining the same standards of service or gaining higher ones. This can be done in two ways: increasing efficiency and increasing the population of the jurisdiction. The first may be accomplished through combining certain county offices; the second, through consolidating counties. The decreasing population of many counties is making the need for administrative reform urgent. Counties containing fewer than 10,000 people should not maintain the same administrative structure as that used by counties of more than 50,000 population (Farber, 1963:1-4).

Demographic Variable B: Population Density

Population density is a more realistic base for differentiating among the several classes of counties than population alone. Although the number of classes of counties in any particular state should be determined by the density range of its counties, a fourfold classification is suggested. "Rural" would be reserved for counties with a population of 100 or fewer persons per square mile. Citizens in such counties receive only a minimum of county governmental services and customarily are not very vocal in demanding the newer, urban-type services. "Semi-rural" would embrace counties with densities ranging from 101 to 250 persons per square mile. As counties approach the upper limit of the density range of semi-rural, citizen demands will mount for such services as health, welfare, and law enforcement. "Semi-urban" would include counties with densities ranging from 251 persons per square mile to a maximum of 1,000. Counties in this group perform a number of services and functions not provided by their more rural counterparts. The fourth classification, "urban," is reserved for counties with population densities of 1,001 or more persons per square mile. These counties are truly units of urban government and are called upon to perform all the urban services. This fourfold classification avoids a stereotyped approach to counties, their organization, problems, and prospects. It also enables us to differentiate meaningfully among the three major roles counties undertake: administrative district of the state, unit of local government, and coordinating agency (Blair, 1964:174-175, 177).

Slightly over half of the population of Illinois is in Cook County. This density and size of population call for deviations from the patterns and functions of county governments elsewhere in the state (Garvey, 1958:539).

Demographic Variable C: Proportion of County That Is Urban

Two of every three Americans live in 300 of our largest counties. In these urban counties the magnitude of traditional county services rendered as a political arm of the state government, such as recordkeeping, elections, administration of justice, penal administration, and public health, has increased tremendously. A large portion of the growth in county personnel and expenditures is caused by the need to provide municipal services to people who have moved outside cities (Hillenbrand, n.d.:3).

Demographic Variables D and E: Proportion of County Population That is Farm or Non-Farm and Living in Unincorporated Areas

In some counties in Maryland, most notably those in metropolitan areas, the increase in county population from 1940 to 1960 has not been accompanied by gains in municipal population. There are no municipalities in Baltimore County, and in the other metropolitan counties (Anne Arundel, Montgomery, and Prince George's), municipal population as a percentage of the county total has dropped. In most counties in the state, there was no increase, or only a modest one, in the number of municipalities between 1940 and 1960. Excluding Baltimore and Howard counties, which have no incorporated places, the percentage of the population in municipalities went down in ten counties and increased in eleven during this period. Thus, there has been a substantial amount of population growth in the unincorporated portions of counties.

A relatively large number of unincorporated urban places exists in Maryland. In 1960, 18 such places had populations ranging from 1,001 to 9,999 and 21 other had 10,000 or more people. Four of the later group had more than 50,000.

The population shift from incorporated to unincorporated areas in Maryland has caused the entry of some county governments into traditional responsibilities of municipal governments: the provision of such basic municipal services as water, garbage and sewage disposal, planning and zoning, and fire and police protection. No new municipalities have been created in the state since 1953. (These Maryland findings are also relevant to *Governmental Variable D: Number of Incorporated Places in the County.*) (Spencer, 1965:8, 11-12).

Increased urbanization, with the consequent emergence of unincorporated fringe areas, has caused counties in Illinois to be confronted with the necessity of assuming many responsibilities of *de facto* municipalities, and the General Assembly of Illinois has expanded county powers to permit them to exercise increased services and controls in these areas. Such expansions include enactment of county zoning laws, authorization to provide garbage disposal facilities, and extension of licensing controls over lodgings for transients and places of amusement or recreation (Garvey, 1958:533).

Demographic Variable F: Regional Location

Governmental institutions characteristic of one region are insignificant or unused in another. Take the county as an example. In the South and West it is a very important governmental unit, but in New England its role is minimal, and in two of the New England states it has disappeared entirely (Lockard, 1963:7).

Major sectional differences are present in both the context and form of urban growth. In the Northeast and Near West, the central cities are declining in population while the suburbs are growing. In the Northwest, both central cities and suburbs are increasing. In the South, new metropolitan areas are developing, and, in a number of instances, are consolidating metropolitan governmental functions at the county level in the traditional southern pattern of reliance on county government. In the Southwest, large-scale annexation programs are extending central cities at the expense of suburban areas, transforming the former into very sizable municipalities. (Elazar, 1966:132).

ECONOMIC VARIABLES

Comments

The variables included within the economic category are:

A. taxable resources

B. value added by manufacturing

C. retail and wholesale trade as a percentage of total activity

D. the proportion of those employed who are in the service sector

E. unemployment rate

An illustration of a possible relationship between an economic factor and the index of political vitality may be shown by considering Variable E in the economic category. We may define the unemployment rate as the percentage of the total labor force that is not employed. This rate should indicate the level of demand placed upon counties to expend their resources on public health and welfare purposes, poverty projects, vocational training programs, and other means of human resource development. Seemingly, high unemployment would stimulate increased demand for these services which would result in turn in greater utilization of available resources by the government in order to finance these undertakings.

ECONOMIC VARIABLES

Selected Findings

Economic Variable A: Taxable Resources

Underassessment is a major problem with the property tax; elected county assessors experience continuing pressure from constituents to keep assessments low. Consequently, assessments generally are far below true market value, and in many states the ratios of assessed to true value vary among counties. A second major problem with the property tax is the extensiveness of exemptions from it (Duncombe, 1966:110, 113).

In some instances the national government has withdrawn vast tracts of land from sale, thereby reducing the taxable property, or it has so greatly reduced its productivity that income to the county has been affected. Shifts of population and decline in mining have taken away from several counties their principal sources of income (Mack et al., 1953:312-313).

Although federal properties are exempt from property taxes, counties in Wyoming assess oil production from them for property tax purposes. In addition, the national government makes payments to state and local governments, including counties, from revenue received by leasing grazing and timber lands (Jacobs and Company, 1954:30).

GOVERNMENTAL VARIABLES

Comments

The variables included within the governmental category are:

A. degree of liberality of state constitutional and statutory provisions (relative to county exercise of powers, etc.)

B. use of county home rule or optional state-prepared county charters (optional state laws)

C. partisan elections

D. number of incorporated places in the county

E. number of special districts, towns, and townships in unincorporated areas

Variable C may be used to demonstrate a possible correlation between a factor in the governmental category and the index of political vitality. In some counties, elections for county offices are held on a partisan basis: a party affiliation appears opposite the name of each candidate and political parties are sometimes active in providing campaign workers and financial support for their candidates. In other counties, elections are nonpartisan; party designations on the ballot are legally prohibited, and political parties, at least openly and usually not even secretly, provide no aid to candidates.

In partisan elections, there is usually a candidate from each political party for at least every major county elective office (the principal exception is in one-party areas). In contrast, in nonpartisan elections, incumbents frequently have no substantial opponents or even no contenders at all. Political parties also generally are more likely to develop platforms, which candidates use to varying degrees as benchmarks for discussions of issues in their campaigns. It seems likely, therefore, that partisan elections generate increased competition for public office and a greater amount of voter participation, which together constitute a component of the index of political vitality.

GOVERNMENTAL VARIABLES

Selected Findings

Governmental Variable A: Degree of Liberality of State Constitutional and Statutory Provisions

Constitutional county home rule, which provides for the writing of a locally-drafted county charter, is available to all or some counties in thirteen states. They are, with the dates of adoption of the constitutional section: California, 1911; Maryland, 1915; Ohio and Texas, 1933; Missouri, 1945; Louisiana, for East Baton Rouge Parish, 1946, and for Jefferson Parish, 1956; Washington, 1948; Florida, for Dade County, 1956; Minnesota, New York, and Oregon, 1958; Alaska, for boroughs, 1959; and Hawaii, 1959. Optional county charters, which consist of two or more alternative plans prepared by the state legislature, enable counties to choose a particular organizational form. Montana, New York, North Carolina, North Dakota, and Virginia have made such charters available (Duncombe, 1966:242-244).

State constitutional provisions exist that prevent or make it difficult to decrease the number of local governments and to increase their size. These restrictions include (1) freezing the existence of townships or other units smaller than counties; (2) declaring the existence of specific counties; (3) locating the county seat; (4) regulating the change of county boundaries; and (5) requiring special popular majorities in consolidations and mergers. Twenty-one state constitutions have one or more restrictions of this nature concerning counties. In addition, these limitations may in some instances bar city-county merger and retard interlocal cooperation.

There are also state constitutional sections restricting executive management and election of county governing boards at large. They call for (1) election of county boards from townships or districts; (2) uniformity of government for all counties; and (3) burdening of the adoption of optional forms by methods not essential to the democratic process. Eleven state constitutions have one or more restrictions of this nature.

State legal limitations on local debt and taxes have handicapped local governments severely. The frequent state constitutional prohibition against the extension of state credit or the making of state appropriations to local governments has restricted the ability of local units to meet changing needs and has stimulated federal aid.

Twenty-five state constitutions impose one or more of the following restrictions on county officials and personnel: (1) requiring an unnecessarily long ballot and imposing conditions that may handicap operations, such as not providing authority for office consolidations; (2) requiring officials to be residents of the jurisdiction of their employment; (3) limiting the salaries of officials;

and (4) prescribing the details of a merit system (Advisory Commission on Intergovernmental Relations, 1962b:38-40).

Thirty-seven states limit the property taxing powers of counties for general government purposes. In addition, Virginia limits county taxing powers for school purposes only, and California imposes tax limits on counties for certain specified purposes, but not for general purposes. State restrictions on local fiscal powers generally take the form of maximum limitations on the allowable tax rate related to the assessed value, not the actual market value, of taxable property, although statewide equalized value is occasionally specified. Most states permitting their local governments to impose nonproperty taxes have restricted the authority to particular local units and to specific types of taxes. With few exceptions, use of four important nonproperty taxes (general sales, income, cigarette, motor fuel) is confined largely to municipalities. All 57 counties and the city-county of San Francisco in California and 65 of the 102 counties in Illinois levy general sales taxes; otherwise county use of nonproperty taxes is sparse (Advisory Commission on Intergovernmental Relations, 1962c:44, 1, 11, 79).

If county government in the United States is weak, it is because of the effects of provisions in state constitutions (Duncan, 1950: 417).

Governmental Variable B: Use of County Home Rule or Optional State-Prepared County Charters (Optional State Laws)

Although nearly 400 counties may frame and adopt their own home rule charters, only 14 had done so by 1960. Ten are in California, two in Maryland, and one each in Missouri and New York. In addition, single counties in a few states, such as Dade County, Florida, and Jefferson Parish, Louisiana, have been constitutionally authorized to adopt home rule charters and have used the authority. County home rule does not substantially increase the power and functions of counties, but it does give counties some discretion relating to structure and powers that might not otherwise exist. It may also be a means for working out more satisfactory arrangements for the sharing of power with other local units (Blair, 1964:192-193).

In some states the legislature has provided two or more alternative forms of county government (often called optional county charters) which may be adopted at the discretion of counties. Certain counties in Montana, New York, North Carolina, North Dakota, and Virginia have exercised such options (Duncombe, 1966: 244).

The constitutional home rule provision in Ohio permits a locally-drawn county charter that changes only county organization to be adopted by majority countywide vote. However, any charter granting a county the exclusive exercise of any municipal or township powers must obtain multiple popular majorities. Although efforts have been made, particularly in Cuyahoga County (Cleveland), to adopt a county charter, none has succeeded (Greene, 1961:49).

The battle for county home rule in Texas reached a climax in 1935 with adoption of a constitutional amendment designed to give certain counties (those of over 62,000 population) a home rule option. The battle has turned out to be largely a waste of time and energy. A county charter must obtain two separate majorities: in the incorporated places and in the unincorporated sections. Resistance is strong in the latter. Moreover, the amendment is a classic in ambiguity and obscurity, especially as to how far a charter may go in overhauling the existing county structure. Since the opportunity to make structural changes is a primary reason for seeking county home rule, the likelihood of judicial interpretation prohibiting certain fundamental changes has enervated the entire movement. There is still no county in Texas operating under a home rule charter (McClesky, 1963:257-258).

Four counties in Virginia have changed their form of government by making use of the Optional Forms Act of 1932, which requires a countywide referendum to be activated locally. Two counties took action in 1933, another in 1945, and the fourth in 1952. Subsequently, one of the four has passed from county to city status (Gibson and Overman, 1961:8-9).

Governmental Variable C: Partisan Elections

In Onondaga County (Syracuse), the concurrence of members of the dominant political party who occupy governmental positions makes it possible for a Republican mayor of Syracuse, who is also Republican county chairman, to integrate welfare functions in the county and further makes the Republican state legislative leadership highly responsive to the wishes of Onondaga County. The reverse is also true. In Oneida County (Utica), the absence of partisan identity between the central city administration and the county governing board apparently has produced conflicts that sometimes have acted as barriers to interlocal cooperation (Munger, 1966:200-201).

The principle of minority party membership on the county board of commissioners (the county governing body) is required by the Pennsylvania constitution. As a consequence, the majority party throws a few votes in each election district to one of the two minority candidates for county commissioner and thus controls the outcome. The recipient of this favor is well aware of the arrangement and of his role as minority commissioner. He seldom, if ever, disagrees with his associates of the opposing party on the board (Cooke, 1965:53-54).

Local nonpartisan elections—the practice of listing the names of candidates for any local public offices on the ballot without party affiliation—have been increasingly attacked in California in recent years, although so far without success in the state legislature. Most incumbent city and county elected officials oppose the change from nonpartisan to partisan local elections, a stand that many Democratic state legislators attribute to the fact that Republicans are predominant in holding county and city elective offices. Opponents of partisan local elections argue that most local issues are unrelated to state and national policies and only remotely related, if at all, to any identifiable political philosophy. Advocates of partisan local elections contend that political parties are the only mechanism for focusing sufficient power to gain adoption of the kinds of local legislation needed to allow local governments to deal effectively with the problems facing them. Efforts to eliminate nonpartisan elections in California county and city governments will likely be made in future legislative sessions. Meanwhile, political party organizations and party personalities are playing an increasingly vigorous role behind the scenes in certain local contests (Crouch et al., 1967:243-245).

Governmental Variable D: Number of Incorporated Places in the County

In the period of heavy urbanization from 1942 to 1952, the number of municipalities in the United States increased by less than 3.5 per cent. In California, the number of incorporations in the thirty years after 1920 was less than one-half the number in the preceding twenty years, despite the largest population growth in the state's history. Many people settled in cities which had incorporated earlier, but many others located in urbanized areas which did not incorporate. Incorporation is not keeping pace with fringe area expansion, chiefly because of negative decisions or inactions by urban fringe residents (Bollens, 1957:100).

(See also the Maryland entry by Jean Spencer under *Demographic Variables D and E.*)

Governmental Variable E: Number of Special Districts, Towns, and Townships in Unincorporated Areas

A large volume of district laws usable in urban fringe areas has been enacted in many states, particularly since the 1940's. Moreover, much of this legislation has been designed exclusively for such areas. This is evident by its provisions, which endow the district with urban functions but restrict its area to unincorporated territory, and sometimes even restrict the district territory to a certain radial distance from the legal city limits or require it to be adjacent to a city. There are several thousand urban fringe districts operating in unincorporated areas bordering cities. These districts are geographically widespread but are not evenly distributed throughout the United States. The unevenness of their geographical distribution may be traced partly to differences in the intensity of urban fringe needs and in the success of other governments in meeting those needs. In New York, for example, numerous fringe demands are satisfied by dependent districts which are part of the town government, a solution which makes it unnecessary to create separate and independent urban fringe districts (Bollens, 1957: 103, 98).

About one half of the 131 counties in Virginia have no special districts. The lack of widespread growth of these units in this state may be due to the long-time history of strong county government in Virginia and to the ability of Virginia counties to establish county-subordinate taxing areas. In the United States in general, special districts have been established when traditional local governments have neglected to provide services or have been constitutionally prohibited from furnishing them (Smith, 1968:59-60).

SOCIAL VARIABLES

Comments

The variables included within the social category all relate to the extent of heterogeneity of the population of a county in terms of:

A. ethnic and racial composition

B. personal income

C. occupations

D. levels of education

E. life styles (single-family and apartment dwellers, home owners and renters, women of child-bearing age in the labor force)

F. family income

G. age composition

H. family structure (single heads of households with dependent children)

Utilizing Variable A as an example, it is possible that different segments of a county population which is highly varied in ethnic and racial backgrounds would have differing public wants and demands and thus would produce a greater interest in and turnout for county elections than would be the case in a homogeneous county. Also, it is assumed that a high degree of ethnic and racial heterogeneity provides an environment for the development of an increased number of issues and conflicts, solutions to some of which are sought through office-seeking. It is further assumed that a county of extensive ethnic and racial heterogeneity will tend to have a larger governing body to reflect the diversified interests (when governing body size may be determined by local option). A larger governing body may or may not result in more adequate public accountability, depending in important part upon whether an executive committee of the board is organized and plays a crucial role in the making of many decisions. Extent of voting and office competition, and adequacy of public accountability are both components of the index of political vitality.

SOCIAL VARIABLES

Selected Findings

Social Variable A: Extent of Heterogeneity (Ethnic and Racial Composition)

Whatever phase of the southern political process about which understanding is sought, the trail of inquiry leads quickly or eventually to the Negro. The politics of individual states in the South vary roughly with the Negro proportion of the population. If the politics revolve around a single theme, it is the role of the black belts. The white residents of the black belts are few in number, but their unity and political skill have enabled them to exercise decisive power at critical junctures of political history in the South (Key, 1962:5-6).

The political participation of Negroes in Florida has been highest and their solidarity most pronounced in opposition to avowed white supremacy candidates and in support of municipal and county officials such as mayor, sheriff, or school superintendent who are regarded as favorable in their treatment of Negroes, and in national contests (Price, 1966:37).

Interparty competition for county offices in North Carolina definitely decreases as the percentage of nonwhite in the total population rises (Gatlin, 1968:234, 238).

Social Variables B and F: Extent of Heterogeneity (Income)

In 200 urbanized areas (each containing at least one city of 50,000 people, as well as adjacent closely-settled incorporated places and unincorporated territory), none of the cities in the two largest population classes (1,000,000 and over and 500,000 to 1,000,000) exceeds its suburbs in median family income, but increasing proportions of such cities do so as one moves down the size range to the smallest urbanized areas. Also, suburbs consistently register higher median family incomes in the older urbanized areas (measured by the number of decades that have passed since the central city first reached 50,000 inhabitants); none of the thirty-one cities attaining a population of 50,000 in 1880 or earlier has a higher average income than its suburbs. On the other hand, the newer urbanized areas tend consistently to show increasing proportions of central cities with higher incomes. Moreover, statistical analysis reveals that even when population size is held constant, age of an urbanized area continues to exert a major influence upon the direction of the differences between central cities and suburbs (Schnore, 1965:206, 208, 211).

The classic dichotomy of the poor, underprivileged, nonwhite central city in contrast to the comfortable white suburb does not hold true throughout the United States. Although racial disparities are large everywhere, the other elements of the dichotomy – income, education, employment, and housing – fit the stereotype consistently only in the large metropolitan areas, many of which are intercounty, and in those located in the Northeast. The Northeast includes 41 of the 190 standard metropolitan statistical areas studied, and outside that region there are 39 metropolitan areas with populations of more than a half million. For the remaining 110 metropolitan areas, many of which are intracounty, this dichotomy does not generally apply.

In the small and medium sized metropolitan areas outside the Northeast, some elements of both high and low socioeconomic status tend to be equally prevalent in both central cities and suburban areas, while other low-status characteristics predominate in the suburbs and some high-status ones are more significant in the central cities. In many metropolitan areas of the South and West, poverty, especially among nonwhites, is more typical of the suburbs than of the central city (U.S. House Committee on Government Operations, 1966:19).

Social Variable C: Extent of Heterogeneity (Occupations)

As the percentage of population in working class occupations in North Carolina counties rises, interparty competition for county office also rises (Gatlin, 1968:229-231, 238).

Social Variable D: Extent of Heterogeneity (Levels of Education)

In North Carolina counties, as the proportion of the total population over twenty-five years of age with less than a fifth-grade education rises, the extent of interparty competition for county offices decreases (Gatlin, 1968:231, 238).

REFERENCES

ADVISORY COMMISSION ON INTERGOVERNMENTAL RELATIONS. (1962a) Measures of State and Local Fiscal Capacity and Tax Effort (Washington) (October).

______(1962b) State Constitutional and Statutory Restrictions on the Structural, Functional, and Personnel Powers of Local Government (Washington) (October).

______(1962c) State Constitutional and Statutory Restrictions on Local Taxing Powers (Washington) (October).

ALEXANDER, HENRY M. (1959) Government in Arkansas: Organization and Function at State, County, and Municipal Levels. Little Rock: Pioneer Press.

ALFORD, ROBERT R., and HARRY M. SCOBLE. (1965) "Political and socioeconomic characteristics of American cities." Pp. 82-97 in Municipal Year Book: 1965. Chicago: International City Managers' Association.

BANFIELD, EDWARD C., and JAMES Q. WILSON. (1963) City Politics. Cambridge: Harvard University Press and M.I.T. Press.

BEALL, CHARLES P. (1961) "Wyoming: the equality state." Pp. 335-355 in Frank H. Jonas (ed.) Western Politics. Salt Lake City: University of Utah Press.

BLAIR, GEORGE S. (1964) American Local Government. New York: Harper and Row.

BOLES, DONALD E., and HERBERT C. COOK. (1959) An Evaluation of Iowa County Government. Ames: Community Research Center, Iowa State College.

BOLLENS, JOHN C. (1957) Special District Governments in the United States. Berkeley: University of California Press.

"Bridges and building blocks." (1966) American County Government, 31 (September): 55, 63.

CAPE, WILLIAM H. (1967) The Emerging Patterns of County Executives. Lawrence: Governmental Research Center, University of Kansas.

COKE, JAMES G., and THOMAS J. ANTON. (1962) Planning in the Penjerdel Region. Philadelphia: Pennsylvania-New Jersey-Delaware Metropolitan Project, Inc.

COLMAN, WILLIAM G. (1965) "Techniques of intergovernmental cooperation." Iowa Municipalities, 20 (November): 22-25.

COOKE, EDWARD F. (1965) Pennsylvania Politics. New York: Holt, Rinehart, and Winston.

CRITTENDEN, JOHN. (1967) "Dimensions of modernization in the American states." American Political Science Review, LXI (December): 989-1001.

CROUCH, WINSTON W., JOHN C. BOLLENS, STANLEY SCOTT, and DEAN E. MCHENRY. (1967) California Government and Politics, 4th ed. Englewood Cliffs: Prentice-Hall.

DAVIS, CLYDE J., EUGENE R. ELKINS, CARL FRASURE, MARVIS REEVES, WILLIAM R. ROSS, and ALBERT STURM (1963) West Virginia State and Local Government. Morgantown: West Virginia University.

DAWSON, RICHARD E., and JAMES A. ROBINSON. (1965) "The politics of welfare" in Herbert Jacob and Kenneth N. Vines (eds.) Politics in the American States: A Comparative Analysis. Boston: Little, Brown.

DONNELLY, THOMAS G. (1947) The Government of New Mexico. Albuquerque: University of New Mexico Press.

DRURY, JAMES W. (1961) The Government of Kansas. Lawrence: University of Kansas Press.

DUNCAN, JOHN P. (1950) "County government—an analysis." Pp. 417-443 in Oklahoma State Legislative Council, Constitutional Survey and Citizen Advisory Committees, *Oklahoma Constitutional Studies*. Guthrie: Cooperative Publishing.

DUNCOMBE, HERBERT S. (1966) County Government in America. Washington: National Association of Counties Research Foundation.

DYE, THOMAS R. (1966) Politics, Economics, and the Public: Policy Outcomes in the American States. Chicago: Rand McNally.

——— (1967) "Governmental structure, urban environment, and educational policy." Midwest Journal of Political Science, XI (August): 353-380.

ELAZAR, DANIEL J. (1966) American Federalism: A View From the States. New York: Thomas Y. Crowell.

EULAU, HEINZ, and ROBERT EYESTONE (1968) "Policy maps of city councils and policy outcomes: a developmental analysis." American Political Science Review, LXI (March): 124-144.

FARBER, W. O. (1963) "Improving county government: reorganization and consolidation." Public Affairs. Vermillion: Governmental Research Bureau, University of South Dakota, No. 14 (August 15).

FAVOR, WILLIAM H., CLYDE WOODALL, GEORGE AULL, and CALVIN C. TAYLOR (1960) The Impact of Economic Change on Local Government in South Caolina. Clemson: South Carolina Agricultural Experiment Station.

FENTON, JOHN H. (1966) Midwest Politics. New York: Holt, Rinehart and Winston.

GARVEY, NEIL F. (1958) The Government and Administration of Illinois. New York: Thomas Y. Crowell.

GATLIN, DOUGLAS S. (1968) "Toward a functionalist theory of political parties: inter-party competition in North Carolina." Pp. 217-245 in William J. Crotty (ed.) Approaches to the Study of Party Organization. Boston: Allyn and Bacon.

GIBSON, FRANK K., and EDWARD S. OVERMAN. (1961) County Government in Virginia, 2nd ed. Charlottesville: League of Virginia Counties and Bureau of Public Administration, University of Virginia.

GOSNELL, CULLEN B. and C. DAVID ANDERSON (1956) The Government and Administration of Georgia. New York: Thomas Y. Crowell.

GREENE, ALEXANDER. (1961) Ohio Government. Englewood Cliffs: Prentice-Hall.

HILLENBRAND, BERNARD F. (n.d.) "Counties—too little almost too late." Washington: National Association of Counties (unpublished paper).

HOWARDS, IRVING and ROBERT W. RICHEY (1959) A Citizen's Handbook of County Government in Illinois. Carbondale: Local Government Center, Southern Illinois University.

IDAHO GOVERNMENTAL COST AND TAX STRUCTURE COMMITTEE (1954) Report, Volume 5: State and Local Problems and Relationships. Boise.

ILLINOIS COUNTY STUDY AND SURVEY COMMISSION. (1961) Source Book on Illinois County Government. Carbondale: Local Government Center, Southern Illinois University.

JACOB, HERBERT, and MICHAEL LIPSKY (1968) "Outputs, structure, and power: an assessment of changes in the study of state and local politics." The Journal of Politics, 30 (May): 510-538.

JACOB, HERBERT, and KENNETH N. VINES. (eds.) (1965), Politics in the American States: A Comparative Analysis. Boston: Little, Brown.

J. L. JACOBS AND COMPANY. (1954) State of Wyoming, Impacts of Federal Grants-in-Aid on the State and Local Governments: Report and Recommendations Prepared for the Commission on Intergovernmental Relations (Chicago).

JONES, VICTOR. (1963) "Urban and metropolitan counties." Pp. 57-82 in Municipal Year Book: 1962. Chicago: International City Managers' Association.

KEY, V. O., JR. (1949) Southern Politics in State and Nation. New York: Alfred A. Knopf.

_____ (1962) Southern Politics in State and Nation, First Vintage Edition. New York: Random House.

KITSOS, THOMAS. (1968) "The 1966 county elections." Illinois Government. Urbana: Institute of Government and Public Affairs, University of Illinois.

LANCASTER, LANE W. (1952) Government in Rural America. Princeton: D. Van Nostrand.

LANGLEY, JAMES N. (1948) "The end of an era: county government has become obsolete in New Hampshire." Durham: Institute of Public Affairs, University of New Hampshire (unpublished paper).

LINEBERRY, ROBERT L., and EDMUND P. FOWLER (1967), "Reformism and public policies in American cities." American Political Science Review, LXI (September): 701-716.

LOCKARD, DUANE. (1959) New England State Politics. Princeton: Princeton University Press.

_____ (1963) The Politics of State and Local Government. New York: Macmillan.

MCCLESKY, CLIFTON. (1963) The Government and Politics of Texas. Boston: Little, Brown.

MACK, EFFIE M., IDEL ANDERSON, and BEULAH E. SINGLETON. (1953) Nevada Government. Caldwell, Idaho: Caxton Printers.

MARTIN, ROSCOE C. (1957) Grass Roots. University: University of Alabama Press.

MICHIGAN STATE UNIVERSITY, BUREAU OF SOCIAL AND POLITICAL RESEARCH. (1959) The County Board of Supervisors (East Lansing).

MUNGER, FRANK. (1966) "Community power and metropolitan decision-making." In Frank Munger (ed.) American State Politics. New York: Thomas Y. Crowell.

NEW YORK OFFICE FOR LOCAL GOVERNMENT. (1966) Reapportionment: Local Government Legislative Bodies. Albany: Information Bulletin No. 2 (March 24).

PENNIMAN, CLARA. (1965) "The politics of taxation." Pp. 291-329 in Herbert Jacob and Kenneth N. Vines (eds.) Politics in the American States: A Comparative Analysis. Boston: Little, Brown.

PORTER, KIRK H. (1945) "The deserted primary in Iowa." American Political Science Review, XXXIX (August): 732-740.

PRICE, HUGH D. (1966) "The Negro and Florida politics, 1944-1954." In Frank Munger (ed.) American State Politics. New York: Thomas Y. Crowell.

SCHNORE, LEO F., and ROBERT R. ALFORD (1963) "Forms of government and socioeconomic characteristics of suburbs." Administrative Science Quarterly, VIII (June): 1-17.

SCHNORE, LEO F. (1965) The Urban Scene: Human Ecology and Demography. New York: Free Press.

SHARKANSKY, IRA. (1967a) "Economic and political correlates of state government expenditures: general tendencies and deviant cases." Midwest Journal of Political Science, XI (May): 173-192.

______ (1967b) "Government expenditures and public services in the American states." American Political Science Review, LXI (December): 1066-1077.

SMITH, ROBERT G. (1968) "County service districts and special districts." In National Association of Counties, Guide to County Organization and Management (Washington).

SNIDER, CLYDE F. (1957) Local Government in Rural America. New York: Appleton-Century-Crofts.

SPENCER, JEAN E. (1965) Contemporary Local Government in Maryland. College Park: Bureau of Governmental Research, University of Maryland.

U. S. HOUSE COMMITTEE ON GOVERNMENTAL OPERATIONS, SUBCOMMITTEE ON INTERGOVERNMENTAL RELATIONS. (1966) Metropolitan America: Challenge to Federalism. Washington: Advisory Commission on Intergovernmental Relations (October).

U.S. SENATE COMMITTEE ON GOVERNMENTAL OPERATIONS, SUBCOMMITTEE ON INTERGOVERNMENTAL RELATIONS. (1965) The Federal System as Seen by Federal Aid Officials (Washington) (December).

VANLANDINGHAM, KENNETH E. (1964) The Constitution and Local Government. Frankfort: Kentucky Legislative Research Commission.

WARD, G. D. (1965), "Reapportionment a 'must' for county boards in Michigan." The County Officer, 30 (January): 1.

WEIDNER, EDWARD W. (1960) Intergovernmental Relations As Seen by Public Officials: Intergovernmental Relations in the United States As Observed in the State of Minnesota. Minneapolis: University of Minnesota Press.

WILSON, JAMES Q. (ed.) (1968) City Politics and Public Policy. New York: John Wiley & Sons.

WOLFINGER, RAYMOND E., and JOHN OSGOOD FIELD. (1966) "Political ethos and the structure of city government." American Political Science Review, LX (June): 306-326.

WOLLENZIEN, HAROLD J. (1965) "Wisconsin county boards must be elected on population basis." The County Officer, 30 (April): 44-45.

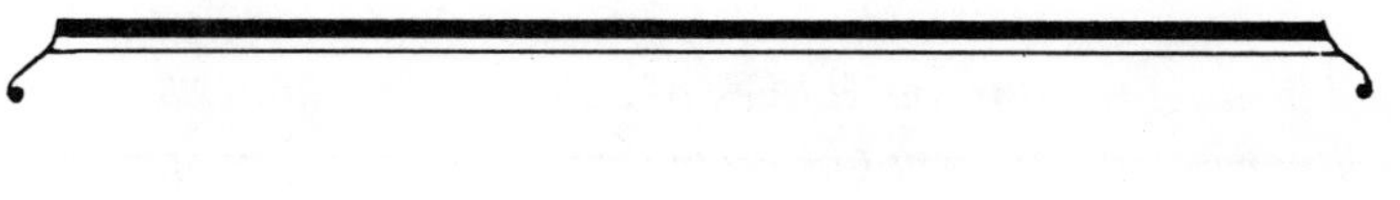

PART THREE

A BIBLIOGRAPHICAL COMMENTARY

All items in the bibliographical commentary are nationwide or statewide in scope. It would have been impossible within the limits of this publication to consider studies of individual counties; however, when a general study mentions them, note usually has been made of this fact. In cases where items about counties in specific states are plentiful, which is the definite exception rather than the general rule, the procedure has been to stress variety and not to duplicate comparable publications.

The commentary is organized under seven major headings (general, finance, intergovernmental relations, organization, politics, reform, and services), all of which have subdivisions. The nationwide items are presented first under each heading and subdivision, followed by an alphabetical arrangement by states and authors within them.

PART THREE

A BIBLIOGRAPHICAL COMMENTARY

COUNTY GOVERNMENT

General

United States

Richard S. Childs in RAMSHACKLE COUNTY GOVERNMENT: THE PLAGUE SPOT OF AMERICAN POLITICS (New York: National Municipal League, 1925, 27 pp.) writes in a muckraking vein about county government in the early twentieth century. He chides county government for its inadequate political responsiveness, deplores the low level of public knowledge about counties, and discusses how their legal advertising is sometimes padded to subsidize certain local newspapers owned by "county bosses." Lack of professional administration, inflexibility of boundaries, and the antiquated and diffused nature of organizational structure are criticized.

Mr. Childs discusses the confusing maze of general and specific state legislation concerning county government, the reasons for its enactment, and its consequences. He examines the problem of obscurity of elective county officers in a long ballot and explores the ways in which the long ballot has led to bossism and inadequate popular control. The concluding section pertains to county reform, including the short ballot, county home rule, and chief executives. The failings of county government are seen as improper political motivation, corruption, obsolete structure, and the long ballot; little attention is given to functions.

Written in a popular style, the pamphlet is readable and entertaining. Many examples from individual counties are given, but there are no footnotes or bibliography. At the time of this publication, the author was a department manager at A. E. Chew Company. He is past president of the National Municipal League, where he is now a full-time volunteer staff member, and former chairman of the Institute of Public Administration, New York.

One of the first thorough studies of county government in the United States was written by John A. Fairlie and Charles M. Kneier, COUNTY GOVERNMENT AND ADMINISTRATION (New York: D. Appleton-Century, 1930, 585 pp.). Typical of much political science writing of the early twentieth century, this volume takes a legalistic-descriptive-structural approach to the subject. It begins with an interesting and extensive treatment of the historical development of county government from its Anglo-Saxon origins to its status in late nineteenth-century America. Emphasis is on the development of regional patterns of county organization in the United States.

The second part of the book concerns county relations with the states. The authors emphasize the quasi-corporate (quasi-municipal) legal status of county government and its dependence on the state of which it is simply a subdivision. State constitutional provisions for county government, county powers, and state judicial and administrative control are examined.

The third part focuses on the organization of county government. It considers boards, officers for the administration of justice, finance and other officials, politics and elections, and employees and the merit system. The powers and responsibilities of various officers and boards and the use of the county as a unit for political party organization and election administration are treated at length.

The fourth part describes the functions of county government, including their administrative, financial, organizational, and intergovernmental aspects. The officers, boards, and employees engaged in the administration of each function are discussed. The functions examined are: justice; jails; poor relief (or public welfare); health, including hospitals; education; highways; and revenue.

The final section is titled "Special Problems." Here the authors examine New England towns; townships; county service districts and special districts; villages, boroughs, and towns; and county government in metropolitan areas. Under the last named subject, city-county consolidation and the general problem of local government in metropolitan areas are scrutinized.

The authors used a wide variety of primary and secondary sources, including many public documents and publications of research bureaus. At the time of this publication, the authors were Professors of Political Science, University of Illinois.

John P. Duncan in "COUNTY GOVERNMENT—AN ANALYSIS," a section in Oklahoma State Legislative Council, Constitutional Survey and Citizen Advisory Committees, *Oklahoma Constitutional Studies* (Guthrie: Co-operative Publishing Company, 1950, pp. 417-448), analyzes the constitutional provisions for and actual operations of county government in the United States in general and in Oklahoma specifically. He begins by setting out a number of criticisms of county government throughout the nation. His first topic of discussion is the diffusion of administrative responsibility and policy-making powers among the county governing body, the elected administrative officers, and semi-independent boards. He then chastises the county for its lack of technical expertise and its insufficient responsiveness to popular demands. Next, the author levels a series of criticisms against the county governing board and cites assessing practices as an example of the laxities of county administration. The problems of the discretionary authority held by county administrators are examined, and intercounty functional consolidation is considered. Finally, he discusses the interrelated problems of inadequate county departmentalization and the governing board's lack of fiscal control over county operations.

The author then examines a second topic: the inadequacy of constitutional provisions for county government in most states. He discusses the role of the county as a subdivision of the state and analyzes constitutional provisions concerning county boundaries and governmental structure. He then discusses county government in Oklahoma specifically. (*See* County Government—General: Oklahoma.)

Professor Duncan is extremely critical of county government and suggests extensive changes in its constitutional and statutory provisions in every state. The content reads easily and is quite interesting, since it is written in a flowing and almost muckraking style. As a chapter in a book containing constitutional studies on various subjects by several authors, it is descriptive, analytical, and prescriptive. At the time of this publication, the author was Professor of Government, University of Oklahoma.

COUNTY GOVERNMENT ACROSS THE NATION (Chapel Hill: University of North Carolina Press, 1950, 817 pp.), edited by Paul W. Wager, is a massive study of county government in the United States at mid-twentieth century. An introductory general section on county government is followed by discussions of each of the then forty-eight states, grouped into four sections—New England, eastern and north-central, southern, and western states. (*See* County Government—General: Eastern and North Central, New England, Southern, and Western.) After discussion of a given state, a detailed case study of one county in it is presented.

The general introductory section to the book, authored by the editor, starts with a treatment of the origins of the county which Professor Wager traces through its English beginnings and colonial development and into the five systems which have developed in the nation: the New England town, the southern county (the Virginia system), the New York system, the Pennsylvania system, and the Rocky Mountain and Far West plan. He also gives a brief explanation of the legal nature of counties.

Professor Wager then describes the governmental pattern of the county. He explains the different types of governing bodies utilized and the extent of their use. He next considers collateral boards, particularly the effect of their creation on the powers of the general governing bodies of the county, and the number of states in which fourteen types of special boards are employed and the reasons for their growth. The focus then turns to officials associated with the courts—sheriff, prosecuting attorney, clerk of the court, coroner, county judge, probate judge, and justices of the peace—and to various non-judicial offices—county clerk, recorder or register of deeds, auditor, treasurer, assessor, surveyor or engineer, superintendent of schools, and constables.

In discussing functions handled by the county, the author points out the ones usually required by state law. He then examines the developing trend of state assumption of functions traditionally considered county responsibilities, and he discusses the limited number of activities the county may initiate and new programs, such as hospitals and other health facilities, resulting from state and federal aid. Finally he explains the trend toward conferring upon county and township governments those duties ordinarily performed by municipalities, notably zoning, housing and regulatory activities.

The discussion of finances begins with a listing of the different sources of county revenue. Detailed breakdowns are given of the expenditure of funds for public assistance and highways, and a balance sheet is included on all county government revenues and expenditures.

Before presenting the different types of state supervision over local government, Professor Wager explains the reasons for this trend and why local government has become inadequate. He follows this with detailed interstate comparisons of state supervision in education, public welfare, highways, fiscal operations, property assessment, and local personnel. He concludes this general discussion of the county by pointing out structural inadequacies and offering suggestions for reform and change.

Discussion of the county by region and state is preceded by a description of the operation of town, township, and school district government across the nation and their relations to the county.

The substance of the material in the regional groupings is discussed under separate entries in this bibliography and follows the format noted above. The common characteristics of each region and the pertinent differences from other parts of the country are discussed in an introductory section to the region; particulars about each state are then given in the separate chapters and in the county case study.

Basically, the organization of the book is from a very general (nationwide) to a somewhat more limited discussion of a region, then to a more specific consideration of each state, and, finally, beyond any generalization, to the organization and operation of a particular county in each state. Professor Wager mentions in the preface that all but one (the town of Guilford in Maine) of the case studies were written from direct field research and familiarity with the unit. In addition to Dr. Wager, the contributors to this volume are Emmett G. Asseff, Donald B. Hayman, George H. Deming, Alan R. Richards, Mavis A. Mann, Harding Hughes, Melvin C. Hughes, Elwyn A. Mauck, Oka Stanton Flick, Fred A. Clarenbach, Edward W. Weidner, Lloyd W. Woodruff, George W. Spicer, Paul Tanner, Lee S. Greene, Evan A. Iverson, George R. Sherrill, William L. Bradshaw, A. J. Bartley, A. G. Breckenridge, T. C. Geary, Walter E. Kaloupek, R. R. Renne, Henry J. Peterson, Leo C. Riethmayer, Thomas C. Donnelly, Jack E. Holmes, Paul Kelso, Ellsworth E. Weaver, S. M. Vincour, Claude C. Smith, Hobert P. Sturm, Paul Beckett, and Herman Kehrli.

This is the most comprehensive and detailed study written on county government throughout the nation. The only comparable work, which is more recent, is Herbert Duncombe's *County Government in America*; its geographic breakdown is not as complete or detailed, however. The Wager study is mainly descriptive, particularly in the case studies, although analysis and some prescription do appear in the introductory sections. At the time of this publication, the editor was Professor of Political Science, University of North Carolina.

Clyde F. Snider summarizes the major problems and trends in county government in the early 1950's in his article, "AMERICAN COUNTY GOVERNMENT: A MID-CENTURY REVIEW," *American Political Science Review,* 46 (March, 1952), 66-80. He shows both the weaknesses and the emerging strengths of county government throughout the United States. Discussion centers first on the virtual numerical stability of counties since the turn of the current century and then turns to intercounty and city-county consolidation.

Much space is devoted to the problems of reforming the organization and processes of county government. The subject is introduced with an analysis of the dependence of the counties upon the states for improvement measures and is followed by an examination of county home rule and optional forms of county government laws. In this connection, Professor Snider presents an interesting discussion of the limitations of county home rule. State administrative control and supervision of county activities comprise the next subject of discussion; then modernized forms of county organization – the county manager plan, county administrative forms, and the elected chief executive form – are considered. There is also an exploration of the need for consolidation of county offices and the introduction of county merit systems. This section concludes with a treatment of the problems of county governing boards, particularly large ones.

The author discusses county functions and revenues at length. He examines the increase in number and variety of functions, giving particular emphasis to the increasingly important role of counties in highway construction and maintenance. He stresses that many new functions of counties have resulted from transfers from other local units, especially townships. This discussion of functional expansion leads into an exploration of county revenue sources. The author considers the problems of great dependence on the property tax and state aid and gives much attention to the need for expansion of nonproperty-tax sources. This section ends with a treatment of the desirability of modern purchasing, auditing, and personnel practices and is followed by a brief section exploring the emerging trend of functional consolidation, which includes city-county, intercounty, and special district arrangements. The concluding section summarizes the need for reform of county government and lists the specific means of attaining it.

Professor Snider deals with county government in a reformist manner, and the article is generally concise and well-written and utilizes many primary and secondary sources. At the time of this publication, the author was Professor of Political Science, University of Illinois.

Lane W. Lancaster says in the preface to his book, GOVERNMENT IN RURAL AMERICA, 2nd edition (New York: D. Van Nostrand, 1952, 375 pp.), that his purpose is "to construct a picture of government in rural areas as a going concern and to describe the government and administration of the rural county, township and school district in the United States." He succeeds in this endeavor.

The book begins with a general discussion of the social and economic conditions of rural life and follows with the effects of this environment and of public attitudes on rural government administration. The problem of area is analyzed at length, specifically the inability of present geographic jurisdictions to provide adequate and economical services. The author first relates this general problem to the New England town, outlining the historical reasons for its present organization as well as the modifications which have been instituted in order to adapt to modern conditions. He also analyzes the reasons for the decline of townships in the middle Atlantic and midwestern states, condemns these units, and urges their abolition. In discussing the problem of area and structure in county government, Professor Lancaster analyzes how traditional structure and processes operate under present conditions. He emphasizes that county government has many real and important powers and duties and concludes that counties should be reformed, not abolished.

The author discusses the important functions of rural government: financial administration, law enforcement, highways, education, public welfare, and public health. After analyzing the trends and changes in fiscal patterns in rural units, he presents suggestions for reform of local administration and for a new pattern of intergovernmental fiscal relations. Under law enforcement, he describes the offices of sheriff and coroner, the operation of the court system, the office of prosecutor, various legal processes, and the administration of local prisons. He concludes with suggestions for reform which would involve greater state control.

Professor Lancaster describes the various patterns of local highway administration, pointing out the difficulties caused by a multitude of small units and indicating how and why leadership is passing to higher units of government. He discusses the traditional values which underlie small school units and the problems which arise from their use, and describes the county unit and the office of county superintendent. He analyzes state interest in and responsibility for education and explains why he believes the local units have been able to resist extensive state supervision and control. His discussion of public welfare contains an extensive consideration of pre-depression local relief practices, and an analysis of how attitudes toward and procedures followed in public welfare have changed. Finally, he describes the organization of rural health machinery and points out the effect of state interest and activity on the operation of county units.

The book also contains very interesting and analytical considerations of local-state-federal relations (*see* Intergovernmental Relations – General: United States) and of the need for and possibility of reform at the local level (*see* Reform – General: United States).

This volume presents an excellent discussion of the theory and practice of local government and the positive and negative aspects of the traditional philosophy of local government adhered to in rural America. It is superior to many other studies of local government, for it is far more than a mere cataloguing and description of structures and functions, its primary purpose being to lay the groundwork for a call for reorganization of local government – abolishing many of the smaller units, transferring their functions to the county, and concurrently establishing a new and more viable pattern of state-local relations.

Extensive reliance is placed on primary sources, including research reports and interviews with government officials. At the time of this publication, the author was Professor of Political Science, University of Nebraska.

In an article, "A NEW LOOK AT THE DARK CONTINENT OF AMERICAN POLITICS," *The County Officer*, 19 (September, 1954), 182-186, George S. Blair evaluates county government. He discusses the slow pace of county consolidation, the growing number of county managers, the increasing transfer of functions from the county to the state, and the provision of municipal services by counties. Professor Blair compares present-day county government with the suggestions for reform made many years ago by H. S. Gilbertson; he concludes that the county no longer deserves the title of the "Dark Continent of American Politics." The article is analytical and makes use of secondary sources.

Clyde F. Snider's LOCAL GOVERNMENT IN RURAL AMERICA (New York: Appleton-Century-Crofts, 1957, 584 pp.) is a general discussion of counties, townships, towns, and special districts, although the author delineates and gives particular emphasis to wholly rural examples of these units whenever possible.

The author first describes the history of local government and the pattern of its use that has developed in the United States, and the constitutional and statutory restrictions on and authorizations for local governmental activity. He discusses the methods of both judicial and administrative control, argues the merits of compulsion and persuasion, points out the extent of use of state departments of local government, and explains and gives examples of county home rule.

Professor Snider then reviews the organization of county government. He describes the different types of governing bodies utilized in the nation and then discusses how the members are chosen and the boards organized, listing their different powers. Finally, he debates the merits of small and large boards. In discussing county officers and employees, Professor Snider lists the various elective and appointive officers, mentions many of their duties, and considers the operation and use of special boards and commissions. Various types of personnel practices are discussed, including compensation, recruitment, in-service training, retirement and social security. His analysis of the county executive begins with his pointing out the general lack of such an officer. He enumerates the duties of a manager and argues the advantages and disadvantages of manager government and its workability in rural counties. He describes elective executives in general and gives specific examples. He concludes the section on county government organization by explaining the commissioner, supervisor, and executive forms of government.

In describing the New England town, the township, and the special district, Professor Snider points out the county's possible relations with them. His interesting explanation of the political importance of the county in the state election and party system includes an entertaining description of rural bossism. He also discusses the electoral process in the county.

In the section on judicial administration, the local courts of the state judiciary are described: general trial, probate, and justice of the peace, with consideration of alternatives to the last named. Relative to law enforcement, the author describes the offices of sheriff, constable, coroner, and prosecuting attorney. He explains various legal processes, including the grand jury, indictment and information, and defense of the indigent, and concludes with an explanation of the current usage of county jails.

The section on highways opens with a comparison of state and local responsibilities and continues with a scrutiny of the trend toward centralization, financing methods, and the extent of state supervision and control. An interesting general description of rural health conditions, particularly the shortage of medical personnel and facilities, introduces the section on health and housing. Here the author gives a detailed description of the organization and administration of local health services and the use of rural hospitals and explains the operation of local housing authorities and farm housing programs. Next, he describes both general outdoor and indoor public welfare assistance. He points out improvements in institutional care, emphasizing county nursing homes, and describes the organization and financing of local welfare administration.

A comparison of state and local responsibilities introduces the section on education. Detailed descriptions are given of the county unit, county boards of education, county superintendent, and financing. Rural and urban schools are contrasted, and rural library service is described.

Another section of the book contains an informative and detailed discussion of agricultural and conservation practices. (*See* Services—Agriculture and Conservation: United States.)

The section on taxation and finance considers the various sources of local government revenue: property taxes, nonproperty taxes, and state aid. Various financial procedures, including budgeting, accounting and auditing, purchasing, borrowing, and debt retirement, are discussed.

The concluding discussion is a presentation of possible methods of reform and reorganization of local government. (*See* Reform—General: United States.)

In general, this book presents a very complete discussion of rural local government. The author devotes most of his discussion to descriptions of structure and activities but still includes enlightening analysis and interesting background material. Particularly useful are his explanations of social and economic conditions contributing to present problems of rural government.

In the preface the author states that interviews and questionnaires supplied by numerous state and local officials were particularly helpful sources, as were publications of the Governments Division of the Census Bureau and the *National Municipal Review* (now the *National Civic Review*). At the time of this publication, the author was Professor of Political Science, University of Illinois.

"STATE ASSOCIATIONS OF COUNTIES IN 1959," *Municipal Year Book: 1960* (Chicago: International City Managers' Association, 1960, pp. 63-68), was the first of Alastair McArthur's annual articles for this publication concerning the activities of statewide associations of county officials. Each year a section of the article deals with efforts of individual associations to influence state legislation in regard to county government. Other topics frequently considered are changes in the internal organization of the state associations, meetings and conferences, and training programs. A recurring theme in McArthur's discussions of the state associations is the great benefit of their activities and programs to county governments and their officials. At the end of each article is a directory of the state associations of counties. The author has intimate knowledge of the activities of the state associations; he is Deputy Executive Director of the National Association of Counties.

The Advisory Commission on Intergovernmental Relations' report, STATE CONSTITUTIONAL AND STATUTORY RESTRICTIONS UPON THE STRUCTURAL, FUNCTIONAL, AND PERSONNEL POWERS OF LOCAL GOVERNMENT (Washington, D.C.: 1962, 80 pp.), presents a variety of material with specific reference to counties. The report is about local governments in general, but the county is often considered separately from other local units, and sections of various chapters are devoted to it.

There is good historical material about counties in colonial times and a discussion of the constitutional restrictions under which they operate. The possibilities of consolidations or other transfers of functions between cities and counties or among counties are considered. The report shows the number of states whose constitutional provisions affect local government; it then illustrates some of the less direct effects of the restrictions. A late chapter is devoted to recommendations for state legislation which would lead to efficient and effective local government. Several of these recommendations specifically relate to counties. The report is a scholarly treatment of the subject.

Herbert S. Duncombe's COUNTY GOVERNMENT IN AMERICA (Washington: National Association of Counties Research Foundation, 1966, 288 pp.) is an up-to-date summary of the workings of county government, covering the following categories: history, officers, services, revenues and finances, intergovernmental relationships, five case studies, and the future of American county government.

The introductory chapter, an overview of the general characteristics of counties, includes statistics on size and population, a description of political organizations in the county, a summary of forms of governmental organization, and lists of services and three organizational charts.

Professor Duncombe's description of the historic role of the county starts with its English heritage. The county's history in the United States is divided into five periods: colonial, post-American Revolution, pre-Civil War, Civil War to World War I, and post-World War I. The effect of urban growth on the county and the resultant changes in functions and structure are examined and explained.

The chapters describing and analyzing officers, services, revenues and finances, intergovernmental relationships, and reform are thorough and timely. (*See* Organization—Officers and Special Boards; Services—General; Finance—General; Intergovernmental Relations—General; Reform—General: United States.)

The five case studies pertain to Petroleum County, Montana; Latah County, Idaho; Montgomery County, Maryland; Davidson County, Tennessee; and Milwaukee County, Wisconsin. In total, they provide an interesting sampling of important types of counties. Petroleum is a small rural county with a county manager form. Latah, a farming county with a fairly large urban center, retains the traditional plural executive form. The case of Montgomery County illustrates how a county can provide efficient, low-cost municipal services for an expanding suburban area. Davidson, the center of a metropolitan area, has a consolidated city-county government. Milwaukee County is entirely incorporated, and the county government has undertaken many areawide, urban functions. An appendix gives a complete, comparative list of services provided by each county.

The book's main value lies in its timeliness. It is a superior summary of counties in general, and the case studies give equally good summaries of five different types. However, the book does lack depth: the author touches on certain political aspects, something neglected by most general books, but the content is not sufficiently penetrating or analytical to fill completely the existing need for material on the county. Basically, the book provides a framework for gathering data and an outline for more intensive investigation.

In the foreword, William G. Colman, executive director of the Advisory Commission on Intergovernmental Relations, points out that with the increasing emphasis on developing and improving intergovernmental relations in the United States, the county may emerge as the preferred device to utilize at the local level. "This book by Professor Duncombe," he concludes, "is not only excellent in content, but most timely in the evolution of local government in the United States."

This volume was written under the auspices of the National Association of Counties which provided many of the sources used by the author. At the time of this publication, the author was Associate Professor of Political Science, University of Idaho.

Rosaline Levenson, in the introductory chapter to her book, COUNTY GOVERNMENT IN CONNECTICUT—ITS HISTORY AND DEMISE (Storrs: University of Connecticut, Continuing Education Service, Institute of Public Service, 1966, 237 pp.), discusses the nature of county government throughout the United States. She starts with an examination of the role of the county as an areawide and, particularly, a rural local government. She considers the diversity of counties in a state and among the states and then refers to the increase in the number of county functions and to criticisms of counties with respect to finances, organizational structures, and administrative management. Finally, she discusses five trends in county government: administrative reform, evolution toward metropolitan government, assumption of municipal services, intensified intergovernmental cooperation, and increased vitality as a local unit.

"CONGRESS AND THE COUNTIES: A VIEW FROM CAPITOL HILL," is the title of a speech by Edmund S. Muskie, chairman of the Senate Subcommittee on Intergovernmental Relations, before the National Association of County Federal Aid Coordinators, which appeared in *American County Government*, 31 (July, 1966), 15-18. Senator Muskie explains the ways in which the county can be a "viable unit of local government" in both urban and rural areas. He describes the role of the county in an intergovernmental context and stresses the need for county federal aid coordinators or urban advisors.

Frederick D. Stocker has developed a design for the study of the adequacy of local government services in a mongraph, THE ROLE OF LOCAL GOVERNMENT IN THE ECONOMIC DEVELOPMENT OF RURAL AREAS (Washington: United States Department of Agriculture, Economic Research Service,

1966, 20 pp., Agricultural Economic Research Report No. 94). He states that since counties are the primary rural governments in most of the United States, such a study might well focus on them. He states four objectives in the study of rural government and develops a framework in which to examine the contributions of local government services and facilities to the economic development of rural areas. He also proposes analysis of the per capita expenditures of rural local governments as they differ with respect to economic, social, and demographic variables of localities.

Professor Stocker cites similar previous research of rural counties in Iowa and Missouri and proposes, also, research on local government borrowing. He briefly examines a number of related topics, including county reform and reorganization and the effects of federal grant-in-aid programs on the finances and organization of local government.

The proposed research design is carefully thought out and adeptly presented. The author's discussion of rural local government provides a framework within which the need for the suggested research is easily understood. His style, however, is verbose. The monograph utilizes both primary and secondary sources, but consists mainly of the author's original ideas. At the time of this publication, Stocker was Professor of Business Research, College of Commerce and Administration, Ohio State University.

The National Association of Counties has brought together a number of original articles about various aspects of county government in a volume, GUIDE TO COUNTY ORGANIZATION AND MANAGEMENT (Washington: 1968, 453 pp.). In the foreword to the book, Bernard F. Hillenbrand, the Association's executive director, states that the collection is a "down-to-earth, realistic, and practical guide to improved county administration." The articles are written by representative county officials, professors, and other persons knowledgeable about a variety of county affairs.

The volume is divided into seven parts, the first of which is entitled "Tools for Administrative Reorganization." The first two articles, called chapters, in this initial part deal with county home rule. One examines how state enabling legislation for home rule should be constructed; the other considers how to organize and carry out the duties of a county charter commission. The third chapter concerns the experience of three counties—Davidson,

Tennessee; Dade, Florida; and East Baton Rouge Parish, Louisiana—with metropolitan government, and the fourth examines in depth the borough governments of Alaska (*see* County Government—General: Alaska). The fifth chapter looks at the operation of the Lakewood Plan in Los Angeles County, California, while the sixth is an informative summary of the nature and use of special districts and county service districts, with emphasis on their relations with counties. The seventh chapter of Part I is a brief, general discussion of regional councils of governments. The final chapter is a general treatment of the nature of county involvement in intergovernmental relations.

Part II which contains four chapters is entitled "County Legislative Functions." The first considers the organization of county governing boards; the second is concerned with county reapportionment and includes a useful table. The third chapter is a rather impressionistic article on the use of advisory bodies in county government. The fourth chapter is a "do-it-youself" guide on county public relations.

Part III consists of two chapters concerning county chief executives. One is on elected chief executives; the other, on appointed administrators. Both are largely based on the experience of the authors as chief executives of Westchester County, New York, and Sacramento County, California, respectively.

Part IV considers county housekeeping functions. The first chapter focuses on budgeting and is largely concerned with explaining line-item, performance, and program budgeting; it also briefly considers county organization for budgeting. The next four chapters are "do-it-yourself" guides to county personnel administration, centralized purchasing, finance, and information and data processing.

Parts V and VI contain articles on county line operations and service functions, the former dealing with traditional county functions. The first chapter of Part V is a concise, informative description and analysis of county recordkeeping activities. The second chapter treats county administration of elections in both a theoretical and a descriptive framework. The third chapter describes the process of and organization for property assessment. County law enforcement from the viewpoint of a county sheriff is the subject of the fourth chapter. The fifth briefly considers the problems of county jail administration, and the sixth analyzes in a legalistic vein the duties and functions of the county attorney throughout the United States. The seventh chapter analyzes the relations of the county courts with county government. The eighth article in Part V is a "do-it-yourself" guide to rural county development and planning.

Part VI is entitled "County Functions of Today and Tomorrow." Its early chapters are also of the "do-it-yourself" variety and consider the administration of county programs for traffic and general safety, transportation and public works, and public welfare respectively. The fourth chapter is an excellent analysis of the history, administrative organization, and programs of county public health agencies. All but the chapter on county planning take the guide-to-action approach. They deal with public education, housing and community development, code administration and enforcement, parks and recreation, and environmental pollution control. Although the chapter on county planning also has some aspects of the "do-it-yourself" approach, it largely seeks to describe and analyze the organization and substance of county planning.

Part VII has three chapters which set out sources of help for county officials in organizing and administering their programs. The first of these chapters discusses federal and state assistance programs and emphasizes the means by which counties can coordinate these programs with their own local efforts. The next chapter lists organizations of public officials which are located in New York, Chicago, and Washington, D.C. The final chapter is a directory of state associations of county officials.

The chapters in this book vary from mediocre to excellent in quality. The best, in terms of gaining a knowledge of the organization, administration, processes, and services of county government, are: "Local Legislative Apportionment," by Herbert S. Duncombe and Clifford I. Dobler; "Alaskan Boroughs," by Claude Millsap, Jr.; "County Service Districts and Special Districts," by Robert G. Smith; "Recordkeeping," by Eunice Ayers; "Legal Functions," by Harold W. Kennedy; "Public Health," by Maurice Kamp; and "Planning," by Ralph M. Barnes. The chapters which take the "do-it-yourself" (guide to action) approach are valuable to county officials in evaluating organization and management of the activities of their own counties but are of only limited value in learning about actual county operations. The many authors use a wide variety of secondary and primary sources; several of the individual chapters are based on their personal experience and knowledge.

Most of the text of Charles R. Adrian's STATE AND LOCAL GOVERNMENTS, 2nd edition (New York: McGraw-Hill, 1967, 607 pp.) is devoted to a discussion of state governments and local governments generally.[1] However, at times the author distinguishes the county from the other local units.

In the first chapter, on all forms of government used in a state, the author explains and compares the different types of government utilized at the county level in the United States. He begins by analyzing the criteria, which include much more than efficiency, that must be employed in evaluating the county as a governmental unit. He then presents some generalizations about the form of county government and analyzes and compares the two prominent types of organization: the commissioner and supervisor forms of county government. Next, he traces the historical development of the use of the many and various categories of officers still functioning in counties. Finally, he describes and analyzes three trends which he sees developing in county government: the growth in the number of urban functions performed by the county, the increasing cost of county government, and the slow but steady move toward reorganization.

The next chapter is devoted exclusively to government in metropolitan areas. Here again the county is singled out for separate discussion. The author analyzes the utility of city-county consolidation and city-county separation as possible solutions to the problems of metropolitan-area government. After a brief introduction to metropolitan federation, he evaluates the county as a metropolitan unit, presenting the handicaps to this plan and briefly describing three cases where this type of governmental system is in use: Los Angeles County, California; Westchester County, New York; and Dade County, Florida.

Although most of the material in the chapter on executive officers centers on state and city governments, Professor Adrian does indicate the many corresponding county officers. He explains policy-making power enjoyed by various county officers: county

---

1. The general state and local government books considered here constitute a representative sample.

clerk, auditor, sheriff, county prosecutor, and assessor. No extended discussion is presented on the county in the chapter on the bureaucracy and personnel practices, but scattered examples from counties are given for comparison of patronage and merit systems.

Regrettably for the purposes of this bibliography the county is not distinguished from other local units in the chapters on the functions performed by government. However, the material may profitably be used in analyzing and evaluating hard data on the county obtained from other sources.

As in *Governing Urban America,* which he wrote with Charles Press, Professor Adrian has approached the subject of state and local government from other than a traditional perspective. Instead of focusing on a description of the structure and functions of units of government, he presents an in-depth and wide-ranging analysis of the entire process and environment of government. He discusses the social, political, and personal factors affecting both the organization and operation of government. Rather than concentrating only on the governmental system, he has described the myriad of inputs, the system itself, and the outputs.

The text is well-footnoted, and an extensive bibliography is included at the end of each chapter and at the conclusion of the book. At the time of this publication, the author was Professor of Political Science, University of California, Riverside.

THE 50 STATES AND THEIR LOCAL GOVERNMENTS (New York: Alfred A. Knopf, 1967, 603 pp.), edited by James W. Fesler, primarily emphasizes state government; local units, including the county, are discussed in a separate section toward the end of the book and are referred to in the various functional chapters.

In a general discussion of the functions of state and local governments, Harvey C. Mansfield summarizes the primary functions of the county. He points out the effects that technology and federal intervention in civil rights have had on changing these activities. In the discussion of state-local and federal-local relations, Professor Mansfield does not distinguish the role of the county specifically from that of other local units.

The section on personnel and money, authored by York Willbern, contains an interesting discussion of why the number of county employees per 10,000 people drops as county population rises, and this phenomenon is compared with the case of the city, where the reverse is true.

Although the only local government discussed in a separate chapter is the city, a general description of the governmental pattern of the county is included in a chapter on local governments by Robert L. Morlan. He first presents statistics on the size and population range of counties and then describes the different structures of government used in counties, pointing out problems of representation and apportionment. He explains the need for reform of county government, emphasizing that similar systems are followed both in small rural and in large urban counties. In his discussion of possible reforms, he concentrates first on merger proposals: county consolidation, city-county consolidation, and functional consolidation, and then tackles the problems of lack of internal integration and of a central executive. He discusses the practice in Los Angeles County of the county government's providing contract services to the cities.

Contributors other than the editor are: Allan R. Richards, Harvey C. Mansfield, Dayton D. McKean, Karl A. Bosworth, York Willbern, Victor G. Rosenblum, and Robert L. Morlan. The sections vary in style but are of a generally good quality. Over-all, the book is a competent discussion of state and local government in the United States, with local government taking a secondary place to that of the state, and the county to that of the city. At the time of this publication, the editor was Professor of Government, Yale University.

As in all textbooks on state and local government, Daniel R. Grant and H. C. Nixon, authors of STATE AND LOCAL GOVERNMENT IN AMERICA, 2nd ed. (Boston: Allyn and Bacon, 1968, 596 pp.), give local government, particularly the county, less attention than the state. However, in this book, although the amount of discussion on the county is limited, the material and the approach are of a higher quality than often found in general texts.

In Chapter 1, "The Changing Environment of State and Local Government," the authors discuss the ramifications and possible effects which the centrifugal push to the suburbs may have on the county, pointing out that either new vigorous government or pathetic paralysis may result. In a later chapter on administrative reorganization, they discuss the slow pace of change in county operation and structure. In the chapter on law enforcement, Professors Grant and Nixon describe the various county authorities and activities in this field, giving emphasis to the office of sheriff. They stress the political base of this office and describe the various inducements that increase its attractiveness. The positions of coroner, public prosecutor, and public defender are also described.

Chapter 16, which is devoted entirely to the county, opens with an overview of its scope, heritage, and growth. Then a brief description is given of the structure and operation of the county governing board. A very interesting discussion follows of a case study of the county board, written by a former member. A brief summary of the other offices of county government is then presented. A subsequent discussion of county reform efforts begins with an outline of the criticisms leveled against county government. Next, the authors explain various proposals for improving county government: county consolidation, increased city-county relations, updating and change of administrative practices, use of home rule, installation of merit systems, and modernization of financial management. Grant and Nixon conclude this section with a warning not to sacrifice all of the old ways merely to further efficiency. In Chapter 18, the authors spell out the problems encountered in governing metropolitan areas and propose various remedies many of which center on the county, such as contractual agreements, federation, and the urban county. They point out shortcomings in county government that must be overcome before the urban county can be effectively used as a metropolitan government.

Although Professors Grant and Nixon have not neglected the traditional emphasis on description of structure and organization, they have included many of the newer findings and ideas on government and politics. They are to be commended for including these innovations which make their book one of the most worthwhile in the field. The footnotes and chapter-end bibliographies are extensive and up to date and include citations to many recent studies as well as to the classics. At the time this publication was written, Grant and Nixon were both Professors of Political Science, Vanderbilt University.

Duane Lockard's book, THE POLITICS OF STATE AND LOCAL GOVERNMENT (New York: Macmillan, 1963, 566 pp.), is an interesting and illuminating analysis of that subject. However, the title is somewhat misleading as the volume deals primarily with state and city government politics. When discussing governments below the state level, Lockard often subsumes and categorizes the various types as "local" and does not distinguish between the different local units. Also, the illustrations and examples seem to indicate that he is concerned mainly with the city in these general local discussions and only secondarily with other local units. (In the perspective of this bibliography, this is the overriding criticism of the book.) However, despite the author's lack of direct reference to the county, many of the conceptual schemes, trends, problems, and analytical tools used in the book can easily be applied to the county.

Early in the book Professor Lockard points to the difficulties of trying to formulate answers to problems facing local government today, caused by its diversity. He cites the varying uses and strength of the county throughout the nation as a prime example and explains four basic challenges with which all non-national governments must cope in the next few decades: population pressure, social, economic, and political challenges.

The author subsequently tackles the problem of decentralization and distribution of power. He questions the idea prevalent in many circles that the power of non-national government must decrease as the power of national government increases or vice versa. He cites the concurrently increasing power at all levels and the hesitancy at the federal level to exert extreme pressure on the others. He suggests three values to be considered in analyzing arguments about the proper allotment of political power in our system: minimizing arbitrariness in governmental rule-making; maximizing democratic control over government; and maximizing efficiency in governmental operations. He analyzes the reasons why these value factors will always be present.

Turning to structure and forms of government, Professor Lockard discusses why the historic distinction between the municipal corporation and the state agent unit is of declining significance. He then takes a closer look at the county, discussing its general uses and the recent interest in its employment as a metropolitan government.

When discussing local politics, the author points out how the fragmented system of governments may tend to create separate centers of powers which may only with difficulty be brought together for effective cooperation. He discusses bossism, focusing on the reasons why it has declined in most sections of the United States and why and how it still operates in some areas. He discusses the objectives of advocates of reform and nonpartisanship and analyzes some patterns of local politics found in the United States.

Professor Lockard also examines governmental operations at the local level. He looks at the local legislative process, citing the activities which sustain legislative power and discussing how the character of the community's political system may affect the political position of the local governing body. (This is one of the discussions in which Professor Lockard's concern, though he does not so specify, seems to be primarily with the city.) He then considers the problems and shortcomings of collegial administration and follows with a most useful discussion of metropolitan government and the future of the county in it. (*See* General – Reform: United States.)

Although this book is primarily concerned with providing an in-depth analysis of state and local government and only secondarily with describing structure and prescribing specific reforms, Professor Lockard's study does point out areas to be investigated when changes are being considered. The author's experience as a state legislator has been helpful in his analysis of local political phenomena and in his reassessment of political dogma. At the time of this publication, he was Professor of Politics, Princeton University.

G. Theodore Mitau, author of STATE AND LOCAL GOVERNMENT: POLITICS AND PROCESSES (New York: Charles Scribner's Sons, 1966, 641 pp.), discusses the county in a special section of the chapter on local governments and also in many of the functional chapters.

In the specific section on the county, Professor Mitau is primarily concerned with governmental organization. He begins by presenting statistics on the size and population of counties generally, emphasizing migration patterns. He then describes the functional development of counties, distinguishing the newer municipal-type functions from the traditional ones. He next sets forth and explains four characteristics of organization which are common to most counties: a county governing board, a large number of elected officials, a larger number of appointive officers, and numerous boards and commissions. He describes the dearth of legislative power vested in the county governing board and the lack of a central executive in most county governments. Brief profiles of various offices are given: sheriff, auditor, county attorney, coroner, treasurer, county clerk, and assessor. This section concludes with a discussion of certain trends developing in county government, particularly the use of home rule charters, centralization of administration, and transfer of functions to the county from smaller units.

Professor Mitau is interested in the county when analyzing the government of metropolitan areas. Two of the proposals he discusses for reorganizing local government within metropolitan areas center on the county. First he outlines and gives specific examples of the main features of city-county consolidation. The second proposal he describes and evaluates is metropolitan federalism and the urban county. He discusses the federation plan, dwelling at length on its employment in Dade County, Florida, and then considers the urban county, focusing on the Lakewood Plan and Los Angeles County, California.

In the chapter on state constitutions, the author points out the various types of articles which affect the county—its governmental structure, representation in state legislatures, and power to perform certain functions.

The chapter on law enforcement includes a separate subsection on countywide police systems. The effect of metropolitan and suburban population growth on the development of adequate county police service is stressed. Discussion of the judiciary includes brief descriptions of the county court and other special courts, particularly the juvenile court.

In the chapters on education, public transportation and conservation, and health and welfare, the author only infrequently distinguishes the county from other units of local government. He uses this same generalizing approach in the discussion of finance and taxation.

Throughout the book, Professor Mitau traces the history of many of the activities and structures he discusses, emphasizing trends he foresees. Although descriptive in his approach, he does not follow the traditional emphasis on structural and legal characteristics of government: rather, his organization of the book reflects his interest in environmental, social, and political characteristics. The text is well-documented, a selected bibliography is included at the end of each chapter, and a general bibliography appears at the conclusion of the book. At the time of this publication, the author was Professor of Political Science, Macalester College.

Clyde F. Snider, in AMERICAN STATE AND LOCAL GOVERNMENT, 2nd edition (New York: Appleton-Century-Crofts, 1965, 735 pp.), avoids a failing of many authors in general texts on both state and local government; he does not sacrifice the specific for the general. In addition to a very comprehensive discussion of government in the American states, he has included both a separate chapter and other extended discussions on the county.

In Chapter 12, "Units of Local Government," Professor Snider describes in general all the types of governments functioning at the local level, including the county. These abbreviated treatments, along with a later general discussion of the legal position and powers of all local government, provide a general basis for comparing and contrasting the functions and positions of these units.

The next chapter is devoted solely to the county. The author first explains the composition, organization, and powers of the county governing board and then compares the merits of small and large board membership. The offices of sheriff, coroner, county clerk, county treasurer, recorder or register of deeds, and county superintendent of schools are then explained and analyzed in detail and are followed by briefer descriptions of the county highway superintendent, auditor, assessor and agricultural agent. Miscellaneous other offices are discussed only in the appropriate functional chapters.

Professor Snider analyzes two pressing problems in the organization of county government today: the lack of integration and coordination of functions performed, and the need for a county executive. He discusses the extent to which elective county executives are used and their functions. A more extensive discussion follows on appointive executives, both managers and quasi-managers. Many examples from different states, particularly California, are given.

In the chapter on the reorganization of local government, Professor Snider explains and evaluates many of the proposals for reform which center on the county. He describes the roots of opposition to county consolidation and the benefits resulting from such a move. He explains how a county may be deorganized but emphasizes the difficulties in garnering the necessary support for such a step. He describes the transfer of functions to the county from smaller units of government. Particular emphasis is given to the process of functional consolidation. When discussing metropolitan areas specifically, the author describes the procedure to be followed in city-county consolidation and how it has worked in specific cases. He explains the role of the urban county in any plan for local federalism. This chapter also contains a section on internal organization: in it, Professor Snider explains why the problem is most acute in the county. He discusses suggestions for reform of office consolidation and extension of the merit system.

In addition to this extended discussion of the structure of county government, there are references of note on the county in many of the functional chapters in the book. In the explanation of state-local administrative relations generally, the author cites the county specifically. He also includes a brief, though separate, discussion of county home rule. A description of the various associations of county officers is contained in his consideration of interlocal relations. In the chapter on law enforcement, Professor Snider lists the uses of the county jail and appraises the criticisms which have been leveled against this institution. The chapter on public welfare contains many references to the role of the county in administering the various assistance programs and in maintaining welfare institutions, particularly county nursing homes. He also makes clear the extent and importance of county activity in the administration of public health activities. In the chapter on education, the organization of the county-unit system of administration is explained in a separate section. When discussing highways, Professor Snider points out the amount and type of mileage for which the county has responsibility. Throughout the entire section on agriculture and natural resources the importance of the county is pointed out. A brief section in the chapter on government and business lists the number and types of business enterprises owned by counties.

As in his book, *Local Government in Rural America,* Professor Snider has in this book on state and local government employed essentially a descriptive approach in presenting the material. Analytic and prescriptive materials usually appear in separate sections rather than intertwined throughout the text. The book is scholarly and well-documented and would appeal more to the student of government than to the layman. This book and Professor Charles Adrian's *State and Local Governments* use very different approaches to the same subject, but they are complementary, not contradictory. Together they comprise a complete, well-rounded picture of state and local government, and, for our purposes, of the county.

This book is well-footnoted and includes extensive subject bibliographies at the end of each chapter. At the time of this publication, the author was Professor of Political Science, University of Illinois.

AMERICAN LOCAL GOVERNMENT (New York: Harper & Row, 1964, 619 pp.), by George S. Blair, covers the major units of local government—cities, counties, townships, towns and school and other special districts—but it emphasizes cities and counties.

Like most other books on local government, this study opens with a discussion of the tradition and history of local government in England and the United States. Also by way of introduction, Professor Blair presents statistics on the number and size of local units and includes a proposal, first suggested by William Anderson, for reducing the number of local units.

He then discusses intergovernmental relations, listing the different forms of state control over counties—legislative, administrative and judicial—and outlines the possible scope of interlocal relations. Although his discussion of federal-local relations deals mainly with the city, the author does discuss both informal arrangements and grant programs that involve the county directly with the national government.

Dr. Blair discusses the voting requirements that are administered by the county, describes the organization of political parties at the county level, mentions the extent of partisan activity in local elections, and stresses the lack of competition for county offices. He develops an interesting typology for classifying counties according to whether they are rural, semi-rural, semi-urban, or urban. He elaborates on the criteria for deciding on the class in which to place a county and presents a table on the proposed classification of counties in ten selected states.

In his discussion of different types of county boards and the typical elective and appointive officers, the author explains why and in what functional areas special boards and commissions are used and discusses their pros and cons. Interesting charts and maps on the organization and structure of county government add effective illustration.

Professor Blair discusses home rule for counties, comparing similarities of home rule movements in various parts of the United States. He examines the limitations on counties as well as their freedom. He then analyzes seven trends he perceives as underlying an increasing acceptance of the county as a legitimate government in its own right, in contrast to its being merely a traditional unit for state administration. He points out the various difficulties faced by rural and urban counties in establishing this legitimacy.

Other discussions concern the legislative, executive, and judicial processes generally followed in the county. The author then explains the different functions carried on by local governments. He describes the rural police, including the sheriff-constable system, and the organization of fire departments in the small number of counties that operate them. He includes a description of public and mental health facilities. When considering intergovernmental relations in welfare, he includes the principles adopted by the County Supervisors Association of California in 1957 on county home rule and intergovernmental relations. Brief mention is given to the role of the county in administering education. Stating that the county is the most important local unit of highway administration, the author lists its general responsibilities and gives a detailed description of Los Angeles County. His discussion of county planning revolves around the suggestions of the National Municipal League's *Model County Charter*. The book concludes with a section on local government in metropolitan areas in which emphasis is given to the important role that the county can play.

This book contains very comprehensive coverage of local governments, although space limitations preclude in-depth attention to any one type of unit, such as the county. The thorough discussion of the history and development of county government contains interesting and unusual facts. Theory is included throughout the book, and mere descriptions of structures and functions are not overplayed. Both primary and secondary sources are used extensively. At the time of this publication, the author was Professor of Government, Claremont Graduate School.

ALSO TO BE NOTED:

William E. Dennison, "Our President Speaks." *The County Officer,* 25 (May, 1960), 141.

L. L. Friedland, "The County as a Unit of Government," *The County Officer,* 21 (May, 1956), 95-96.

Mitchell Gordon, "Counties' Comeback, Local Units Experience a Revival Unexpected by Political Scientists," *The County Officer,* 28 (November, 1963), 432-433.

David H. Grubs, "What is Happening to County Governments?" *Tennessee Planner,* 23 (March, 1964), 77-83, 96.

Bernard F. Hillenbrand, "Counties and the National Domestic Crisis," *The County Officer,* 30 (April, 1965), 9.

______, "County Government is Reborn," *Public Administration Survey,* 7 (May, 1960), 1-8.

Hubert H. Humphrey, "Local Government's Great Opportunity," *Portia Law Journal,* 3 (Spring, 1968), 115-122.

A. F. Lemans, *The County, Underdog of American Politics* (The Hague, Netherlands: International Union of Local Authorities, 1959, 8 pp.).

Conrad L. McBride, "Local Self-Government: A County Challenge," *The County Officer,* 20 (June, 1955), 122-124.

National Association of Counties, Washington, *The County Letter,* July 22, 1963 to present.

"Nation's Hope Held Resting in Rural-Urban Cooperation," *American County Government,* 30 (February, 1966), 14.

Kirk H. Porter, *County and Township Government in the United States* (New York: Macmillan, 1922, 362 pp.).

Helen M. Rocca, *County Government,* 2nd edition (Washington: National League of Women Voters, Department of Efficiency in Government, 1932, 58 pp.).

Harold Sheffelman, "County Government—Is It Obsolete or the Answer to Urban Growth?" *The County Officer,* 26 (August, 1961), 256-257, 287-289.

United States Bureau of the Census, *County and City Data Book* (Washington: U. S. Government Printing Office, 1967, 673 pp.).

John F. Willmott, *The Coming Change in County Government* (Houston: Tax Research Association of Houston and Harris County, 1958, 7 pp.).

Eastern and North Central Region

Twelve states are discussed in the section on the eastern and north-central states (pp. 150-341) in COUNTY GOVERNMENT ACROSS THE NATION (Chapel Hill: University of North Carolina Press, 1950, 817 pp.), edited by Paul W. Wager.

In the introductory section Professor Wager discusses the two primary systems of county government (the New York and Pennsylvania plans) operative in the region. He points out that in many of the midwestern states the township is losing its importance. He considers the different types of county governing bodies, collateral boards, and chief administrative officers which are used in various states. He explains the causes of the long ballot which is used extensively in this region.

Statistics on the number and size of counties are given in the individual state chapters. Also, the author usually discusses the governing body and main functions of the county in the state. The states and the county case studies described are: New York (Schuyler), New Jersey (Mercer), Pennsylvania (Bucks), Delaware (Sussex), Maryland (Wicomico), Ohio (Clark), Michigan (Genesee), Indiana (Hancock), Illinois (Douglas), Wisconsin (Dodge), Minnesota (Aitkin), and Iowa (Grundy). Other authors in this section, in addition to Professor Wager, are Emmett G. Asseff, Elwyn A. Mauck, Harding Hughes, Oka Stanton Flick, Fred A. Clarenbach, Edward W. Weidner, and Lloyd W. Woodruff.

New England Region

Rosaline Levenson examines the nature of county government in New England in her article, "NEW ENGLAND COUNTIES EXAMINED; STRONG TOWN TRADITION STILL PREVAILS," *American County Government,* 30 (May, 1965), 20-21,

64-65. She looks first at some of the reasons for the weakness of New England counties, particularly in relation to the strength of town governments in the region. She then describes the status of county government in each of the New England states in which county government exists, lists their functions, and relates their relative importance. She discusses the organization and officers of the county governments in each state and enumerates the total number of counties, county employees, and the size of the payrolls of counties in each state. In addition, she describes the unique form of government of Suffolk County, Massachusetts, which is dominated by the City of Boston. Of the six New England states, Connecticut and Rhode Island do not have county governments.

Professor Levenson is largely descriptive in her presentation of the structure and functions of county government but analytical in her examination of the reasons for the weakness of counties in the region. She has a straightforward, lucid style of writing. The article relies mostly upon primary sources, particularly state documents. At the time of this publication, the author was a professor on the research staff of the Institute of Government, the University of Connecticut.

Before delving into the history and abolition of county government in Connecticut, Rosaline Levenson explores the nature of county government in New England in her book, COUNTY GOVERNMENT IN CONNECTICUT–ITS HISTORY AND DEMISE (Storrs: University of Connecticut, Continuing Education Service, Institute of Public Service, 1966, 237 pp.). She starts with a brief treatment of the origins and present extent of county government in New England and then turns to a discussion of how development of strong town government in New England has retarded the growth of strong counties. A description follows of the structure and functions of county governments in each of the four New England states with operating county governments. The author examines the general weakness and decline in functions of the counties in the region. In this connection, she reviews a study of county government in Maine which concludes with recommendations that would virtually eliminate county government there. Studies of county government in Massachusetts and New Hampshire, which are done in a similar vein, are also mentioned.

The New England section (pp. 46-147) in COUNTY GOVERNMENT ACROSS THE NATION (Chapel Hill: University of North Carolina Press, 1950, 817 pp.), edited by Paul W. Wager covers six states. These states and their county and town case studies are: Maine (Piscataquis County, Guilford Town), New Hampshire (Hillsborough County, Wilton Town), Vermont (Orange County, Randolph Town), Massachusetts (Middlesex County, Sudbury Town), Rhode Island (Washington County, North Kingstown Town), and Connecticut (Middlesex County, Durham Town).

The introductory section to the region begins with a discussion of why and how the town is the primary unit of local government. The author explains how the government of the town is organized and how it functions and gives detailed descriptions of its activities relating to schools, highways, and public welfare. After thus establishing the supremacy of the town, he explains why the county is of limited importance and lists the relatively few county officers active in these states.

Each of the state chapters contains statistics on the size and population of the counties within its boundaries and considers the local governmental functions handled by counties. In addition to Professor Wager, Emmett G. Asseff and George H. Deming are contributors to this section.

Southern Region

Paul W. Wager, the editor of COUNTY GOVERNMENT ACROSS THE NATION (Chapel Hill: University of North Carolina Press, 1950, 817 pp.), has included thirteen states in Section III (pp. 344-551), which deals with the South.

Professor Wager begins the discussion of this region by describing the history of local government in the South from revolutionary times to this century. He then explains the different titles and variations in composition and method of selection of the county governing boards. Next, he describes the duties of the counties in the assessment and collection of taxes, school administration, and the administration of highway work. He then explains that although a marked tendency toward state centralization exists in the South, counties are increasingly assuming new functions. He gives examples of these new activities and points out the states in which county activity is most pronounced. Finally, he explains the difficulties and inadequacies of county government which result from the large number of counties and their consequent small size. He documents the success and failure of attempts to remedy these faults.

The states and the county case studies discussed are: Virginia (Albemarle), West Virginia (Raleigh), Kentucky (Franklin), Tennessee (Washington), North Carolina (Orange), South Carolina (Richland), Georgia (Wilkes), Florida (Polk), Alabama (Marengo), Mississippi (Claiborne), Louisiana (De Soto), Arkansas (Lafayette), and Missouri (Callaway). Other contributors to this section are George W. Spicer, Mavis A. Mann, Paul Tanner, Lee S. Greene, Evan A. Iverson, George R. Sherill, Melvin C. Hughes, Emmett G. Asseff, William L. Bradshaw, and A. J. Bartley.

Western Region

Section IV (pp. 554-808) in COUNTY GOVERNMENT ACROSS THE NATION (Chapel Hill: University of North Carolina Press, 1950, 817 pp.), edited by Paul W. Wager, deals with the western region of the nation and includes studies of the following states and counties: Texas (Harrison), Oklahoma (Pushmataha), Kansas (Saline), Nebraska (Seward), South Dakota (Clay), North Dakota (Grand Forks), Montana (Fergus), Wyoming (Albany), Colorado (Boulder), New Mexico (Bernalillo), Arizona (Pima), Utah (Weber), Nevada (Washoe), Idaho (Bannock), Washington (Whitman), Oregon (Lane), and California (Orange).

Professor Wager begins by pointing out the relative lack of towns in these states and the importance of the county. He also compares the average size of counties in this region with that in the rest of the country. He then cites the near uniformity in title and composition of the county governing boards in these states. He presents statistics on the types of executives and points out the great similarity in elective officers used in the counties, citing the number of states which use many of the most common ones. He discusses at some length the educational system used in most of these states, emphasizing the fairly low level of county activity in this field. Then, after demonstrating how similar the states and counties in this region are, Professor Wager itemizes and discusses the unique features that differentiate the systems of government of the states.

Authors of the individual state chapters include Emmett G. Asseff, Donald B. Hayman, A. G. Breckenridge, T. C. Geary, Walter E. Kaloupek, R. R. Renne, Henry J. Peterson, Leo C. Riethmayer, Thomas C. Donnelly and Jack E. Holmes. Also included are Paul Kelso, Ellsworth E. Weaver, S. M. Vincour, Claude C. Smith, Hobert P. Sturm, Paul Beckett, Herman Kehrli, and Allan R. Richards.

Alabama

James D. Thomas has prepared a study of county government in Alabama within the framework of the statutory provisions for county governmental structure, officers, activities, and processes. As the author states, this monograph, A MANUAL FOR ALABAMA COUNTY COMMISSIONERS (University: University of Alabama, Bureau of Public Administration, 1963, 96 pp.), "is a manual – a factual, descriptive study – designed to make available to the county commissioners basic information concerning the state's system of county government. It consists largely of descriptions of the various agencies and functions of county government."

The first chapter, which deals with the legal status of counties in the state, includes an analysis of court cases leading to the definition of counties as quasi-corporations with a status distinctly different from that of municipalities. In this connection, it explores the consequences of this legal status, centering on the nature of county liability for torts, the strict control of the state legislature over county government, and limitations on such control. The constitutional provisions for changing county boundaries and for the creation of new counties are also presented in this chapter.

The second chapter is devoted to the organization of Alabama county government. The three basic types of governing boards – the probate judge form, the board of revenue form and the commission form – are described. Provisions for board meetings are laid out, and the lengthy list of powers and responsibilities of the boards is outlined. There follows a more general discussion of the governing boards, which emphasizes connection with various county activities and relationships with other county officers and boards. The remainder of the chapter looks at the nature, powers, and duties of various county officers and boards. Included are judge of probate, chairman of the governing board, county judges and their courts, register and clerk of the circuit court, solicitors (prosecuting attorneys), sheriff, justices of the peace, constables, coroner, jury commission, and tax assessor; others are board of equalization, tax collector, treasurer or depository, license inspector, board of registrars, board of pensions and security, library board, farm agent, home demonstration agent, board of education, superintendent of education, and board of health.

Chapter III and Chapter V examine county services. (*See* Services—General: Alabama.) Chapter IV looks at county finance. (*See* Finance—General: Alabama.)

Although this monograph is largely descriptive, the author often analyzes the effects of the statutes he describes and at times presents their historical background. His style is simple and concise, and he uses mostly primary sources, almost all of which are statutes and constitutional provisions.

ALSO TO BE NOTED:

Association of County Commissioners of Alabama, Montgomery, *Mr. County Commissioner*.

Alaska

The Alaska Local Affairs Agency has printed the text of the BOROUGH ACT OF 1961 AS AMENDED (Juneau: 1962, 37 pp.). This legislation contains the statutory provisions for the organization and structure, governing boards, chief executive, general powers, and elections of Alaskan boroughs.

Chapter 5 is concerned with unorganized boroughs and the establishment of service areas within them, while Chapter 10 deals with the incorporation of organized boroughs and details the process by which a borough may be incorporated. It describes the requirements regarding borough size and area and sets out the provisions for the apportionment of the governing board of the borough, the borough assembly. The dissolution of special districts upon borough incorporation and the establishment of borough areawide functions are also specified.

Chapter 15 lists the general powers of organized boroughs, including those of taxation and indebtedness. This chapter provides for the establishment of special service areas within organized boroughs, borough school districts, and borough planning and zoning powers. There are extensive provisions for borough exercise of municipal powers outside incorporated areas, jointly with cities, and within incorporated areas after the transfer of specified powers from cities.

Chapter 20, concerned with the borough assembly, considers such matters as the reapportionment of borough assemblies; their organization and procedures, meetings, quorum, voting and weighting of votes of members; their legislative powers and limitations; ordinances; and auditing.

Chapter 25 provides for borough chief executives. Boroughs may have an elected chief executive, a borough chairman, or an appointed borough manager. The powers and responsibilities of the borough chief executive are detailed. This chapter also includes sections on conflict of interest, nondiscrimination, and bribery.

Chapter 30 is concerned with borough elections. It specifies the qualifications and dates for voting in borough elections. It provides for special elections, procedures for nominating candidates, filling office vacancies, the initiative, referendum and recall, and reapportionment of assembly and school board districts.

The final chapter sets out the procedures and requirements for consolidation, dissolution, classification, and reclassification of boroughs.

Before passage of the Borough Act of 1961, the Alaska Local Affairs Agency and the Legislative Council issued their FINAL REPORT ON BOROUGH GOVERNMENT (Juneau: 1961, 97 pp.). This report contains the recommendations of both of these agencies for legislation implementing the provisions for borough government in the state constitution. The chapter titled "Constitutional Intent" is particularly useful. It analyzes the section of the state constitution providing for borough home rule and appraises the intent of the constitutional convention in placing nonrestrictive provisions for borough government in the constitution.

Ronald C. Cease has briefly described Alaska's experience with borough government in his article, "ALASKAN BOROUGHS ESTABLISH ROLE," *National Civic Review,* 54 (July, 1965), 379-381. The author discusses the problem involved in getting boroughs to organize in the state. He outlines and analyzes the provisions of the Mandatory Borough Act of 1963 and some of the problems faced by the boroughs in establishing their governments. Also included is an examination of city-borough relations and of the areawide and municipal powers of boroughs. At the time of this publication, the author was Director, Alaska Local Affairs Agency.

Claude Millsap, chairman of Greater Juneau Borough, examines the role of the borough in Alaska in his article. "ALASKAN BOROUGHS" in a volume published by the National Association of Counties, *Guide to County Organization and Management* (Washington: 1968, pp. 36-48). The author first outlines how borough government came about and emphasizes the crucial role of the Mandatory Borough Act which required the creation of boroughs in certain regions of the state. A short discourse on the nature of the borough as a flexible regional government follows.

In the article, a major section, "Functions of the Borough Government," treats the borough chairman, borough assembly, borough school board, services areas, and general government. Stating that the functions of all boroughs are identical, the author confines much of his discussion to Greater Juneau Borough. He details the method of election and general powers and responsibilities of the borough chairman, who is the borough chief executive, and stresses that functionary's role in administration. The selection method, organization, powers, and functions of the borough assembly which is the governing body are also considered. The political controversies which have developed around the weighted vote formulas, which must be used by borough assemblies, and the results of their use are explained and analyzed.

The borough school board's functions and relations with the borough assembly and borough chairman are described. Next explored is the use of service areas by boroughs to provide individual municipal services in particular portions of the borough. Finally, the general functions of the borough are described, including the duties of the officers and boards responsible for them, with areawide planning and zoning given special emphasis. Other functions include areawide dog control, public health and hospitals, fire prevention, police protection, areawide sewage collection and disposal, and activities of the county attorney and clerk-treasurer. The article concludes with an analysis of the experimental nature of the use of boroughs as an intermediate level of government between the state and its cities.

The article is readable, interesting, and analytical, giving a general impression of the problems of establishing a new governmental level. Information for the article is derived largely from the author's personal experience and knowledge.

A section of a report by the Public Administration Service, LOCAL GOVERNMENT UNDER THE ALASKA CONSTITUTION (Chicago: 1959, 82 pp.), describes and analyzes the provisions for borough government in the Alaska constitution and speculates on the role borough government will play in the governmental structure of the state.

ALSO TO BE NOTED:

Ronald C. Cease and Jerome R. Saroff (eds.), *The Metropolitan Experiment in Alaska: A Study in Borough Government* (New York: Frederick A. Praeger, 1968, 449 pp.).

Wendell G. Schaeffer, *Does Alaska Need County Government?* (Juneau: Alaska Statehood Committee, 1955, 16 pp.)

"A Short Summary on the Borough Legislation," *Alaska Local Government,* 1 (May, 1961).

"The Whys and Wheres of Organized Boroughs," *Alaska Local Government,* 1 (November, 1961), 1-4.

Lyman Woodman, "Unique Style of Government Sought by Alaskans," *Western City,* 43 (May, 1966), 44-45.

Arizona

This monograph, THE STATE OF ARIZONA (1963, 81 pp.), prepared by the League of Women Voters of Arizona, presents a brief overview of both state and local government in that state. Chapter 10 is devoted entirely to the county; other county material is included in the chapter on political parties, the judiciary, and education. The monograph explains the division by the county board of supervisors of the county into justice-of-the-peace precincts. The duties and jurisdiction of these courts are explained as are the organization and jurisdiction of the superior courts, which sit in each county. The organization and conduct of the meetings of the county central committees and a complete list of duties, both those legally required and those politically expedient, are included. In the section on education, the requirements for office and the duties of the county school superintendent are explained, and the procedure to be followed in establishing a county union high school is described.

The introductory section to the chapter on the county (six pages with one page a map) contains a brief history as well as a description of the constitutional and statutory limitations on the counties, particularly the classification scheme. Next, both the sources of revenue and the financial administration procedures are described. In the discussion of the organization of the county government, the method of selecting the supervisors and their duties are presented. Brief descriptions of the duties and salaries of the sheriff, county attorney, clerk of the superior court, county treasurer, county recorder, county assessor, and county superintendent of schools (which is discussed more fully in the chapter on education) are given.

Although this monograph touches only the surface and is entirely descriptive, it does provide an outline of the structure of county government in Arizona. No sources are cited and no bibliography is included; thus the publication, which was prepared for citizen information, cannot be used as a guide to more detailed research.

Bruce B. Mason and Heinz R. Hink devote a chapter to county government in their book, CONSTITUTIONAL GOVERNMENT IN ARIZONA, 2nd edition (Tempe: Arizona State University, Bureau of Governmental Research, 1965, 223 pp.). The chapters on the court system and political party organization also contain information on Arizona county government.

The chapter on county government summarizes the relevant Arizona constitutional provisions, which pertain to the county's quasi-corporate legal status, number of counties, county officers, county boards of supervisors, and county finance. The method of selection, term of office, procedures, compensation, and thirty specific duties required by law of the board of supervisors are set out in detail. The functions and duties of officers serving the board are also described, and an organization chart of the typical Arizona county is presented. Finally, the chapter describes the functions and duties of the elected, constitutional county officers: sheriff, recorder, treasurer, county attorney, assessor, and clerk of the superior court. In the discussion of the functions of the county assessor, some of the problems of county property assessment practices are examined. Certain appointive county officers and boards receive brief mention.

The chapter on political party organization describes the organization and method of selecting the county central committees. The authors speak of the relationship of these committees to the nomination of party candidates for the boards of supervisors, and the endorsement of the Arizona Democratic Council is also considered. The chapter on the state court system deals with the county courts as part of that system. It tells of the jurisdictions of the various courts and the method of choosing their judges. The relation of the county courts to the county government, particularly to the board of supervisors, is examined.

This book contains very detailed legal descriptions of county government and county officers in Arizona. In fact, legal detail is emphasized to the point that the functioning of county government is largely neglected; little attention is given to services. The detail is handled in a scholarly and straightforward manner; most of the sources are primary, consisting principally of constitutional and statutory provisions. At the time of this publication, both authors were staff members of the Bureau of Governmental Research, Arizona State University.

Arkansas

Henry M. Alexander, author of GOVERNMENT IN ARKANSAS: ORGANIZATION AND FUNCTION AT STATE, COUNTY, AND MUNICIPAL LEVELS (Little Rock: Pioneer Press, 1959, 264 pp.), describes county government extensively in both a separate chapter and many functional chapters.

In the section on politics, the author touches only briefly on the operation of the Republican Party at the county level. However, he describes in detail the organization and functions of the Democratic county conventions and county committees. He also describes the conduct of the election machinery by county-level party and governmental officials and briefly discusses the representation of the county in the state legislature.

The coverage of the judiciary and law enforcement agencies in Arkansas begins with a description of the jurisdiction, functions, and personnel of various courts which sit in the county: justice of the peace, corporation, common pleas, juvenile, circuit, and chancery. The operation of the grand jury, the duties of the sheriff and the constable, and the uses of the county jail are discussed.

The author explains the powers of the county in regulating the sale of liquor and points out the functions the county performs in the administration of education and libraries. He considers the role of the county in the maintenance and construction of highways and touches upon the relation between the state and county in the administration of welfare services and the county's specific duties.

Taxation and financial administration are thoroughly explained. The extent and limitations on the taxing power of the county are described, with particular emphasis on the property tax. The county's power to borrow, the extent and character of the state's supervision over the county's financial procedure, and the different taxes and the amount distributed to counties are considered.

The chapter on the county opens with a few statistics on the size and population of the counties and then a brief explanation of their legal position. The author points out the dual capacity of the county as an arm of the state and as a local unit and the provisions in the constitution affecting the county. He explains the use of locally-initiated salary acts which place most county officers in some counties on a salary rather than fee basis.

Structure is the next topic discussed in the county chapter. Professor Alexander describes at some length the composition, meeting procedure, and powers of the quorum court, which is the governing body of the county. In his treatment of the officers of the county, the author emphasizes the duties and general importance of the county judge and describes other offices: circuit clerk, county clerk, sheriff, coroner, assessor, board of equalization, collector, delinquent tax board, treasurer, depository board, surveyor, highway commission, hospital board, board of education, supervisor of schools, library board, and health officer. In addition he describes the composition and duties of the county health units and the county department of public welfare. Brief attention is given to the duties of the county in the field of agriculture.

It is difficult to glean the sources used in the writing of this book, as none is cited in the text and no bibliography is given; it appears that the author relied on the constitution, statutes, and court decisions for much of his support. This book is useful for its description of county structure and functions. However, it does not give much indication of the scope of the services provided. At the time of this publication, the author was Professor of Government, University of Arkansas.

ALSO TO BE NOTED:

Arkansas, Legislative Council, Research Department, *County Government in Arkansas and Selected States,* Research Report No. 79 (Little Rock: 1957, 35 pp.).

California

CALIFORNIA GOVERNMENT AND POLITICS, 4th ed. (Englewood Cliffs: Prentice-Hall, 1967, 318 pp.), by Winston W. Crouch, John C. Bollens, Stanley Scott, and Dean E. McHenry, covers many important aspects of state and local government in

California. The county is discussed in a separate chapter and is mentioned often throughout the book.

The authors point out the duties of county officials in the operation of election machinery and in the organization and responsibilities of the county party committees. They discuss personnel systems which have been established in some counties, and consider state aid to local governments, local sources of revenue, general financial administration, and particular fiscal characteristics of counties. They describe the functions of the justice and superior courts which sit in the counties, emphasizing the Executive Office of Los Angeles Superior Court, and the composition and functions of the grand jury.

The chapter on counties begins with a general overview of their nature and scope. First, the authors point out "dark corners" remaining in county government in California and then describe the evolution of counties. They discuss the county's duties in aiding the state government, delineate the diversified functions and varying service areas of the modern county, and consider problems that arise when services are supplied to unincorporated areas. They explain how the misunderstanding and confusion about counties result partly from variations in areas or zones of county activity.

Three services receive extended treatment: public assistance, roads, and protection. The authors also include a complete list of the remaining services, pointing out the relative financial support given to each one.

Problems of area, population, and reform receive considerable analysis. (*See* Reform—General: California.) The extent of and reasons for nonpartisanship at the local level are scrutinized and the arguments for and against it presented. The chapter concludes with a prognosis on the county of the future.

In a section on metropolitan areas, the authors point out the different local government patterns that characterize the metropolitan areas: Los Angeles, the metropolitan county; San Francisco Bay Area, a possible example of metropolitan federation; and the predominantly single-county metropolitan areas of San Diego, Fresno, Bakersfield and Stockton. They conclude with an explanation of the Commission on Metropolitan Area Problems.

The authors of this book have included both description and analysis and have incorporated anecdotes and pertinent incidents which contribute to the book's readability.

At the time of this publication, Winston W. Crouch and John C. Bollens were Professors of Political Science, University of California, Los Angeles; Stanley Scott, Assistant Director, Institute of Governmental Studies, University of California, Berkeley; and Dean E. McHenry, Chancellor, University of California, Santa Cruz.

Jane Gladfelder wrote CALIFORNIA'S EMERGENT COUNTIES (Sacramento: County Supervisors Association, 1968, 121 pp.) as a master's thesis. Subsequently she submitted it to the County Supervisors Association of California whose staff members edited and updated the original study.

The first chapter is an introduction to the geography, history, and legal position of counties in California, with particular emphasis on the distinction between charter and general law counties. Before describing the organization and functions of the various county offices, Mrs. Gladfelder divides them into three categories—mandated elective, mandated appointive, and permissive appointive. The mandated elective offices described are the board of supervisors, district attorney, sheriff, coroner, public administrator, surveyor, county clerk, treasurer, tax collector, recorder, assessor, and superintendent of schools. Attention is given to the duty of the board of supervisors to adjust the boundaries of supervisorial districts.

The duties of five required appointive offices are then described: probation officer, road commissioner, sealer of weights and measures and agricultural commissioner, welfare director, and health officer. In the third category, permissive appointive officials, the author describes in much detail the county administrative officer. Other officers considered in this category are the public defender, county counsel, hearing officer, and public works director; miscellaneous other officials are listed. Boards and committees used in counties are discussed briefly.

In her discussion of functions handled by the county, Mrs. Gladfelder explains how they have changed and expanded during this century and points out both the extent of and the reasons for this development. Her discussion of welfare is particularly informative; she notes how the character of and the attitude toward county welfare services have changed. Her descriptions of hospitals, mental health services, and health are also somewhat analytical, although not to the degree found in the section on welfare.

Education is discussed under three topics: school administration, library services, and agricultural education. Then, the current role of the county in the judicial process of the state and the jurisdiction and powers of the various courts located in the county are depicted; a separate section is devoted to a discussion of why the state legislature has increased court fees. The focus in the discussion of law enforcement and police protection is on detention and correction; here, the duties of the principal officials and the purposes of the different types of institutions are explained. Finally, under the heading, "Protective Services," the functions of the county in fire protection, flood control, and soil and water conservation are presented. The author then describes the character of the county's activity in highway maintenance and construction, particularly financing procedures, and closes the section on functions with a detailed discussion of parks and recreation.

A separate chapter, devoted to the role of the county in environmental planning, starts with a brief discussion of the rural counties of the state and then proceeds to the environmental problems of metropolitan counties. The work of the Association of Bay Area Governments and the Southern California Association of Governments, two regional multigovernment planning organizations, is emphasized.

The author describes how the county government may institute the creation of special districts, and the districts' relation to general governments. She summarizes and analyzes the work of the Assembly Interim Committee on Municipal and County Government (1963-65) which was concerned with the problem of special districts. She explains the provisions of two earlier pieces of legislation, the County Service Area Law of 1963 and the Community Services District Law of 1955, which provide alternative methods by which unincorporated areas may receive governmental services. She discusses the purposes and work of local agency formation commissions, established in each county to review and approve all proposals for municipal incorporation and annexation and district formation and annexation. Case studies illustrate the work being done on the metropolitan problems of air pollution, traffic congestion, and water.

The difficulty of finding revenue to finance the new and expanding services provided by counties is discussed, as are the different sources of revenue, the different types of expenditures, and the extent, purposes, and limitations on county indebtedness. The budgetary process followed in counties is traced through its cycle. The author concludes by analyzing three financing problems confronting counties: the inadequacy of the property tax, how to finance the increased responsibilities assumed by counties, and the difficulties arising from an increasing and shifting population.

A chapter is devoted to county personnel systems. The author describes the recommendations of the civil service commission of Ventura County and discusses the charter provisions of Los Angeles County regarding personnel practices. She presents an overview of the various types of workers employed in counties and the different types of retirement systems used. Four problems—recruitment, the right of county employees to strike, the position of the veteran, and political involvement—are analyzed.

The book concludes with a look at the future of the county in California. The author questions what changes may occur in the role of the board of supervisors and to what extent administrative officers may be used. She discusses the possibility of appointing traditionally elective officials. The question of the degree of representativeness of the board of supervisors is viewed from the perspectives of apportionment of districts, size of the board, and nonpartisanship. She points out why county-city contracts have developed and spread.

Mrs. Gladfelder's book is a timely account of California counties. The author does not limit herself to description; she analyzes, compares, projects into the future and points out the relations between structural and functional changes and environmental conditions in which the county operates. Although no bibliography is provided, the text is extensively footnoted.

ALSO TO BE NOTED:

County Supervisors Association of California, Sacramento, *County News*.
———, *County Observer*.

Clyde E. Jacobs and John F. Gallagher, *California Government, One Among Fifty* (Boston: Allyn and Bacon, 1962, 209 pp.).

Henry A. Turner and John A. Vieg, *The Government and Politics of California*, 3rd edition (New York: McGraw-Hill, 1967, 290 pp.).

Colorado

The Colorado Governor's Local Affairs Study Commission has published the proceedings of the 1965 Governor's Conference on Local Government and Urban Affairs in REPORT OF THE GOVERNOR'S CONFERENCE ON LOCAL GOVERNMENT AND URBAN AFFAIRS: LOCAL GOVERNMENT IN TRANSITION (Denver: 1965, v.p.). Included in this report are three speeches made at the conference containing information concerning county government in Colorado. Fred J. Schneider, then General Counsel, Colorado County Commissioners Association, discusses the powers of county government generally. More specifically, he examines the problems confronting Colorado counties in their efforts to provide urban services to unincorporated urban areas. Another point of emphasis concerns the difficulties experienced by Colorado counties due to their lack of home rule powers.

Mrs. Edward G. Fisher, at that time President, League of Women Voters of Colorado, explores a variety of topics related to Colorado county government: the historical process of growth in the number of counties; their organizational structure, officers, and functions; and county finance. Melvin J. Roberts, president of the Colorado Public Expenditure Council, examines the sources of county revenues in the state. All three speakers sought to be analytical in their presentations; none gave the sources of his information.

ALSO TO BE NOTED:

Colorado, Governor's Local Affairs Study Commission, *Local Government in Colorado; Findings and Recommendations: Final Report* (Denver: 1966, 140 pp.).

Connecticut

Rosaline Levenson has made a comprehensive study of the history and abolition of county government in Connecticut. This study, which she has published in a book, COUNTY GOVERNMENT IN CONNECTICUT—ITS HISTORY AND DEMISE

(Storrs: University of Connecticut, Continuing Education Service, Institute of Public Service, 1966, 237 pp.), includes a general overview of the status of county government in the United States (*see* County Government – General: U. S.) and of county government in New England specifically (*see* County Government – General: New England) in order to provide a background for analysis of the Connecticut situation.

As a first step in her study of the Connecticut experience, she describes the status of county government in that state at the time the counties were disbanded in 1960. She explains the very limited role the counties were playing in the state's governmental structure and examines their limited functions. She gives a more detailed analysis of Connecticut county functions in her lengthy historical treatment of the rise and decline of county government. The functions of county government in Connecticut at the time of its demise are listed as: the operation of jails (the only significant function); maintenance of state courthouse buildings; inspection of weights and measures; adjustment of road disputes; and administration of certain kinds of trust funds. Additionally, immediately before their abolition, counties made financial contributions to agriculture extension services and forest firefighting but did not actually perform these services themselves. Throughout the book, considerable attention is given to the history of county administration of the jails.

The author next devotes particular attention to the politics involved in the appointment of the county boards of commissioners by their respective county delegations in the state legislature and describes the meager powers and responsibilities of the boards. She next focuses on the county sheriff, the only elected county officer and the only one having extensive duties, and discusses his powers and functions at some length. His four prime functions – supervision of the county jail and appointment of the jail staff, limited law enforcement duties, various court responsibilities, and serving civil processes – are considered. Attention is also given to amounts and methods of compensation of the sheriff. The powers and duties of the two appointive county officers – the sealer of weights and the treasurer – are examined.

The final section of the chapter on Connecticut counties at the time of abolition deals with county personnel and finance. In this chapter, there is only a brief sketch of matters relating to county employment and personnel practices. However, in later chapters, Miss Levenson gives much detail on county employment trends for various functions and discusses county personnel practices as a "spoils system." In relation to county finance, the author treats auditing and accounting of expenditures, the roles of the county board of commissioners and the county delegation to the state legislature in budgeting and appropriations, county revenue sources, and the objects of county expenditures. At the end of the chapter, there is an organizational chart of the typical Connecticut county at the time of abolition.

The author examines the history of county government in Connecticut in terms of the growth and subsequent lessening of county functions and the evolution of county structure. The first chapter lays out the colonial foundations of county government and considers the establishment of counties as an intermediate level of government between the towns and the colonial government for the administration of the courts and operation of the jails. Expansion in the number and functions and the evolution of the structure of counties during the colonial period are then traced. The next chapter relates to the further expansion and addition of certain county functions and the decline and elimination of others during the nineteenth and early twentieth centuries. Finally, the net numerical loss of county functions during the twentieth century is described.

Two other chapters dealing with certain historical aspects of county government are more closely related to the discussion of the abolition of government in Connecticut and its aftermath: one considers the need for county jail reform, and the other discusses the circumstances surrounding the transfer of county public welfare functions to the state. Six chapters—those just mentioned, plus four on the abolition of county government, state assumption of county functions, the effects of the abolition, and the prospects for some sort of governments to replace counties—treat the circumstances surrounding the abolition of county government and the aftermath of abolition. (See Reform—Abolition: Connecticut.)

Professor Levenson has done an excellent job of description and analysis of one of the most unusual of government phenomena—the statewide abolition of a unit of government. Her historical approach to the subject results in a much greater understanding of how and why Connecticut counties were abolished than would a nonhistorical treatment. She demonstrates great insight into the political environment of the state in her analysis of the actual abolition. The book utilizes both primary and secondary sources. The primary sources consist largely of state documents, census data, and personal interviews. Secondary sources include reports of several state commissions and committees and of private groups concerned with county government in Connecticut generally and with selected functions of county government. At the time of this publication, the author was Assistant Extension Professor, Institute of Public Service, University of Connecticut.

Delaware

Paul Dolan, in his book THE GOVERNMENT AND ADMINISTRATION OF DELAWARE (New York: Thomas Y. Crowell, 1956, 396 pp.), presents an integrated look at both the institutional and informal characteristics of state and local government in Delaware, The county is important to all governmental and political activities of the state. This importance, which Dolan labels "countyism" and analyzes in depth throughout the book, stems from the fact that three counties cover the entire state.

In a brief chapter devoted entirely to the county, Dolan describes the historical and constitutional basis of the county; its structure and offices; fiscal operations; the organization of health and welfare; public works; planning and zoning; utilities; a few miscellaneous activities; and the county's relation to municipalities.

Throughout the remainder of the book Dolan emphasizes the impact countyism has on both the political and governmental organization of the state. In discussing the political sphere, the author describes countyism's effect on apportionment, party activity, the electoral process, and the nomination procedure for statewide offices. (*See* Politics—General: Delaware.) In sections dealing with governmental activities, he explains why the responsibility for traditional county functions such as public welfare, health, highways, and education has been taken over by the state. He discusses the county's role in the administration of these programs and reiterates the rationale for and methods of county representation on these state administrative boards as well as on most others.

In the chapter on the judiciary, Dolan describes both the judicial and administrative activities of the various courts which sit in the counties, and the different court personnel. In the discussion on law enforcement, he discusses the duties of county law enforcement agencies, including the sheriff, coroner, rural police, constables, and probation officers. He touches briefly on the county's role in the maintenance of correctional institutions and jails.

The book contains a very comprehensive analysis of planning in Delaware counties, focusing on the work in New Castle County and its role in the development of regional planning. (*See* Services – Planning: Delaware.) Another chapter deals with the county's role in intergovernmental relations with both federal and state levels. (*See* Intergovernmental Relations – General: Delaware.)

Dolan constantly stresses the need for a complete reorganization of the local political and governmental arrangement; however, he does not formulate a specific plan.

At the time of this publication, the author was Associate Professor and Chairman of the Department of Political Science, University of Delaware. He seems to have relied extensively on his previous and firsthand knowledge of the state, as footnotes and references are quite limited. The primary sources cited are the revised code of the state, the constitution, and newspaper articles.

This book is a member of the Crowell American Commonwealths Series which was originally planned to include books on the government of each state. Intended as a text and reference book on Delaware government, this volume is an intensive and technical treatment.

Florida

In their book, THE GOVERNMENT AND ADMINISTRATION OF FLORIDA (New York: Thomas Y. Crowell, 1954, 444 pp.) Wilson K. Doyle, Angus M. Laird, and S. Sherman Weiss have comprehensively described the structure and functions of county government in that state.

Chapter 22 is devoted entirely to a description of the structure and primary activities of county government. The authors first consider the composition and powers of the board of commissioners. A general discussion of the duties and compensation of the constitutional, statutory, and school officers of the county follows; emphasis is given to the office of the clerk of the circuit court. A section of this chapter on the reconstruction of local government focuses on county reorganization and city-county consolidation.

In another section of this chapter, dealing with county finances, the authors discuss the offices of tax assessor and collector, the procedure for levying taxes, the preparation of the county budget, the sources and collection of revenue, and the county debt. State auditing of county accounts and records is briefly considered in a later chapter on state financial administration.

The chapter on the county also contains a section dealing with county government services; here the authors discuss highways, health and welfare, education, agriculture, land use and zoning, law enforcement, and miscellaneous minor activities. The scope of county activity in some of these and other fields is also treated in other chapters which look at state administrative duties, including education, public health, public welfare, agriculture, conservation, and highways. The duties of the sheriff are treated at length in the chapter dealing with law enforcement in the state. In the chapter on the state judiciary, the authors describe the judicial process in the county, discussing the composition and functions of the various courts which sit in the county; special attention is given to the duties of the county judge.

Consideration is given in the chapter on municipal government to the county's role in municipal activities. The chapter on intergovernmental relations in the state covers both federal-local and state-county relations. (*See* Intergovernmental Relations – General: Florida.)

The historical and constitutional position of the county is briefly treated early in the book. The discussion of political and electoral activities in the state includes short descriptions of local party organization, and county registration and election officials and their duties. Mention is made of the role of the county in the apportionment of the state legislature and of the problem of local legislation at the state level.

Intended to serve primarily as a textbook at the college level and as a source of information for government officials and the public at large, this book is technical and encyclopedic. The bulk of the references cited are from the state constitution, statutes, and state government studies. Although the authors have been very complete in their description of the structure and functions of county government, they have not included substantial analytic or prescriptive material.

This book is one in the American Commonwealths Series edited by W. Brooke Graves. At the time of this publication, the authors held positions in the higher education system and government of Florida. Doyle and Laird were Professors of Public Administration at Florida State University; Weiss was Director, Legislative Reference Bureau, State of Florida.

ALSO TO BE NOTED:

Florida State Association of County Commissioners, Tallahassee, *Florida County Official.*

Georgia

Cullen B. Gosnell and C. David Anderson's book, THE GOVERNMENT AND ADMINISTRATION OF GEORGIA (New York: Thomas Y. Crowell, 1956, 403 pp.), is designed to provide information concerning the structure, functions, and problems of government in Georgia at state and local levels. The county is treated both in its own chapter and in other pertinent chapters throughout the book.

A brief background sketch and statistics on size and population of counties open the chapter on the county. The authors then describe the three forms of county government in Georgia: executive, commission, and county manager-commission. They describe the composition and organization of each, designate the suitability of the three forms for different types of counties in the state, and conclude with a description of the pros and cons of each form. A general listing of the powers and functions of county government then follows.

The authors next classify the county offices as elective and appointive and give brief descriptions of the terms and duties of each of the offices in the two categories. Their subsequent section on county finances is filled with statistics on revenues, expenditures, and debt. They suggest better budgeting and recordkeeping systems. When considering county reorganization, the authors discuss county consolidation, functional consolidation, and state centralization.

The county's role in the state's conservation, liquor control, transportation, and planning activities are mentioned briefly in appropriate chapters in the book. In the chapter on finances, particular emphasis is given to state-county cooperation in taxation and to the participation of particular county personnel in the state retirement system. When explaining education in the state, the authors emphasize the importance of the new county unit system of organization. They also point out how the state common school funds are apportioned among the counties and the relation of the state School Building Authority to the county district.

In the chapter on public health, the authors trace the development of local health boards since the passage of the Ellis Health Law in 1914. They discuss state grant-in-aid programs for counties, which were inaugurated in 1939, and the relation of the state Division of Local Health Organizations to the local health units. The progress in the organization of county welfare departments is traced from their inception in 1932. The authors describe the composition of the local welfare boards, their local functions, and their work as units in administration of state welfare programs. They consider the work of the state Division of Finance and Statistics which distributes state and federal funds to the county, and the work of the divisions of Public Assistance and of Child Welfare which supervise county administration of these two programs.

The civil and criminal jurisdiction, administrative work, and judge of the county courts are adequately described in the section on the state judiciary. Brief mention is given to the functions of the juvenile court which sits in the county. When covering law enforcement in the state, the authors discuss the functions of the sheriff, coroner, local police, solicitor general, and grand jury, stressing the last named's power to investigate county administration.

The chapter on intergovernmental relations in the state covers state-county, intercounty, and city-county activities. (*See* Intergovernmental Relations – General: Georgia.)

The authors discuss the historical position of the county in the state constitution. Emphasis is given to the provisions of the 1945 constitution which affect local government and to the constitutional amendment ratified in 1952 which permits local governments to submit amendments relating only to a particular locality.

The chapter on popular control of government adequately covers the county's role in the political party process and in election activities, with particular emphasis on the effect of the county unit system. (*See* Politics – General: Georgia.).

Throughout the book the authors cite the need for change in generalized terms. The book is quite complete in its description of county government organization and activity, but analysis of the ramifications of many of these activities is lacking. Since the authors have been diligent in pointing out the areas of state-county relations, the need for a complete analysis of the effect of this contact on the county is particularly evident. Their best analysis appears when they are discussing the county unit system. The adequacy of analysis in this area can easily be explained since Professor Gosnell was active in the fight to abolish the system.

This book is one in the Crowell American Commonwealths Series which is intended to fill a void on scholarly work in state government. At the time of this publication, the authors were scholars at the college level in Georgia. Gosnell was Professor of Political Science and Director of the Institute of Citizenship, Emory University; Anderson was Instructor of Social Studies and Chairman of the Department of Social Studies, Emory-at-Oxford.

The speech, "THE TRADITIONAL RIGHT ARM OF THE STATE," by Governor Carl E. Sanders of Georgia before the 51st Annual Convention of the Association of County Commissioners of Georgia, has been summarized in *Georgia County Magazine,* 16 (May, 1965), 12-14. The Governor briefly mentions some problems confronting Georgia counties, but the main theme of his speech is a plea to the counties to undertake several kinds of reforms so that they can continue to function effectively as "the traditional right arm of the state."

ALSO TO BE NOTED:

Association of County Commissioners of Georgia, Atlanta, *Georgia County Government.*

Robert L. Stoyles, *Handbook for County Commissioners* (Athens: University of Georgia, School of Law, Institute of Law and Government, 1962, 157 pp.).

Hawaii

An excellent description and analysis of the role of county government in the governmental system of Hawaii are contained in a report by the Public Administration Service, STATE AND LOCAL GOVERNMENT RELATIONS IN THE STATE OF HAWAII (Chicago: 1962, 234 pp.). This monograph begins with a general introductory discussion of the nature of counties and their legal status. Hawaii counties are compared with those on the "mainland," and some of the functions performed by counties are outlined. (*See* Services—General: Hawaii.) The introduction also includes a description of the constitutional basis for the apportionment of governing boards of the four counties. A final portion is devoted to the weaknesses of the county as a basis for political organization in the state.

Following the introduction is a general discussion of the structure and powers of counties. The administrative organization of the counties is handled in greater detail in a later section of the monograph. (*See* Organization—General: Hawaii.) The history of county government is traced, and the structure, officers, boards, and powers of the City and County of Honolulu, which operates under a home rule charter, are outlined. There is also brief mention of state-county relations (*see:* Intergovernmental Relations—State-County: Hawaii), a subject also handled in detail in a later section. This section concludes with an analysis of the viability of counties as units for local self-government.

Another section is concerned with county revenues. The sources of county revenues are described and analyzed in detail. Particular emphasis is given to the dominant role of excise taxes, which the counties share with the state, and the property tax. A chart showing the trends in county and state revenues is presented.

The report is particularly insightful in its discussions of county administration and functions. Throughout the report, the importance of state-county relations is stressed and the effects of these relations on all county activities are analyzed. The monograph was prepared by administrative analysts on the staff of Public Administration Service. This research staff relied largely on primary sources, particularly state documents.

Idaho

Herbert S. Duncombe and Katherine D. Pell have prepared a study of county government in Idaho which largely concentrates on the constitutional and statutory provisions for this unit. In addition, the authors analyze the implications of some of the statutes and point out actual practice. This book, HANDBOOK FOR COUNTY OFFICIALS IN IDAHO (Moscow: University of Idaho, Bureau of Public Affairs, 1966, 191 pp.), begins by setting out the provisions of the Idaho constitution relating to county government and follows with a general discussion of the statutory provisions for the structure of county government in the state. An organizational chart of the Idaho county, a list of elected county officers, and a number of statutory provisions concerning all elective officers are presented. Chapter 2 lists statutory provisions for the creation of new counties, the changing of county boundaries, the location of county seats, and the consolidation of counties.

The third chapter pertains to the county governing board, the county commissioners. In its first section, the authors present the general statutory provisions regarding the commissioners: these include compensation, meetings, chairman of the board, clerk of the board, legal counsel for the board, records and publication of proceedings, summoning of witnesses, and administering oaths. The next section deals with the county commissioners as a legislative body and includes ordinance and rule-making powers, budgeting and tax powers, corporate powers, and legislative review of administration. Finally, after a general discussion of the executive and administrative role of the county commissioners, the authors present a long list of more specific executive and administrative powers, including such matters as accounting and auditing; agriculture; appointments, salaries, and other personnel matters; buildings and property; civil defense; elections; fairs; finance; fire protection; forestry; hospitals and health; highways, roads, and bridges; housing; jails and corrections; judicial proceedings; judicial administration; libraries, museums and historical societies; licensing and regulation of business; parks and recreation; planning, zoning, subdivision controls, and urban renewal; safety; taxes; veterans' affairs; and welfare. The following six chapters examine the statutory powers and responsibilities of the elected county officers: clerk, auditor, recorder, treasurer, assessor, sheriff, coroner and constables, and prosecuting attorney.

Five other chapters are devoted to provisions for county functional responsibilities. The chapter on judicial administration outlines the state court system and sets out the major statutory provisions for each type of court—supreme, district, probate, justice, and police. County responsibilities with regard to these courts are emphasized. The next chapter examines county services in the field of agriculture and conservation, including agricultural extension services, county fairs, and weed control.

Chapter 12 includes an examination of statutes which provide for county health services to the general public through multicounty districts. In this connection, county boards of health, county physicians, and county health officers are discussed. Other county health and welfare services which are explored in the chapter are emergency relief and medical services, nursing homes, children's homes, hospitals, and mental health clinics. The number of counties providing each service is indicated.

Chapter 13 is concerned with county planning, zoning, subdivision, and urban renewal programs. Its first section explains the nature of county planning, planning law in Idaho and how it applies to counties, joint or regional planning commissions, and federal aid for planning. The nature of county zoning, county zoning law in Idaho, and airport zoning are examined in the next section. A shorter section explores the logic of subdivision regulations and Idaho law concerning such regulation. The final section of the chapter looks at state enabling law for county urban renewal activities and briefly outlines the nature of federal aid for urban renewal.

Chapter 14 deals with county public works and other functions, primarily county road administration. This section begins with a general overview, followed by an examination of variations among counties in their responsibilities for highway administration. Then come subsections on highway and "good road" special districts, the highway powers of the board of county commissioners, county road superintendents, and county roads. Other county public works functions which are considered in the chapter are land surveys, construction and maintenance of county buildings, and airport administration. Some other functions handled in the chapter are civil defense, parks and recreation, promotion of industrial development, and provision of water, sewerage and refuse collection.

Two chapters are devoted to county finance. A long chapter deals with tax administration; its largest section is devoted to description of the various statutory provisions for assessing the value of real and personal property for tax purposes; another section concerns the equalization of the tax rolls. Subsections consider county equalization through means of a board, state equalization by the state tax commission, and appeals from improper assessment. Other sections examine taxing districts and tax levies, and computation and collection of taxes.

The second chapter on county finances discusses county revenues and budgeting. It analyzes each revenue source in some detail, particularly state and federal aid programs. Two brief sections handle county expenditures and indebtedness. The statutory provisions for the county budgetary process are explained in detail and include budget preparation, review by the county board of commissioners, public hearings and final decisions on the budget, interim and emergency appropriations, expenditure controls, and lapse in appropriations. The final subject of the chapter is county auditing.

Another chapter discusses the following information sources for county officials: experienced officeholders, employees, and citizens; Idaho state laws; handbooks on county government; Idaho Municipal League; Idaho Association of County Officials; National Association of Counties; and federal and state agencies. The final chapter analyzes trends affecting the future of counties in the state: the rapid growth of county government; increasing urbanization of Idaho; and the growing number of urban and suburban counties becoming involved in county-city cooperation.

This descriptive handbook deliberately centers on formal structure and processes and serves as a guide to county officials as to what state law requires of counties and county officers and what it permits them to do. Throughout the volume the authors make specific reference to the statutes of the state, which are their primary source. At the time of this publication, Herbert Duncombe was Associate Director, Bureau of Public Affairs Research, University of Idaho, while Katherine Pell was a research assistant at the Bureau.

ALSO TO BE NOTED:

Idaho Association of Commissioners and Clerks, Preston, *Newsletter*.

Illinois

SOURCE BOOK ON ILLINOIS COUNTY GOVERNMENT (Carbondale: Southern Illinois University, Local Government Center, 1961, 120 pp.), prepared by the County Study and Survey Commission, begins by distinguishing between state- and municipal-type functions of the county. The legal background and justification for this distinction are explained, and the different types of functions in each category are described.

Next, the Commission discusses the structure of county government. It identifies the three types of county governing boards: the three-member board in nontownship counties, the supervisor board in township counties, and the fifteen-member board in Cook County. Brief descriptions are given of the standard and most common offices, and the justification and criteria for classification of counties are set forth.

The section on county financial procedures is quite extensive. Limitations on county indebtedness are explained, the budget process described, the duties of the auditor and treasurer discussed, and the procedure to be followed in financial reporting depicted. The report analyzes the fiscal problems facing the county, notably the lack of sufficient resources, and explains some possible solutions, such as consolidation of county offices.

The Commission considers the duties of and rationale for the office of coroner and summarizes the complaints lodged against this office. It explains the division of responsibility among levels of government for maintenance and construction of highways. The operation and effect of matching programs for financing are discussed.

The report covers the problem of representation and apportionment of county governing boards which follow the township system and points out the extent and nature of population growth. The possibility of using population multiplies in limiting the size of county boards is noted, and the shortcomings of this method of apportioning and deciding the number of representatives are indicated.

This publication is primarily devoted to a description of the structure and functions of county government and of some problems plaguing it. The authors have analyzed the causes and effects of these problems and have presented suggestions for changing and improving the situation.

Neil F. Garvey's book, THE GOVERNMENT AND ADMINISTRATION OF ILLINOIS (New York: Thomas Y. Crowell, 1958, 602 pp.), which is concerned with both state and local government in Illinois, contains two separate chapters about the county, one on rural local government and the other on Cook County. These chapters stress the structure and organization of county government, although they do not ignore services. More in-depth discussions of the services provided by the county are included in appropriate problem-area chapters throughout the book. In such chapters, brief attention is given to the constitutional background of the county, the personnel practices and the agricultural functions. More extensive treatment is given to the activities discussed below.

In the chapter devoted to popular control of government, the composition and duties of county central committees and county conventions are described. The role of the county in the registration and election machinery is delineated.

The county revenue system receives extensive coverage in the discussion of state fiscal operations. The author covers the constitutional limitations on property taxation; the administration of the inheritance tax; allocation of state funds; the assessment, review, equalization, levying, collection, and distribution of the general property tax; and the constitutional limitations upon taxing and borrowing by counties.

County judicial functions are included in the discussion of the judicial system in the state. When discussing the county court, Professor Garvey covers its civil and criminal jurisdiction and the local administrative duties of the county judge. He also describes the special probate courts which sit in some counties. Then he explains the judicial duties of the probation officer, county clerk, clerk of the circuit court, sheriff, state's attorney, public defender, and public administrator. Special attention is given to the compensation and powers of the county judge. The petit jury system in the county is briefly described.

Law enforcement in the county is treated in Chapter 12. The relation of the state Bureau of Criminal Identification and Investigation and of the Attorney General to county officials is covered. Individual subsections describe the office of sheriff, coroner, state's attorney, and the grand jury. The county's functions regarding probation and parole are mentioned.

When discussing the role of the county in education, the author focuses on the duties and qualifications of the county superintendent, the work of county school survey committees, and the creation, composition, and responsibilities of boards of school trustees established for each county. In his discussion of public health in the state, Professor Garvey includes the general health powers of the county. He covers the creation of full-time county health departments, methods of their management and composition, and similar activities of the county governing body when the county does not have a full-time health department. He also discusses federal-state-local health relations, with particular emphasis on finances.

In the chapter on public welfare, Dr. Garvey discusses the purposes, composition, and relations with the state of county departments of public aid. He also explains the work of an appointed or *ex officio* supervisor of general assistance. The methods of channeling public funds to the county through the Illinois Public Aid Commission are explained. The work of the county in administration of general assistance and maintenance of institutions is considered.

Chapter 18 on transportation in Illinois includes a description of the county secondary road system, the financing of county road work, and the responsibilities of the county board in this field. The method of selection and responsibilities of the county superintendent of highways are covered. The chapter on planning discusses the duties of the county governing board in planning activities, the county's role in regional planning commissions, and zoning powers and procedures of the county.

In the chapter on rural local government, the author describes the two streams of migration into Illinois—from the South and from the East—analyzing the effect of their differing conceptions of local government on county organization in Illinois. He explains the distinction made by the Illinois Supreme Court between municipal and quasi-municipal corporations and its effect on the development of the county. He includes statistics on size and population of the counties.

In his discussion of the organization of county government, Professor Garvey describes the three different types of county governing boards operating in Illinois. He lists the powers conferred upon county boards by the state and gives special mention to a board's discretionary legislative powers regarding fiscal matters. He develops the trend to confer general municipal powers upon the county through its regulatory functions. He discusses the effect of classification by the legislature on the composition of county government and points out which officers do not appear in all counties. Descriptions are provided of various elective officers: county clerk, county judge, county treasurer, sheriff, state's attorney, auditor, and recorder of deeds. A brief discussion follows of the appointive officers, including the surveyor, superintendent of highways, county welfare superintendent, and various boards. The chapter concludes with an informative discussion of the realignment of functions in rural local government, in which the increasingly large role of the county and state is explained. Special attention is given to clerical functions, fiscal problems, law enforcement, highways and public works, health and welfare, and education.

There is a separate chapter on Cook County. Its governmental framework and distinctive organizational pattern are described, and attention is given to the office of president of the board of commissioners, including its powers, the selection of the chief executive, and the limiting factors on his executive power. The staff agencies found only in Cook County are described. Functions performed by Cook County are explained: specifically, the duties of the county clerk; the recording practices in the county; the conduct of elections; law enforcement and administration of justice; education; the county department of welfare; health activities; recreational service; transportation; and the regulatory functions, which are becoming increasingly important.

In the chapter on intergovernmental relations, the author gives a comparatively short description of federal-local relations. State-local relations are treated more extensively and the fiscal and nonfiscal relations are delineated from each other. (*See* Intergovernmental Relations—General: Illinois.)

In addition to the obvious distinction made in individual chapters between Cook and the other counties, Professor Garvey also points out differences in other parts of the book. He has been very comprehensive in his description of Cook and the other counties and has included much relevant analysis, particularly when discussing state-county relations. In general, the book is very enlightening and wide-ranging.

This book is a member of the Crowell American Commonwealths Series. At the time of this publication, the author was Associate Professor of Political Science, University of Illinois. The main sources cited are Illinois statutes, the state constitution, and Illinois Legislative Council studies.

Irving Howards and Robert W. Richey, in A CITIZEN'S HANDBOOK OF COUNTY GOVERNMENT IN ILLINOIS (Carbondale: Southern Illinois University, Local Government Center, 1959, 60 pp.), describe the organization and functions of Illinois county government.

The book opens with a description of the history of the county. The differences between the supervisor and commissioner types of boards, both of which are used in the state, are pointed out, and the duties and powers of the board are listed.

Next, the authors describe the administration of a variety of activities carried on by the county: public health, welfare, education, highways, law enforcement, judicial functions, and elections. They list miscellaneous functions performed by the county. In each of the above-mentioned fields, the officers involved and their duties are explained. The duties of the auditor and coroner, not included in the discussion of functions, are described later in the book.

The authors discuss the assessment, collection, and equalization of property taxes. They set forth the steps followed in the property tax process and list nonproperty tax revenue sources.

The extent of administrative integration in county government is described, and separate charts on Cook and downstate counties are presented. Finally, the problems of urban and rural counties are pointed out, and different proposals are put forth as possible remedies.

This monograph is primarily descriptive. Only a minimum of analysis appears in the text, and the only prescriptive material is at the end of the handbook where the authors present their suggestions for change in internal administration and external reorganization of the county. At the time of this publication, the authors were researchers at the Local Government Center, Southern Illinois University.

ALSO TO BE NOTED:

Theodore L. Carlson, *Illinois Government and Institutions* (Boston: Allyn and Bacon, 1962, 209 pp.).

Illinois, Secretary of State, *Government in Illinois, State, County, Local* (Springfield: 1964, 29 pp.).

Illinois Association of County Supervisors and Commissioners, Springfield, *Illinois County and Township Official.*

Clyde F. Snider and Irving Howards, *County Government in Illinois* (Carbondale: Southern Illinois University, Local Government Center, 1960, 171 pp.).

University of Illinois, Institute of Government and Public Affairs, *Illinois Local Government: Final Report and Background Papers, Assembly on Illinois Local Government* (Urbana: 1961, 91 pp.).

Indiana

HERE IS YOUR INDIANA GOVERNMENT, Indiana State Chamber of Commerce, (Indianapolis: 1967, 152 pp.) contains a very detailed chapter describing the organization, functions, and offices of county government.

The chapter begins with a few statistics on the size and population of the counties and a brief outline of the legal framework in which the counties operate. The first aspect of county government discussed is the board of county commissioners. A brief description is given of the terms, salaries, and general responsibility of the commissioners, and a detailed, complete list is then presented of twenty-eight general functions of the board. Some of these functions and other more unique ones are treated in detail.

Next discussed are the financial powers of the county council which serves as a check on the board of commissioners. Detailed attention is given to its powers to approve real estate sales, set the budget estimate form, and authorize the borrowing of money.

Extensive descriptions are provided of the qualifications and duties of many elective county administrative officials: auditor, treasurer, recorder, clerk of the circuit court, surveyor, sheriff, prosecuting attorney, coroner, and assessor. Equally extensive coverage is then given to appointive officers and boards: highway supervisor, highway engineer, superintendent of schools, extension agent, attorney, inspector of weights and measures, physician, purchasing agent, superintendent of county homes, board of review, board of tax adjustment, election board canvassers, board of education, board of public welfare, health officer, commission on public records, alcoholic beverage board, planning commission, general and tuberculosis hospital boards, and the board of aviation. Other county boards and agencies discussed in less detail are drainage board, miners' examination board, board of memorial trustees, library district, capital improvement board of managers, coliseum directors, mental health clinic board, department of parks and recreation, central data processing agency, department of buildings, Indianapolis Historical Preservation Commission, Mass Transportation Authority of Greater Indianapolis, and port authority. A list is provided of remaining county officers as is a complete table of annual salaries of county officials. A complete and worthwhile chart is included on the organization of a typical Indiana county government.

The last part of the section devoted to the county explains the county court system. Three types of courts are described: circuit, superior, and various special ones, such as probate, juvenile, and criminal courts. A chart is included on the annual salaries of judges.

The duties and method of selection of jury commissioners and the duties of the county grand jury are considered.

In the section on school corporations, the county unit method of school administration is explained. Included in the discussion of how local governments obtain money is a chart which shows exactly how the process is carried out in counties. The appendix of the study contains a descriptive narrative on the origins of the county, and a table is included that gives the date of organization, the county seat, and the origin of the name of each county. Another section in the appendix also describes in some detail the organization of the political parties in the state. The county organization is explained with emphasis on the duties of the county chairman.

This book is a clearly-written and encompassing description of Indiana county government. It deserves an excellent rating on the quality and quantity of its factual information. Although written for the information of the interested citizen, it is of a much higher caliber than many similar civic publications reviewed.

Most of the material relating to the county in Pressly S. Sikes's INDIANA STATE AND LOCAL GOVERNMENT, 3rd edition (Bloomington: Principia Press, 1946, 246 pp.) is contained in Chapter IV. The only other references of merit are a description of the county central committees of the political parties and an explanation of county representation in the state legislature.

The chapter on the county opens with a history of its legal position. Then the author presents statistics on the number and size of Indiana counties and outlines the procedures to be followed in creating new counties and in changing the county seat.

After a general introduction to the type of functions performed by the county, the author describes in detail a number of functions: law enforcement, administration of justice, highways, education, relief and public welfare, public health, assessment and collection of taxes, suffrage and elections, recordkeeping, and the extent of miscellaneous other activities.

The discussion then turns to county activity from the viewpoint of county officers and boards. The qualifications and duties of the following officials are explained: auditor, treasurer, clerk of the circuit court, recorder, sheriff, coroner, surveyor, county commissioners, county council, assessor, superintendent of schools, attendance officer, health officer, highway supervisor, agricultural agent, inspector of weights and measures, physician, and attorney. The operations of special boards operating in the county are described: board of review, board of tax adjustment, election board, board of education, board of hospital trustees, board of managers of the tuberculosis hospital, library board, miners' examining board, jury commissioners, county board of public welfare, county alcoholic beverages board, and board of registration. Differences in use of these offices and boards between counties of different size are pointed out in the discussions.

This book contains very complete descriptions of the structure and functioning of county government but virtually no analysis of the quality of service and operation; nor does the author supply prescriptions for change. However, as a repository of factual information, the book is highly useful. Although a bibliography appears at the end of the book, no sources are cited in the text. At the time of this publication, the author was Professor of Government and Director of the Bureau of Government Research, Indiana University.

Iowa

Donald E. Boles and Herbert C. Cook set forth a general discussion of county government in Iowa in AN EVALUATION OF IOWA COUNTY GOVERNMENT (Ames: Iowa State College, Community Research Center, 1959, 78 pp.). In part, the authors take a descriptive, traditional approach to the discussion of county government in Iowa. They describe the method of selection, compensation, term of office, functions, and responsibilities of the county board of supervisors, as well as of ten other county officers and ten other county boards and commissions. The county officers include the county attorney, auditor, treasurer, sheriff, county recorder, coroner, clerk of the district court, county superintendent of schools, county engineer, and county assessor. The boards are the board of education, board of review, board of social welfare, county agricultural extension council, soldiers' relief commission, county drainage board, county board of health, county hospital board, county zoning commission, and the county fair association.

The discussion also includes a discourse on the history of county government in Iowa since 1838 and tells of the origin of Iowa counties, the subsequent expansion in their number, and the evolution of their structure. The monograph also considers the legal status of county government in the state. It sets forth the constitutional restrictions on county size, boundaries, and debt, and on the legislature's ability to shape the structure and organization of county government. The legal basis of the classification of counties as quasi-corporations is laid out.

The authors become more analytical when they examine other aspects of county government. They explore the problem of lack of information about county governmental operations as a source of citizen and state legislative apathy toward county government. The major analytical section of this monograph deals with the development of a model for the examination of the determinants of county government administrative costs and its application to the cost of Iowa county government administration. (*See* Finance—General: Iowa.) The volume contains an interesting discussion of problems involved in county financial administration, particularly budgeting. (*See* Finance—Administration: Iowa.) Other administrative problems are also considered. The weaknesses of the system of multiple justices of the peace are considered at length, and administrative problems involved in the duties of the assessor, sheriff, auditor, and the board of supervisors are also explored.

The need for various kinds of administrative reorganization are presented. The kinds of reorganization studied include consolidation of the counties into larger units of government; converting elective administrative offices to appointive status; establishment of a state agency of local affairs; and establishment of an executive head, either elective or appointive, for each county government. The volume concludes with specific reform measures to solve county administrative problems and to help bring about reorganization. These reform measures involve a number of state constitutional amendments and state legislative enactments. Throughout the monograph there is a lack of discussion of the functions of Iowa county government. Emphasis is on the structure, general administration, and administrative costs of Iowa county government.

Written in a clear, concise, straightforward manner, there is little excess verbiage in this monograph. The authors use many charts, graphs, and tables that are closely related to and usually well-integrated with the text. They use mostly primary sources, which include a large number of state documents, such as the state auditor's records and the state examiner's reports on county offices, as well as statutes and constitutional provisions. At the time of this publication, the authors were both Professors of Political Science, Iowa State College.

ALSO TO BE NOTED:

Iowa Legislative Research Bureau, *County Governments: What Are They, What Do They Do, How Are They Organized?* Bulletin No. 13A (Des Moines: 1958, 18 pp.).

Iowa State Association of County Officers, Independence, *The Iowa County Officer.*

Russell M. Ross, *The Government and Administration of Iowa* (New York: Thomas Y. Crowell, 1957, 382 pp.).

Harry R. Smith, *A Handbook for County Supervisors* (Iowa City: University of Iowa, Institute of Public Affairs, 1962, 125 pp.).

Kansas

James W. Drury and Associates in THE GOVERNMENT OF KANSAS (Lawrence: University of Kansas Press, 1961, 393 pp.) have been very thorough in their coverage of the county. The chapter devoted to the county and township contains information on the organization of county government and a sketch of its activities. Throughout the book, other chapters devoted to a particular activity in the state give in-depth coverage of county functions.

First the authors trace the organization of the political party county committees through the election of precinct committeemen, the choice of two of their number as chairman and chairwoman, and their representation of the county at the state level. Mention is made of the functions of the county committee; and the election procedure in the county is explained by focusing on the work of the county clerk or election commissioner.

The authors mention the county's representation in the state House and Senate. When discussing the powers and procedures of the legislature, they explain its power to enact local legislation and mention the number of lobbyists from the counties and their influence on the legislative process.

In the chapter on the state revenue system, state supervisory powers over local taxing procedures are considered. The recommendations of the Kansas Citizens' Commission on Assessment Equalization are described, and the apportionment of state collected taxes to the counties is discussed. (*See* Finance – General: Kansas.)

In the chapter on the judiciary, the authors give concise descriptions of district courts, probate courts, county courts, justices of the peace, and small debtor courts. In the chapter on law enforcement, they discuss the problems of ill-defined jurisdiction, inadequate personnel, and insufficient financial support.

The various county property taxes levied to support the elementary and high schools in the county are discussed, and a full explanation is provided of the office of county superintendent of public instruction, including qualifications, duties, financial resources, and weaknesses. The authors explain the procedure for establishing a county health department, give statistics on the number of such units established and the number of people served by them, and analyze the deficiencies of the present system and mention suggested alternatives.

Extensive coverage is given to the county's role in public welfare services, with mention of its activity in the various welfare programs of the state, the operation of the county board of social welfare, the duties of the county welfare director, and financial procedures. Past trends and possible future developments in this field are explained. (*See* Services – Public Welfare: Kansas.)

The representation of the county on the state Board of Agriculture and the county's work in weed eradication and extension services are indicated. The creation by the county of various special districts pertaining to conservation are scrutinized. In the chapter on transportation, the two systems of classification of county roads used in the state are explained, and local highway administration and financing are discussed.

A number of statistics introduce the chapter on the county, followed by a discussion of the organization of county government, which begins with a description of the board of county commissioners. The duties of some officials—county clerk, treasurer, sheriff, attorney, coroner, register of deeds, probate judge, clerk of district court—are considered, and miscellaneous appointive officials are mentioned. The lengthy discussion of the county clerk includes his various duties: secretary to the board of commissioners, assessment, and election administration. There is also an organizational chart of the county structure. In a section of this chapter on finances, sources of revenue and the problems resulting from too-heavy reliance on the property tax are fully discussed. (*See* Finance—General: Kansas.) The need for and difficulties in attaining reorganization are noted. The chapter concludes with a discussion of the future of the county.

The discussion of intergovernmental relations includes an analysis of state-local relations, brief mention of nation-local relations, and a description of various types of interlocal relations. (*See* Intergovernmental Relations—General: Kansas.)

The Government of Kansas is a scholarly, rigorous treatment of government at all levels in the state. In it James Drury and his associates have succeeded in giving balanced coverage to the various aspects of county government. Analysis and prescription are generously interlaced, but description does not suffer. The structural and organizational aspects of county government and activities are adequately described. The actual procedure followed is also detailed.

As a point of interest, it should be noted that the index is very complete in references to sections dealing with the county. The primary references cited are the state statutes, constitution, various government publications, and studies by the Governmental Research Center of the University of Kansas. The Kansas Citizens' Commission on Assessment Equalization was the source of much tax information.

ALSO TO BE NOTED:

William H. Cape, *County Government in Kansas,* Citizens Pamphlet No. 23 (Lawrence: University of Kansas, Governmental Research Center, 1958, 35 pp.).

"County Platform Represents Consolidation of Position," *Kansas Government Journal,* 51 (January, 1965), 8-9.

Kentucky

John E. Reeves's monograph, KENTUCKY GOVERNMENT (Lexington: University of Kentucky, Bureau of Government Research, 1955, 87 pp.), is a brief treatise on the constitution and government of this state. There is no separate section devoted to the county, although this unit is mentioned in various sections, and its historical development and present constitutional position are explained. The section on politics and elections in Kentucky contains the most material relevant to the county. Here the author explains the county's function in registration procedures, including canvassing, and the appointment of the county boards of registration. The composition and duties of the county board of election commissioners are described in the discussion of nominations and elections. The role of the challengers appointed by the county party committees is explained. The composition of the political party county committee, the role of its chairman, and its five most important duties are indicated.

Discussion of the general assembly includes a brief mention of districting and the representation the county possesses in the legislature. In the section dealing with the state administration, the author mentions the relation of the Kentucky Tax Commission, the state Department of Revenue, and the Department of Highways to the county. The circuit courts which sit in the county are discussed, with the focus on the criteria which determine the number of circuit districts and judges in a county. The civil and criminal jurisdiction of the county court is also considered. The author explains the functions and qualifications of the county judge and the composition of the fiscal court, the governing body of the county over which the county judge presides. Brief mention is given to the justice of the peace courts in the county and to the makeup and role of the grand jury.

Kentucky Government is a brief descriptive monograph intended only as a supplement to more extensive works. Many secondary references are listed at the end of the chapters, but the citations throughout the text are primarily from the constitution and statutes of Kentucky.

Kenneth E. Vanlandingham discusses the need for Kentucky constitutional revision of provisions relating to county government in his monograph, THE CONSTITUTION AND LOCAL GOVERNMENT (Frankfort: Kentucky Legislative Research Commission, 1964, 63 pp.). One chapter is devoted to a discussion of the constitutional provisions for local government, including counties. The author explains the overrestrictiveness of the provisions and explores the need for constitutional change to give the legislature more flexibility in dealing with county government. Some constitutional changes which have taken place in other states are reviewed, and proposals for change in Kentucky are examined.

Another chapter deals with the general nature and problems of county government in Kentucky – a discussion that is also oriented toward the need for reform. The general structure of county government is described and analyzed briefly, and suggestions for constitutional renovation are made. In particular, the organization of the two forms of county governing boards is analyzed, and the problems involved in the justices of the peace form are pointed out. The general lack of county merit systems is scrutinized, and the constitutional provisions and court interpretations that are barriers to the institution of merit systems are explored. This chapter also includes an extensive examination of the fee system of compensating county officers. The operation of the fee system for certain county officers is described and the problems of its use are analyzed. State constitutional reforms which have abolished the fee system in other states are considered, and recommendations for change in Kentucky are made. Another chapter examines local finance. Constitutional restrictions on county powers to tax and to incur debt are examined, and the financial bind which they place on counties are noted. Recommendations for reform are also made.

This monograph is well-written and very readable. The author backs up his recommendations with evidence of the defects of county government in Kentucky. He does not give specific reference to sources of his information, but it can be assumed that much of his source material comes from state constitutions and statutes and personal observation in the state of Kentucky. At the time of this publication, the author was Professor of Political Science, the University of Kentucky.

ALSO TO BE NOTED:

Kenneth E. Vanlandingham, "County Government and Constitutional Change in Kentucky," *Review of Government*. 2 (Lexington: University of Kentucky, Bureau of Government Research, March, 1963), 1-4.

Louisiana

William C. Havard's short book, THE GOVERNMENT OF LOUISIANA (Baton Rouge: Louisiana State University, Bureau of Public Administration, 1958, 194 pp.), portrays the governmental system of that state. It contains a separate chapter on parish government and scattered references to the parish throughout the text.

When discussing the political and electoral process in Louisiana, the author includes a detailed description of parish registration procedure, concentrating on the work of the parish registrar of voters. He also presents a brief discussion of the composition and duties of parish political party organizations as well as a description of the selection of the commissioners for primaries, and the selection, composition and duties of the parish board of supervisors in general elections. He describes the representation enjoyed by the parish in the state senate and house of representatives, and the influence of localism in the legislature.

There is also description of the organization of the district, juvenile, and justice of the peace courts, all of which sit in at least some of the parishes. Brief mention is given to the office of district attorney and clerk of the district court.

The author discusses the state's interest in the property tax and its effect on the parish.He touches on the effect of the civil service law at the parish level and mentions state supervision of parish school districts, distribution of state funds in the parishes, and the centralization trend in public welfare. Reference is made to the influence of parishes in deciding on the composition of the state highway board and distribution of state funds to parishes for road work.

The chapter on the parish opens with statistics on the size and population of parishes. The author then discusses the composition of the police jury, the governing body of the parish, and the selection of its president. He lists the duties of the jury, with emphasis on its administration of the parish road system. He mentions other methods of organization of the governing body: the commission form established by the legislature as an optional form, and the consolidated city-parish government of New Orleans and Baton Rouge. He describes the office of sheriff, clerk of the district court, assessor, and coroner. He outlines how education, welfare, public health, libraries, and agriculture are handled in the parish and discusses how a special district may be formed in a parish. The chapter closes with a discussion of the impediments to reform of parish government and a brief general description of the few current examples of the county manager plan.

The discussion of the parish in this book is only descriptive and rudimentary. There is no attempt at analysis; in fact, only the bare outlines of the structural components of parish government are given. The author does not deal at all with the informal aspects of government. It is difficult to determine his main sources since no citations are included in the text. Bibliographical notes at the end of each chapter give a very brief description of suggested references for further reading. The study was written as a project for the Bureau of Public Administration, Louisiana State University.

The Louisiana Legislative Council's book, THE GOVERNMENT OF LOUISIANA (Baton Rouge: 1959, 405 pp.), is a narrative about all branches and levels of government in Louisiana. It contains a separate chapter on local government in Louisiana, which emphasizes the parish, and also separate discussions of the parish throughout the remainder of the book.

When discussing party organization, the authors briefly mention how the parish is represented on the state central committee and describe in more detail the composition, chairman, and duties of the parish executive committee. The chapter on the electoral process includes a description of the registration process, which stresses the duties of the registrar of voters, and of the conduct of elections, particularly the efforts of the parish election commissioners. The discussion of apportionment of the state legislature explains the representation enjoyed by the parish.

When explaining the judicial process in the state, the authors describe the jurisdiction of the courts – district, juvenile and family, justice of peace – which sit in the parishes. The court-related duties of district attorney, clerk of district court, sheriff, constables, and coroner are treated, with particular attention to the office of clerk of district court and the sheriff.

The chapter on intergovernmental relations contains only very general comments on the nature of state-local and federal-local relations. The organization and activities of the parish school board are described, with emphasis on the office of superintendent of education, whose holder is executive officer of the parish board. Separate discussion follows on state funds available to the parish and on the extent and methods of local financing. The book gives extensive consideration to parish highway activity. Methods of administration, state and local financing, state technical assistance, and interparish cooperation are discussed. (*See* Services – Public Works: Louisiana.)

Public welfare administration is inadequately covered, with the duties of the state division of local welfare services receiving only brief mention. The division of effort between state and parish government regarding public health is delineated. Then the authors describe the composition, organization, and functions of the parish health boards, focusing on the duties and importance of the parish health officer. The planning and coordinating activities of the state division of local health services are covered.

Brief mention is given to the parish fire-fighting activities and property ownership and management. The non-judicial duties of the district attorney and sheriff are explained in the section on law enforcement. The section on fiscal procedure includes a brief description of the duties of and restrictions on local assessors and the duties of the state Supervisor of Public Funds who examines local records.

The chapter on local government opens with a discussion of the four systems of rural government which developed in America. Then the authors describe the historic development of parishes in Louisiana, which were originally based on the Virginia system. This introduction concludes with a description of the present status of the parish.

Mention is then given to the normal method of organization of parish government. Deviations from this normal pattern in Orleans, East Baton Rouge, and Jefferson parishes are explained more fully. The principal functions of the police jury and the different elective and appointive officers are listed. Brief descriptions are given of the activities of the registrar of voters, the treasurer, the local library boards, and surveyor. The rationale for the creation of parish-planning and development commissions is explained, as are their composition and duties. The chapter also includes a detailed consideration of home rule in Louisiana. (*See* Organization – Home Rule: Louisiana.)

Throughout the book the authors are careful to point out deviations from the general pattern of parish activity, particularly those found in East Baton Rouge and Orleans parishes. In general this is a legalistic description of government in Louisiana and lacks the factor of analysis: like William C. Havard's book, *The Government of Louisiana.* However, it is more detailed and complete in its description of parish activities than Havard's work. Lack of analysis of state-local interaction is its weakest point. The book contains no bibliography and only scattered citations throughout the text, although in the preface the executive director of the Louisiana Legislative Council which prepared the book states that it relied heavily on previous reports of the Council. The book was originally presented to the members of the state legislature as a research study.

A staff report issued by the Louisiana Legislative Council, LOUISIANA: ITS HISTORY, PEOPLE, GOVERNMENT, AND ECONOMY (Baton Rouge: 1955, 285 pp.), is descriptive and emphasizes structure. Only a brief portion of the report is directly related to county government; it gives a history of such government in the state as well as presenting the functions and responsibilities of county officials.

ALSO TO BE NOTED:

L. E. Chandler, *A Study of Parish Government in Louisiana* (Hammond: Southeastern Louisiana College, 1960, 27 pp.).

Police Jury Association of Louisiana, Natchitoches, *Louisiana Parish Government.*

Maine

Edward F. Dow begins his monograph, COUNTY GOVERNMENT IN MAINE: PROPOSALS FOR REORGANIZATION (Augusta: Maine Legislative Research Committee, October 1952, 121 pp.), by pointing out the declining and restricted role of the county in New England. He then traces the historical development of Maine counties from colonial days, pointing out how their distinctive traits originated.

Before describing the government of the counties, the author points out why they are not suitable for the manager plan. He then outlines their functions as an administrative agent of the state. When discussing the officers of the county, he mentions the existence of the judge of probate, register of probate and clerk of courts and suggests their conversion to appointive status. He explains the duties of the county attorney, the county police force, treasurer, commissioners, register of deeds, and bail commissioners. Tables are included on county resources, county expenditures, and per capita costs of county government.

The author describes at length the court system operative in the Maine counties. He points out which courts sit in the counties, their personnel and duties. A long section on county jails follows, in which the author describes their quality, emphasizing their more serious shortcomings.

In a very extensive description, Dow explains the constitutional and statutory provisions affecting county government. He emphasizes the restrictions on and requirements for county offices. Throughout this discussion, he also notes the supervision exercised over county activities by the state government.

All through his description and analysis of county government in Maine, the author points out weaknesses needing change and improvement and indicates the character of this reform. Unfortunately, when indicating the type of change needed, he does not always spell out exactly how it would be accomplished or the nature of the improvements that would result. However, the book serves as a good source on the nature of and limitations on county government in the state of Maine.

COUNTY GOVERNMENT (Augusta: 1966, 29 pp.) is a report with recommendations on the nature of county government in Maine by the Maine Intergovernmental Relations Commission. Part One of the report begins with the evolution of county structure and administration from 1670 to the present. This historical presentation emphasizes the subordinate status and the limited powers of county government throughout the state's history. In addition, the major functions and responsibilities of county governments are outlined, the county as the basis for organization of the courts described, and the county officers and boards examined.

Part Two compiles the results of detailed questionnaires sent by the Commission to the sixteen counties in the state. The resultant data include the number of court cases heard; the expenses of the clerks of the courts; the volume of county recording work done by the registers of deeds; and information relating to county probate courts, law libraries, the county commissioners, county medical examiners, and county civil defense operations. In addition, detailed information is given about the purposes and amounts of county cash disbursements.

Two lengthy sections of Part Three make statistical comparisons of the county sheriffs' departments with the state police, and of county jails with state penal institutions. A third section examines the role of the county attorney and includes the results of a questionnaire to county attorneys: statistics on the output of their offices, and their opinions on such matters as the nature and jurisdiction of their offices. Part Four briefly presents the Commission's recommendations for legislation which would change various aspects of county government in Maine. The Commission calls these suggestions its "10-Point Program."

This report itself is statistical, and it uses statistics as the basis for the analysis. Its analysis of the county attorneys' opinions is particularly interesting. The Commission consists of two municipal officials, who serve as chairman and vice-chairman, two state senators, two state representatives, and one public member.

ALSO TO BE NOTED:

Maine, Legislative Research Committee, *County Government,* Publication No. 103-9 (Augusta: 1967, 36 pp.).

Maryland

Jean E. Spencer has written an excellent description and analysis of the status of county government in Maryland in CONTEMPORARY LOCAL GOVERNMENT IN MARYLAND (College Park: University of Maryland, Bureau of Governmental Research, 1965, 116 pp.). An interesting introductory section mentions the traditional role of county government in the state and examines trends in population and municipal incorporation and their implications for county government; it includes four tables of data on population trends, which are significant to county government.

The introduction is followed by an enlightening discussion of the unusual situation in Maryland with respect to legislative control over county government and to county home rule. This section begins with an analysis of the provisions in the Maryland constitution which give the state legislature extensive control over county government and leads to an exploration of the way in which a Maryland county's legislative delegation acts, to some extent, as its legislative body. The author analyzes the consequences of this situation for the public accountability of county government.

Relating the above discussion to an examination of county home rule, the author extensively describes and analyzes the county home rule constitutional amendment and places special emphasis on how certain provisions of the amendment have resulted in little expansion of home rule powers by those counties which have adopted home rule charters. In this connection, the author discusses the Express Powers Act at some length. In a similar vein, the book deals with the proposed Code Home Rule Amendment, which was subsequently passed. She describes the nature of the limited, non-charter home rule powers which the amendment would grant counties adopting it. She also lists the reasons why the amendment is desirable.

Many other aspects of county government are considered in detail. These include an examination of the roles of the county governing boards and chief executives and analysis of the interrelationships between them (*see* Organization – Governing Boards: Maryland); discussion of elective and appointive county officials and boards and their relationship to the county governing board (*see* Organization – Chief Executives, General: Maryland); and an exploration of the functions of county government in Maryland (*see* Services – General: Maryland). A subject given more cursory attention is the authority of the county governing board over municipal incorporation and dissolution.

This excellent book describes institutional arrangements and constitutional and statutory requirements and also analyzes the effects of such arrangements and requirements upon the actual operation of county government. The author stresses the relationships among county officers and boards and gives constant attention to the important matter of county relations with the state. County-municipal intergovernmental relations are also a matter of concern to the author, particularly in the discussion of county functions. The book's one weakness is that it does not include political aspects in its otherwise thorough coverage of all phases of county government.

The sources of information for the book are largely primary. They include, in particular, constitutional and statutory provisions, state documents, and field research done by the staff of the Bureau of Governmental Research at the University of Maryland. At the time of this publication, the author was Research Associate and Lecturer, Bureau of Governmental Research, University of Maryland.

ALSO TO BE NOTED:

Don L. Bowen and Robert S. Friedman, *Local Government in Maryland* (College Park: University of Maryland, Bureau of Governmental Research, 1955, 143 pp.).

Maryland County Commissioners Association, College Park, *Courthouse News Letter*.

Massachusetts

A section of Elwyn E. Mariner's THIS IS YOUR MASSACHUSETTS GOVERNMENT: CITY, TOWN, COUNTY, STATE; A DESCRIPTION OF THE STRUCTURE AND

FUNCTIONS OF THE STATE AND LOCAL GOVERNMENTS OF THE PEOPLE OF THE COMMONWEALTH OF MASSACHUSETTS (Arlington Heights: Mariner Books, 1959, 172 pp.) is devoted to county government in Massachusetts. This section starts with a treatment of the history and legal status of county government in the state. Emphasis is placed upon the nature of the county as a subdivision of the state and upon the county's lack of legislative authority. There follows an examination of the officers and functions of county government. The variation among counties in their adequacy as administrative units and in the number and variety of functions they perform is noted.

The role of the county boards of commissioners is analyzed and their powers and functions are outlined. The author describes the status of the county as a "middleman" in the construction of secondary roads. There is also an interesting analysis of the very limited nature of county financial powers, and the sources of county revenues, county budgeting, and county intergovernmental fiscal relations are examined. The final portion of the section is devoted to an extensive consideration of the special role of tuberculosis sanitariums in county government.

The author is largely descriptive in his discussions of county government, although he undertakes analysis at certain points. Both primary and secondary sources are used. The author has been a member of several taxpayer groups.

COUNTY GOVERNMENT IN MASSACHUSETTS (Boston: 1962, 167 pp.), prepared by the Massachusetts Legislative Research Council, is largely an in-depth study of the functions of county government in that state. An introductory chapter presents an overview of county services, and later chapters examine individual county services in detail. (*See* Services – General: Massachusetts.) Considerable attention is also devoted to county history, structure, officers, and court organization. Within this examination of county services, the powers and duties of the various county officers are explained, and the county budgetary process is outlined. The study reaches some conclusions about the nature of county administration and examines proposals for the abolition of county government.

This excellent study analyzes the effectiveness of counties in their administration of services as well as the nature of the services themselves. The House of the Massachusetts General Court commissioned the Legislative Research Council to prepare the monograph. The authors largely use primary sources, including interviews with county officials, questionnaires, and state documents. Throughout the study a wide variety of data relating to various aspects of county services is presented.

PROCEEDINGS OF THE 12TH GOVERNOR'S CONFERENCE (Amherst: 1960, 49 pp.), published by the Bureau of Governmental Research of the University of Massachusetts, includes four papers which deal with Massachusetts county government. The paper by Donald P. Tullock, Sheriff of Barnstable County, concerns county jails and houses of correction; he briefly explains the uses of these institutions and the administrative practices of county sheriffs.

A second paper explains the abolition of Connecticut county governments and some weaknesses characteristic of counties in that state. The author of this paper, James J. St. Germain, Professor of Political Science at Merriack College, notes that most of these same weaknesses are present in Massachusetts counties; therefore, he advocates the abolition of county government in that state.

Massachusetts county government is defended in a third paper by Thomas B. Brennan, a county commissioner of Middlesex County, who talks about the history, structure, functions, officers, and budgetary processes of Massachusetts counties. He argues that county government should be strengthened rather than abolished, so that government may be kept "close to the people" and democratic.

The fourth paper also takes the position that county government in Massachusetts is obsolete and should be abolished. In addition, the author, John J. Beades, a state senator, describes the methods of selection, terms, and duties of the various county officials and employees. In a final section of his paper, he discusses the possible use of greatly reformed counties as metropolitan governments in certain areas, but emphasizes that in most areas, county government should be abolished.

Except for the first paper, which was completely descriptive, the authors seek to be analytical and prescriptive as well as descriptive. The authors generally use secondary sources as well as their personal knowledge and experience as the basis for their papers.

ALSO TO BE NOTED:

Massachusetts Legislative Research Council, *Report Relative to Succession and Continuity in State and County Government,* Senate No. 520 (Boston: 1959, 37 pp.).

Joseph Zimmerman, "The Role of Local Government in Massachusetts," *Municipal Voice*, 2 (November, 1964), 4-8.

Michigan

Floyd C. Fischer's book, THE GOVERNMENT OF MICHIGAN (Boston: Allyn and Bacon, 1965, 230 pp.), is a short, simple treatment of government at all levels in that state. Except in the chapter devoted to county government, only minimal references are made to the county. These include mention of county agricultural agents, the county as a basis for apportionment of the state legislature, jurisdiction of circuit and probate courts, equalization of assessments, organization and duties of county party committees, and election activities. The only reference of more than minimal coverage concerns assessment equalization in Bay County and its "Operation Fair Play." But this too needs much more development to be adequate.

The chapter on county government opens with a brief background sketch, including statistics and relevant constitutional provisions. Next, the author explains the composition and lists the administrative and financial functions of the county board of supervisors. The following four-year-term county offices are described: sheriff, clerk, treasurer, register of deeds, and prosecuting attorney. Then the author explains the duties of the surveyor, drain commissioner, and coroner, who are elected for a two-year term in most counties.

When examining local activity in education, the author discusses the 1948 law which replaced county school commissioners with a county superintendent of education. He explains an act passed in 1962 which replaced traditional county school districts with intermediate school districts. In a later chapter on education in Michigan, mention is made of the trend toward consolidation of school districts and the authority of counties to establish community colleges.

In the chapter on county government, the author briefly describes the organization and operation of county health departments. Regarding highways, he mentions the organization of the county road board and explains its authority and powers under the general highway law. He also notes the offices of road superintendent and highway engineer, both of which are filled by the board. In discussing county reorganization, he cites the limitations and weaknesses of the present system and notes suggested changes in organization. He focuses on county home rule, discussing the rationale for its creation and the article of the 1963 constitution which authorizes its use. In the chapter on townships and villages, mention is made of their points of contact with the county.

This book contains only basic description and has value solely as an outline. It is simply written and seems to be intended for use as a high school text. The author is a high-school civics teacher and a city commissioner in Bay City, Michigan. No sources are cited in the text, and there is no bibliography.

The Bureau of Social and Political Research at Michigan State University has made a legalistic study of county government in Michigan, entitled THE COUNTY BOARD OF SUPERVISORS (East Lansing: 1959, 152 pp.), in which special emphasis is placed on the role of the board of supervisors. As pointed out in the introductory section of the book, the work "is largely a study of the relevant provisions of the Constitution and statutes, as interpreted and applied by the Supreme Court and Attorney General."

The first section deals with the historical evolution of the general provisions for county government under the Michigan state constitution. This discussion includes an examination of the counties as units for representation in the state legislature and of the quasi-corporate status of the county government. There follows an extensive examination of the role of the board of supervisors. (*See* Organization—Governing Boards: Michigan.)

When the study focuses upon the functions of county government, county involvement in education is examined first. The organization of county or multicounty school districts is discussed, and the method of selection, term of office, and functions and duties of the county school board are explored. The role of the county superintendent of schools is described. The relationships between the school board and the board of supervisors and between the school board and the local school districts are considered.

The preparation of a study of educational conditions in the county by the school board and its special educational services are also discussed. The financial relationships of the local school districts, the county, and the state to the county education function is the final topic examined. The means of establishing county and multicounty regional libraries are explained, and the method of selection, and functions and duties of the county and regional library boards are discussed as a function closely related to education.

Brief consideration is given to the establishment and duties of the office of county agricultural extension agent. County participation in the ownership and maintenance of public agricultural produce markets and county fairgrounds is also briefly explored. The regulatory powers of the county board of supervisors over the erection of dams and bridges is mentioned. The authority of the board of supervisors to establish county parks is considered, and the method of selection and duties of the county park trustees are set forth. The activities of the county in the field of forestry are delineated, and the method of selection and duties of the county forestry commission are described.

The power of the board of supervisors to adopt a zoning law is examined. The method of selection and functions and responsibilities of the county zoning commission and the board of zoning appeals are then discussed. The method of selection and powers and duties of the register of deeds are set out, while the office of county surveyor receives only brief mention. The subdivision regulation powers of the county are described, and the composition and functions of the county plat board are laid out.

Another summary examination concerns the county court system. The circuit court system and its relationship to county government are explained, the roles of the circuit court judge and the circuit court commissioners examined, and the office of probate judge discussed.

The book also describes very briefly the powers and responsibilities of the elective county officers who had not been previously considered: the sheriff, county clerk, and treasurer. There is then a discussion of matters relating to county officers and employees: compensation, oath of office, method of removal from office or position, recall petitions, appointive powers of the board of supervisors, civil service systems, and employee benefits. The book additionally explores several functions in detail: highways and public works (*see* Services—Public Works: Michigan); public health (*see* Services—Public Health: Michigan); and public welfare (*see* Services—Public Welfare: Michigan).

Several matters relating to county real property are discussed: location of the county seat, taxation for capital construction, the legal responsibility of the board of supervisors to provide and maintain certain county buildings, and erection of joint city-county buildings. Closely related to this discussion is an examination of the county planning function. The book deals with the county planning commission, the planning director and his staff, and county plans. County purchasing powers are briefly described, and county finance is examined in detail. (*See* Finance—General: Michigan.)

The final topic is county accounting and auditing. The means of establishment, method of selection, and term of office of the county board of auditors are explained. The compensation, meetings, functions, and responsibilities of the board are then detailed. The functioning of the board of supervisors as the board of auditors, if there is no separate board, is briefly discussed. The various county funds are explained. The auditing of claims against the county by the board is given special emphasis.

It should be kept in mind that the book does not seek to study how county governments in Michigan actually operate, but rather that its purpose is to examine the constitutional and statutory provisions for their operation. Throughout the volume, emphasis is placed on the legal role of the board of supervisors in the various county functions and responsibilities. Although written in a legalistic style, the book reads easily. It is a staff study of the Bureau of Social and Political Research at Michigan State University.

Kenneth Verburg's A STUDY OF THE LEGAL POWERS OF MICHIGAN LOCAL GOVERNMENT (East Lansing:

Michigan State University, Continuing Education Service, Institute for Community Development, 1960, 46 pp.) examines the constitutional and statutory powers of local governments in Michigan. This publication rarely, however, deals with county government separately from local government generally. One instance where county government is handled individually is in an analysis of the powers of the county boards of supervisors over municipal annexations and incorporations. Another is in a discussion of state aid to the county highway function. This work is largely descriptive, although the author does at times undertake analysis. At the time of this publication, the author was Coordinator for the Institute for Community Development and Services at Michigan State University.

ALSO TO BE NOTED:

Dean L. Berry, *The Powers of Local Government in Michigan: An Outline and Discussion of the Government, Powers and Finances of Counties, Townships, Cities, and Villages* (Detroit: 1961, v.p.).

Michigan State Association of Supervisors, Lansing, *Michigan Courthouse Review.*

———, *Newsletter.*

Michigan State University, Institute for Community Development, *The Michigan County* (East Lansing: 1962, 28 pp.).

Minnesota

The Minnesota Legislative Interim Commission to Study County and Township Government, in its publication, simply titled REPORT (St. Paul: 1961, 40 pp.), lays out its recommendations for reform of Minnesota county government. In the process of making these recommendations, it has analyzed some aspects of the structure and operations of county government in the state. The commission concentrates largely on rural counties in analyzing county government. In addition, the study contains an appendix which shows recent trends in county government. The trends examined are: increasing use of alternative forms of county government through the use of home rule charters and optional state laws; consolidation of county offices or functions; joint exercise of powers;

rising qualifications for certain county offices; administrative improvements in county government; and increasing county involvement in metropolitan fringe-area problems.

In the main body of the study, the Commission first notes the vigorous support which county officials give to the concept of home rule and the great adaptability of local government in Minnesota. Next is a discussion of the role of the county surveyor and recommendations for renovation of this office. The system of county real property assessment is examined and proposals are made. The recommendations of the Commission for county centralized purchasing are then outlined. The need for change of the classification system for counties used in state legislation is analyzed. Finally, the report explores several topics which need further attention: compensation of county officials, relationship of the county board to other county boards and commissions, implementation of the home rule amendment of the state constitution; county home rule charters; and county financial procedures.

This publication is largely prescriptive, but its recommendations are based on an extensive study of county government in the state. The substance of this study is not presented in the *Report.* The Legislative Interim Commission to Study County and Township Governments was established by the Minnesota Legislature in 1959 to review the structure and operations of county and township governments, with special reference to changes suggested by the constitutional home rule amendment adopted in 1958.

ALSO TO BE NOTED:

Association of Minnesota Counties, St. Paul, *Newsletter.*

League of Women Voters of St. Paul, *You Are the Government: A Handbook for Minnesota Citizens* (St. Paul: H. M. Smyth, 1958, 79 pp.).

Mississippi

THE GOVERNMENT AND ADMINISTRATION OF MISSISSIPPI (New York: Thomas Y. Crowell, 1954, 414 pp.), by Robert B. Highsaw and Charles N. Fortenberry, surveys state and local government in Mississippi. Although the emphasis is on the state level, the authors have included descriptions of the county in a separate chapter devoted to it and in many other chapters throughout the book.

When considering the conduct of political parties and election procedure throughout the state, the authors describe the party organization at the county level. They discuss the composition and duties of the county executive committee and the convention system. They examine the role of the county in the registration procedure, conduct of primary and general elections, and enforcement of prohibitions against corrupt practices. They mention the representation of counties in the state legislature.

The authors discuss the role of the county in its relationship to various statewide functions: revenue, judicial procedure, law enforcement, education, public health, public welfare, agriculture, conservation, transportation, and regulation of business and labor. The following are the only chapters which contain more than cursory treatment of the county's role. The judiciary section covers the jurisdiction of the justice of the peace, county circuit, and chancery courts. Officers of the court who are discussed are the judge, sheriff, and clerk. In examining education, the authors describe the various types of districts, the operation of the county school board, the functions of the county superintendent of education, and the financing of education at the local level. For both health and welfare, the authors explain how the county serves as a unit of state administration, particularly the organizational arrangements established to effectuate this administration. In the chapter on transportation, they explain the responsibilities of the county boards of supervisors for local highway activities and the administrative and financial links between the state and county.

The chapter on the county opens with a brief description of the historical background, legal development, and present position of the county. The authors then describe the various subdivisions established in the county for administrative purposes. First they discuss the arrangement whereby the county is divided into five districts called "beats." They also mention the large number of school and special districts which have been formed in counties and explain the court districting which exists in nine counties.

Attention is then given to the board of supervisors, its membership, organization, and general powers. The authors consider the duties and powers of a number of county officers: sheriff and tax collector, a combined office; chancery clerk; tax assessor; circuit clerk; superintendent of education; county attorney; coroner; and surveyor. They then list miscellaneous offices. They outline the scope of a variety of primary functions carried on by the county—finance, education, highways, justice and law enforcement, and elections—and list the functions the county performs as a unit of state administration. The authors mention that county government in the state has changed little in the past 160 years and discuss the three main principles that any plan of reform should embody—consolidation of units, integration of internal administration, and extension of state supervision.

In the chapter on intergovernmental relations, the authors explain very extensively the relations of the county with other local units, the state, and the national government. (*See* Intergovernmental Relations—General: Mississippi.)

Highsaw and Fortenberry are descriptive in their approach throughout the entire book. More interpretation and analysis of the county would have been useful; however, they have included enough to tie the description together and make it meaningful. As with all other books in the Crowell American Commonwealths Series, this volume is intended primarily for students of state and local government and only secondarily for the public at large. Therefore the authors have been more technical than popular in their treatment of the subject though they have not become overly legalistic or particularistic.

The main sources used are the constitution and statutes, although the authors frequently cite secondary works by Professor Highsaw on both state and local government in Mississippi. At the time of this publication, Dr. Highsaw was Professor of Public Administration and Dr. Fortenberry was Professor of Political Science at the University of Mississippi.

ALSO TO BE NOTED:

Dana B. Brammer, *A Manual for Mississippi County Supervisors,* County Government Series No. 9 (Oxford: University of Mississippi, Bureau of Governmental Research, 1966, 192 pp.).

Mississippi Economic Council, County Administration and Finance Committee, *Is This Your County? A Study of Mississippi County Government with Recommendations* (Jackson: 1953, 44 pp.).

Missouri

Robert F. Karsch, in THE GOVERNMENT OF MISSOURI, 9th Edition (Columbia: Lucas Brothers, 1966, 215 pp.), discusses the county both in a separate chapter on counties and special districts and in earlier chapters on voting patterns and political parties.

Maps and tables depicting the success, by county, of the two parties in national, state, and county elections are presented. The author analyzes the significance of these maps and compares and contrasts the strength of the parties in elections at the different governmental levels. He also describes the composition and duties of the county party committees and describes and presents maps on voter turnout by county for presidential and senatorial elections.

Karsch begins the chapter on the counties by pointing out the number of duties delegated to local government generally by the state. He gives statistics on the number of the various different types of local government in the state and on the number and size of counties. He describes the articles of the constitution applying to counties.

The four categories into which counties are classified are described, and the differences between the form of government used in St. Louis County and that in the rest of the state are indicated. The qualifications for and duties of a large number of county offices are described—county court, circuit clerk, county clerk, recorder of deeds, prosecuting attorney, sheriff, assessor, collector of revenue, treasurer, coroner, public administrator, superintendent of public schools, county surveyor, highway engineer, county auditor, county counselor, board of equalization, county planning and zoning commissions, and health trustees.

The book in general is very informative, and the analysis, although limited, is enlightening. However, since the chapter on the county and the other references to it are so brief, the author has described only the county's basic elements. An extensive list of sources for future reference is provided at the end of the chapter on the county.

MISSOURI VOTERS' HANDBOOK (St. Louis: 1967, 82 pp.), prepared by the League of Women Voters of Missouri, is basically an annotated outline of the organization and operation of government in that state.

The chapter on political party organization includes a brief description of the structure of the county committee and a list of its functions. When discussing public education, the authors of this study explain the duties of the county superintendent of education and of the county board of education. Mention is also made of the role of the county in the administration of public health and welfare programs.

Chapter Five is on the county and is devoted primarily to a description of the structure of its government. It begins with a list of the typical functions performed. It lists and gives the criteria for the four classes of counties. Then the provisions of the 1945 constitution for changing county organization are set forth. The bulk of the chapter is devoted to a listing of the main duties of the following officials: clerk of county court, circuit clerk, county clerk, recorder of deeds, prosecuting attorney, counselor, sheriff, collector of revenue, assessor, treasurer, coroner, public administrator, superintendent of public schools, surveyor, highway engineer, auditor, and county supervisor. The distinguishing characteristics of St. Louis County are then pointed out. Various special county services are described in brief: health centers, county hospitals, county welfare commission, and libraries. The organization of road, school, soil and water conservation, and fire protection districts, is described.

This publication is intended only as an aid to the general citizenry and is written simply and with little detail. Also, no prescriptive material on the county is included. No sources are cited in the chapter on county government and the general bibliography for the book is very limited.

Carl A. McCandless in the preface to his book, GOVERNMENT, POLITICS AND ADMINISTRATION IN MISSOURI (St. Louis: Educational Publishers, Inc., 1949, 261 pp.), states that his purpose is to describe in some detail the governments of the state. The county is included, both in a separate chapter on local government and in scattered references throughout the book.

Professor McCandless explains the apportionment of the legislature as it affects the county and discusses the practice and ramifications of special legislation. He makes clear the role of the county in the state judicial system in terms of the circuit, magistrate, and probate courts which sit in the county. The book contains an interesting discussion of county political party organization and activity. (*See* Politics – Political Parties: Missouri.) The discussion of county election procedures is very legalistic. The author briefly lists the duties of county election officials in the conduct of primary elections and describes the filling of vacancies, the appointment and duties of general election officials, and registration requirements.

Professor McCandless explains the functions performed by the county in public health and welfare, education, highways, agriculture, and finance. However, only the chapters discussed below contain more than rudimentary information. In the chapter on public health and welfare, he emphasizes state-local relations, particularly in the maintenance of institutions, and the duties of the county welfare commission. The discussion of highways includes a description of the work of county highway commissions and their relations with the state and national governments, particularly in financing. He explains the reasons for the creation of road districts and the work carried on in them. He explains how special road districts can be formed and the financing methods which are used. When discussing law enforcement in the state, he mentions the geographic and experience handicaps of the sheriff.

The chapter on local government opens with a discussion of the constitutional position of the county – aspects of county government established and controlled by state statute and constitution and those delegated to the county government itself. The author then discusses the procedure a county must follow to frame and adopt a charter for its own government. Then he explains the forms of government provided for all counties not operating under home rule charters. He lists and describes the four established classifications of counties and points out that the general assembly may provide alternative forms.

The county court is a county's chief legislative and administrative authority. Professor McCandless discusses briefly its composition, selection of the presiding judge, classification of salaries, and duties. An extensive section follows in which the duties of all officers and boards operating in any or all counties are presented.

Following this, the author describes the operation of township government vis-a-vis the county. He includes in this chapter on local government a discussion of the problems which occur in the administration of governmental services in St. Louis City and St. Louis County. He lists the provisions in the constitution regarding possible solutions to the problem. The chapter concludes with a brief evaluation of the present system of county government, emphasizing weaknesses and limitations.

Professor McCandless is very complete in his description of the structure and organization of county government. Since his discussion in the local government chapter revolves around description of offices, and since the program chapters in general do not include extensive discussion of the county, an adequate description of county program activity is not always forthcoming. What analysis is undertaken can be very helpful, particularly in the discussion of politics and the evaluation of the county. At the time of this publication, the author was Assistant Professor of Political Science, Washington University, St. Louis.

ALSO TO BE NOTED:

Association of County Judges of Missouri, Warsaw, *Missouri Official.*

Montana

In his book, THE GOVERNMENT AND ADMINISTRATION OF MONTANA (New York: Thomas Y. Crowell, 1958, 508 pp.), Roland R. Renne presents a very complete picture of the county.

Dr. Renne covers many areas of county activity in much of the book in addition to the chapter devoted specifically to county government. He discusses the technicalities of the procedure for assessing property taxes. He points out the problems arising in assessment and the efforts of the State Board of Equalization to equalize the varying assessments among the counties. He also covers the procedure by which county treasurers collect property taxes. He mentions other sources of revenue for the county and the present county indebtedness. In a brief appraisal of Montana's revenue system, he includes specific comments on the viability of present county revenue sources. He discusses financial administration in the county, particularly bonding procedure and state supervision.

In the chapter on the judicial process, the author covers the jurisdiction of the justice of the peace, police, and district courts. He mentions the process by which county officials may be removed from office, lists the duties of the sheriff as an officer of the court, and describes the selection of juries. When discussing law enforcement, he mentions the supervisory powers of the attorney general over county matters and lists extensively the duties of the sheriff and the county attorney. He describes the operation and use of the county jail.

Dr. Renne covers the county's role in the provision of public education, first describing the requirements for the office of county superintendent and then the duties of the officeholder. He explains the function of the county board of commissioners when it serves *ex officio* as the board of school budget supervisors. He explains the minimum foundation program which provides for state aid to local school districts. He discusses the procedure by which county commissioners may establish free libraries. He explains the method by which a county high school district may establish a junior college.

The author outlines the composition of the county board of health and describes the duties of the county health officer, who also acts *ex officio* as secretary of the board. The procedure by which a county may establish a full-time county health unit is described and the method by which a city may participate is pointed out. He describes the organization of a county board of health in counties having a full-time county health unit. The organization and operation of public welfare administration are treated at great length, including brief descriptions of the various programs. (*See* Services—Public Welfare: Montana.)

Various agricultural functions of the county are covered: livestock disease control, meat inspection, livestock inspection, protection of livestock from predators, and pest control. Mention is made of the ability of the county board to create a county forest, and of the organization and work of county rural fire departments.

When discussing transportation in the state, Dr. Renne points out which roads are included in the secondary road system. He explains the supervision over highways exercised by the county boards and describes how local improvement districts may be formed and how their administration is organized. The maintenance of bridges and creation and administration of airports by the county are discussed.

Brief attention is given to the county's activities with regard to labor and business regulation, licensing, planning, and personnel practices. The procedure followed by the county commissioners in incorporating a city is described, and the method of effecting city-county consolidation is considered.

The author begins the chapter on the county with a discussion of its constitutional status. He then presents in detail and analyzes the statutory framework within which the county operates. His description of the structure of county government is very complete. First he presents a general overview of the entire organization, mentioning all the different types of officials, their relation to each other, and when and how many deputies and assistants are allowed for many officials. He gives a detailed description of the scope of functions engaged in by the county commissioners, including their many *ex officio* duties. Subsequently, he considers the duties of three fiscal officers: assessor, treasurer, and auditor. He explains how different financial procedures are handled. He traces the full development of the preparation and acceptance of the budget, pointing out the different limitations on and earmarking of certain expenditures. He lists all the areas in which the county makes expenditures, and the extent of indebtedness of counties in general.

Dr. Renne then turns to the judicial and law enforcement officers in the county. He describes the duties of the sheriff, coroner, constable, justice of the peace, county attorney, clerk of district court, and public administrator. He presents in detail the duties of three additional officers: clerk-recorder, superintendent of schools, and surveyor. The chapter concludes with a valuable section on the need for and methods of reorganizing county government. (*See* Reform – General: Montana.)

This book by Dr. Renne on government in Montana is one of the best volumes in the Crowell American Commonwealths Series. The author has been thorough in his description of both the organization and operation of county government. Moreover, his description is not simply legalistic; he constantly connects the various activities and officers with each other and with other levels of government so that a dynamic, not static, picture emerges of the operations of county government. Although the book is primarily descriptive in nature, the author has provided sufficient analysis to supply depth and insight. Some prescription is included, specifically in his discussion of reorganization.

The main sources cited are the state constitution and statutes, and government monographs and reports. At the time of this publication, the author was President, Montana State College.

Nebraska

A. C. Breckenridge, in his article "NEBRASKA COUNTY GOVERNMENT: 100 YEARS," in *The County Officer,* 19 (April, 1954), 80-88, describes the structure and functioning of county government in that state.

He opens with statistics on the size and population of the counties and then traces their historical development. He points out the extent to which traditional offices and activities have persisted, and the effect this rigidity has had on the operation ot the county. He describes the different sources of county revenue, emphasizing the property tax. The budgeting and accounting procedures are explained briefly.

Professor Breckenridge delineates the differences between the two types of governing board used in Nebraska—the supervisor and commissioner forms—and points out the board's primary activities. Next, he presents a detailed discussion of the various officers used in the county and lists the important duties of most of them. Particular emphasis is given to the county clerk.

At the time of this publication, the author was Associate Professor of Political Science, University of Nebraska.

ALSO TO BE NOTED:

Nebraska, Legislative Council, *Report of the Nebraska Legislative Council, Committee on County Government,* Committee Report No. 149 (Lincoln: 1966, 34 pp.).

Nebraska Association of County Officials, Ravenna, *Newsletter.*

Nevada

In the preface to their book, NEVADA GOVERNMENT (Caldwell, Idaho: The Caxton Printers, 1953, 384 pp.), Effie M. Mack, Idel Anderson, and Beulah E. Singleton describe their work as a comprehensive analysis of the administration and politics of the state, county, township, and city government. However, they present little more than a general outline of county government. The chapter devoted to county and township government is short, and only scattered, brief references are made to the county throughout the rest of the book.

The authors mention the apportionment of state representatives among the counties. The county's role in the judicial process receives concise treatment in terms of district courts, grand juries, and justices of peace. A very short description of local election procedure and local party organization is included, and the bare outlines of the organization of local school districts are presented in the chapter on education. In the chapter on state boards, commissions, departments, and agencies, mention is made of the relationships of the state tax commission, state planning board, state health department, and state welfare department with the county. The book includes passing references to the place of the county commissioners in the constitution, the relation of state-elected officials with local government, state-local financial relations, the creation of special districts, and the effect of state-federal relations on the county.

The chapter on the county and township starts with a discussion of the history of the county in the United States in general and in Nevada in particular. The authors then discuss the authority of the legislature over the county and the limits on local indebtedness and action specified in the constitution.

Discussion of the organization and administration of the county begins with a description of the composition and powers of the board of commissioners. Brief descriptions follow of the county clerk, district attorney, assessor, auditor and recorder, treasurer and tax collector, sheriff, public administrator, surveyor, and county engineer. The authors also discuss the work carried on by the county probation board and the county planning board. They outline the scope of the county's welfare functions and note the responsibilities of the main officials. The activities of the county health departments and health officer are discussed; specific examples of organization are given from Washoe and Clark counties. Administration of libraries, recreational areas, and agriculture and conservation activities is discussed briefly.

The chapter on planning near the end of the book contains a discussion of county efforts. The possibility of county consolidation, county-city merger or office consolidations, and the use of the county manager plan are discussed.

At the time of this publication, the authors of this volume were high school teachers. The book is very simply written; it is descriptive and historical, and little analysis is included. No sources are cited in the body of the text; the list of readings at the end of the book is very short.

New Hampshire

James M. Langley, in "THE END OF AN ERA: COUNTY GOVERNMENT HAS BECOME OBSOLETE IN NEW HAMPSHIRE," a paper presented to the Sixth Annual Institute of Public Affairs at the University of New Hampshire (Durham: 1948, 14 pp.), gives an analytical-prescriptive view of county government and presents an argument for its abolition. Its thesis is that economy in government and increased quality of service may be achieved by transferring county functions to towns. At the time of this publication, the author was publisher of the *Concord Monitor*.

STRENGTHENING LOCAL GOVERNMENT IN NEW HAMPSHIRE: A SURVEY REPORT (Chicago: Public Administration Service, 1964, 114 pp.) is a staff report which discusses the history of local government in that state. The sections of the report that separate county government from other local governments deal with history, intergovernmental relations and welfare. The historical section discusses the creation of counties in New Hampshire in 1769 and describes the county's increasing role in welfare activities in later years. Welfare is treated from its beginnings, with county participation commencing in the early nineteenth century, to its current operations. The various sections, including the one on intergovernmental relations, point out suggestions for improving local government. The last named section points out that the service functions of New Hampshire counties are largely restricted to public welfare activities.

New Jersey

James M. Collier examines the organization, services, and finances of New Jersey county governments in his monograph, COUNTY GOVERNMENT IN NEW JERSEY (New Brunswick: Rutgers University, Bureau of Government Research, 1952, 64 pp.). He begins his treatment with a brief sketch of the history of counties in the state since 1664. A short but interesting section on the nature of the county-state relationship follows.

Chapter 2 explores the organization of county government. A lengthy section of this chapter is devoted to the board of chosen freeholders. The author explains the central position of this board as the executive-legislative or policy-making body of county government. The method of selection, term of office, and number of chosen freeholders are also given attention. The author very briefly describes the general powers of the board, of which there are two types: large and small. The author relates their differences and astutely analyzes, from a political perspective, the arguments for and against each type. The role of the director (chairman) of the board is scrutinized. Then the author describes the nature of board meetings and the board's use of committees. This chapter also explains the position of the county supervisor as the elected chief executive in Essex and Hudson counties and outlines his powers and responsibilities. The final subject of the chapter is county personnel administration, the characteristics of which are briefly outlined.

Chapter 3 deals with the county court system and law enforcement. Other county services are discussed in Chapter 4. (*See* Services – General: New Jersey.) The third chapter outlines the structure of the state court system; included is a diagram depicting this structure. The organization and jurisdiction of county-related courts—county, district, juvenile and domestic relations, and surrogate—are described. Chapter 5 examines county finance at some length. (*See* Finance—General: New Jersey.) Throughout the chapters on county services and finance, the powers and responsibilities of the various elected and appointed county officers and special boards are described.

The author draws a number of conclusions about county government in the state in Chapter 6. He looks at trends that are making counties more effective units: establishment of civil service systems and increasing areawide powers. He also examines a number of county problems involving county relations with the state and municipalities, the need for more efficient organization, and the realignment of county functions to keep abreast of changing economic and social conditions. Some proposals for solutions to such problems are mentioned.

This monograph is a useful, excellent study. It covers nearly every aspect of county government, although to some extent it slights county intergovernmental relations. This very readable study includes astute political, organizational, and administrative analysis, along with useful factual description. At the time ot this publication, the author was Associate Professor of Law at Baylor University.

ALSO TO BE NOTED:

New Jersey Association of Chosen Freeholders, Trenton, *New Jersey County Government.*

New Mexico

Thomas C. Donnelly's book, THE GOVERNMENT OF NEW MEXICO (Albuquerque: The University of New Mexico Press, 1947, 330 pp.), begins by describing the history of New Mexico during its territorial period and includes many interesting references to the status and growth of the county.

In the chapter on parties and elections in the state, the author presents in detail the county's activities regarding registration, absentee voting, and the conduct of primary and general elections. In discussing political activities, he considers the now defunct convention system of nominations and the present organization of the parties at the county level. In the chapter on the legislature, mention is made of how apportionment affects the county.

The author describes the organization and operation of district health units which are composed of two or more counties; a helpful organization chart is included. Only brief mention is given to the county's role in public welfare administration. A very insightful analysis of the activity of the county commissioners in county road work is presented. When discussing law enforcement, the author analyzes briefly the conflict of authority between local and state police and the limits to administrative reform in this area. His description of educational activities at the county level is extensive. He explains the dual system of administration in operation, which includes both an elected superintendent and an appointed board; their duties are treated at length. He also includes an interesting discussion of the arguments for a county unit system and a technical description of financing. Administration of the property tax and state supervision of financial procedures at the county level are described in the chapter on finances. When he considers the judicial system in the state, Professor Donnelly discusses the justice of the peace, probate, juvenile, and district courts. He also describes the qualifications and duties of the district attorney.

At the outset of the chapter on the county, the author presents statistics on size and population and gives an interesting picture of the background of the county. He enumerates the principal constitutional limits on the county and analyzes the political support the county enjoys in its fight to prevent further state centralization.

Professor Donnelly gives a descriptive list of the ten principal divisions of the functions of county government. He describes the criteria for the five classes into which the counties have been divided. He analyzes the effectiveness of the classification system and presents and rebuts the main criticisms of it. He presents analytical and descriptive accounts of the board of county commissioners, county clerk, assessor, treasurer, sheriff, and surveyor. These descriptions, with the exception of that on the surveyor, are very detailed, include the informal as well as legalistic aspects of the position, and trace the historical development whenever relevant.

The author presents an illuminating discussion of county reform. He describes the defects in the present system, emphasizing the personal and political factors which have retarded improvement. He sums up the trend to take functions away from the county and vest them in the state. Finally, he analyzes the most frequently suggested remedy – the county manager system. He discusses the necessary prerequisites for successful implementation of the plan and describes its operation in one county. He traces the development of attempts to institute county consolidation, discusses the reasons for its failure, and suggests a method that might be more successful in the future.

This is an interesting, insightful, and worthwhile book. The author does not give a detailed recital of the facts about structure of county government to the exclusion of analysis, which is the failing of many books on county government. He also includes a picture of the attitudes and informal arrangements existing in the county. His analyses of county government are very helpful because they include consideration of the human and political factors. He also includes interesting and relevant history on the county and its government. At the time of this publication, the author was Professor of Government and Citizenship, University of New Mexico.

New Mexico Legislative Council's A PARTIAL CONSOLIDATION OF COUNTY OFFICES (Sante Fe: Information Memo No. 202.98, January 1953, 5 pp.) provides only a brief outline of county government. It acknowledges the fact that counties have assumed new functions, lists the principal officers and their primary duties, and mentions a few of the constitutional and statutory limitations on counties. Some suggestions for consolidation of county offices are made.

ALSO TO BE NOTED:

Theresa A. Shepro, *Handbook for County Commissioners – New Mexico, Publication No. 75 (Albuquerque: University of New Mexico, Department of Political Science, Division of Research, 1967, 37 pp.).*

New York

In his book, THE GOVERNMENT AND ADMINISTRATION OF NEW YORK (New York: Thomas Y. Crowell, 1954, 506 pp.), Lynton K. Caldwell describes the organization and operation of county government. The material included in the chapter on the county primarily pertains to the organization and structure of county government. References to the county in the remainder of the book are to functions performed in the county and to political and intergovernmental aspects of the county.

In the beginning of the chapter on the county, the author describes the legal basis of the county before 1935 and then discusses the adoption of charters in specific counties in the state. He describes laws and amendments passed since 1935 which affect the county's governmental powers. When discussing the administration of the county, he briefly deals with the organization and functions of the board of supervisors. He lists the various officials in the county, dividing them into appointive, mandatory constitutional or statutory elective, and judicial. He lists the primary functions undertaken by the county government. The relative importance of each function is indicated on a chart which shows the distribution of expenditures.

The author describes the history of the county and its present position in the state and includes statistics on size and population. He mentions the functions of county boards of elections and describes the representation of counties in the legislature. When discussing state-local relations, the author devotes much of his attention to the statutory and constitutional connection between the two levels. He also mentions the role of statewide associations of local officials and of party organizations.

In the chapter on the judiciary, Professor Caldwell describes the organization and jurisdiction of the county, surrogate, and children's courts in the county and considers how the judges are selected. In discussing finance, he lists the different sources of local revenue and describes the limitations on taxes and indebtedness. He covers briefly the administration and equalization of local property taxes. State assistance to local government is depicted, although inadequate distinction is made between the county and other local units. The author covers law enforcement by district attorneys, and protection by the sheriff. He also mentions fire protection and civil defense work carried on in the county.

Professor Caldwell describes the distribution of social welfare financing and the optional plans for local welfare administration that have been adopted: county unit plan, two modified county unit plans, and combined county-city unit. He mentions the probation and parole activity carried out in the county.

This book does not give a detailed description of the county, although there is some coverage. Lacking are analysis of the material presented and discussion of the informal aspects of county government. Often, too, the author does not distinguish clearly between the role of the county in particular and of local government in general. Often the county is simply subsumed in a discussion of local government.

Many of the references cited are primary sources, mainly the constitution, statutes, and legislative reports. Secondary historical sources are also used extensively. At the time of this publication, the author was Professor of Political Science, Maxwell Graduate School of Citizenship, Syracuse University. This volume is a member of the Crowell American Commonwealths Series.

Robert Reinow has devoted a section of his book, NEW YORK STATE AND LOCAL GOVERNMENT (Albany: University of the State of New York, Bureau of Secondary Curriculum Development, 1959, 239 pp.), to an examination of county government in New York State. He begins with comments about the county's legal status under the state constitution and follows with an examination of county functions; particular emphasis is given to county responsibilities in public welfare, public health, law enforcement, and judicial administration.

A lengthier section is devoted to county structure. The author explores the causes of the dispersion of responsibility in county government and discusses the organization of the county board of supervisors. The methods of selection and responsibilities of the various county administrative and judicial officials—the county judge, surrogate, judge of the children's court, sheriff, district attorney, coroner or medical examiner, clerk, treasurer, and commissioner of public welfare—are also outlined.

The author next looks into the interrelated topics of structural reorganization, home rule, and optional forms of county government. There is a discussion of the restrictiveness of the state constitution concerning county structure. In this connection, the establishment of elected county chief-executive forms of government in Westchester and Nassau counties through a constitutional amendment is given brief consideration. The implications of the county home rule constitutional amendment are analyzed at some length. The author briefly describes the optional forms of county government established by the state legislature, as required by the home rule constitutional amendment. These forms are county administrator, county manager, county director, and county president. As a final topic in his section on county government, the author comments on the nature of county political organization and its implications for county governmental reform.

Three other sections of the book have information about certain aspects of county government. One describes the organization, functions, and method of selection of county central committees of political parties. Another deals with county responsibilities in the administration of elections, with emphasis on the role of county boards of elections. The third section defines the nature and jurisdictions of the three county-related courts.

The author is both descriptive and analytical in his treatment of county government in New York. His clear and concise language enhances the readability of the book. Most sources used are secondary. At the time of this publication, the author was a professor at the State University of New York, College for Teachers, at Albany.

ALSO TO BE NOTED:

Franklin M. Bridge, *Local Government Today: The New York Pattern,* Pamphlet Series No. 2 (Albany: New York State, Executive Department, Office for Local Government, 1965, 12 pp.).

New York State, Temporary State Commission on the Constitutional Convention, *Local Government,* Report No. 13 (Albany: 1967, 150 pp.).

North Carolina

Henry W. Lewis has written a monograph, AN INTRODUCTION TO COUNTY GOVERNMENT (Chapel Hill: University of North Carolina, Institute of Government, 1963, 21 pp.), which briefly sets forth the history, legal status, nature and powers of governing boards and municipal functions of county government in North Carolina. The author's treatment of the history of North Carolina counties is an analysis of the evolution of the three different forms of county government that have been used since 1776. He begins his discussion of the legal status of North Carolina counties by quoting at length a North Carolina supreme court decision which defines the county as a "body politic and corporate" and as an administrative unit of the state. The functions assigned to counties by the state are listed in an analysis of the legal relation between the counties and the state.

The powers, organization, method of selection, and method of compensation of the governing board are described. Emphasizing the limitations on the county board imposed by the state legislature, the author examines the powers delegated to the county board. The other officers of county governments are then briefly mentioned, and some of the controls over them exercised by the state and the county board are examined. Finally, some of the municipal services of counties are noted.

This monograph is written in a legalistic style and emphasizes state limitations on county powers and activities. It is both analytical and descriptive and is based largely on secondary sources. At the time of this publication, the author was Professor of Government and Public Law, University of North Carolina.

John Alexander McMahon opens his monograph, NORTH CAROLINA COUNTY GOVERNMENT: ITS HISTORY, ORGANIZATION, ACTIVITIES (Chapel Hill: North Carolina Association of County Commissioners, 1964, 27 pp.), by presenting statistics on the size and population of the 100 counties in the state. He begins his description of the county board by comparing its historical and present composition and then considers its powers. He points out the functions for which the responsibility for administration is shared with either an independent board or an officer. He discusses the activities of three officials, the county attorney, the clerk of the board, and the county manager, who all work closely with the board. Particular emphasis is given to the duties of the manager.

The monograph includes an extensive discussion of county finances. Sources of revenue are listed, and the duties of the primary financial officers—tax supervisor, tax collector, county treasurer, county accountant, and purchasing agent—are described.

The author considers the office of sheriff, noting both the required qualifications and the duties of the officeholder, and outlines the duties of the register of deeds. He discusses the jurisdictions of the courts in the county and explains the duties of the different officers of the court.

Certain activities carried on by the county are described in detail: public welfare; education; public health; administration of libraries, hospitals, airports, and correctional institutions; inspection of electrical installations; agricultural extension; rural fire protection; civil defense; and elections. Miscellaneous other activities are listed. In each area the author points out in what respects the county is acting either as an agent of the state or on its own discretion. He describes the extent of state supervision and responsibility.

This monograph primarily describes the structure and activities of county government. In this endeavor, it is an excellent work. However, it does not include any in-depth analysis or evaluation. In writing this study, the author relied on both primary and secondary materials. At the time of this publication, the author was General Counsel, North Carolina Association of County Commissioners.

Robert S. Rankin, in his book, THE GOVERNMENT AND ADMINISTRATION OF NORTH CAROLINA (New York: Thomas Y. Crowell, 1955, 429 pp.), describes government at all levels in North Carolina. He covers the county in a separate chapter on its government and also in chapters describing its various functions and activities.

In the beginning of the chapter on the county, Professor Rankin describes the historical background and legal position of the county.

Next, he briefly analyzes the fragmented governmental system in the county and the intercounty differences in the state. He explains and analyzes the powers of the county governing body, the board of county commissioners. He describes and contrasts the two plans for county government provided by state law – the commissioner and the commissioner-manager plan. He explains the power exercised in county affairs by the members of the legislature. When describing the officers in the county, he first offers a general explanation of their relation to each other and to the governing body and then gives more detailed descriptions of the sheriff, register of deeds, clerk of superior court, treasurer, coroner, county accountant, tax officials, and county attorney. He explains the powers of collateral boards and special districts and their relationship to the county board. The county boards of health, welfare, education, and elections are given particular emphasis. Then he lists the principal functions of the county.

Professor Rankin discusses the financial powers of the board of commissioners and the restrictions placed on it by state laws and delineates the sources of revenue and expenditures. He presents a detailed explanation of the work of the Local Government Commission, a state agency that controls and renders assistance to units of local government in financial matters. (*See* Finance – General: North Carolina.)

The county is discussed frequently in the remainder of the book. Only brief mention is given to political party organization at county level. The technicalities of county activity in the conduct of nominations and of primary and general elections are given. The requirements for county representation in the legislature are explained, and mention is made of the relation of the state revenue and personnel systems to the county and to county activity in agriculture, conservation, and regulation of the sale of alcoholic beverages.

The judicial system in the county is explained fully. The author describes the activity of the justice of the peace, county-city recorder, municipal, county, recorder, juvenile, and superior courts. He discusses the composition and work of the grand and trial juries. Problems in local law enforcement are explained, with special emphasis on the upkeep of county jails.

When discussing education in the state, the author points out the different areas of state control, supervision, and assistance to local units. He discusses at length the powers of local officials and describes the duties of the county board of education and the county superintendent of education (a list of all duties is included). An interesting point made by the author is the state's efforts to overcome federally-ordered integration by returning to the local boards authority to assign pupils.

The discussion of public health is also quite complete. The activity of county boards of health and of state supervision of local units is described. The scope of mental health activity is pointed out. State financial and technical supervision of and assistance to local welfare activity are described. The composition and duties of the county board of welfare and the duties of the county superintendent of welfare are explained. (*See* Services – Public Welfare: North Carolina.) The historical development of highway activity, which is now centralized in the state, is traced. Brief mention is given to state assistance to local units in their planning activities. The scope of state-local relations is briefly summarized, with the trend toward centralization being emphasized.

Probably because of the trend toward centralization in North Carolina, the author concentrates on the scope of state activity in functions in which the county participates. As a result, a clear picture of county participation does not emerge. His description of the structure and organization of the county in the separate chapter, however is very complete, somewhat prescriptive, and quite analytical.Yet, since he does not approach the discussion by focusing on functions, actual county activity is again neglected.

This book is a member of the Crowell American Commonwealths Series. The main sources cited are the state constitution, statutes, and secondary historical works. The bibliography is quite extensive. At the time of this publication, the author was Professor of Political Science, Duke University.

Paul W. Wager states in the preface to his short book, NORTH CAROLINA: THE STATE AND ITS GOVERNMENT (New York: Oxford Book Company, 1947, 124 pp.), that it has been prepared to assist the citizens of North Carolina to acquire a simple over-all picture of the agencies and services of their state and local governments. In the book he has presented a comprehensive, though not detailed, picture of county government. In addition to preparing a separate chapter on the county, he has included information on this unit in chapters devoted to particular services and to politics.

Professor Wager begins the chapter on the county with a short history of its growth and legal position. He then explains its dual nature as a civil division of the state and as a unit of local self-government. He notes why there is no separation of powers in the organization of county government and describes the actual organization. First, he discusses the board of commissioners – its composition, functions, and bases of powers. He then describes the duties of a number of elective officials – sheriff, register of deeds, clerk of superior court, treasurer, coroner, county court officials, and the board of education. He then summarizes the functions of various officers appointed by the county commissioners – tax supervisor, county accountant, assessors, tax collector, county attorney, and county physician and superintendent of the county home. He explains at slightly greater length the scope of county activity in numerous fields – administrative and fiscal services, education, public welfare, public health, correction, and agriculture. The more important officials in each field are noted. His discussion of county finances is divided into two sections – a description of sources of revenue and a discussion of the composition of the county budget. Before closing the chapter, he outlines the phenomenon of county loyalty, which is quite strong in North Carolina.

In the chapter on the constitution, Professor Wager points out the more important sections of the various constitutions of the state which have dealt or deal with the county. He mentions the role of the county in apportionment of seats to the state legislature. He discusses the superior and justice of the peace courts which sit in all counties and lists other courts that sit in some counties.

The subject of business in the state comprises another chapter. Here, the author describes the functions of the county boards of alcoholic control in twenty-five counties which have legalized the sale of liquor. When discussing public welfare, he describes the day-to-day administration at the county level and the eligibility requirements for federal funds, and emphasizes the supervision over local action by the state welfare department and divisions. He describes the work of the Division of Local Health Administration, a state body which organizes and assists local health departments. He discusses the work of the county board of education, which is primarily administrative, and the financial powers of the county board of commissioners. The chapter on state finances contains a section dealing with local debt and its control, focusing on the work of the Local Government Commission which exercises administrative control over the power of local units to contract debt.

In the chapter on parties and elections, Professor Wager describes the organization of the Democratic county committees and county conventions, the representation of county delegates in district and state committees, and the Republican party's organization. He then gives a thorough description of the work of the county board of elections.

This short book provides a good general description of the role of county government in North Carolina but its brevity precludes in-depth or detailed discussion. By excluding detailed technicalities, the author has used available space to include interesting and worthwhile analysis. No sources are cited in the text and no bibliography is included, but in the preface the author notes that the main sources were the constitution and statutes, official departmental reports, and the state manual. The author's qualifications to write on county government are indisputable: three years after the publication of this book he wrote *County Government Across the Nation.* At the time of this publication, the author was Professor of Political Science, University of North Carolina.

ALSO TO BE NOTED:

Albert Coates, "North Carolina; the Land, the People, the State, and the Counties," *Popular Government,* 26 (September, 1959), 1-7.

John A. McMahon, "The Traditional Role and Modern Problems Influence Future Direction of Counties," *American County Government*, 30 (November, 1965), 14-15, 25.

North Carolina Association of County Commissioners, Chapel Hill, *Newsletter.*

University of North Carolina, Institute of Government, *County Government in North Carolina* (Chapel Hill: 1965, v.p.).

______, *1959 School for Newly Elected County Commissioners in North Carolina* (Chapel Hill: 1959, 275 pp.).

North Dakota

The pamphlet, NORTH DAKOTA STATE GOVERNMENT: A HANDBOOK FOR NORTH DAKOTA CITIZENS (Fargo: 1962, 40 pp.), prepared by the League of Women Voters of North Dakota, contains only brief and scattered references to counties.

In the section on fiscal management in the state, the report points out the duties of the county board of equalization. Later it mentions that county welfare boards must operate under the state merit system.

The section on the judiciary and the state system of courts contains the most material relevant to the county. When discussing the district court, the report briefly describes the office of clerk of the district court, which is elective in each county. The jurisdiction of the county court and the qualifications and duties of the county judge are listed. The procedure for increasing the jurisdiction of a county court is explained. The report describes how justice courts may be authorized by the county board of commissioners.

Only one brief paragraph is devoted to the activities and powers of the county. State restrictions on county financial activities are pointed out. This report is of limited use in the study of counties. The references to the county are scattered throughout the text, and no effort is made to develop even a systematic outline of county structure and activity. The report was intended only as a reference for the general public and contains no analysis.

Ohio

Francis R. Aumann and Harvey Walker's book, THE GOVERNMENT AND ADMINISTRATION OF OHIO (New York: Thomas Y. Crowell, 1956, 489 pp.), is intended as a comprehensive guide to the organization and functioning of state and local government in Ohio. The authors have treated the county both in a separate extensive chapter and in various functional chapters throughout the book.

The chapter on the county opens with a complete description of the historical and present constitutional and legal position of the county. The authors include a listing of all the references in the present constitution relating to counties. They give a very detailed explanation of Article X, which pertains to county home rule, including form and method of approval. They then present a general overview of the government organization. Next, detailed description and analysis are given of the board of county commissioners, its composition, method of operation, and powers. The authors emphasize and explain at length the board's power to enter into agreements with other governments and districts, its quasi-municipal authority in planning and zoning, and its health, welfare and finance duties. (*See* Organization – Governing Boards: Ohio.)

Aumann and Walker describe the offices of prosecuting attorney, sheriff, coroner, county engineer, county recorder, auditor, and treasurer. The duties of various boards and commissions are explained: trustees of sinking fund, county budget commission, county board of revision, board of elections, and board of education. A fairly detailed description is included on the operation and financing of libraries.

Early in the book the authors describe the organization and duties of the county central committee and discuss the importance of the chairman's duties. The method of selection of the board of elections is described and a detailed list of its duties provided.

The effect of the state revenue system on the county is explained. The authors discuss the constitutional and statutory restrictions on financial powers of the county and the apportionment of state funds to the county. The relevance of the state civil service law to counties, the progress in classification of county public service positions, and payroll requirements are described.

The jurisdiction and organization of the common pleas court – the court of general jurisdiction – are considered. Brief descriptions are given of the probate, juvenile and domestic relations courts, and the judicial duties of the clerk of the court of common pleas. The duties of a number of law enforcement officials are discussed: prosecuting attorney, grand jury, sheriff, and coroner.

Duties of the county board of education are presented in a general fashion, and the supervision undertaken by the state department of education over local schools is explained. The educational work of the state agricultural extension service at the county level is discussed and the inspection of apiaries by the county commissioners is described. A general outline is provided of the activity of the county commissioners in managing county highway work.

The division of labor among the state, counties, and cities in the administration of public health services is explained, and the weaknesses of local units are pointed out. The organization of general health districts, which embrace only unincorporated areas, is described, and the reasons for and success in creation of local welfare boards are explained. The cooperation between state and county levels and the duties of the county in administering certain programs are discussed: aid to blind, aid to aged, mental health clinics, and probation and parole.

This book on Ohio government varies in its quality. The descriptions of structural aspects of county government, the board of commissioners, and other officers, are very complete. However, discussion of particular activities and processes are often subsumed under a discussion of structure; sometimes only a list of duties appears. Intermittent analysis appears in the book, but, here again, it is devoted mainly to structure and not to function. Little attention is devoted to political and informal aspects of the county. The authors do make a point of tracing the historical development of many of the features they discuss. Although the book is intended primarily as a college-level textbook, it could be of interest to the layman.

This volume is a member of the Crowell American Commonwealths Series. The book's main sources are the state constitution and statutes, although secondary works of interest are included in the bibliography. At the time of this publication, the authors were Professors of Political Science, Ohio State University.

Alexander Greene's OHIO GOVERNMENT (Englewood Cliffs: Prentice-Hall, Inc., 1961, 105 pp.), which covers state and local government, provides only a bare outline of county government in Ohio.

Outside the chapter on the county, the author touches briefly on a few of the more important aspects and functions of this unit. He mentions the representation each county is entitled to in the lower house of the state legislature and points out the connection between both the state department of agriculture and state department of highways and the county. He briefly considers the jurisdiction of the county court and provides a descriptive list of the other courts which sit in the county. Mr. Greene describes the composition of the county board of education and lists its duties. He mentions the assessment duties of the county auditor and the supervision over local assessments exercised by the Ohio Board of Tax Appeals. He briefly indicates the composition of county election boards and lists their duties.

The chapter on the county opens with a short background discussion of the legal position of the county and of size and population statistics. The author then mentions the qualifications of commissioners and the composition of the board of county commissioners and discusses its general powers. Next he gives short descriptions of certain offices: auditor, clerk of court, coroner, engineer, prosecutor, recorder, sheriff, treasurer, the county budget commission, the county board of revision, dog warden, and county director of welfare. The chapter concludes with a discussion of reorganization covering the problems of county government that have prompted a need for reform and an explanation of the home rule amendment to the constitution.

This book provides only a rudimentary description of county government in Ohio. No analysis is included and no attention given to informal characteristics. However, the book is obviously intended to be a high school text and thus a rigorous treatment would be extraordinary. No sources are cited and no bibliography is included. At the time of this publication, the author was affiliated with South High School, Cleveland.

COUNTY GOVERNMENT IN OHIO by Matthew Holden, Jr. (Cleveland: Metropolitan Services Commission, Study Group on Government Organization, 1958, 23 pp.) presents a structural-functional analysis of county government in the state. The first part cites legal cases and the Ohio constitution in considering the legal basis of county government and its organization. There is a description of county offices and of the role of special boards and commissions, the latter of which may become involved in many types of county governmental activities. The author stresses that the county is largely treated as an agent of the state. The presentation is both analytical and prescriptive, using primary and secondary sources.

ALSO TO BE NOTED:

County Commissioners Association of Ohio, Columbus, *County News*.

Albert H.Rose, *Ohio Government, State and Local*, 3rd edition (Dayton: University of Dayton Press, 1966).

Harvey Walker, *Form and Function in Local Government in Ohio*, Special Report No. 15 (Columbus: Ohio State University, Engineering Extension Station, Office of Community Development, 1959, 6 pp.).

Oklahoma

Although an introductory section deals with county government in the United States generally (*see* County Government—General: United States), most of John P. Duncan's "COUNTY GOVERNMENT—AN ANALYSIS" in Oklahoma State Legislative Council, Constitutional Survey and Citizen Advisory Committees, *Oklahoma Constitutional Studies* (Guthrie: Co-operative Publishing Company, 1950, pp. 417-443) deals with constitutional provisions for county government, county officers, and criticisms of county operations in Oklahoma.

Under the topic of constitutional provisions, the author begins with an examination of the status of the county as a quasi-municipal corporation and as a subdivision of the state. There is then a lengthy description of constitutional provisions for the changing of county boundaries, followed by a delineation of constitutional provisions in relation to the structure and functions of county government, including a listing of the twelve county officers provided for in the constitution. The discussion of this topic ends with an examination of the provisions concerning county finance.

The section on the powers and functions of county officers considers possible consequences which could result from the fact that the constitution does not list the duties of the county officers it prescribes. The remainder is concerned with the statutory and constitutional powers and duties of the county board of commissioners.

The final and longest section of the work sets out a series of criticisms of county government in Oklahoma, mainly dealing with its costs. In this connection, several studies of the factors determining per capita costs of county government are discussed. This examination of per capita costs is closely related to an exploration of the need for and feasibility of intercounty functional or total governmental consolidation. Other criticisms listed concern lack of home rule provisions, the multiplicity of elected county officials, lack of merit systems, and inadequacy of assessment practices. Another set of criticisms pertains to statutory and constitutional provisions about county finances and county financial administration. Finally, the author criticizes county administration of justice, especially the operation of the county sheriff's office, and administration of the county road system.

Sections on county government organization and officers, state and local finance, and the court system in Hurschel V. Thornton's AN OUTLINE OF OKLAHOMA GOVERNMENT (Norman: Rickner's Book Store, 1956, 144 pp.) present a general view of county government in the state. Emphasis is on the structure and finance of county government, with little attention given to its functions, intergovernmental relations, or political characteristics.

The author begins the section on county government organization by stressing the role of the county as a subdivision of the state government and as a quasi-municipal corporation, and he includes an organizational chart of the typical Oklahoma county. He proceeds to examine the qualifications, terms of office, and powers and functions of the county commissioners and twelve elective and five appointive county officers. The elective officers are constables, justices of the peace, county judge, county attorney, court clerk, county clerk, superintendent of schools, county assessor, county treasurer, county sheriff, county weigher, and county surveyor. There is a discussion of numerous appointive officers: county agricultural agent, county home demonstrator, county engineer, superintendent of the poor farm, and county physician. Information on the county judge and the justices of the peace is presented in the section on the court system in the state.

In the description of the powers and duties of county officers, the main emphasis is on the role of the county commissioners. Their powers are specifically listed, and mention is made of their ability to control other county officers. The functions of county government are given some attention, but only incidentally to the description of the duties of county officers. The author thus takes a traditional, legalistic approach to county government. He does, however, become more analytical in his discussion of county finance in the section on state and local finance. (*See* Finance—General: Oklahoma.)

Professor Thornton writes in a straightforward, lucid style. Much detail is given about the duties of county officers, but the work is not overburdened by it. The sources of information are largely primary, consisting particularly of statutory law and constitutional provisions. At the time of this publication, the author was Director of the Bureau of Governmental Research and Professor of Government, University of Oklahoma.

ALSO TO BE NOTED:

Hurschel V. Thornton, *The Government of Oklahoma* (Oklahoma City: Harlow Publishing, 1960).

Oregon

REPORT: FINDINGS AND RECOMMENDATIONS (Salem: 1956, 204 pp.) by the Oregon Legislative Interim Committee on Local Government contains a wide variety of information on county government in Oregon. Part Three examines the legal status, organization, functions, finances, and intergovernmental relations of local governments, including counties. It explains the quasi-corporate status of the county as a subdivision of the state. A section of this part summarizes the state statutes governing county government: the kinds of provisions included relate to organizing new counties, the discretion of the county court in organizing units of government, the changing of county boundaries, the county governing boards and administrative officers, the functions of counties, and county finances. The subsection on governing boards and administrative officers briefly sets out their statutory powers and responsibilities and considers the following officers and boards: judge, commissioners, sheriff, district attorney, clerk, assessor, treasurer, coroner, superintendent of schools, recorder, auditor, engineer, health officer, constables, budget committee, board of equalization, welfare commission, board of health, district boundary board, and hospital board. It also includes an organizational chart of the legislatively-prescribed structure of county government. Another section scrutinizes county functions and finances in actual practice.

The study analyzes the provision by counties in unincorporated areas of various municipal-type services: planning, zoning, and subdivision control; fire protection; police protection; parks and recreation facilities; residential street construction; sewage disposal; and refuse disposal. A much briefer section describes county revenue sources and purposes of expenditures.

There is also an extensive consideration of county participation in intergovernmental relations. Contracts among counties for the provision of various kinds of services are scrutinized. Extensive examination is also made of county-city and county-special district relations. The county is also included in an analysis of state-local relations.

Part Two of the report examines local government organization, finances, and services in the state's metropolitan areas. Discussion of the role of counties in these areas is found throughout this part. Emphasis is placed upon county services in unincorporated areas. The multicounty Portland metropolitan area is given the lengthiest treatment.

In Part Four, the report reaches conclusions about the role of the county in the governmental system of the state and makes recommendations for legislation about county government. These recommendations concern county special service districts, county home rule, county bonded indebtedness, and county planning and zoning.

Although examining the organization, functions and finances of all counties in the state, this report is particularly oriented to the problems of metropolitan, primarily suburban, counties. The report strikes a unique balance between description of structure and analysis of functions and processes. It was authorized by a joint resolution of the state legislature in 1955.

ALSO TO BE NOTED:

Association of Oregon Counties, Salem, *AOC Bulletin.*
———, *AOC Legislative Report.*

Pennsylvania

George S. Blair briefly examines county government in Pennsylvania in his article, "SOME CURRENT COMMENTS ON COUNTY GOVERNMENT IN PENNSYLVANIA," *The County Officer*, 19 (August, 1954), 158-160. He begins with a treatment of the history, method of creation, size, and resources of counties in Pennsylvania and follows with an outline of the method of classification of counties used by the state legislature. The author discusses the general powers of counties, lists county functions, and describes state constitutional, statutory, and administrative controls over county governments. Lengthier consideration is given to the powers and responsibilities of the county governing board and to the various types of elected and appointed county officials. A description of the county court system is presented. The final topic is the consolidation of the city and county of Philadelphia in 1854 and the evolution of its structuie since that time.

The author is largely descriptive in this structural approach to county government in Pennsylvania and mainly uses secondary sources. At the time of this publication, the author was Assistant Professor, Institute of State and Local Government, the University of Pennsylvania.

A description of county government in Pennsylvania is given in INTRODUCTION TO PENNSYLVANIA GOVERNMENT AND POLITICS (Harrisburg: Pennsylvania State Chamber of Commerce, November, 1959, 28 pp.). The monograph includes sections on finance, political party organization, and elections.

There is a section on county officials, which includes a listing of elected and appointed officers, and a discussion of the system of classification of counties used in the state. The monograph is descriptive and uses secondary sources.

ALSO TO BE NOTED:

Jacob Tanger, Harold F. Alderfer, and M. Nelson Geary, *Pennsylvania's Government, State and Local,* 3rd edition (State College: Penns Valley Publishers, 1950, 442 pp.).

South Carolina

J. David Palmer, in "CHANGES FORESEEN FOR SOUTH CAROLINA COUNTIES," *University of South Carolina Governmental Reviews,* 8 (February, 1966), 1-4, discusses the future of county government in the state. The article is both analytical and prescriptive, giving a brief history of county government in the state and suggesting remedies for some of its weaknesses. These defects – overlapping functions, jurisdictional disputes and "buck-passing" – would be ameliorated, according to the author, if there were county managers. Both primary and secondary sources are used. At the time of this publication, the author was Assistant Professor of Political Science, University of South Carolina.

ALSO TO BE NOTED:

South Carolina Association of Counties, Georgetown, *News Bulletin.*

South Dakota

William O. Farber, Thomas C. Geary, and William H. Cape discuss both state and local government in GOVERNMENT OF SOUTH DAKOTA (Sioux Falls: Midwest-Beach Company, 1962, 211 pp.).

In a chapter on all types of local government in South Dakota, the authors give general material on the county. The distinction is made between its quasi-municipal functions and administrative duties, and the primary sources of revenue and expenditures are explained. A very brief description follows of the county board of commissioners, and the elective and appointive officers are listed. An interesting discussion of reorganization follows. The authors describe the reasons for reform and the proposed methods.

In discussing parties and elections, the authors describe the organization of political parties, nominating procedures, and the conduct of elections at the county level. They discuss the bases of representation in the legislature. The jurisdiction and organization of the county court and the circuit court which sits in each county at least twice a year are described, and brief attention is given to the jury system. State-local cooperation in law enforcement and limitations on local law enforcement are discussed, and mention is made of the duties of the state's attorney (county officer) and coroner.

State supervision of assessment procedures and the preparation of the budget and apportionment of several state taxes are discussed. When considering education, the authors describe the organization of the county board of education, the duties of the county superintendent of schools, and school district reorganization.

Administration of general assistance by the board of county commissioners and the duties of county welfare officers are explained. The reasons for increased county expenditures in health and welfare and the problems this development has caused the county are discussed. A detailed explanation is given of the administration of old-age assistance, including financing statistics. Financing and administration of county highway work are concisely described.

This book gives an overview of the operation and organization of the county in South Dakota. The material presented is descriptive and some analysis is included. However, the brevity of coverage prevents in-depth analysis or detailed description. Written mainly as a textbook, the book is also intended to interest the lay reader. It is simple and straightforward in presentation. No sources are cited in the text, but it appears from the bibliography that the *Journal of County Government,* published monthly by the South Dakota Association of County Commissioners, and W. H. Cape's

Handbook for South Dakota County Officials (1961) were heavily relied on for the material on the county. At the time of this publication, Dr. Farber and Dr. Geary were Professors of Government, University of South Dakota, and Dr. Cape was Associate Director, Governmental Research Center, University of Kansas, after having been Professor of Government, University of South Dakota.

STUDY OF COUNTY GOVERNMENT IN SOUTH DAKOTA (Pierre: Legislative Research Council, September 28, 1961, 31 pp.) discusses the number of counties in the state, their history, and the concentration of each county's population in the county seat. The fee system for the payment of sheriffs is discussed. There is a consideration of the possibilities of reorganization, through either office consolidation or intercounty consolidation, and a listing of states possessing such powers. The report is of an analytical-descriptive nature, using primary sources. It was prepared by the staff of the Legislative Research Council.

ALSO TO BE NOTED:

South Dakota Association of County Commissioners, Pierpoint, *Journal of County Government.*

University of South Dakota, Governmental Research Bureau, *Handbook for South Dakota County Officials* (Vermillion: 1961, 264 pp.).

Tennessee

"Some features of Tennessee affairs still await further study. This is notably true of county government; certain studies being pursued by the Bureau of Public Administration of the University of Tennessee are not yet complete." Despite this disclaimer in the preface, the book by Lee S. Greene and Robert S. Avery, GOVERNMENT IN TENNESSEE (Knoxville: University of Tennessee Press, 1966, 2nd edition, 371 pp.) gives extensive coverage to the county.

A separate chapter on the county begins by explaining that its functions are a mixture of statewide and purely local interest; the authors include two examples of counties to illustrate this mix. They analyze the problems that have occurred in providing certain services and the reason for a trend toward centralization. They provide a breakdown for financial resources, discuss the procedure for property tax assessment, and outline the reasons suggested by the Tennessee Taxpayers' Association for the deplorable conditions in this procedure.

Greene and Avery trace the lack of uniformity and the confusion in the administrative structure of the county. They point out the discrepancies among the counties as well as the confusion within a single county. The composition and operating procedure of the county court (the governing body) are explained. A list of duties follows. The authors analyze the criticisms leveled against the court and the suggestions made to remedy these weaknesses. The problem of lack of an executive and the unofficial, political methods used to overcome this difficulty are discussed. (*See* Organization – Governing Boards: Tennessee.) Brief descriptions are given of various offices: sheriff, trustee (financial officer), register, county court clerk, and circuit court clerk. The existence of the tax assessor and county superintendent of schools is mentioned, and the budgeting, accounting, and personnel procedures are described. The problems of the counties calling for reform and the possibility of instituting reform through consolidation, redistricting, and administrative reorganization are analyzed.

At the beginning of the book, a brief background of the pattern of county government is given and the historical development of relevant constitutional provisions traced. A very complete explanation of parties and elections in the county is presented as part of a statewide discussion. The authors consider registration, nominating procedures, and election administration in the county, and mention the organization and influence of special county-based interests. They briefly analyze the importance of the county as a basic unit in the state political party machinery, noting the effects of patronage on policy outcomes.

Brief discussions are included on the relation of state fiscal and administrative operation to the county. The review of the judicial system in the state covers the justice of the peace and general sessions courts, and the county court of monthly sessions which sit in the county. The criticism of lack of experience and of professionalism among the personnel in these county courts is presented. Brief attention is given to criticisms of the sheriff as a law-enforcement official.

Selection of county road administrators and the operating procedure in the districts is considered, and state-county relations, particularly the financing of highway work, are described.

Mention is made of agricultural extension services in the county and of the subsidiary position of the county in health and welfare administration. The authors describe the complex web of fiscal and administrative relationships between the city and county school systems and explain the operation of the county board of education. The qualifications, powers, and duties of the county superintendent are outlined. The conduct of county planning, the county zoning enabling act of 1935, and the extent of county planning are discussed.

In this book, *Government in Tennessee,* Professors Greene and Avery have combined description, analysis, and prescription in their treatment of the county. In general, they have presented thorough coverage. One area, however, that is possibly underdeveloped is state-county cooperation and relations in the administration of functions of joint interest. This book was written primarily as a college text, although it has been presented in a form that will appeal to the lay reader.

Heavy reliance for source material was placed on the state constitution and statutes, various county government reports, and studies by the Bureau of Public Administration, University of Tennessee. At the time of this publication, the authors were Professors of Political Science, University of Tennessee.

ALSO TO BE NOTED:

Tennessee County Services Association, Nashville, *Tennessee Counties Today.*

Texas

Clifton McCleskey's book, THE GOVERNMENT AND POLITICS OF TEXAS (Boston: Little, Brown and Company,

1963, 427 pp.), covers both the formal and informal aspects of county government.

One section of the chapter on local government is devoted to the county. The author gives a historical description of the relation of the county to the state and explains the results of the battle for home rule, emphasizing both its actual provisions and opposition to the idea. State authority over the powers of the commissioners court (governing body) as well as the functions of the court are discussed. The extent of discretion afforded the court is pointed out, and the duties of the county judge, who is the presiding officer of the commissioners court, are explained.

Brief descriptions are given of the duties of the many elective offices: sheriff, county attorney, county clerk, tax collector and assessor, county superintendent of schools and county board of school trustees, justice of the peace (coroner), treasurer, surveyor, and constable. Existence of appointive offices is mentioned, and the requirements directing their use explained.

The author discusses reform. First he points out the problems of the present system, notably the lack of any central administrative authority, and then discusses possible solutions to this problem. Other problems resulting from decentralization that he discusses relate to personnel and purchasing practices, duplication of time and effort, and proliferation of spoils as a result of district division of road administration.

Throughout the rest of the book, only brief mention is made of the effect on the county of the state constitution, state finance, and special districts. However, the discussion of the activity of the county in parties and elections is quite complete. The method of selection of election officials and their duties are explained. The administration of the poll tax and its formal and informal uses are discussed. Nominating procedures and requirements are described briefly, followed by a detailed description of the organization and functions of the party committees. The role of the chairman is explained, and an organization chart of the political party in Texas is included. Representation accorded the county in both the Senate and the House is pointed out. The extent of local legislation and its evils are discussed. The jurisdictions of justice of the peace, county, juvenile, and small claims courts are described, and brief mention is made of other special courts which may sit in one or more counties. Problems associated with the present judgeship requirements are pointed out and the selection of jurors is briefly explained.

The role of the county in administration of highway work is traced through its historical development, and the extent of centralization in the state pointed out. The author explains the intermediate position of the county board of school trustees between the local school district and the state authorities and analyzes the inadequate delineation of duties of the county.

Next, the background of the office of county school superintendent is described, various ways of filling the office pointed out, and the functions of the office discussed. The author indicates how countywide districts for operation of junior colleges may be established. Brief mention is made of the relation between state and local health authorities.

The main weakness of this book is the lack of discussion and analysis of the administration of many functions at the county level. More detail on county structure would be useful, too. The book does contain good political analysis, both in chapters dealing specifically with political aspects and also in descriptions of the county in general—as when discussing the commissioners' powers. Information from state and local officials, newspaper articles, and the state constitution and statutes are apparently the most important sources. The book is intended as a college text but could be easily appreciated by the lay reader. At the time of this publication, the author was associated with the University of Houston.

ALSO TO BE NOTED:

Wilbourn Benton, *Texas: Its Government and Politics,* 2nd edition (Englewood Cliffs: Prentice-Hall, 1966, 562 pp.).

County Judges and Commissioners Association of Texas, Edinburg, *County Progress.*

William J. David and William E. Oden, *Municipal and County Government,* Arnold Foundation Monograph No. 8 (Dallas: Southern Methodist University, 1961, 130 pp.).

Utah

JeDon A. Emenhiser's UTAH'S GOVERNMENTS (Palo Alto: The National Press, 1964, 79 pp.) is a concise treatment of all levels of government and as such does not go into detail on many aspects of the county. However, the author has included discussion of the county both in a separate chapter on local government and elsewhere in the book.

In the chapter on local government, the author explains the dual role of the county as a unit of local government and an organ for state administration. The effect of the past on boundaries and organization and the classificatory scheme of general law are mentioned. A list of county officials is included, and the combination of certain offices in some classes of counties is pointed out. The author discusses the organization of the county board of commissioners and explains its general function. The trend in administration of functions at the county level is considered, and a chart showing receipts and expenditures of the county included. The need for reorganization and possible methods of rectifying the lack of coordination are discussed.

In the beginning of the book, the author explains the representation accorded the county in the state legislature. The organization and jurisdiction of the justices' and district courts are explained. The author includes a good discussion of national-local, state-local, and interlocal governmental relations. (*See* Intergovernmental Relations – General: Utah.)

Due to its brevity, this work does not contain much description. Particularly lacking is depth of discussion on the organization and functions of the county government. However, the inclusion of diagrams somewhat alleviates this lack. Although rudimentary in nature, the author's comparisons of Utah's county government with that of the rest of the nation and the western states in particular is commendable in view of the space limitations. The book is intended to serve as an outline and basis for further investigation on the part of the citizen, and it fulfills this function admirably. The main sources cited are the state constitution and statutes. At the time of this publication, the author was associated with the Department of History and Political Science, Utah State University.

A report by the staff of the Utah Foundation, STATE AND LOCAL GOVERNMENT IN UTAH (Salt Lake City: Utah Foundation, 1962, 233 pp.), includes discussion of county government, although more emphasis is given to local government in general. A section in this report contains information on county officials and their responsibilities and on the legal status of Utah counties.

ALSO TO BE NOTED:

Roy V. Peel, *Forms and Problems of Local Government* (Salt Lake City: University of Utah, Institute of Government, 1956, 307 pp.).

Utah Association of Counties, Salt Lake City, *County Bulletin.*

Utah Local Government Survey Commission, *Local Government in Utah: A Report to the Utah Legislative Council* (Salt Lake City: 1956, 217 pp.).

Virginia

A concise description and analysis of county government in Virginia are presented by Frank K. Gibson and Edward S. Overman in COUNTY GOVERNMENT IN VIRGINIA, 2nd edition (Charlottesville: League of Virginia Counties and University of Virginia, Bureau of Public Administration, 1961, 38 pp.). This monograph begins with a short section on the geographic, economic, and demographic features of Virginia counties. The legal status of counties as administrative units of the state is explained and compared with that of cities.

The traditional form of county government is described, with special emphasis on the role of the board of supervisors whose powers and responsibilities are explained and analyzed. New forms of Virginia county government as set forth in the Optional Forms Act are examined in detail. (*See* Organization—Optional Forms: Virginia.) County functions are explained in some depth, along with the status, powers, and duties of the county officers responsible for their administration.

The role of the county electoral board in the administration of elections is examined, the circuit court system described, and the powerful role of the circuit court judge in county government explained. The authors tell of the multiple roles of the county clerk — as recorder of important public documents, clerk to the board of supervisors, and clerk of the circuit court. The duties of the county board of assessors, county commissioners of revenue, and the county treasurer in county financial administration are set forth. The authors discuss the commonwealth's attorney and the county sheriff relative to their responsibilities in county law enforcement. Virginia counties have extensive responsibilities in public education, and the monograph details the role of the circuit court judge, the board of supervisors, the county school board, and the division superintendent of schools in this activity. The manner in which the county welfare board administers the county welfare function is given attention. The functioning of the county health department under the county health officer is considered. The activities of the county agricultural extension agent are examined, and the objectives and aims of agricultural extension work are set forth in detail. The authors explain the powers and duties of the county planning commission and the board of supervisors in relation to the county's planning, zoning and subdivision activities.

At the time of this publication, Overman was Associate Professor of Political Science and Assistant Director of the Bureau of Public Administration, University of Tennessee, and Gibson was Associate Professor of Political Science, University of Georgia. The main emphasis is placed on description of the structure and functions of county government in Virginia, but there is also analysis of the roles of the county officers and boards, chiefly the board of supervisors, the circuit court judge and the county clerk. Although the authors at certain points go into much detail, the work is not bogged down with it. The sources of the authors' information are not given, but many seemingly are primary. The monograph is well-integrated and uncomplicated, which makes for easy reading and understanding.

Washington

THE RESEARCH COUNCIL'S HANDBOOK: A COMPENDIUM OF STATISTICAL AND EXPLANATORY INFORMATION ABOUT STATE AND LOCAL GOVERNMENT IN WASHINGTON (Seattle: Washington State Research Council, 1968, 647 pp.), prepared by the Washington State Research Council, discusses the county quite extensively in a section on local governments (pp. 523-620).

This section commences with a general introduction to the legal position of counties, with emphasis on the powers of home rule counties. Mention is made of combined city-county government. Then the criteria for classification of counties are presented, the classification of each county given, and the procedure for a change of classification explained.

The offices required by state law are listed and the duties of the following elective ones described: county commissioners, auditor, county clerk, treasurer, sheriff, assessor, prosecuting attorney, and coroner. The compensation of officers according to class of county is itemized.

In a subsection on local government finance, the handbook describes the different sources of county income. Restrictions on county taxing powers are noted, and the extent of revenue received by the county from the state is pointed out. Particular attention is given to the procedure for assessing, collecting, and equalizing the property tax. Types of and limitations on bonded debt of local (including county) governments are described. The report also includes a budget calendar for counties and tables on expenditures for various activities.

In a very interesting, brief discussion of public employees, the report describes a 1967 law which authorizes collective bargaining for local government (including county) employees. The report also discusses the duties of the county, under a law of the same year, to coordinate services for the mentally retarded. The Interlocal Cooperation Act of 1967 which authorizes local government contracts is described and examples of its initial use in 1968 by various counties are given.

This book describes very well the structure and operation of county government and is particularly useful, since it discusses many of the 1967 laws passed by the state legislature which apply to county government. In general, the book provides a basis of factual information for further reference or research.

Donald H. Webster, Ernest Howard Campbell, and George Duncan Smith have written WASHINGTON STATE GOVERNMENT: ADMINISTRATIVE ORGANIZATION AND FUNCTIONS (Seattle: University of Washington Press, 1948, 113 pp.) as an outline of the state government, which mentions the county merely in passing.

The apportionment of state representatives among the counties and the practice of having vacancies in either house filled through appointment by the board of county commissioners are mentioned. The supervision exercised by state offices, such as the Election Division, auditor, attorney, and superintendent of public instruction, over county officials is described. The authors briefly explain the supervision exercised by the following appointive state officials over the county: Game Commission, Department of Health, Division of Medical Care in the Department of Public Welfare, Board of Education, Tuberculosis Building Commission, Public Welfare Committee, State Humane Bureau, and gubernatorially-appointed notaries public. The authors also give brief descriptions of the justice of the peace, superior, and juvenile courts which sit in the county, and of the judicial duties of the county clerk as clerk of the superior court.

This monograph is descriptive in its references to the county; moreover, even in regard to the state government, only basic information is given. According to the authors, the publication was prepared as a concise, over-all report for the benefit of laymen and public officials. The state constitution and statutes were the main sources. At the time of this publication, Webster was Director, Campbell, Assistant Director, and Smith, Research Associate, Bureau of Governmental Research and Services, University of Washington.

ALSO TO BE NOTED:

Washington State Association of County Commissioners, *County Government in Washington State* (Olympia, 1957, 218 pp.).

______, *The County News-Advocate.*

Washington State Association of Elected County Officials, Olympia, *The Courthouse Journal.*

Washington State University, Division of Governmental Studies and Washington State Association of County Commissioners, *Proceedings of the Institute for County Commissioners* (Pullman: 1965, 50 pp.).

West Virginia

Claude J. Davis, Eugene R. Elkins, Carl M. Frasure, Mavis Mann Reeves, William R. Ross, and Albert L. Sturm, in WEST

VIRGINIA STATE AND LOCAL GOVERNMENT (Morgantown: Bureau for Government Research, West Virginia University, 1963, 477 pp.), give considerable coverage to the county both in a separate chapter and in specific discussions in other parts of the book.

The background sketch at the start of the chapter on the county provides statistics on size and population, a brief history of the development of the county, and a discussion of its legal position. The authors give a brief overview of the organization of county government, citing the extensive control exercised by the legislature. They briefly explain the magisterial districts, which are subdivisions of the county. They discuss the composition and duties of the county court (governing body), emphasizing its supervisory, financial and judicial powers. Concise discussions follow of the duties of the clerk of county court and clerk of circuit court. Other elective officers are listed. The appointment of certain other officials is discussed, and the process of removing county officers described.

The authors consider the changes and the trends in the performance of functions by the county, pointing out the reasons for the addition of new duties and distinguishing between them and traditional ones. Separate descriptions are given of various functions performed at the county level: recording and licensing, law enforcement, judicial administration, elections and party organization, health and hospitals, and welfare. The duties of the officers responsible for each area are pointed out. The range of activity in newer services, particularly libraries and recreation, is described, and the trend toward consolidation of functions among various local units mentioned. A very complete discussion of county finances follows. (*See* Finance – General: West Virginia.) The need for and obstacles to reorganization are discussed. The authors describe the Optional Forms Act of Virginia and explain why and how a similar system could be used in West Virginia.

When discussing intergovernmental relations in the state, the authors consider state-local legal, administrative, and fiscal relations, and interlocal relations. In a chapter on the constitution, they point out the sections of the previous and present constitutions concerning the county.

The authors briefly describe the representation of the county on district and state party committees, the organization and duties of the county committees, and party conventions. They then explain the county-level activity in the following electoral areas: registration, primaries, creation of voting precincts, the duties of election commissioners and clerks, the care of voting machines, canvassing, filling of vacancies in governmental offices, and filing of campaign expenses. The apportionment of seats to the counties in the legislature is explained, and the representation accorded rural counties is compared to that of urban areas. The scope of local legislation enacted by the legislature, the inadequacy of present limitations on such legislation, and the matters which should be returned to the locality are explained.

The chapter on taxation and finance contains a good description of the tax limitation amendment applying to localities. Other financial matters, particularly education revenue and equalization of assessment, are covered. The advisory and supervisory powers of the state Sinking Fund Commission and state Board of School Finance are pointed out. (*See* Finance – General: West Virginia.)

The limited use of the merit system at the county level is mentioned. The jurisdictions of the circuit, special inferior, and justice of the peace courts which sit in the county are described. In the chapter on law enforcement, the authors explain the duties of the sheriff, constable, prosecuting attorney, grand jury, and coroner and medical examiner. They also consider the extent of county responsibility for maintenance of jails. Regarding education, the authors discuss the creation of the county unit system and its effect on the educational program and explain the state assumption of educational costs. Brief mention is given to the progress of integration of schools in the counties. State supervision in public health is briefly discussed, and the operation of local health units, including combined units and county and city units, is described.

Public welfare administration before and after the depression is contrasted briefly. The authors describe the present local organization of relief programs and explain the administration of general assistance. They discuss briefly the activity of county staffs in agriculture and extension work and the creation of soil conservation districts in a county. The trend toward and extent of state supervision of highway work is described. Finally, the areas of labor and business regulation in which the county has some responsibility are pointed out.

This book gives a very complete descriptive account of the organization and functions of county government and includes analysis of certain trends and functions. It does not, however, include much analysis or discussion of political and informal aspects of the county. Written both as a text and as a guide for the citizen of West Virginia this volume is more than adequate in approach to satisfy both needs.

The more important sources are the constitution, statutes, and studies prepared by the Bureau for Government Research, West Virginia University. At the time of this publication, Davis was Director, Bureau for Government Research, West Virginia University; Elkins was Senior Research Analyst, Bureau for Government Research; Frasure, Dean, College of Arts and Sciences, West Virginia University; Mrs. Reeves, Associate Professor of Political Science, University of Louisville; Ross, Associate Professor of Political Science, West Virginia University; and Sturm, Director, Institute of Government Research, Florida State University. Dr. Reeves and Dr. Sturm formerly were at West Virginia University.

Oscar D. Lambert in WEST VIRGINIA AND ITS GOVERNMENT (Boston: D. C. Heath, 1951, 491 pp.) covers many aspects of government in the state. Directly relevant to counties are the sections on the history of their formation, their importance in electoral matters, and a description of intergovernmental relations. In many parts of the book the county is not delineated from local governments in general. At the time of this publication, the author was Professor of History, West Virginia University.

ALSO TO BE NOTED:

Harold J. Shamberger, *County Government and Administration in West Virginia* (Morgantown: University of West Virginia, Bureau of Government Research, 82 pp., 1952).

Wisconsin

Ruth Baumann has written an excellent report on Wisconsin county government, COUNTY GOVERNMENT IN WISCON-

SIN (Madison: University of Wisconsin, Bureau of Government, 1962, 23 pp.). A brief introduction traces the evolution of county government in the state since the early 1800's and discusses its general role as a governmental and political unit. A related section examines the broad forces affecting county government in the state, including the increasing multiplicity of local governmental units, rural to urban population shifts, the change in the state's economy from agrarian to industrial, the increasing number of functions performed by counties, and the increase in intensity of long-established functions.

Another section is devoted to an examination of the relative importance of the various county activities. In this connection, there is an extensive discussion of the nature of county responsibilities and of the level of county output in the fields of welfare services and highway construction and maintenance. The report also looks at county-state relations by illustrating the county-state "partnership" in three functional areas—education, planning, and traffic-law enforcement. A short section examines multicounty cooperation; numerous examples are given.

A large portion of the report considers the organization and officers of county government. The powers of the board of supervisors, the use of an elected chief executive in Milwaukee County, representation on the county board, compensation of the supervisors, role of the chairman of the board, and use of committees by the board are all presented. The powers and duties of each of the elected county officials are also discussed. These officials are the county clerk, county treasurer, register of deeds, district attorney and corporation counsel, sheriff, coroner, surveyor, county superintendent of schools, and county judge. There is also brief mention of the "political nature" of these offices. The appointed county officials, who vary in kind and number from county to county, are likewise given brief mention.

A short section is devoted to county finances. The variations among the counties in their financing is pointed out. County revenue sources are outlined, with emphasis on the nature of state aid. The purposes of county expenditures are discussed. The dominant role of welfare and highway expenditures is stressed. A table presents county revenues by source and expenditures by purpose. The concluding section contains a general assessment of the role of the counties in the state and discusses the need for county reform.

The report is concise and readable, although at certain points it becomes somewhat overgeneralized. The occasional lack of detail because of space limitations does not hamper the author in her general purpose—a brief overview of county government in the state. At the time of this publication, the author was Assistant Director, Bureau of Government, University of Wisconsin. She does not cite the sources of her information.

The Wisconsin Taxpayers Alliance, THE FRAMEWORK OF YOUR WISCONSIN GOVERNMENT (Madison: Wisconsin Taxpayers Alliance, 1955, 69 pp.), presents a descriptive view of government in the state. Approximately ten pages are devoted to specific discussion of the county and describe its governmental forms and responsibilities.

ALSO TO BE NOTED:

University of Wisconsin, Bureau of Government, *County Government Activities in Wisconsin* (Madison: 1961, 72 pp.).

Wisconsin County Boards Association, Madison, *Wisconsin Counties*.

Wyoming

Herman H. Trachsel and Ralph M. Wade, in THE GOVERNMENT AND ADMINISTRATION OF WYOMING (New York: Thomas Y. Crowell, 1953, 381 pp.), give a general outline of county government in that state. The authors discuss the county both in a separate chapter and in other chapters throughout the book.

The chapter on the county is structural, beginning with a brief description of its historical, constitutional, and legal position. The authors then discuss the organization of county government and give an overview of all officers. They describe the composition, operating procedure, and powers of the board of county commissioners. The procedure for filling vacancies on the board is explained. Various offices are described—assessor, county clerk, county and prosecuting attorneys, treasurer, surveyor, and superintendent of schools. The sheriff, coroner, and clerk of district court are also mentioned. The chapter concludes with a discussion of the need for and methods of improving county government, with its focus on the county-manager plan.

Throughout the remainder of the book, reference is made to various county functions. The authors discuss the organization of county central committees, representation of the county committee on the state committee, and the operation of county conventions. Some of the electoral duties for which county officials have responsibility are discussed, including handling of nominating papers, election administration, canvassing, hearing and determining the results of contested local elections, and filing of financial statements. The effect of the apportionment of the legislature on the county is discussed.

The authors mention the governor's power to remove county officials. They describe the apportionment of state-collected funds to local governments, giving details on the gasoline and motor vehicle license taxes. Licensing of liquor dealers by the county is briefly explained. Limitations on local taxing power are pointed out, and the increasing tendency to shift the property tax to local units is mentioned. County personnel services are explained briefly.

The authors describe the justice of the peace, district, and juvenile courts which sit in the county; they describe the judicial duties of the clerk of courts and judges and the selection of jurors for the petit jury. They discuss the compensation and duties (both judicial and enforcement) of the sheriff and the duties of the constable, coroner, and county and prosecuting attorneys. The responsibility of the county to assign counsel and to maintain correctional institutions is explained.

Professors Trachsel and Wade mention the qualifications of the office of county superintendent of education, fully describe its duties, and consider the control and power vested in the local boards of school trustees. They discuss the method of creating a county health department and the appointment of a health officer and look at the composition and duties of the county department of public welfare. A relatively brief description is given of the duties of the county director of public welfare. Tax levies for welfare, and apportionment of federal, state, and county funds to the programs are described. The authors discuss the agricultural inspection activities handled through the county, especially those of the county livestock inspector. The financial problems facing the county in maintaining its system of highways, and a breakdown of revenue from the state are presented. The county's responsibilities for enforcing state labor laws are mentioned. The process for collecting fees and furnishing licenses is described. The requirement for the health officer to inspect barber shops is discussed briefly.

The main value of this book comes from the outline it provides of county government; only minimal analysis is included. The book is intended primarily as a textbook at the college level, but it is sufficiently uncomplicated to be easily understood by the lay reader.

The main sources cited relating to the county are the state constitution and statutes and Paul W. Wager's *County Government Across the Nation.* This book is a member of the Crowell American Commonwealths Series. At the time of this publication, the authors were Professors of Political Science, University of Wyoming.

ALSO TO BE NOTED:

Wyoming Association of County Officials, Lander, *WACO – Your County Newsletter.*

Urban Areas

In GOVERNING URBAN AMERICA, 3rd edition (New York: McGraw-Hill, 1968, 530 pp.), Charles R. Adrian and Charles Press have focused their investigation and analysis on the city rather than on the county. However, some worthwhile material on the county is included.

In their discussion of the various forms of government used in metropolitan areas, the authors explain and evaluate the county as a metropolitan unit. First, they present the disadvantages which result from the county being used as a supergovernment for urban areas. On the pro side of the argument, they point to the use of this approach in Los Angeles County, California, and Westchester County, New York. Then they describe alternative approaches for urban government, specifically functional consolidation and joint city-county administration of activities.

Scattered references to the county appear in the chapters which discuss the functions performed by metropolitan area governments. The authors point out the increased use of joint city-county planning commissions and explain the case for countywide health units rather than smaller municipal departments in metropolitan areas.

Governing Urban America is a well-written, informative book which breaks away from the traditional descriptive, structural approach. Instead, the authors have analyzed and evaluated the entire political process which occurs in urban areas. Environmental and social factors as well as governmental ones are discussed at length. It is unfortunate for purposes of this bibliography that relatively little attention has been given in this volume to the county. A book which concentrated on the county written in the same style and method, would be of immeasurable benefit to students of the field. The text is liberally footnoted, and a geographically arranged bibliography is included at the end. At the time of this publication, Adrian was Professor of Political Science, University of California, Riverside, and Press was Professor of Political Science, Michigan State University.

Three chapters in John C. Bollens and Henry J. Schmandt's THE METROPOLIS: ITS PEOPLE, POLITICS, AND ECONOMIC LIFE (New York: Harper & Row, 1965, 643 pp.) deal directly with the question of the urban county. These chapters cover the role of the county in the cooperative, one-government, and two-level approaches to metropolitan problems.

In Chapter 13 the authors are concerned with forms and methods of interlocal cooperation in metropolitan areas. They point to the widening role of the counties in these efforts. They single out for extensive consideration the governmental system operative in Los Angeles County. Before discussing Los Angeles as an urban county, Bollens and Schmandt describe five practices which are often considered to be forms of urban county development. They then analyze at length the fourth of these practices, service contracts between the county and its cities, which is used most extensively in Los Angeles County. Later in their discussion of metropolitan councils, the authors refer often to the role of the county in these cooperative efforts.

Chapter 14 deals with one-government approaches, notably

annexation and consolidation. The form of county action in these approaches is city-county consolidation. The history of this movement is traced from its nineteenth-century beginnings, and the plan is described as it functions in Baton Rouge City and Parish and in Nashville-Davidson County.

In Chapter 15 the authors explain the two-tier approaches to metropolitan government; district, comprehensive urban county, and federation. They begin the section on the comprehensive urban county plan with a brief overview of the scope and operation of the concept. Following this introduction they outline the plan as it was advanced in four areas—Cuyahoga County, Ohio; Allegheny County, Pennsylvania; Harris County, Texas; and Montgomery County, Ohio. They then discuss five obstacles which must be overcome before the plan may be put into effect: legal authorization, county reorganization, composition of county governing body, assignment of functions, and financial powers. Finally, they present an in-depth and comprehensive analysis of urban county government in Metropolitan Miami (Dade County, Florida).

In these three chapters the authors have covered comprehensively all the major approaches to government in metropolitan areas, including a history of their development. In addition to explaining how the plans operate, they analyze the effectiveness and problems of current operations. Also, the authors have presented insights about the future courses of these plans, pointing out possible problem areas. At the time of this publication, Bollens was Professor of Political Science, University of California, Los Angeles, and Schmandt was Professor of Urban Affairs, University of Wisconsin—Milwaukee.

William N. Cassella analyzes trends in urban and suburban counties through the review of ten publications which deal with county government in nine urban and suburban counties. This book review, "COUNTY GOVERNMENT IN TRANSITION," *Public Administration Review,* 16 (Summer, 1956), 223-231, emphasizes structural change, administrative adequacy, expanding services, and intergovernmental relations. Through a comparative study of these publications, Dr. Cassella appraises the adequacy of the counties as metropolitan, suburban, and moderate-size urban governments. At the time of this publication, Cassella was associated with the National Municipal League and the Government Affairs Foundation.

W. Brooke Graves made a study of suburban county governments in CHANGE IN SUBURBAN COUNTIES (Washington: National Association of Counties Research Foundation, 1968, 28 pp.). Much of the study is based upon case material from eighteen suburban counties in eleven states. The author introduces the subject with a discussion of suburban problems, including the rapid influx of population, the financial "squeeze" on suburban local governments, and the unhealthy suburban psychological climate.

The second chapter examines the changing nature of county government. The slowly-developing trend toward changing the legal basis of county government is explored briefly in terms of the increasing number of county home rule charters. The problem of the traditional organizational structure is mentioned and some examples of change in this structure are given, as is an example of county progress without structural change. The county governing board as a representative body is analyzed, and the subject of reapportionment of county boards is given attention. There follows a brief discussion of the headless nature of county governmental structure and the increasing interest in county chief executives. The author then considers the nature of the county court system and the problem of reform of the county judiciary. The final topic of the chapter is the expansion in scope of the older county functions and the addition of new ones. The author lists the traditional and the new county functions.

Chapter 3 of the monograph looks at the financial problems of county government. The author examines four sources of county financial problems particularly evident in suburban counties—fast growing populations which result in more than proportional increases in expenditures; legal barriers to tapping tax sources; overdependence on the property tax, and inefficient financial administration, particularly relative to assessment practices. Possible remedies to county financial difficulties are proposed.

The next chapter deals with county personnel problems. Generally, the author does not treat these problems as distinct from state and local personnel problems. The matters considered specifically are: the need for higher quality personnel; the need for improvement of personnel administration; and employee-employer relations, particularly those concerning strikes and unions.

The final chapter is devoted to intergovernmental relations. Means for developing areawide policies are discussed: internal reorganization of county governments; new local governments, particularly areawide multipurpose special districts; federal support for areawide plans; councils of governments; and metropolitan "super-governments." The author concludes the chapter with examples of intergovernmental cooperation involving the eighteen counties.

To some extent this is a study of suburban county government since the examples used are drawn from the eighteen suburban counties. However, most problems which the author discusses apply to many nonsuburban counties and to other urban local governments. The work lacks a sense of continuity and completeness. Many secondary sources and some primary sources are used. At the time of this publication, the author was a staff member of the Library of Congress.

Beginning with his article, "URBAN COUNTIES IN 1957," *Municipal Year Book: 1958* (Chicago: International City Managers' Association, 1958, pp. 56-59), Bernard F. Hillenbrand wrote an annual article on urban county developments in this publication for eight years. Each year the article usually includes a section on recent types of county intergovernmental relations. Another section considers county functions and services, although in some years specific services such as recreation, planning, and community colleges are handled separately. In three articles, there are sections dealing with state legislative actions affecting counties. Another subject sometimes given attention is county home rule charter activity. The 1962 article is particularly extensive; in addition to the topics mentioned above, it considers the roles of the metropolitan county, population trends, and county government organization.

The author illustrates trends in urban counties through the use of numerous examples of county developments. Although the articles are largely descriptive, the description is interspersed with analysis. The style is fluid and readable. At the time of these publications, the author was executive director of the National Association of Counties.

At the beginning of "URBAN COUNTIES," an article in *The Municipal Year Book: 1954* (Chicago: The International City Managers' Association, 1954, pp. 133-147), Victor Jones states that his purpose is "to point up the close relationship of cities, counties, and metropolitan areas as indicated by demographic, geographic, and governmental data." For the first time, he explains, the metropolitan county has been considered an urban government, and data about it have been included in the *Municipal Year Book.*

He presents and analyzes data about various aspects of urban counties: population characteristics; other census data on size, per cent of land in agriculture, number of dwelling units constructed, number of employees, and size of payroll; services in unincorporated urban areas; county utilities; county planning; organization of county government; and the county as the center of metropolitan government. Under this last point, he lists four considerations as to why the county should be the unit around which to construct a metropolitan governmental system.

Two tables contain the data used in the above discussion. One includes statistics on population, dwelling units, land area, employees, and payroll for 174 counties with populations over 100,000. The other contains governmental and planning data for urban counties and includes statistics on the number of local governments, types of governing bodies, services in unincorporated urban areas, county-owned utilities, planning agencies, planning directors, number of full- and part-time employees, expenditures for 1953, comprehensive zoning ordinances, and comprehensive subdivision regulations for the same 174 counties.

The article is of continuing interest as the first statistical investigation of the county as an urban unit. Also, the framework and mode of analysis may profitably be used in interpreting more recent data on the same subject. At the time of this publication, the author was Professor of Government, Wesleyan University.

The metropolitan counties Victor Jones considers in "URBAN AND METROPOLITAN COUNTIES" in *The Municipal Year Book: 1962* (Chicago: The International City Managers' Association; 1962, pp. 57-87) have increased to 263 from the 174 he considered for a similar study and analysis in 1954 of the characteristics of the counties.

Before presenting and discussing the census data on which most of this article is based, Professor Jones describes four roles he sees for the metropolitan county: administrative agent of the state, provider of urban services, metropolitan areawide government, and leader in interlocal cooperative ventures.

Subsequently he turns to a discussion of the statistics and data from the 1960 census. He first examines the population trends in these counties, including absolute growth, and changes in the amount, proportion, and distribution of population in unincorporated areas. He compares the 1960 figures with those of 1950. He then investigates the changes in government organization and services. He examines the governing boards, the executives and managers, services rendered to unincorporated areas, services provided countywide, and operation of utilities. He analyzes county planning activity, specifically zoning, subdivision regulation, and number and use of county and regional planning agencies.

As in the 1954 report, Professor Jones presents and explains two tables. The first compares the data from 1950 and 1960 in population, per cent of population change, per cent urban, change in per cent urban, and the per cent age distribution of 1960 urban population between urbanized areas and other urban territory. The second table gives governmental and planning data for urban counties in 1962. It includes information on governing bodies, county administrators, utilities owned and operated, county services, planning agencies, planning directors, number of full-time employees, expenditures, zoning ordinances, subdivision regulations, improvements required, and land grant required.

The value of this report lies not only in the comparisons he makes with 1954 and the trends he points out but also in that the data are of basic interest to persons interested in county affairs; these he has explained and analyzed very well. At the time of the publication of this article, the author was Professor of Political Science, University of California, Berkeley.

PROCEEDINGS OF THE URBAN COUNTY CONGRESS (Washington: 1959, 152 pp.) is a compilation of papers delivered at the first such congress held by the National Association of County Officials (since renamed National Association of Counties). In these proceedings, as Bernard F. Hillenbrand,

NACO's executive director, states in the foreword, "In broad outline and sometimes in detail there is unveiled a general urban development plan that most certainly indicates a wider role for county government."

These proceedings start by covering the general approaches to the problem of metropolitan area government and services. They then turn to the problem areas themselves: urban transportation; county administration; health, education, and welfare; county finance; community facilities; and planning and development. Under the general approaches, the papers tackle city-county federation, county-service agreements, city-county cooperation, city-county consolidation, multicounty functional consolidation, special service districts, informal city-county agreements, and state-county cooperation. The congress concludes with reports which discuss and prescribe future methods of action: increased federal-county cooperation, strengthening the county by streamlining its administration, increased use of state associations of county officials, and, finally, a greater use of the benefits which NACO itself can offer.

Although the papers in this book differ in quality, specificity, and usefulness, collectively they point out clearly the role the county can play in solving metropolitan problems and possible courses of action open to them. Most of the authors were active county officials at the time of this publication, and their reports are based on their experiences. This approach complements the often more theoretical bent of much of the academic literature and is a necessary contribution toward insuring a complete understanding of the problem.

THE PROCEEDINGS OF THE SECOND URBAN COUNTY CONGRESS (Washington: 1963, 75 pp.), held by the National Association of Counties, opens with a unanimous resolution by the delegates in support of greater effort to strengthen local self-determination. This resolution includes five proposals regarding the machinery of local government, particularly the county, which should be followed to realize this self-determination.

The various papers in the proceedings are geared to this objective and reflect the viewpoints of officials from all levels of government as well as those of business and labor leaders. Early essays investigate the role of the county in an urban environment and the effect of this urbanization on counties. A separate workshop, encompassing three reports, is devoted to the problem of urban transportation. Other functional areas of activity investigated are recreation, juvenile delinquency, mental health, and employment. The final general session is concerned with the development of county officials to provide effective urban leadership. The papers at this session cover fiscal and economic leadership roles for the county, uses of state associations of counties, the county's role in voluntary regional cooperation, the impact of federal urban programs, and a look at state-local cooperation.

As is true of the papers from the first Urban County Congress, these papers vary in quality and usefulness. However, they, too, provide an interesting insight into the attitudes and beliefs of people actively participating in urban developments. Comparing this congress with the first also indicates the direction in which action and thought about the urban county is moving.

In "EMERGENCE OF A NEW GOVERNMENTAL FORM: THE SERVICE COUNTY," *Georgia Local Government Journal*, 4 (September, 1955), 8-9, Louis H. Cook presents an analytical discussion of urban counties in the state. The rapid growth of metropolitan areas in Georgia has led to demands on county government which severely burden this unit, as counties have not been given adequate authority to handle these new problems of a municipal character. The author's solution to this problem is the "Service County." The development of such a county eliminates the advantages of municipal incorporation since the county becomes the dominant force and a *de facto* municipality in organization and functions. At the time of this publication, the author was Planning Director of DeKalb County, Georgia.

The State of New York, Joint Legislative Committee on Metropolitan and Regional Areas, GOVERNING URBAN AREAS: REALISM AND REFORM (Albany: March 31, 1967, 122 pp.) contains three chapters which deal in varying degrees with the role of the county as a unit of urban and metropolitan government in New York State.

Chapter One lays out the ways in which counties can help to

resolve the problems which now face local government in metropolitan areas and emphasizes the benefits to accrue from discarding the traditional piecemeal approach to urban government and substituting an areawide unit. This chapter describes at length the increasingly important role of the county in providing local services in metropolitan areas and the resulting necessary growth in revenue and spending. In addition, the report points out the change in type, as well as expansion in amount, of county services and discusses at length how they are becoming more urban in type. Asserting their belief that reapportionment of county legislative bodies is the most important change now influencing the future course of county government, the authors trace its recent history and speculate as to the effects it will have on the county political process. Finally, the ability of charter counties in New York to tackle urban problems is pointed out and recommendations presented to expand further the adoption and revision of charters.

Based on the assumption that high quality planning is necessary in metropolitan areas, Chapter Two examines the problems confronted by local government in this field and suggests a possible step toward their solution – strengthening county agencies and enlarging their ability to make land use decisions. The report points out the existing role of the county in metropolitan area planning, analyzes the problems now troubling county planning efforts, and delineates the need for improvement. The possible benefits to be derived from a bill to provide planning assistance to local areas are discussed. The report summarizes current discussion regarding the proper extent of county planning powers and explains how the Committee's planning review bill enhances the influence of county planning.

The third chapter in the report is concerned with regionalism. Here the authors emphasize the shortcomings of the present local tax system and suggest possible remedies, including reliance on the county to perform all local assessment. Also, areawide services are discussed, and possible methods of providing them – quite often through the county – are described.

This report is a well-reasoned and realistic call for relying heavily upon the county in the struggle to improve our urban areas. It describes the past and present conditions of the metropolis, analyzes the types and extent of its problems, and prescribes the action to be followed by the agencies of government.

James W. McGrew in his article, "THE TEXAS URBAN COUNTY IN 1968: PROBLEMS AND ISSUES," *Public Affairs Comment,* XIV (Austin: University of Texas, Institute of Public Affairs, March 1968), 1-4, investigates the possibility of the urban county as a practical solution to the problem of government in metropolitan areas.

He briefly traces the history of approaches to metropolitan government, explaining why these earlier solutions were not satisfactory and why attention then turned to the county. He discusses the negative features of utilizing the county and looks at encouraging developments in this approach, describing the practices in Los Angeles County, California, and Monroe County, New York. He presents three reasons offered by the Texas Research League for taking an areawide approach to metropolitan problems and concludes that the county is the closest approximation to the needed governmental mechanism. The remainder of the article is devoted to explaining and substantiating this conclusion.

The author explains that sweeping reform will not be needed in Texas and discusses why the county there can be developed as an urban unit either through extensive use of contractual arrangements or assumption of areawide services. He analyzes why the main barrier to areawide service is the financial one and how the present restrictions on the county may be overcome. He discusses the problem of rural-urban slums in many counties and emphasizes that new powers must be granted to the county in order to prevent the spread of this problem. He traces the attempt to reorganize county government in Texas—a step he explains must be taken before the county can function adequately as a metropolitan government. He presents the arguments both for and against internal reform. He concludes by discussing signs of hope that point toward an increasing willingness on the part of county officials to break with tradition.

This brief article is a penetrating analysis of the feasibility of adopting an urban county approach in Texas. It is well-documented with recent government reports and newspaper articles to substantiate the proposals and conclusions. At the time of this publication, the author was Research Director, Texas Research League.

METROPOLITAN TEXAS: A WORKABLE APPROACH TO ITS PROBLEMS (Austin: 1967, 79 pp.) is a study of local governmental services in the state's metropolitan areas, prepared by the Texas Research League.

The report begins by surveying Standard Metropolitan Statistical Areas (SMSA's) generally and in Texas in particular. The authors then turn to the problems facing Texas metropolitan areas: growth, pockets of stagnation and poverty, lack of coordination and integration of governmental effort in these areas, the conflict between the inner core and the growing fringe, and a need for areawide services. They examine the growth in number of local governments, the use of special districts, and the increase in federal activity as current methods of handling these problems. They analyze the desirability of comprehensive and coordinated planning procedures as an important solution to many difficulties. They emphasize that the county commissioners court would be the central actor in promulgating and enforcing land and building regulations. How to provide economical and efficient services is the next problem the report tackles. Here the authors present and explain recommendations for increased interlocal cooperation in provision and administration of these services.

Chapter V is entitled "The Urban County as an Answer." First, the authors explain why the county's authority to act should be broadened and how this could be accomplished. They describe the way in which many counties now provide services on an areawide basis and analyze the effect of present tax restrictions and limitations on the county's ability to secure the needed financing. They investigate the effect of the proliferation of special districts on county government. After this survey, the authors recommend the strengthening of counties. They present a suggested amendment to the constitution empowering this move, discuss a variety of alternatives for action that the urban county plan would offer for solving many metropolitan problems, and attack the problem of internal reform of the county government which is needed before this approach can be successful.

This study is a well-reasoned, analytical prescription for solving the problems of the metropolitan areas in Texas. The authors investigate the problem thoroughly; consequently, when they present their proposal for an urban county plan, it is solidly supported by and logically consistent with the analysis of the difficulty and the present conditions. This study should be read in conjunction with the preceding entry in this bibliography, the article prepared by James W. McGrew for *Public Affairs Comment.*

ALSO TO BE NOTED:

General

"The Changing County: Urbanization Bringing Increased Services, Greater Discretion, Larger Importance," *National Municipal Review*, 45 (October, 1956), 433-437.

Richard S. Childs, "Counties in the Metropolitan Area Problem," *The County Officer,* 21 (September, 1956), 208, 210.

"The County As a Regional Government," *American County Government,* 31 (September, 1966), 6, 66-67, 72-73.

James R. Donoghue, "Problems of Urban Growth; County Government and Urban Growth," *Wisconsin Law Review*, 1959 (January, 1959), 30-54.

Mark B. Feldman and Everett L. Jassy, "The Urban County: A Study of Approaches to Local Government in Metropolitan Areas," *Harvard Law Review*, 73 (January, 1960), 526-582.

Bernard F. Hillenbrand, "Counties and the Metropolitan Problem," *The County Officer,* 26 (August, 196l), 252-253, 291.

______, "Recent Trends in Urban Counties," *Public Management,* 40 (April, 1958), 86-88.

______, "Urban Counties in 1958," *Public Management,* 41 (May, 1959), 106-109.

Victor Jones, "The Changing Role of the Urban County in Local Government," *Public Affairs Report,* 4 (June 1963), 1-4.

______, "Urban Counties—Suburban or Metropolitan Governments?" *Public Management,* 36 (May, 1954), 98-101.

Gladys M. Kammerer, *The Changing Urban County* (Gainesville: University of Florida, Public Administration Clearing House, 1963).

David Mars, *The Urban County* (Milwaukee: Metropolitan Study Commission of Milwaukee, Research Coordinating Committee, 1960, 37 pp.).

Individual States

New Jersey County and Municipal Government Study Commission, *Creative Localism: A Prospectus* (Trenton: 1968, 104 pp.).

University of Wisconsin, Bureau of Government, *County Government and the Problems of Urban Expansion: A Report to the Wisconsin County Boards Association* (Madison: 1959, 95 pp.).

FINANCE

General

United States

In its report, STATE CONSTITUTIONAL AND STATUTORY RESTRICTIONS ON LOCAL TAXING POWERS (Washington: October, 1962, 121 pp.), the Advisory Commission on Intergovernmental Relations considers both historical and current problems and makes recommendations for increased revenues and greater rationalization of local taxing powers. Little specific attention is given to counties. Chapter 3 includes a discussion of the county and its property tax restrictions. Chapter 5 contains a brief treatment of the ability of counties to use nonproperty taxes.

The sources used in the report include both state and national documents. Various state officials reviewed the legal provisions of their states regarding property taxation and commented on the limitations. The report is well-written and substantially documented.

In STATE CONSTITUTIONAL AND STATUTORY RESTRICTIONS ON LOCAL GOVERNMENT DEBT (Washington: September, 1961, 98 pp.), the Advisory Commission on Intergovernmental Relations makes recommendations for state action on local indebtedness. The report considers three major types of restrictions—limit on indebtedness, limit on tax rates imposed for debt service, and requirement of local referendum to authorize issuance of bonds. The county is not generally delineated in the report from other local governments, but many of the problems discussed pervade all local units.

Chapter 5 of Herbert S. Duncombe's COUNTY GOVERNMENT IN AMERICA (Washington: National Association of Counties, Research Foundation, 1966, 288 pp.) describes county revenues and finances.

The author first examines sources of revenue and lists the types of property taxes; then he examines problems of assessment and equalization. He describes the recommendations of the Advisory Commission on Intergovernmental Relations to strengthen the property tax and explains and cites examples of the use of various nonproperty taxes: county sales, selective sales, and business licenses and business. He discusses the extent and importance of revenue from intergovernmental sources, both state and federal.

Professor Duncombe examines the reasons for the continuing upward trend in county government expenditures. He points out the restrictions on counties in their control over their own expenditures and provides statistics on county debt. The author considers the restrictions in state constitutions and laws on incurring debt and outlines the recommendations of the ACIR in this area. He describes the ways in which county indebtedness may be authorized, referring again to the recommendations of the Advisory Commission.

Financial administration is covered extensively. The author describes the county budget process, emphasizing differences between large and small counties. He then explains the procedure followed in cash accounting and auditing. He discusses purchasing and lists the advantages of centralized purchasing. The procedure used in management analysis and data processing is explained and examples of their use are cited.

By way of summary, Professor Duncombe analyzes the revenue squeeze faced by the counties. He explains the divergence between the levels of revenue and the demand for new and expanded services and increased prices.

Four important tables are included: county general revenue, 1962; per cent distribution of general revenues of county government by source in selected states, 1962; expenditures for functions of county government 1913-1962; and per cent distribution of general expenditures of county government by function in selected states, 1962.

Alabama

Chapter IV of James D. Thomas' monograph, A MANUAL FOR ALABAMA COUNTY COMMISSIONERS (University: University of Alabama, Bureau of Public Administration, 1963,

96 pp.), examines county finance. The first section of the chapter describes county revenue sources. Extensive treatment is given to the property tax and state aid. The kinds of property which are taxable are explained, the mill levy limitations for various purposes listed, and statutes relating to the property tax assessment process described. The various kinds of state grants-in-aid and shared revenues are outlined. There is also some mention of other county revenue sources, including license fees and taxes on gasoline, beer, tobacco, and general sales.

This chapter includes other shorter sections. One sets forth statutory requirements on the budgetary process. Two others outline the requirements for the custody of county funds and the process of their disbursement. The County Financial Control Act of 1935, which deals with county accounting practices, is explained. Another section explores various statutes which require county financial reporting. County powers to incur indebtedness and state constitutional and statutory limitations on county debt are treated in a further section. A final section scrutinizes the nature of state supervision over county financial administration.

California

FINANCING COUNTY GOVERNMENT IN CALIFORNIA: SUMMARY COMPARISONS FISCAL YEAR JULY 1, 1960 TO JUNE 30, 1961, 1959-60 BUDGETS COMPARED WITH 1960-61, TEN YEAR COMPARISON OF BUDGETS WITH 1960-61 (Sacramento: County Supervisors Association of California, February 1, 1961), by Vincent T. Cooper, discusses finances and the distribution of aid in California in relation to counties. The entire range of county activities is considered in this monograph. At the time of this publication, the author was Assistant General Manager of the County Supervisors Association of California. Primary sources are used extensively.

Idaho

STATE-LOCAL PROBLEMS AND RELATIONSHIPS (Boise: Idaho Governmental Cost and Tax Structure Committee,

Volume V, 1954, 29 pp.) considers the problems of county collection of state taxes and the varying fiscal years for county and state operations. This report was written by a group composed of state senators, citizens, a representative of the League of Women Voters, Associated Taxpayers, and the University of Idaho. Using primary sources, the report is both descriptive and prescriptive.

Illinois

Irving Howards examines county finance as part of his discussion of county-state fiscal relations in Illinois in SELECTED ASPECTS OF STATE SUPERVISION OVER LOCAL GOVERNMENT IN ILLINOIS (Carbondale: Southern Illinois University, Public Affairs Research Bureau, 1964, 109 pp.). His first topic of discussion is sources of county revenue; he places particular emphasis on county dependence on the property tax. He compares county and municipal expenditure and revenue trends, particularly as they relate to balanced budgets. A more extensive section deals specifically with the county property tax: the author explores constitutional and statutory limitations on the property tax rate, special funds set up from property tax revenues, the use of rate limitations for specific purposes as a means of state supervision over county operations, and the actual effect on county fiscal operations of state rate formulas. Howards is also concerned with various aspects of county debt, including constitutional and statutory debt limitations, referenda on county bond issues, and statutory limitations regarding interest on county bonds.

Iowa

A model for the examination of determinants of costs of county government has been developed by Donald E. Boles and Herbert C. Cook in AN EVALUATION OF IOWA COUNTY GOVERNMENT (Ames: Iowa State College, Community Research Center, 1959, 78 pp.). In the application of this model to Iowa counties, major focus is on the administrative costs of the board of supervisors. Incidental examination is made of the administrative costs of other county agencies and selected county services, including those of official publications, the courthouse, poor relief, bounties, care and aid for the insane, and soldiers' relief. Multiple regression analysis was made of the factors which might be expected to cause variations in total and per capita county government costs among the Iowa counties. The factors examined included area, total population, proportion of workers engaged in agriculture, proportion of county population which is urban, and several others. During their discussion of the costs of the boards of supervisors, the authors explain how the boards operate through committees.

Kansas

Financial procedures engaged in by the county are very adequately explained in James W. Drury and Associates's THE GOVERNMENT OF KANSAS (Lawrence: University of Kansas Press, 1961, 393 pp.). In a chapter on finances throughout the state, the authors discuss the limitations on supervisory powers of the state Department of Property Valuation and the state Board of Tax Appeals over counties and officials. They explain the large role of the county assessor in establishing the assessing procedure and appointing local assessing officials. The great variance in county rates is mentioned. The authors cover the recommendations of the Kansas Citizens' Commission on Assessment Equalization, related to county procedure and state supervision. They indicate how the county collects the inheritance tax and explain the apportionment of cigarette, liquor, motor vehicle, license and grain taxes among the counties.

In the section on finances in the chapter on the county, the authors describe the relative importance of various county functions in terms of their expenditures. They explain and analyze the effect of the reliance on the property tax at the county level. A discussion of the amount and type of state-collected, locally distributed taxes and the method of distribution closes the section which also contains many interesting and useful tables.

Maryland

William P. Walker, in his monograph, RECENT TRENDS IN TAX RESOURCES OF COUNTY GOVERNMENT IN

MARYLAND (College Park: University of Maryland, Agricultural Extension Station, Department of Agricultural Economics, 1968, 19 pp.), analyzes property tax data from nine Maryland counties and seeks to accomplish four objectives: (1) determine trends in farm real estate property taxes; (2) compare the relative impact of both real and personal property taxation upon farm and nonfarm populations; (3) evaluate property tax exemption policies; and (4) determine areas where property tax resources are not fully utilized.

The author's approach to his fourth objective is of particular interest. He explores the weaknesses in legislation and administration which have caused increases in property tax revenues to lag behind gains in "taxable resources." In the discussion, he points out the relationship between property tax revenues and state aid to local governments. Data comparing "potential lag" among the nine counties are set out in two tables.

This study is empirical and analytical, and the author has developed some useful methodologies for evaluating county property tax resources and the impact of such taxation on farm and nonfarm populations. At the time of this publication, the author was Professor of Agricultural Economics, University of Maryland.

Michigan

An examination of the constitutional and statutory provisions dealing with county finance in Michigan is found in a section of a book by the Michigan State University, Bureau of Social and Political Research, entitled THE COUNTY BOARD OF SUPERVISORS (East Lansing: 1959, 152 pp.). This section (pp. 117-132) explores county borrowing and the principal steps involved in levying property taxes—assessment, equalization, preparation of the budget, allocation of tax rate, and apportionment of taxes to the local governments, and spreading the tax rolls. Village, city, and township involvement in property assessment is explained, and the functions of the county assessment department are described. The board of supervisors' role in proper assessment equalization is considered. The discussion then turns to the property tax rate and the role of the property tax allocation board. The composition, meeting procedures, powers, and functions of the property tax allocation board are detailed. The setting of tax rates on areas of local jurisdictions by the board of supervisors is discussed.

County debt is examined at length with attention first to county debt limitations. Then the borrowing powers of the board of supervisors are explained, including a delineation of the purposes for which the board may incur county debt. Other subjects considered are interest on debt, referenda on issuance of bonds, state supervision of county debt, and the county sinking fund and the board of sinking fund commissioners.

New Jersey

Chapter 5 of James M. Collier's monograph COUNTY GOVERNMENT IN NEW JERSEY (New Brunswick: Rutgers University, Bureau of Government Research, 1952, 64 pp.), is concerned with county finance. The first topic of discussion is the nature of state administrative supervision over county finance. Next, each source of county revenue is examined: state grants-in-aid, state-levied taxes shared with the counties, and the property tax. Extensive consideration is given to the various aspects of administration of the property tax. In this connection, the role of the county board of taxation is explored. The author then reviews the characteristics of the county budget and the budgetary process as prescribed by the local budget law, including the functions of the county treasurer. The pre- and post-audit of county accounts, including the office of county auditor, are considered. A final section scrutinizes the issuance and redemption of county bonds for capital improvements.

New York

The report by the New York Temporary Commission on Fiscal Affairs of Government, A PROGRAM FOR CONTINUED PROGRESS IN FISCAL MANAGEMENT, (Albany: 1955, 2 vols., 672 pp.), is largely concerned with improved state fiscal management and makes very little direct reference to counties.

However, what does apply to them is useful and emphasizes finance, functional changes, and highways. This study shows the way in which urbanization of certain counties in the state and the subsequent transfer of former municipal functions to them has prompted a search for an expanded financial base. Exclusive of these above-mentioned sections there are only scattered references to the county, including historical material which furnishes perspective about changes in the county over time.

North Carolina

The discussion of county finance in Robert S. Rankin's THE GOVERNMENT AND ADMINISTRATION OF NORTH CAROLINA (New York: Thomas Y. Crowell, 1955, 429 pp.) is worth noting because of the detailed description of the Local Government Commission, a state agency which supervises local units.

The author explains the reasons for the creation of the Commission in 1931, describing at length the financial problems of the counties during the 1920's. He describes the organization of the Commission and discusses its primary activities—approval of proposed issues of local units, assistance in refunding operations, and a brokerage service that handles the sale of all securities issued by local governments. The lesser, or more routine, functions of the commission are regulation of sinking funds, operation of a reminder service on local debts, approval of auditing contracts, collection of reports on remittances from local units, appointment of administrators for units in default, and installation of uniform accounting systems. The section closes with an interesting appraisal and analysis of the Commission's work.

Oklahoma

An extensive discussion of county finance in Oklahoma is contained in a section on state and local finance in Hurschel V. Thornton's AN OUTLINE OF OKLAHOMA GOVERNMENT (Norman: Rickner's Book Store, 1956, 144 pp.). An analysis is made of the process of property tax assessment, with special emphasis on the role of the county assessor and the county equalization board. A chart showing the process of property tax assessment and equalization is presented. The weaknesses of the property-tax assessment system are reviewed. An examination is made of the manner in which property tax rates are set; the role of the county excise board is set out in detail. A diagram setting forth the process through which property tax rates are established is presented. Mention is also made of county debt. Throughout the discussion, constitutional provisions relating to local finances are stressed.

South Carolina

A very informative study of the trends in county expenditures and revenues in South Carolina has been made by William H. Favor, Clyde E. Woodall, George H. Aull, and Calvin C. Taylor in their monograph, THE IMPACT OF ECONOMIC CHANGE ON LOCAL GOVERNMENT IN SOUTH CAROLINA (Clemson: South Carolina Agricultural Experiment Station, 1960, 58 pp.). The authors divided the counties of South Carolina into four categories – urban, urban – non-farm, mixed, and farm – and examined expenditure and revenue trends for each group from 1940 to 1957. Since school expenditures make up a very large proportion of county expenditures in the state, examination is first made of the trends in the patterns of school expenditures both on a total and on a per capita basis. Similar study is made of expenditures for other county purposes. The authors also consider the patterns of indebtedness for school and other county activities.

The authors analyze trends in county revenue by county groups. Revenue is divided into three categories – property taxes, state aid, and other revenue – but particular emphasis is given to the role of the property tax as a source of county revenue. In this connection, the authors examine the variations in the property tax base among the county groups. Part of this study is an analysis of the effective property tax rate by county group as divided between school and other county purposes. Finally, a brief study of state aid as a source of county revenue is presented.

Throughout this examination of county expenditures and revenue, eighteen tables, charts, and graphs serve as bases for illustration of most of the analysis in the study. Also included in the monograph is an appendix in which the data presented in the text are broken down into much greater detail. The monograph is well-written and uses concise and simple language. It is a scholarly presentation, based largely on primary sources, particularly census data and state documents. At the time of publication of the monograph, Mr. Favor and Mr. Woodall were assistant agricultural economists and Mr. Aull was head of the Department of Agriculture Economics, South Carolina Agricultural Experiment Station, Clemson Agricultural College, and Mr. Taylor was Agricultural Economist, Farm Economics Research Division, Agricultural Research Service, United States Department of Agriculture.

South Carolina Fiscal Survey Commission's Report, STATE-LOCAL RELATIONS (Columbia: November 30, 1956, 53 pp.), focuses on financial problems of local units in South Carolina. The county is not generally delineated from other local governments. The report concludes that counties are structurally defective, wastefully administered, and lack sufficient authority. The present system of financial reporting is criticized because it fails to give a complete, accurate picture of county financial conditions. Primary sources are used in the report, which is both descriptive and prescriptive in nature.

West Virginia

WEST VIRGINIA STATE AND LOCAL GOVERNMENT (Morgantown: Bureau for Government Research, West Virginia University, 1963, 477 pp.) by Claude J. Davis, Eugene R. Elkins, Carl M. Frasure, Mavis Mann Reeves, William R. Ross, and Albert L. Sturm adequately covers the financial powers, functions, and limitations of the county.

When discussing statewide finances, the authors describe in much detail the Tax Limitation Amendment of 1932. They explain the four classes into which this amendment divided property and discuss a defeated amendment that in part would have allowed counties to assume a greater portion of the financial burden for education. The allocation of aid to the counties by the state Department of Education is pointed out. A 1958 act to provide for reassessment of all property is discussed. The work of the state Sinking Fund Commission relating to counties and the assistance rendered by the state Board of School Finance are briefly explained.

The chapter on the county also contains a detailed discussion of finances. The sources of revenue are broken down into their proportionate shares, the restrictions and limitations on county taxing ability discussed, and expenditures itemized. The areas in which counties are required to expend revenue and those in which they have discretion are delineated. The extent and limitations of county indebtedness are described. Then the authors consider financial administration at the county level and point out the duties of particular offices. They describe very completely the following procedures: assessment; budgeting; collection, custody, and disbursement of funds; and accounting and auditing. A detailed expenditure chart is included.

ALSO TO BE NOTED—FOR FINANCE:

General

"Editorial—County Tax Squeeze," *The County Officer,* 21 (October, 1956), 222.

United States Bureau of the Census, *Census of Governments, 1962: Finances of County Governments,* Vol. IV, No. 2 (Washington: 1964, 196 pp.).

Philip Warren, "County Outlays Continue to Rise; Aggregate Total Near $10 Billion," *The County Officer,* 29 (July, 1964), 306-307.

______, "Fiscal Problems Still Plague Most Counties," *The County Officer,* 29 (January, 1964), 43, 56.

Individual States

"County Finance in Florida," *The County Officer,* 25 (January, 1960), 34.

University of Iowa, Institute of Public Affairs, *Trends and Variations in Local Finance—The Case of Iowa Counties* (Iowa City: 1965, 113 pp.).

Oklahoma Public Expenditure Survey, *The Cost of County Government in Oklahoma* (Oklahoma City: 1968, 28 pp.).

FINANCE

Administration

United States

Planning, programming, and budgeting systems (PPBS) are a widely-heralded device for long-range governmental financial planning. The State-Local Finances Project of George Washington University, directed by Selma J. Muskin, has published a series of guides to the development of PPBS in county, city, and state governments: PLANNING, PROGRAMMING, BUDGETING FOR CITY, STATE, COUNTY OBJECTIVES (Washington: January, 1967-July, 1968).

The series is composed of twelve publications. The first, "What is PPB?" outlines the content of such a system for a city, state, or county government. "PPB Notes" is the general title given to the other publications in the series. "PPB Note 1" examines the usefulness of PPBS; Note 2 discusses the administrative framework for establishing PPBS; and Note 3 sets out model guidelines for setting up a PPB system. The subject of Note 4 is staffing and training for the system, and Note 5 examines the development of an object-oriented governmental program structure. Note 6 considers the role and nature of cost analysis in a PPB system; Note 7 focuses on output measures for a multi-year program and financial plan; and Note 8 presents a general discussion of such a program and plan. Note 9 offers demographic and economic data guidelines for PPBS. Highway safety programs are used in Note 10 to illustrate program objectives, effectiveness criteria, and program structure. Note 11 lays out guidelines for development of an "issue paper," a written presentation that seeks to identify and describe the major features of a significant governmental problem.

Georgia

An account of the research findings of Charles Clement, then Associate Professor of Business Administration at the University of Georgia, on property tax revaluation in Georgia is presented in "REVALUATION FOR EVERY COUNTY IN GEORGIA," *Georgia County Government Magazine,* 16 (April, 1965), 6-7. An introductory section tells why property tax revaluation is needed and the extent to which it has been undertaken by Georgia counties. A number of "political benefits of revaluation" are listed and followed by an explanation of some of their political pitfalls. The advantages and disadvantages of contracted professional *vs.* local revaluation are explored. Finally, the need for keeping property valuations up to date after revaluation is noted.

This article is largely analytical but at times becomes prescriptive. It is a good, concise statement of the problem of property revaluation in Georgia.

"THE STATE REVENUE DEPARTMENT REVALUATION ASSISTANCE PROGRAM," an article in *Georgia County Government Magazine,* 16 (April, 1965), 8, describes the Georgia State Revenue Department's program of technical and financial assistance to and nominal supervision of county property revaluation programs. The article also indicates the impact of the state program. This concise and well-written article is a staff effort of the magazine.

"GEORGIA'S EQUALIZED ADJUSTED SCHOOL PROPERTY DIGEST," *Georgia County Government Magazine,* 16 (May 1965), 16-19, is a study involving the comparison of the total assessed valuation of the property in each Georgia county to its total sale or appraised value. One of the most interesting comparisions is of the assessed value as a percentage of total value. The study consists of a three-page chart plus one page of analysis of the data presented in the chart. The single source for the study is *Report of Study of Property Valuations in State of Georgia* by the Georgia Department of Audits.

Illinois

Irving Howards examines county budgeting as a part of his discussion of county-state fiscal relations in Illinois in a monograph, SELECTED ASPECTS OF STATE SUPERVISION OVER LOCAL GOVERNMENT IN ILLINOIS (Carbondale: Southern Illinois University, Public Affairs Research Bureau, 1964, 109 pp.). He describes statutory provisions relating to the county budgetary process, dealing separately with provisions pertaining to Cook County and those relevant to the other counties in the state. He then analyzes why the budgetary processes prescribed in the statutes are not followed. He explores the problems which counties face in developing rational budgeting and accounting processes and concludes with county budgetary practices in other states.

Iowa

Donald E. Boles and Herbert C. Cook discuss the close relation between financial adminstration and policy formation in AN EVALUATION OF IOWA COUNTY GOVERNMENT (Ames: Iowa State College, Community Research Center, 1959, 78 pp.). Examination is made of the problem of independent budget-making by individual county agencies. The authors also discuss the manner in which the state legislature has severely restricted county budgeting through its regulation of county financial administration. In this connection, the authors analyze the county funds system in Iowa which involves the setting up of special funds with specific mill levy limitations: county expenditures for specified purposes must come from these special funds.

ALSO TO BE NOTED—FOR FINANCE: ADMINISTRATION:

General

Joseph S. Holland, "Better Budgets Build Public Understanding of the Cost of County Government," *The County Officer,* 21 (November, 1956), 264-265.

National Association of Counties Research Foundation, *Agricultural Assessing Practices,* Information and Education Service Report No. 26 (Washington: 1963, 8 pp.).

———, *County Financial Reports,* Information and Education Service Report No. 25 (Washington: 1963, 8 pp.).

Individual States

Arkansas Legislative Council, Research Department, *Control of County Finance in Arkansas: A Summary of Constitutional and Statutory Provisions,* Research Report No. 107 (Little Rock: 1962, 14 pp.).

M. E. Gause, "State Supervision Over Local Finance in Colorado," *Municipal Finance.* 36 (February, 1964), 97-99.

John W. Cook, *Fiscal Administration in Pennsylvania Counties* (Harrisburg: Pennsylvania Department of Internal Affairs, Bureau of Municipal Affairs, 1966, 291 pp.).

INTERGOVERNMENTAL RELATIONS

General

United States

Chapter 6 of Herbert S. Duncombe's COUNTY GOVERNMENT IN AMERICA (Washington: National Association of Counties, Research Foundation, 1966, 288 pp.) deals with county intergovernmental relationships.

First, Professor Duncombe discusses county-state relations. He points out the extent of the powers of the state, which are derived from state constitutions and laws. He discusses the constitutional control over structure and describes the different forms that state legislation has taken: special legislation, general laws, classification of counties. He points out the existence of state court influence on counties and considers the types and extent of state aid.

The author discusses county-federal relations and briefly describes different types of assistance. He examines the contacts that arise from the administration of federal grants-in-aid and points out that federal activity may weaken as well as strengthen county government.

Next Professor Duncombe discusses county relationships with other local units. He covers the relationship of counties as a legal and fiscal arm of the state with townships and special districts; counties as vendors of services; counties as purchasers of services; counties as creators of dependent districts and service areas; counties as participants in informal cooperative arrangements not involving a sale; counties as partners in city-county agencies; counties as participants in intercounty agencies; and counties as participants in voluntary regional conferences. He then presents illustrations of county relations with other units of local government: city-parish relations in East Baton Rouge Parish; city-county relationships in Dade County, Florida; and the Lakewood Plan in California.

Only a limited amount of material in Daniel J. Elazar's AMERICAN FEDERALISM: A VIEW FROM THE STATES, (New York: Thomas Y. Crowell, 1966, 228 pp.) is directly relevant to the county, and most of the local government material in the book is too general to be specifically applied to the county. However, the author does give an interesting description of what he calls the "civil community," which includes the county as one of the important elements. In this discussion Professor Elazar explains how local areas circumvent curtailments on their power by the state constitution. He gives examples of such autonomous operation, as in an urban county health department.

Elazar explains the territorial character of the basic pattern of political organization in the United States. A brief description is included of the interchange of personnel between levels of government, for instance, the paying of county agricultural agents from federal, state, and local funds. When discussing the effects of sectional differences on urban growth, Elazar points out that in the South new metropolitan areas are emerging and often consolidating metropolitan governmental functions at the county level. He points out the role of the National Association of Counties as spokesman for the more urbanized counties. He explains the limitations on the county in engaging in intergovernmental relations and how home rule provisions would increase its autonomy and its ability in this endeavor. He points out why the county has recently come to be viewed in a more positive light.

Elazar's analysis of the county results from his interest in investigating the cooperative aspect of federalism. Very little of the book is devoted to a description of governmental structure at any level. Rather, Elazar analyzes the operations of governments which have intergovernmental aspects and the actual techniques of intergovernmental cooperation. As the author states in the preface, this book is based on the best of the recent research into the problem of examining American federalism from the perspective of the states, including the author's own work over the past decade. At the time of this publication, the author was Professor of Political Science, Temple University.

The main purpose of Daniel J. Elazar in THE AMERICAN PARTNERSHIP: INTERGOVERNMENTAL COOPERATION IN THE NINETEENTH-CENTURY UNITED STATES (Chicago: University of Chicago Press, 1962, 358 pp.) is to refute the traditional theory of dual federalism and to propound his thesis that federal-state-local collaboration has existed from the beginning of American government. Although his emphasis is upon federal-state relations, Professor Elazar also points out the active role of the county in these intergovernmental relations throughout the nineteenth century.

Many of the case studies the author uses to buttress his thesis contain information on the part played by county government in general and by various county officials in particular. Professor Elazar's discussion of federal aid for the literary fund and education in Virginia centers around the duties of the county governing board and school officials in administering the education program. When describing the procedure involved in expanding the railroad into Colorado Territory, he emphasizes the role of county governments in providing much of the local capital. Another example from Colorado explains the procedure followed by the general assembly in dividing funds secured from federal land grants to the counties for specific projects. The author describes the competition among the counties to secure this money and the matching-basis apportionment formula used by the state to distribute it. Later he points out the impact of federal funds on internal improvements in Minnesota counties.

These discussions and other similar scattered references to the county throughout the book indicate the active and vital role of the county in nineteenth-century intergovernmental relations. They are also useful in pointing out the impact of federal funds on the activities of county government. In general, Professor Elazar has done an excellent job of supporting his thesis that intergovernmental collaboration, not independent action, characterized governmental activity in the nineteenth century. His examples and the description and analysis of their significance lend much weight to the validity of his ideas. At the time of this publication, he was on the staff of the Institute of Government and Public Affairs, University of Illinois.

THE AMERICAN SYSTEM by Morton Grodzins (Chicago: Rand McNally, 1966, 404 pp.) was essentially completed before the author's death but was later edited by Daniel J. Elazar, a student and close associate of Grodzins. The hypotheses presented by the author are related to the thesis that all governmental functions are shared by all levels of government. These hypotheses are supported by statistical evidence derived from original research. This theory of shared governmental relationships is called the "marble cake" view.

There is very little information presented that relates directly to counties, although chapters 7, 8 and 9 pertain to local government and its interrelationships. In Chapter 5 there is a discussion of recreational programs at the county level. (*See* Services – Recreation: United States.) The scope of the book is that of the total governmental mix of the nation, with a consequent lack of emphasis on any one governmental unit, such as the county. The innovative approach of the author includes a number of prescriptive comments. The author was Professor of Political Science, University of Chicago.

Chapter 14 of Lane W. Lancaster's *Government in Rural America* (New York: D. Van Nostrand, 1952, 375 pp.) is a discussion which the author calls "LOCAL UNITS AND A NEW GOVERNMENTAL PATTERN." Basically it is a call for a transfer of local functions from the small units to larger governments, that is, to the county and the state.

The author begins this chapter with a general summary discussion of why rural institutions are inadequate, a theme which pervades the entire book. He discusses the concepts of centralization and decentralization. He analyzes at length why county home rule has not been as successful as early proponents had hoped and delineates the differing conditions under which it will or will not be useful and productive.

Professor Lancaster compares the practices of administrative supervision in England with those in the United States. Subsequently he points out how state supervision might be utilized in the administration of finance, health authorities, and in other fields generally. He analyzes the principles of supervision and what it should and should not be expected to accomplish. Then he points out the possibility for increased state-local informal administrative cooperation. He discusses the reforms needed at the local level for these techniques to be fruitful.

Finally the author describes the centripetal tendencies at work and analyzes the pressures which are causing the towns to give way to the county, the county to the state, and the state to the federal government. He discusses the effect this trend may have on our system of government and points out how it can be modified and molded to our advantage.

Twenty-six states are covered in the monograph, THE IMPACT OF FEDERAL GRANTS-IN-AID ON THE STRUCTURE AND FUNCTIONS OF STATE AND LOCAL GOVERNMENTS (Washington: June, 1955, 489 pp.), issued by the Commission on Intergovernmental Relations. Each state is treated in an individual chapter, with the quality of the text varying considerably. The chapters are authored by a university professor from the given state or a member of that state's governmental bureaucracy. In general, the county is not delineated from other units of local government. The two chapters of most value to the study of counties are those on Alabama and Ohio. The chapter on the former discusses the impact of federal grants-in-aid on welfare and the resulting changes in the county's role. The chapter on the latter considers this same area as well as the problem of recruiting personnel for rural counties.

The National Association of Counties, in COUNTY DEVELOPMENT COORDINATION (Washington: 1968, 64 pp.), presents a series of six manuals to assist local officials in establishing and administering county development coordination offices. Manual I, "Responsibilities of Elected Officials," explains at the outset that the growing demand on many counties for increased services and facilities has placed great strains on county financial resources and has resulted in increased requests for federal funds. The bulk of the manual is a discussion of the impact on local government of the federal grant-in-aid system and furnishes some basic information about its operation. At certain points direct advice is offered to county officials. In a short final section, the manual proposes that counties establish an office of county development coordinator, chiefly to provide liaison with the national government. The duties and benefits of the position are outlined.

Manual II, "Organization and Administration for Coordination," after briefly sketching the procedure for establishing the office of development coordinator, lays out its responsibilities. Four basic functions are explained: providing information to county officials about possible sources of federal, state, and private aid for county programs and services; coordinating all county activities concerned with applications for state and federal aid; furnishing grant administration advice and assistance to county officials in order that they may get maximum benefits from such aid; and serving as liaison between county officials and administrators and state and national legislators.

This second manual also discusses the factors affecting the form of county organization for development coordination, including the slow institutional response of rural counties. Four kinds of organizational responsibility are examined: an individual appointed by the county chief executive; an elected board member or appointed administrative official with full-time assistance; a county department head; and a community-wide nonprofit organization such as an economic development or community action agency. Examples of each type are given, and the views of a number of incumbents about their positions are presented. This discussion points out a number of the problems and advantages of the various arrangements. Brief case studies of the office in Prince George's and Baltimore counties, Maryland, and Montgomery County, Tennessee, are presented, and the desirable qualifications for a development coordinator are outlined. Finally, the manual proposes an organization for the office, including recommendations to the county officials responsible for its creation.

"Federal Aid Information Systems," Manual III, examines the role of the coordinator as collector and dispenser of information on federal aid programs. It begins by discussing the vastness of the federal aid "administrative jungle," which requires that counties know what aids are available and that applications are prepared correctly. An analysis follows of the kind of information system a coordinator needs to develop. Various published sources of information, as well as the agencies and persons from whom data may be obtained, are discussed. A chart shows the cities in which the regional offices of the major federal agencies are located. Finally, the third manual considers the specific kinds of data which a coordinator must assemble and how these data may be organized into an information system.

Manual IV, "The Necessary Coordinator Contacts," examines the kinds of relationships that development coordinators should maintain outside county government in order to function effectively. It explains that the coordinator should maintain good working relationships with all federal regional offices but generally should avoid contacts with agency headquarters in Washington. The more limited nature of contacts with state officials is discussed. An interesting discussion is presented of how a coordinator may act as a liaison with congressmen and their staffs. The importance of developing similar relationships with state legislators is also briefly considered. The major responsibility of contacts with other local governments is pointed out in a more extensive section. The fourth manual describes how the coordinator may be the focal point for exchanging information and sharing services and grants-in-aid. A lengthy discussion then follows of regional councils of governments and the relationship of coordinators to them. The increasing role of citizen advisory groups in local government and the need for coordinators to maintain close contacts with them are explained. Finally, the contacts of coordinators with community organizations are considered.

The need to coordinate county activities with federal assistance programs is emphasized in Manual V, "Activities and Assistance Coordination." One of the initial steps in a coordination program — the preparation of a comprehensive analysis of past and present federal and state programs in the county—is considered. Interdepartmental coordination, particularly the coordinator's relations with the finance and planning departments, is then discussed. The fifth section is devoted to determining which federal grants to seek. The remainder of the manual consists mainly of a practical guide concerning how departments work with the coordinator in making grant applications. A brief final section outlines the duties of the coordinator in administering state and federal grants.

Manual VI, "County Planning, Budgeting, and Assistance," which is the final one in the series, examines the coordination of county planning and budgetary activities. It first discusses the nature and process of comprehensive county planning and then briefly explains the Planning-Programming-Budgeting System (PPBS). The requirements of many federal programs which assist planning are explored. The sixth manual next considers county capital improvement programs, listing their advantages and analyzing the means of improving them. Using the example of Santa Clara County, California, to demonstrate the proper process, the manual outlines the procedure for capital improvement budgeting. Finally, the way for a coordinator to relate county planning and budgeting to federal assistance programs is discussed and examples from various counties presented.

Information for these manuals was derived from survey questionnaires, field interviews, and national and regional conferences of county development coordinators. These guides include some insightful analysis of the role of counties and their county development coordinator in the federal grant-in-aid system.

INTERLOCAL GOVERNMENTAL COORPERATION: A STUDY OF FIVE STATES, Agricultural Economic Report No. 118 (Washington: U. S. Department of Agriculture, Economic Research Service, 1967, 123 pp.) by John E. Stoner, is an excellent study of interlocal relations in Alabama, Indiana, Nebraska, Pennsylvania, and Wisconsin. Although taking metropolitan areas into account in collecting data, the study largely focuses upon areas of a nonmetropolitan nature. Data were gathered through survey questionnaires answered by local officials.

After explaining the origin, purpose, and scope of the study, the author describes and analyzes the statutory authority for interlocal cooperation in each of the five states. An interesting table presents for each of the states the number of legal provisions permitting cooperation in twenty types of local activities.

The second section of this monograph deals with the survey of local officials, the complete results of which are in tabular form in the appendix. Among the topics on which the appendix tables contain county data are: the frequency of contact of county and other officials; the reasons for this contact; the units cooperating most frequently; opinions of officials about cooperation; and the frequency of cooperation of counties with other units, according to kind of cooperation and type of activity.

The author begins the second section with a methodological discussion of the questionnaire and then analyzes some of the survey's important findings. No particular portion of this analysis is devoted to counties, but there are numerous references to them when significant relationships are discovered. For example, the author notes that of all local units, counties, particularly in Alabama and Wisconsin, have the greatest frequency of contact with other local governments.

This second section, a portion of which is devoted to counties specifically, contains an intensive study of interlocal cooperation in Indiana. (*See* Intergovernmental Relations—General: Indiana.) Then, for each state there are a series of case studies, which usually involve counties, to demonstrate the nature and variety of interlocal relations. (*See* Intergovernmental Relations—General: Alabama, Indiana, Nebraska, Pennsylvania, and Wisconsin.) These case studies are based upon field work done under the direction of the author.

The final section of the monograph features an evaluation of interlocal cooperation which Professor Stoner found in five states. He first classifies and analyzes the various kinds of cooperative arrangements—exchange of information and parallel action, mutual aid, contracts, sale of services, and joint action. An analysis follows of the factors which affect cooperation—for example, level of expenditures, metropolitan versus nonmetropolitan location, density of governments, and functional complexity. The problems of local leadership, the role of legal arrangements, and various financial aspects of cooperative activities are then given detailed consideration; examples from the case studies are used as illustrations. The author follows with some general conclusions about the level of cooperative services and the flexibility of the cooperative device. Although this section does not discuss counties except as examples, the analysis is based on data drawn in important part from counties. In a final section the author makes recommendations for improving interlocal cooperation.

The author used modern research methods and made excellent use of quantitative data. This well-written work is analytical and descriptive and also includes a short prescriptive section. At the time of this publication, Stoner was Professor of Government, Indiana University.

Alabama

John E. Stoner's monograph, INTERLOCAL GOVERNMENTAL COOPERATION: A STUDY OF FIVE STATES, Agricultural Research Report No. 118 (Washington: U. S. Department of Agriculture, Economic Research Service, 1967, 123 pp.), contains several case studies on the variety of interlocal cooperative arrangements in Alabama. Most of the studies involve counties as participants, and are concerned with the following topics: the informal agreement among the municipalities and county government in Lawrence County for mutual aid in firefighting; the establishment of a regional library system jointly by Barbour, Dale, Henry, and Pike counties; the purchase and operation of an airport jointly by Limestone and Morgan counties and the cities of Athens and Decatur; and the participation of Limestone County with seven counties in Tennessee, numerous cities, private enterprise groups, rural electric cooperatives, and private citizens in the Elk River Development Association.

Delaware

In chapter 25 of his book, THE GOVERNMENT AND ADMINISTRATION OF DELAWARE (New York: Thomas Y. Crowell, 1956, 396 pp.), Paul Dolan analyzes the intergovernmental relations of the county. He describes how the trend toward more federal aid to the state has affected the position of the county, and discusses direct federal-local relations. The most interesting part of the chapter deals with state-local relations and analyzes state supervision of local units and state-local fiscal relations.

Florida

Wilson K. Doyle, Angus McKenzie Laird, and S. Sherman Weiss, in their book, THE GOVERNMENT AND ADMINISTRATION OF FLORIDA (New York: Thomas Y. Crowell, 1954, 444 pp.), describe the role of the Florida county in intergovernmental relations. In the chapter on the county, brief mention is given to county functional cooperation and to city-county consolidation. In the chapter on the municipality, the authors discuss the county's activities in boundary adjustment, city-county consolidation, and tax assessment and collection. The chapter dealing with intergovernmental relations in the state has two points of interest for the county. First, federal-local relations are described, with emphasis on public works, housing, and debt adjustment. State-county relations are discussed in the three spheres of legislative, executive, and judicial control.

Georgia

Throughout Cullen B. Gosnell and C. David Anderson's book, THE GOVERNMENT AND ADMINISTRATION OF GEORGIA (New York: Thomas Y. Crowell, 1956, 403 pp.), attention is given to the problem of intergovernmental relations. When discussing finances, the authors explain the dependence of the state on county officials in taxation matters. The importance of finances as a connecting link between the two levels is also emphasized in considerations of apportionment of state funds among counties for education, the financing of public health through state grants-in-aid to counties, and the work of the state Division of Finance and Statistics in disbursing all state, county, and federal funds for public welfare. State supervision of county administrative activity is explained in the discussions of the work of the Division of Local Health Organizations and of the supervisory practices of the state Division of Public Assistance and Division of Child Welfare over local administration of these welfare programs.

Brief mention is given to city-county consolidation in the chapter on municipal government. The chapter on intergovernmental relations includes examinations of state-county, intercounty, and city-county cooperation. In the area of state-county relations, the authors discuss mutual tax assistance, technical and informational assistance to counties by the state, and grants-in-aid. When discussing intercounty relations the authors explain the operation of intercounty functional consolidation. In the section on city-county relations, cooperation between Fulton and DeKalb counties and the City of Atlanta is considered. The authors also explain articles of the state constitution which permit city-county contracts for services.

James L. Greene and Charles D. Clement briefly but analytically discuss the impacts of state and federal grants-in-aid on Georgia counties in their monograph, SOME IMPACTS OF INTERGOVERNMENTAL FISCAL RELATIONS IN GEORGIA (Athens: University of Georgia, Bureau of Business and Institute of Community and Area Development, 1963, 34 pp.). However, the major portion of the monograph is devoted to the impacts of federal grants on state government. The authors rely largely on primary sources, particularly census data. At the time of this publication, Greene was Professor of Economics and Clement was Assistant Professor of Economics, University of Georgia.

Illinois

In Neil F. Garvey's book, THE GOVERNMENT AND ADMINISTRATION OF ILLINOIS (New York: Thomas Y. Crowell, 1958, 622 pp.), particular attention is given to intergovernmental relations. A brief section deals with federal-local relations, but because the author does not distinguish the particular local unit involved, it becomes difficult to judge the relevance of the discussion to the county. In this section, the author emphasizes the collection and dissemination of information by the national government to local units and the development of federal-local contacts as a result of the depression, specifically loans for public projects, debt adjustment, and grants-in-aid.

Professor Garvey's description and analysis of state-local relations are divided into two separate areas, fiscal and nonfiscal, with the emphasis on fiscal relations. He describes and analyzes the interdependence of state and local fiscal machinery for taxation. He discusses the administrative control exercised by state departments and agencies in fiscal matters, giving specific examples. Garvey devotes much space to a discussion of the amount, methods, and limitations of budgetary control exercised by state agencies and departments over local governments. Auditing and accounting controls are also covered. Many details and examples are included in the discussion of state grants-in-aid programs.

When discussing nonfiscal relations, the author points out the great extent and variety of these contacts. He mentions areas of confusion and clouded authority. He devotes particular attention to state-local relations in law enforcement. Complementary material on state-local relations is found scattered throughout the book in most of the service chapters.

Indiana

John E. Stoner's monograph, INTERLOCAL GOVERNMENTAL COOPERATION: A STUDY OF FIVE STATES, Agricultural Economic Report No. 118 (Washington: U.S. Department of Agriculture, Economic Research Service, 1967, 123 pp.), includes a much more extensive inquiry into interlocal cooperation in Indiana than into any of the other four states surveyed. A special study of cooperation in the state contains much specific information about counties. Four tables and accompanying explanations in the text analyze the relationships between the incidence of cooperation (in terms of the number of cooperative activities in which counties are engaged) and the following variables concerning counties: their location in metropolitan or nonmetropolitan areas; total assessed property valuation; population; a majority of their population living in urban or rural areas. In addition, this section contains a general analysis of interlocal cooperation in the state, an assessment that is relevant to the role of the county in such relations.

This work also includes a series of case studies of interlocal cooperation in Indiana, in most of which counties participate. The case studies involving counties are as follows: joint city-county planning by Howard County and the city of Kokomo; the construction of a city-county building to serve both as city hall and county courthouse for New Albany and Floyd County; the selling by Knox County of the services of its tuberculosis hospital to other counties; and the establishment of a cooperative library system by the cities and county government of Grant County.

Kansas

Chapter 25 of James W. Drury and Associates' book, THE GOVERNMENT OF KANSAS (Lawrence: University of Kansas Press, 1961, 393 pp.), contains a very complete description and analysis of the county's intergovernmental relations. In this chapter the authors explain the manner in which many of the county's contacts with the state and national governments are carried on routinely. In the coverage of state-local relations, the authors cover the range and amount of state administrative supervision over the county, how it has increased in recent times, and the conditions under which it takes place. They explain the different forms this supervision may take from function to function. They describe how the problem of efficiency and economy in administering government services has been attacked and the possible causes of future transfer of many functions to the state. They present a very interesting analysis of the attitudes and responses of local officials to state supervision and of the cooperation between the two levels. Only brief mention is made of direct national-local relations.

The authors explain the reason for the numerous contacts between local officials. They describe the various financial ties between the local units and give examples of instances of informal and formal cooperation. They explain how the relations vary from simple to complex and why, with increasing technology, these contacts will probably increase. Various references to intergovernmental relations are also scattered throughout the book.

Mississippi

Chapter 24 of Robert B. Highsaw and Charles N. Fortenberry's book, THE GOVERNMENT AND ADMINISTRATION OF MISSISSIPPI (New York: Thomas Y. Crowell Company, 1954, 414 pp.), is devoted to a discussion of intergovernmental relations in Mississippi. In it the authors have included sections on the county's relations with other local units, with the state, and with the national government.

The authors explain the extent of city-county relations, particularly the cooperative arrangements set up to handle public health work and education. They mention municipal activities which are extended beyond city boundaries to include unincorporated county territory. They explain the problems which creation of special districts presents for the county.

Professors Highsaw and Fortenberry then explain the extent of state supervision of local government. The aspects of state supervision of local finance they consider are taxation, indebtedness, and grants-in-aid. The functional areas of state supervision and state-county relations they discuss and analyze pertain to education, industrial promotion, highways, public health, and public welfare.

Regarding the county's relations with the national government, the authors first discuss federal grants-in-aid and in-lieu-of-tax payments. They explain the operation of agricultural, home economics, and conservation work at the county level and the supervision and control in these fields exercised by the national government. They also mention the areas in which the national government provides information and technical assistance.

Nebraska

A section of John E. Stoner's study, INTERLOCAL GOVERNMENTAL COOPERATION: A STUDY OF FIVE STATES, Agricultural Economic Report No. 118 (Washington: U. S. Department of Agriculture, Economic Research Service, 1967, 123 pp.) sets out a number of case studies of interlocal relations in Nebraska in order to give examples of the variety of cooperative arrangements. Most of these efforts include counties as participants. Those cases in which counties have a role are: the cooperation of seven counties with the Salt-Wahoo Watershed District; the establishment of a regional library system in Phelps, Gosper, Kearney, Furnas, Harlan, and Franklin counties through a cooperative arrangement with the Holdrege-Phelps County Library; the operation of informal cooperation between the city of Holdrege and Phelps County in the provision of police protection; and the furnishing of services and financial aid to school districts by counties.

Pennsylvania

INTERLOCAL GOVERNMENTAL COOPERATION: A STUDY OF FIVE STATES, Agricultural Economic Report No. 118 (Washington: U. S. Department of Agriculture, Economic Research Service, 1967, 123 pp.), by John E. Stoner, includes a series of case studies on various types of interlocal cooperative arrangements in Pennsylvania. Counties are prominent in most of these arrangements. Some case studies in which they are participants are: the furnishing by Berks County of staff services and personnel to local governments and private agencies which maintain recreational facilities; the Mifflin County Library which receives financial support from other governments but operates largely autonomously; and the support by Lehigh and Northampton counties and three cities of an airport authority. Other case studies in which counties are involved are: the establishment by Westmoreland County of a Municipal Water Authority which sells water to many local governments; the establishment by Lebanon County and nine other localities of a regional planning commission for the county's central portion; and the cooperation of local governments in Centre County on several fiscal and school matters.

Texas

In A GUIDE TO UNDERSTANDING STATE-LOCAL RELATIONS (Austin: 1962, 45 pp.), the League of Women

Voters of Texas discusses various program areas and their intergovernmental linkages. The program areas discussed include: public health, school administration, welfare, and highways. Within each area, the county's role and intergovernmental relations are shown. City-county, intercounty, national-local, and state-county programs are discussed in both their formal and informal aspects.

Utah

Chapter VI, "Intergovernmental Relations," in JeDon A.Emenhiser's UTAH'S GOVERNMENTS (Palo Alto: The National Press, 1964, 79 pp.) contains a very good discussion of national-local, state-local, and interlocal governmental relations in the state.

The nature of national-local relationships is described, and the controversy over the question of bypassing the states is analyzed. When discussing state-local relations, the author mentions why the localities have formed associations to protect their interests. A breakdown of state financial grants and payments to the local governments is given. Comparison is made of the extent of dependence on the state by the various types of local governments.

The discussion of interlocal relations begins with an explanation of the difficulties involved in instituting such cooperation. The author covers all the methods of cooperation used to increase relations, from the informal, such as the telephone call, to the formal, such as the Lakewood Plan in California. He discusses the existence and use of formal organizations, such as multicounty groups and associations of county commissioners. He mentions the growth of problems in the metropolitan areas and the different approaches to their solution.

Wisconsin

In his monograph, INTERLOCAL GOVERNMENTAL COOPERATION: A STUDY OF FIVE STATES, Agricultural Economic Report No. 118 (Washington: U. S. Department ofAgriculture, Economic Research Service, 1967, 123 pp.), John E. Stoner presents a number of case studies which illustrate the variety of interlocal cooperative arrangements in Wisconsin. Counties are included in most of these arrangements. They are participants in the following cases: the construction and maintenance of a joint city-county building for Portage County and the city of Stevens Point; the cooperative provision of a bookmobile library service by three impoverished rural counties in the northern part of the state; the operation by these same three counties—Ashland, Bayfield, and Iron—of a tuberculosis sanitorium; and the joint construction and operation of an airport by Oneida County and the city of Rhinelander.

ALSO TO BE NOTED—FOR INTERGOVERNMENTAL RELATIONS:

General

W. Brooke Graves, *American Intergovernmental Relations* (New York: Scribner, 1964, 984 pp.).

Bernard F. Hillenbrand, "Creative Federalism and the Counties," *American County Government,* 30 (May, 1965), 9.

______, "Massive Cooperation," *The County Officer,* 24 (October, 1959), 307.

______, "Why Not a Decent Break for Rural Counties?" *American County Government,* 32 (May, 1967), 6, 26.

"Incentive for Development Coordinators," *American County Government,* 31 (September, 1966), 60-61.

Robert E. Merriam, *The Role of the County in Federal-State-Local Relations* (Washington: United States Bureau of the Census, 1957, 7 pp.).

"White Paper on Role of Counties," *American County Government,* 30 (May, 1965), 15-17.

Individual States

County Supervisors Association of California, *County, State, Federal Partnership and Shared Revenue Programs* [in California]: *A Guidebook* (Sacramento: 1964, 86 pp.).

James V. Burgess et al., *A Study of Intergovernmental Cooperation in Georgia: Legal Basis* (Athens: University of Georgia, Institute of Community and Area Development, 1963, 20 pp.).

INTERGOVERNMENTAL RELATIONS

Officials' Views

United States

THE FEDERAL SYSTEM AS SEEN BY FEDERAL AID OFFICIALS (Washington: 1965, 215 pp.), prepared by the Subcommittee on Intergovernmental Relations of the Committee on Government Operations of the United States Senate, is a study which compiles and analyzes questionnaire returns, dealing with intergovernmental relations, submitted to the federal administrators of 109 programs. The document focuses on local government in general and usually does not specifically delineate the position of the county. However, the material that specifically refers to the county is interesting and useful.

Five main subjects constitute the bulk of the material presented: the purposes and methods of implementing federal aid; federal, state, and local financial administration; the type and caliber of state organizations which handle grants; state and local personnel involved in intergovernmental relations; and the specific problems of metropolitan area relations. The report analyzes the opinions of the federal officials who responded and their attitude toward and interest in the subject matter.

Of particular interest to the study of counties is a section on metropolitan areas which deals with urban fragmentation and the county. Here the Subcommittee specifically asked the federal officials their views on the use of county government in such areas. The difference in the extent and type of contact between government levels for grant-in-aid and other federal assistance programs is pointed out. The differences of opinion about the county between those who do and those who do not deal with it are striking.

This study merits considerable attention by anyone interested in the future of federal-state-local relations. It analyzes extensively and explicitly the attitudes of the federal officials toward other levels of general government. Friction points and problem areas requiring attention become very evident, and the need for both a change in attitude as well as procedure is strikingly clear.

THE FEDERAL SYSTEM AS SEEN BY STATE AND LOCAL OFFICIALS (Washington: 1965, 215 pp.), prepared by the Subcommittee on Intergovernmental Relations of the Committee on Government Operations of the United States Senate, is a study which examines and analyzes the results of a questionnaire on intergovernmental relations distributed to 6,000 state and local officials and certain other authorities. A copy of the questionnaire is included at the beginning of the report.

The text of the report is broken down into four main subject areas: federal grants-in-aid, taxation and revenue, metropolitan areas, and other general problems in the field of intergovernmental relations. For each topic the staff first submits its own analysis of the problem and then presents representative answers to each question from officials of different levels of government. The answers bring to light the attitudes of the officials toward federal aid and problem areas which they believe need improvement.

The report points out differences in opinion between county and other governmental officials and between officials in counties of different size. Responses were received from officials in four categories of counties: below 10,000; 10,000 to 50,000; 50,000 to 250,000; and over 250,000. However, half of the questionnaires returned came from officials in the counties over 250,000.

In its analysis of the problems of metropolitan areas, the staff points out the increasingly important role of the county. The existence and approval of this trend are borne out in the opinions expressed by the state and local officials themselves.

At the conclusion of the study all the respondents are placed in one of four categories, based on their attitudes toward intergovernmental relations. The classifications are: orthodox states righters, neo-traditionalists, pragmatic cooperative federalists, and new nationalists.

As is the case with the companion piece focusing on the federal officials, this study is important not only for the knowledge and description it provides of the operation of intergovernmental relations but also for its presentation and explication of the attitudes of officials who keep the system functioning. It emphasizes and brings to the surface the subjective, personal elements that can spell either success or failure in this area.

Minnesota

An excellent study of intergovernmental relations as viewed by public officials has been conducted by Edward W. Weidner and published as INTERGOVERNMENTAL RELATIONS IN THE UNITED STATES AS OBSERVED IN THE STATE OF MINNESOTA (Minneapolis: University of Minnesota Press, 1960, 162 pp.). This monograph is one of a series on intergovernmental relations published by this university press under the editorship of Professor Weidner and Professor William Anderson.

As the basic sources for this study, the author used the results of a sample survey of local public officials and state and national administrative officials. The state and local officials were from Minnesota and included 474 county officials. The latter were county engineers, superintendents of schools, sheriffs, agricultural agents, assessors, welfare executives, auditors, governing board members, and welfare board members.

The survey consisted of two questionnaires given to the officials: one sought responses to questions dealing with various aspects of intergovernmental relations; the other dealt with questions on participation, awareness, and responsibillty and sought to determine the officials' attitudes toward government and society and their roles therein. The latter questionnaire was used in the analysis only when correlations could be developed between the two questionnaires. The author analyzes the officials' views on intergovernmental relations on the basis of the questionnaire results.

Except for a section in the chapter on horizontal intergovernmental relations, no portion of the monograph deals solely with county officials. However, throughout the monograph the responses of each classification of county official are separated from those of other local officials. In addition, as a part of his analysis of the total responses, the author often analyzes the more significant responses of county officials in general or of a particular type. Thus a very good picture is obtained of the views of county officials on intergovernmental relations. Although some questions in the lengthy intergovernmental relations questionnaire do not pertain to county officers, most of them do apply. Thoughout the text of the monograph, the author makes use of many tables to present the results of the questionnaires. Additionally, the appendixes contain the questionnaires themselves and detailed compilations of answers to every question.

All six chapters of the monograph contain information and analysis on the views of county officials on intergovernmental relations. However, in Chapter 5, only the section on county horizontal intergovernmental relations is relevant to the study of counties. An introductory chapter gives general background information on the officials surveyed, including their educational level and experience in government. There is also a discussion of the special role of the county auditor in Minnesota as a type of weak executive-head of county government. Further information on this matter is given in Chapter 2 which deals with the views of the officials on the allocation of activities to the various units of government. Among the topics considered in this chapter are the attitudes of the officials on the desirable amount of governmental activity; attitudes of county officials on state activities in relation to the county; municipal officials' attitudes on county activities in general; the attitudes of officials toward the level of various kinds of activities; the attitudes of officials toward the general level of activities of the various kinds of governmental units, including counties; the attitudes of welfare officials on the desirable amount of national governmental activity; and the attitudes of local officials on "physical" versus the "social" functions of government.

Chapter 3 is concerned with the views of officials on the frequency of contact with and the cooperativeness of the different types of governmental units. Included among the topics in this chapter are: the rating of cooperativeness of state officials by other officials; rating of the cooperativeness of national officials by other officials; rating of the cooperativeness of other officials by municipal officials; sources of most contacts and best cooperation with state legislators and administrators; and views of local officials on areas of least satisfactory state cooperation. Other topics included are: the efficiency of the state government as rated by municipal, county, and national officials; the efficiency of the national government as rated by municipal, county and state officials; the sources of major problems confronting all the officials from inside or outside their own units; frequency of contacts with state officials as rated by local and national officials; the frequency of contacts with national officials as rated by local and state officials; and the correlations between frequency of contact and cooperativeness and between frequency of contacts and efficiency.

In the fourth chapter, the author is concerned with the views of the officials on vertical intergovernmental relations. Some matters which he considers in this relation are: perceptions by local officials of state-local relations; attitudes of the officials on the desirable amount of state technical advice; attitudes of the officials on the desirable amount of state administrative supervision; attitudes of the officials on whether or not the powers of state administrators over local government should include each of the following—requiring reports, making inspections, giving advice, auditing expenditures, issuing orders, issuing rules, removing local officials, approving local officials, and taking over administration; perceptions by local officials on whether or not they have less "say so" about their affairs as a result of national contacts; and the attitudes of local officials on the desirable amount of contact with national officials.

Chapter 5, on horizontal intergovernmental relations, contains material relevant to county participation. The topics with which this section deals include the views of county and state officials on the adequacy of the areal size of counties; attitudes of county and state officials on expensive county services (as determined by the proportion of officials choosing given alternatives if the services are too costly for a county); attitudes of county and state officials toward township government; and attitudes of state and local officials on assessing and public health activities, as shown by the proportions favoring and opposing the transfer of those activities from municipalities to the county.

Chapter 6 presents a summary and conclusions. It points out possible generalizations to be made on the basis of the compiled data. Some generalizations which are particularly significant in relation to county intergovernmental relations involve the specialization of county functional officials, the professionalism pervading certain functions, and the factors uniting functional officials who administer such a function in all governmental units. Other generalizations concern the unit of government orientation of general executives and governing body personnel and the effects of the creation of independent county boards for particular functions.

Although this study relies upon data gathered from the state of Minnesota, its findings are probably applicable to many states. The monograph is extremely well-written. The tables are particularly well constructed and useful. The behavioral approach which this work uses is extremely rare in studies of intergovernmental relations, especially those relating to counties. At the time of this publication, the author was Professor of Political Science, Michigan State University.

INTERGOVERNMENTAL RELATIONS

National-County

United States

The National Association of Counties Research Foundation has compiled a catalogue of federal programs which can be of assistance to county planners in the development of county plans. This catalogue is entitled COMPREHENSIVE COUNTY PLANNING . . . FEDERAL ASSISTANCE PROGRAMS, Technical Advisory Report Number Two (Washington, D. C.: 1964, 39 pp.). The catalogue lists programs which will assist counties in comprehensive planning, collection of basic data for planning, and administration of planning programs. A number of federal programs give counties assistance in such areas as public and institutional, industrial and commercial, agricultural, and parks and recreation land-use planning. Transportation planning areas include comprehensive planning assistance and aid for port and harbor development. Finally, the national government can give counties many kinds of public-facilities planning assistance. These programs are described in the catalogue and put into five classifications: public buildings and civil defense; health facilities planning assistance; educational facilities assistance; water facilities planning assistance; and polution abatement assistance. This publication also includes a selected bibliography on federal aid programs.

The publication was undoubtedly written for county planning officials and other county functional officials and serves as an excellent reference for them. The sources of information for this work are primarily federal documents.

A report by the National Association of Counties, Federal Aid Advisor Service, GUIDELINES FOR FEDERAL PROGRAMS (Washington: 1966, 7 pp.), examines seven steps counties should take to establish a beneficial pattern of national-county relationships. One of the most interesting prescribed steps is the establishment of county federal aid coordinators. The duties to be performed by such an officer, who acts in a link-pin capacity between his county and the national government, are described. The report notes that such officers have already been appointed in many counties.

California

THE IMPACT OF FEDERAL GRANTS-IN-AID ON CALIFORNIA, by Earl C. Segrest and Arthur J. Misner (Berkeley: University of California, Bureau of Public Administration, 1954), presents an historical discussion of many governmental functions, a number of which are within the province of counties. For example, the section on roads begins with a consideration of legislation passed in 1897 which provided for the establishment of county districts for this purpose; it proceeds with various other actions relating to highways up through the late 1940's. The authors describe how federal grants have strengthened local units.

Kansas

J. L. Jacobs and Company, under a contract with the United States Commission on Intergovernmental Relations (Kestnbaum Commission), undertook a study of the impact of federal grants-in-aid in Kansas: STATE OF KANSAS—THE IMPACTS OF FEDERAL GRANTS-IN-AID ON THE STATE AND LOCAL GOVERNMENTS (Chicago: June 1954, 179 pp.). After a general introduction, the study looks at the individual federal grant-in-aid programs, not all of which are applicable to county government. The programs which are included in the study and are related to the county are public health, maternal and child care, public assistance, child welfare, and public highways.

The introductory chapter of the report deals with matters relevant to county government. One section, a general discussion of county revenue sources in Kansas, emphasizes the role of federal and state grants-in-aid as sources of county revenue. There is a table which lists such revenue from the various sources in 1947 and 1953 and shows the percentage increase between those years. In another section, an examination is made of how county health and welfare employees come under the state merit system. The chapter concludes with an interesting discussion of how federal grants-in-aid have led to more state supervision over county government.

The chapter on the public health program begins with a description of the federal public health grant programs and federal requirements for and administrative controls over these programs. The report then examines the trends in the level of support of public health activities by the national, state, and local governments. Next is a discussion of how the federal grants have spurred the state and local governments to raise the level of public health activities. Then comes consideration of state administration of the public health programs, including examination of the relationship of the state health agency with county and city-county health departments. Finally, there is a discussion of the programs at the local level. There is no discussion of county participation in the Hill-Burton hospital program, since public hospitals are a municipal and township function in Kansas.

A short chapter deals with the maternal and child health care program. It begins with a description of the services for which federal grants are available to states for distribution to county and city-county health departments. The federal requirements of the program are listed. Finally, trends in the financing of the program by the federal, state and local government are explored.

A lengthier chapter is concerned with the public assistance program. After a general introduction the structural arrangements, including the powers of the various county officers and boards, for county administration of the program are described. The federal requirements in the state welfare plan are listed. The extent of federal, state and county support of the program is discussed. This is followed by an extensive description and analysis of state supervision over county public assistance activities, including discussion of the role of the state manual of public assistance as a mechanism of supervision. Federal requirements for a merit system and for periodic reports and reviews are given somewhat shorter analysis. The chapter concludes with an enlightening examination of the consequences of increasing federal support for the public assistance program.

The chapter on the child welfare program begins with a general description of the purposes for which federal child welfare grants are made to the state. There follows a discussion of the federal requirements for a state child welfare plan. This leads to an examination of the state and county responsibilities in the program and its actual operation at the county level. The personnel problems of counties in relation to the program are explored. Finally, mention is made of the effects on state as against county responsibilities for child welfare of federal entrance into the child welfare program.

The final chapter to deal with a federal aid program relevant to county government is concerned with the highway program. The first section explains which county roads and highways are a part of the federal aid system. The responsibilities of counties—including responsibility for provision of a proportion of state matching funds—for roads and highways are examined. The means for county financing of its share of matching funds are described. This description leads to a discussion of the trends in the financing of county roads and highways by the state, county, and national governments. Federal controls over federally-aided roads and highways are listed, and the consequences of federal control assessed.

Throughout the study, emphasis is placed on institutional and financial arrangements for the administration of the federal aid programs. Federal and state statutory and administrative requirements are also stressed. At some points, the study includes analyses of federal requirements on county administration of the programs, but such analyses are generally brief and incomplete. County government is not a major focus of this study; instead, federal-state relations are given the major attention. The staff of J. L. Jacobs and Company used largely primary sources in preparing the study. These sources included official state statistical data, interviews with state, local, and federal officials, statutes, and manuals of administrative regulations.

Michigan

In the early 1950's, the United States Commission on Intergovernmental Relations (Kestnbaum Commission) contracted with various research institutions to undertake studies of the impact of federal grants-in-aid in several states. Public Administration Service was commissioned to undertake the study in Michigan. Its findings are reported in THE FEDERAL GRANT-IN-AID SYSTEM—ITS IMPACT IN THE STATE OF MICHIGAN (Chicago: May, 1954, 163 pp.). Concerning county government, most findings pertain to the channeling of federal aid and federal regulations through the state to the county level in public health, public welfare, and highway programs.

The most important findings are contained in the introductory chapter which examines the impact of federal-state programs in general. However, to comprehend the impact of federal aid on county government programs, our attention must focus on the three above-mentioned programs, since they are the only federally-aided ones discussed which involve counties. Among the topics dealt with in this introductory chapter are: the effect of federal aid as a stimulant to the expansion of the health and welfare programs in the state; the effects of federal involvement on the administration of the aided programs, with particular emphasis on its impact on county administration of the public welfare program; the effects of federal reporting requirements on county administration of the health and welfare programs; the effects of federal participation on county-state relationships, particularly with respect to state regulation of county-aided activities; an analysis of federal auditing of local records and payment procedures; and a general examination of the effects of federal aid on the scope of the three county programs and on the "vitality" of local (meaning county) governments.

The report devotes a chapter to the description of the impact of federal aid on each of several state programs. For reasons mentioned above, the focus in federal aid to county government is on the public welfare, public health, and highway programs. Very little information is given about its effects on county highway and road programs. Some mention is made of the effect that federal aid to secondary road construction has on county road programs. In addition, there is brief mention of the relationship between state sharing of certain revenues earmarked for road purposes with counties and county matching funds for federal highway aid.

This report includes much insightful analysis as well as interesting description of relationships. However, with the expansion of federal aid programs into new areas, including direct federal aid to counties in certain programs, the study probably is out of date as a general study of the impact of federal grants-in-aid on county government. Nonetheless, many intergovernmental relationships which it describes and the analyses it makes of them are probably still applicable, particularly as they apply to the federal aid programs, notably in the health and welfare fields, which are channeled from the national government through the state to the counties.

The report is written in a clear, concise, and simple style. Extensive use is made of examples from particular programs to illustrate the generalizations. Emphasis is placed upon intergovernmental relations in particular programs, rather than upon an effort to develop generalizations about an over-all pattern of intergovernmental relationships; however, it should be pointed out that the latter is not ignored. The Public Administration Service generally used primary sources in preparing the study, including original surveys and field work.

(For other entries on Michigan impact grant studies, *see* Services—Public Health; and Public Welfare: Michigan.)

Mississippi

McKinsey and Company, in THE IMPACT OF FEDERAL GRANTS-IN-AID ON THE STATE OF MISSISSIPPI (Washington: May, 1954, 147 pp.), emphasize the effects of such grants on political institutions and specific program areas. The report considers the impact on the quality of service and the degree of authority possessed by local decision-makers who operate under national standards. The county is not generally delineated from other local units.

South Carolina

The Governments Affairs Institute's IMPACT OF FEDERAL GRANTS-IN-AID ON SOUTH CAROLINA: SUBMITTED TO THE COMMISSION ON INTERGOVERNMENTAL RELATIONS (Washington: 1954, 271 pp.) covers the program areas of health, housing, highways, and welfare. The county is considered in discussions of functions in which it is active. The authors analyze the ways federal grants have affected local units, such as in raising their standards and broadening their services.

Washington

McKinsey and Company's report, THE IMPACT OF FEDERAL GRANTS-IN-AID IN THE STATE OF WASHINGTON (Washington: 1959, 161 pp.), discusses a number of program areas: vocational education, public health, highways, housing, and welfare. It describes how one of the results of the grant-in-aid program has been the growth of "behind the scenes" government. It discusses how each grant program involves a host of interest groups that seek the protection and expansion of their special interests. It also shows how federal grants have aided local politicians by reducing their burden of raising taxes. The county is included in the analyses of functions in which it participates.

Wyoming

STATE OF WYOMING, IMPACTS OF FEDERAL GRANTS-IN-AID ON THE STATE AND LOCAL GOVERNMENTS: REPORT AND RECOMMENDATIONS PREPARED FOR THE COMMISSION ON INTERGOVERNMENTAL RELATIONS (Chicago: 1954, 177 pp.), prepared by

J. L. Jacobs Company, deals specifically with the county in the sections on public health and welfare. The study examines the trend toward intergovernmental sharing of responsibilities in the welfare field, with the national government having an increasingly important role. The author explains that the requirements accompanying federal grants have sharply restricted county discretion.

ALSO TO BE NOTED—FOR INTERGOVERNMENTAL RELATIONS: NATIONAL-COUNTY:

Advisory Commission on Intergovernmental Relations, *The Impact of Federal Urban Development Programs on Local Government Organization and Planning,* Report No. A-20 (Washington: 1964, 198 pp.).

"Agriculture Department Committee System Seen as Weakening County Government," *The County Officer,* 28 (April, 1963), 150, 161.

Bernard F. Hillenbrand, "A County Urban Advisor," *The County Officer,* 27 (January, 1962), 5.

______, "A County Urban Advisor and Federal Aid," *American County Government,* 31 (January, 1966), 6.

______, "More About a County Urban Advisor," *The County Officer,* 28 (November, 1963), 403.

National Association of Counties, Washington, *Washington Report*, July 29, 1963 to present.

INTERGOVERNMENTAL RELATIONS

State-County

Hawaii

State-county relations is a major theme throughout the Public Administration Service's monograph, STATE AND LOCAL GOVERNMENT RELATIONS IN THE STATE OF HAWAII

(Chicago: 1962, 234 pp.), but it is also the subject of detailed examination in one particular section. An important line of emphasis in this discussion is state "paternalism and excessive oversight of local county government operations." The authors discuss the use of counties as administrative arms of the state and give extensive attention to state supervision and control over various kinds of county activities. There is an individual examination of county-state relations in the following activities: civil service and personnel administration; law enforcement (county police departments); planning, zoning, and subdivision control; and capital improvements programs. A final topic in this section is the limited nature of county home rule in the state of Hawaii.

Illinois

County-state fiscal relations is one of the topics Irving Howards considers in his monograph, SELECTED ASPECTS OF STATE SUPERVISION OVER LOCAL GOVERNMENT IN ILLINOIS (Carbondale: Southern Illinois University, 1964, 109 pp.). He refers to this subject throughout the monograph rather than concentrating on it in any one chapter or section. These references can be grouped under four headings: general finance, including an extensive discussion of revenue sources, the property tax, expenditure and revenue trends; debt limitations (*see* Finance—General: Illinois); county budgeting (*see* Finance—Administration: Illinois); and state financial assistance.

In his discussion of state financial assistance to counties, the author explores state aid in the public welfare-general assistance and federal aid highway programs. The major points of emphasis are the state aid formulas and the total extent of state aid. Additionally, the author briefly describes how each program operates.

In his examination of these topics, Howards emphasizes state statutory requirements and analyzes their consequences for county government. His exploration of state requirements for county budgeting is particularly enlightening. At the time of publication, the author was acting director of the Public Affairs Research Bureau, Southern Illinois University.

Nevada

NEVADA COUNTIES AND CITIES (North Las Vegas: March 1966, 8 pp.), prepared by the League of Women Voters of Nevada, is a study on the relationship of the Nevada legislature to county and other local governments. Half of the paper is devoted to counties. The introductory section outlines the purpose and scope of the study and presents statistics on the size, population, and county seats of the counties.

In turning specifically to the relationship between the county and the state legislature, the report describes the articles of the constitution which refer to county government. Then it outlines the basic laws which govern its operations. Next, the specific legislative requirements affecting the board of county commissioners are explained, and a full list of the powers and duties of the board prescribed by law is given. The final section dealing with the county describes the amount and character of local legislation affecting this unit. A table is included which lists the number of local bills introduced and enacted for the seventeen counties in both the Senate and Assembly during 1963 and 1965.

Although this study does not analyze the effects and actual ramifications of legislative control and prescription on the county, it effectively points out the scope of such oversight. More detail, however, is needed, particularly on the relationship between the legislature and offices of county government other than the board of commissioners.

ALSO TO BE NOTED—FOR INTERGOVERNMENTAL RELATIONS: STATE-COUNTY:

Lockheed Missiles and Space Company, *State of California Information System Study: County-State Information Flow* (Los Angeles: 1965, 76 pp.).

League of Women Voters of Kentucky, *Who's in Charge Here: Evaluation of the State's Responsibilities toward County Government* (Frankfort: 1966, 1967, 12 pp.).

INTERGOVERNMENTAL RELATIONS
City-County

Alabama

A good study of the powers of counties in Alabama to engage in cooperative arrangements with cities and towns is Ernie W. Farrar's article, "WAYS ARE CLEAR FOR MORE CITY-COUNTY COOPERATION," *Alabama Municipal Journal,* 19 (July, 1961), 5-6, 10-11. This article discusses the constitutional and statutory provisions for city-county cooperation and the opinions of the Attorney General of Alabama regarding them. The author considers the means of financing various kinds of cooperative functions and enterprises as well as discusses the cooperative arrangements themselves. Among the kinds of cooperative arrangements with which he deals are: joint construction and maintenance of airports; joint public housing projects; mutual aid agreements in civil defense; several varieties of cooperative agricultural programs; reciprocal rental machinery and equipment; joint hospital construction; several kinds of joint economic and industrial development projects and programs; joint library boards and library facilities; many types of joint recreational programs, projects, and facilities; joint public buildings; intergovernmental contracts for care of prisoners; joint sewerage and water projects; several kinds of cooperative arrangements in the field of education; several types of cooperative arrangements in street and highway construction and maintenance; and financial contributions from one government to another for a variety of purposes.

Since the author's purpose is to motivate city and county officials by informing them of their powers to cooperate with each other, he does not seek to analyze these powers. In line with his legalistic style, much detail is given about the specifics of provisions for cooperative arrangements. The author was Mayor of

Reform, Alabama, for ten years and was formerly a county probate judge.

California

In CITY-COUNTY RELATIONS REPORT (Sacramento: March, 1960, 32 pp.), the League of California Cities suggests cooperative solutions for city-county problems. The history of city-county relations in California is discussed, and a summary of cooperative functional programs in thirteen California counties is presented.

Kansas

The Kansas County-City Cooperation Committee has studied the statutory provisions for city-county cooperation in that state and has made recommendations for improvements. The Committee, established jointly by the League of Kansas Municipalities and the Kansas County Commissioners Association, has summarized its findings in an article, "INTERGOVERNMENTAL COOPERATION – KEY TO THE FUTURE," *Kansas Government Journal,* 1 (October 1964), 457-461. It briefly summarizes recommendations by the Committee for two new state laws and a state constitutional amendment, all three aimed at furthering intergovernmental cooperation in general. The article also summarizes the Committee's recommendation for broadening the state's joint powers act.

The final and major portion of the article summarizes, evaluates, and makes recommendations for the revision of statutory provisions for county-city cooperation in many local governmental activities: airports; building construction and maintenance; cemeteries; civil defense; courts; economic development; elections; engineering; fire protection; health; highways; jails; libraries; mental health; planning; police protection; radio communications; recreation and parks; refuse; sewerage; social welfare; utility service; agricultural extension; ambulance service; coyote eradication; and juvenile detention homes.

INTERGOVERNMENTAL RELATIONS

District-County

United States

The very important role of the county is analyzed in John C. Bollens, SPECIAL DISTRICT GOVERNMENTS IN THE UNITED STATES (Berkeley and Los Angeles: University of California Press, 1957, 280 pp.). Throughout the book the author points out the various relations existing between these special authorities and the county government.

In the beginning of the book, Professor Bollens explains the role of the county government in the selection of the members of the governing bodies of various special districts. He describes how the county may singly or in conjunction with city governments appoint the members of the governing body. He points out that members of the county government may serve *ex officio* on a number of district governing boards.

Although Professor Bollens stresses throughout the book that most of these special boards are independent of general purpose governments, in Chapter Seven he explains the circumstances under which dependent districts and authorities do function. Using examples from Los Angeles County, he explains the relationship that exists under such circumstances between the county and these special entities. He also describes the organization and operation of county service areas, which are subsidiaries of county government having no governmental structure of their own.

The great significance of special districts for general purpose governments evolves in Chapter 8. Here, Professor Bollens examines the problems these special districts create for county government, as well as the inadequacies of these units. On the basis of this examination he calls for a wider role and more power for the county. Specifically, he recommends that the general unit absorb many of these special governments.

This book is primarily concerned with describing and analyzing the organization and functions of special districts; yet, the author does not neglect the significance such units have for the entire local governmental system and explains the connections between and interdependence of all these governments. His suggestions for absorption of many special districts into general governing units are substantiated by the material he has presented in the body of the text and deserve consideration. At the time of this publication, the author was Associate Professor of Political Science, University of California, Los Angeles.

The sponsorship by the National Association of Counties of Robert G. Smith's book, PUBLIC AUTHORITIES, SPECIAL DISTRICTS AND LOCAL GOVERNMENT (Washington: National Association of Counties Research Foundation, 1964, 225 pp.), reflects the main concern of this study—the effect of these special types of government on general purpose governments, particularly the county and the city.

First, the author examines the main reasons advanced for establishing these authorities. He then tests these criteria against the actual functioning of public authorities on the county and municipal levels of five states—Connecticut, Delaware, New Jersey, New York, and Pennsylvania. He compares their financing procedure with that used in counties and explores the possibility of placing these authorities under control of the general government in order to avoid "vertical functional autocracy." He examines representation of general government officials on the governing board of the authority as a method of securing political control and responsibility.

After analyzing both the positive and negative aspects of special authorities, the author discusses means of curtailing their continued unrestrained proliferation. He discusses the method established by the California legislature in 1963: the creation of commissions in each county to consider and approve any proposals for formation of a new government or for annexation of any territory to an existing government.

This book is descriptive, analytical, and prescriptive. Professor Smith describes how the public authorities should function and analyzes whether or not their actual operation meets original expectations and whether their use is detrimental or beneficial to effective and efficient government generally. He then presents proposals for integrating and adapting these special authorities to general purpose government. The book is well-written and clearly organized and developed. It is a very useful and informative document on one of the many problems facing county government.

The author cites the previous texts dealing with special districts in the United States and supplements this with extensive use of newspaper articles on the subject and continued first-hand observation of district government in action. At the time of this publication, Smith was Professor of Political Science, Drew University.

ALSO TO BE NOTED—FOR INTERGOVERNMENTAL RELATIONS: CITY-COUNTY AND DISTRICT-COUNTY:

General

Judith Finlayson, "Councils of Government: What Are They and Why Are They?" *American County Government,* 32 (April, 1967), 20-25.

W. Brooke Graves, *Interlocal Cooperation: The History and Background of Intergovernmental Agreements,* Information and Education Research Report No. 23 (Washington: National Association of Counties Research Foundation, 1962, 9 pp.).

National Association of Counties and National League of Cities, *Proceedings of the Workshop on Voluntary City-County Regional Cooperation* (Washington: n.d., 24 pp.).

Individual States

William R. MacDougal, "City-County Cooperation [in California], "*The County Officer,* 25 (December, 1960), 384-385.

Howard J. Grossman, "Counties Come to Life: Newly Developed Partnership with Municipalities Puts 'Dark Continent' in Position of Leadership [in Pennsylvania]," *National Civic Review,* 53 (September, 1964), 429-433.

David H. Grubbs, "City-County Agreements in Our Four Tennessee Metropolitan Areas," *Tennessee Town and City* (August, 1961), 13.

E. W. Meisenhelder and R. A. Lovelace, *Laws for City-County Cooperation in Tennessee* (Knoxville: University of Tennessee, Bureau of Public Administration, 1960, 56 pp.).

League of Virginia Counties, *County-Municipal Cooperation in Virginia* (Charlottesville: 1963, 60 pp.).

ORGANIZATION

General

United States

John P. Duncan summarizes state constitutional provisions for county government in the United States, excluding Hawaii and Alaska, in "COUNTY GOVERNMENT—CONSTITUTIONAL DATA," a chapter in Oklahoma State Legislative Council, *Oklahoma Constitutional Studies* (Guthrie: Co-operative Publishing Company, 1950, pp. 466-490). As a preface to setting out the constitutional data, the author discusses the four regional variations in county governmental forms.

The data are presented in two ways. In the first section, states are presented by type of constitutional provision. The first subsection deals with the formation of counties and considers these points: counties recognized as legal divisions of the states; provisions for changing county boundaries; power granted to the legislature to organize new counties; various substantive limitations imposed on the character of new counties; various substantive limitations imposed on the character of old counties; dissolution and merger provisions; division and consolidation of counties; provisions for city-county consolidation and separation; functional limitations imposed upon new counties; other provisions relating to new counties; and referendum required to change county seat.

Constitutions in relation to the form of county government are examined in the second subsection. The points covered are: provisions authorizing the voters to prepare county charters; provisions for optional forms of county government; provisions relative to townships; provisions relative to the uniformity of county government; provisions directly or indirectly establishing a specific type of governing board; states where all or part of the administrative offices are provided for in the constitution and/or where the provision is made for filling administrative offices by election; and other provisions relating to county officers.

The third subsection is organized around the provisions concerned with the functioning of county government. The subjects covered are: constitutional limitations with respect to county debts; constitutional limits on the tax rates of counties; and restrictions with respect to county lending, credit, and investment in corporations. The fourth subsection deals with constitutional limitations on legislative action relating to counties. Two general areas of limitation are covered: provisions to bar the legislature from imposing tax rates on counties and to prohibit local and special legislation. A table concluding the first section shows the number and terms of various types of officials provided for in the state constitutions.

Section Two of the chapter presents the same basic data, but in more detail and in a different form. Using the same four broad categories—formation of counties, form of counties, functions and functioning of counties, and limitations on legislative actions in dealing with counties—constitutional provisions are examined on a state-by-state basis in tabular form. A table is presented for each category, and a brief description of each state's constitutional provisions under the points outlined above is provided.

This presentation of state constitutional data relative to counties is still useful despite some changes that have occured since it was prepared, because it gives a picture of the kinds of provisions for and limitations on county government which are generally found in state constitutions. Although specific constitutions have changed, the patterns shown in the constitutional data have not changed significantly. These data are set forth in a very clear and usable form.

In a separate chapter on forms of county government (pp. 444-465), Professor Duncan examines modern types of organization. As a model for comparison with modern forms, a chart of the structure of county government in Oklahoma is presented as an example of the traditional type. The forms of county government possessing chief executives are then explored.

The author notes that there have been revisions in county organizational structure without constitutional change in many states.

An examination is made of the county manager plan. An organization chart is presented to show the ideal county organizational structure for this plan. The experience of several counties with this plan is evaluated, and an extensive discussion is presented of Petroleum County, Montana, and Henrico County, Virginia. Other county manager counties examined in some depth are Durham County, North Carolina; Monroe County, New York; Warwick County, Virginia; Hamilton County, Tennessee; and Sacramento County, California.

Other kinds of chief executive plans are also explored, but not in the same depth as is the county manager plan. The county elected executive system is considered, with special attention given to Nassau County, New York. An organizational chart for an ideal elected executive form of county government is laid out. Attention is given to the appointed county executive plan that establishes an executive head with powers less than those of a county manager. Organizational charts for two variations of this plan are diagrammed. Mention is also made of the county president plan, wherein the chairman of the county commission functions as the executive head. An organizational chart of this plan is also presented.

This chapter is an analytical, descriptive presentation of the status of the nontraditional forms of county government. It is one of a number of works which have suggested the extension of these forms to other counties through state constitutional amendment and enabling legislation. Its discussion of individual county formal and informal modification of the traditional structure of county government without constitutional or legislative authority is one of the first of its kind. The work is well-written and makes effective use of examples. The sources of information are generally secondary although the reports of individual counties are sometimes used. At the time of this publication, the author was Professor of Government, University of Oklahoma.

Franklin H. Pierce's "WHAT DOES THE LAW REQUIRE OF COUNTIES?" *American County Government,* 31 (August, 1966), 50-51, 56, discusses the legal status of counties. This article, by the president of the National Association of County Civil Attorneys, is a digest of Chester J. Antieau's book, *County Law*. It discusses the statutory and constitutional powers of the county and its legal position. Tax exemptions and conflicts of interest between counties and other units of government are also discussed.

California

An interesting study of the legal structure of county government in California, with particular emphasis on the legal duties and limitations of the boards of supervisors, is presented by Harold W. Kennedy in "THE LEGAL STRUCTURE OF COUNTIES AND THE RESPONSIBILITIES OF SUPERVISORS," in County Supervisors Association of California, *County Government, 1959: Proceedings, 4th Biennial County Government Institute* (Sacramento: 1959, pp. 6-51).

The sources of information for the paper are primary—the California constitution and the California Government Code. Mr. Kennedy, Los Angeles County Counsel, writes in a legalistic style. Emphasis is on the description of legal provisions; there is very little analysis and no prescription.

The author begins his discussion with an examination of the corporate powers of counties and their status as political subdivisions of the state. The powers of the county set forth in the Governmental Code are detailed, and the county officers enumerated in it are listed. Constitutional provisions for the method of compensation of county officers are discussed. The author then turns to the legal role of the board of supervisors and explains the procedures to be followed at official meetings. The board's legal powers and responsibilities are listed in detail, and some of these powers are developed more fully. Its authority in the negotiation of contracts is detailed. When Mr. Kennedy delineates the powers of the board in county property control he spells out the functions of county purchasing agent. He then looks into a number of miscellaneous matters: county liability for the acts of its employees; the police power of counties; county indebtedness and liability; county licensing powers; and the auditing of financial claims against the counties.

Georgia

An excellent analysis of the legal provisions for county government in Georgia is contained in an article by Harold Sheats, "THE JOB OF THE COUNTY COMMISSIONER," *Georgia County Government Magazine,* 16 (January 1965), 5-7, 14. The article begins with a discussion of the role of the counties as political subdivisions of the state. Then, the author turns to a very interesting examination of constitutional and statutory grants of power to the counties, with particular emphasis on the problem of the use of population classification in legislation dealing with county government. Within an examination of county functions, there is mention of the evolution of governing bodies. Last, the author explores the powers of the county governing body specifically. He deals with legislative limitations on the governing body, including discussion of a judicial decision that Georgia counties have no general welfare powers. He lists the twenty purposes for which county governing bodies may levy taxes.

This is a well-written and interesting article. Although it concerns constitutional and statutory provision, it is not written in dreary, legalistic style, and lay people can easily understand it. Unlike most works dealing with legal provisions for county government, the article is not confined to drab description, but contains a considerable amount of insightful analysis. At the time of this publication, the author was County Attorney, Fulton County, Georgia.

Hawaii

A lengthy examination of county organization and administration is contained in a report by the Public Administration Service, STATE AND LOCAL GOVERNMENT RELATIONSHIPS IN THE STATE OF HAWAII (Chicago: 1962, 234 pp.). Most of the section devoted to this subject is concerned with the City and County of Honolulu, which operates under a home rule charter. The organizational structure of Honolulu is described in detail. The powers and responsibilities of the mayor, managing director, city council, department heads, and other boards and commissions are explained. The functions of the departments are outlined, and a city-county organizational chart is presented.

The report begins its consideration of the other three counties in the state with a chart outlining their organization. This is followed by a discussion of county personnel and employment. There is then an analysis of the role of the county chief executive, the independently-elected county chairman. The powers and duties of the other elected county officers are explored: auditor, treasurer, clerk, and attorney. Other county officers, commissions, and boards are also examined, and the departments or functions under their control discussed: civil service commission and director for personnel administration; planning commission for planning and traffic services; police commission and head of police department for police protection and civil defense; fire chief for fire protection; public works commission and county engineer for the public works department; and other boards and commissions for additional functions which vary among the three counties.

The report analyzes the inefficiency of county government which results from its dispersed administrative structure. The diffusion of policy-making among the board of supervisors, county chairman, elected officers, and appointed commissions and boards is discussed. The report particularly deplores the decentralization of the budgetary process and concludes that the problems of county administration are largely the result of excessive state statutory control over the organizational structure of the counties.

ALSO TO BE NOTED—FOR ORGANIZATION:

General

United States Bureau of the Census, *Census of Governments, 1967: Governmental Organization,* Vol. 1 (Washington: 1968, 460 pp.).

Edward W. Weidner, *The American County—Patchwork of Boards* (New York: National Municipal League, 1946, 24 pp.).

Individual States

Tennessee Legislative Council, *Study on Structure of County Government* [in Tennessee], FR Series No. 1966-B3 (Nashville: 1966, v.p.).

ORGANIZATION

Chief Executives, General

United States

William H. Cape has made a comprehensive study of county chief executives in a lengthy monograph, THE EMERGING PATTERNS OF COUNTY EXECUTIVES (Lawrence: University of Kansas, Governmental Research Center, 1967, 123 pp., Governmental Research Series No. 35). To provide the reader with a perspective within which to view the role of the various kinds of county chief executives, the author begins his work with a general, but concise, discussion of the status of county government throughout the United States. Some of the more interesting points which he considers are: the manner in which state legislatures deal with counties through special legislation; the increasing role of county governments in intergovernmental relations; the conflicting roles of the county as an administrative arm of the state and as a local government; the functioning of the county governing board, particularly in relation to the role of the chairman of the board; and the relationships between the board and elected county officials.

The second chapter of the monograph is a broad overview of the trend toward county chief executives. Attention is first given to why there has been an increasing demand for county chief executives and why such executives are needed in county government. A general examination follows of the various kinds of chief executives established in 450 counties throughout the United States. They are placed in four basic categories: the county manager; the appointed county chief administrative officer; the elected chief executive; and other elected county officers designated as chief executives. Each category is first discussed in terms of the powers and responsibilities generally possessed by that kind of chief executive and his relations with the county governing board and other county officials and boards. The author then delves into the variations in the powers and responsibilities, methods of selection, titles, formal status in county government, and patterns of relationships with the county board and other county officials and boards of each category of chief executive. In this chapter the greatest emphasis is given to appointed chief administrative officers.

Professor Cape devotes a chapter to a more detailed examination of elected county heads. (*See* Organization – Chief Executives, Elected: United States.) Two chapters are concerned with a description and an evaluation of the county manager plan throughout the country. (*See* Organization – Chief Executives, Appointed: United States.) Other chapters deal with proposals for county manager government in Kansas and evaluate the county chief executive systems of selected states. (*See* Organization – Chief Executives, General: Georgia, Maryland, North Carolina; Appointed: California, and Virginia; and Elected: New York.) The operation of the county manager plan in Petroleum County, Montana, and the independently elected county executive in New Castle County, Delaware, is also described.

The final chapter makes general evaluations of the trend toward county chief executives. Much of this repeats the earlier discussion. The author does, however, seek to make some judgments about the various forms of county chief executives and provides three useful appendixes. One is a table listing data on each of the counties with a county board-appointed non-manager chief administrator. Another appendix briefly summarizes state constitutional provisions which permit the county manager plan. The final one presents voter reactions and International City Managers' Association approvals of county manager governments during the period from 1961 to 1962.

This mongraph is a significant contribution to the literature on county government. The author has brought together and has sought to integrate all present sources of information on county chief executives. In addition, he has added to these sources through the presentation and analysis of quotations from letters he solicited from certain county chief executives, concerning their views about their positions. The work, however, contains unnecessary repetition, and the terminology employed in discussing various types of county executives is at times imprecise. At the time of this publication, the author was Research Associate, Governmental Research Center, and Professor of Political Science at the University of Kansas.

"WE NEED COUNTY GOVERNORS!" the editorial by Bernard F. Hillenbrand in *American County Government,* 32 (June, 1967), 8, is a concise, well-reasoned plea for an elected chief executive for the county. He cites the extent to which such an office is already used in counties and then quotes Gerald Saunders, the county mayor of Monroe County, Florida, in support of the plan. Much of this editorial, devoted to explaining why the chief executive should be elected, emphasizes that this office in the county would be a logical extension of our executive system of government, as opposed to the English parliamentary system. Mr. Hillenbrand states that he sees "no conflict between the appointed manager and elected executive ideas," since an elected executive must have the staff aid of a skilled full-time manager.

Georgia

Three Georgia counties—Wayne, Glynn, and Fulton—have county managers, while six others have nonmanager appointed county administrators—Chatham, Dougherty, Floyd, Hall, Muscogee, and Polk. One county, De Kalb, has an elected executive. William H. Cape in a section of his monograph, THE EMERGING PATTERNS OF COUNTY EXECUTIVES (Lawrence: University of Kansas, Governmental Research Center, 1967, 123 pp., Governmental Research Series No. 35), discusses the county manager system of Fulton County at length, while he mentions the other chief executives only briefiy.

Maryland

Maryland has a variety of both elected and appointed county chief executive forms. These include an elected executive director and a director of administration (appointed by the former) in Anne Arundel County; an "administrative director" (county manager) in

Wicomico County; and a county manager in Montgomery County. These chief executives and their counties are given individual consideration by William H. Cape in a section of his monograph, THE EMERGING PATTERNS OF COUNTY EXECUTIVES (Lawrence: University of Kansas, Governmental Research Center, 1967, 123 pp., Governmental Research Series No. 35).

Jean E. Spencer in a book, CONTEMPORARY LOCAL GOVERNMENT IN MARYLAND (College Park: University of Maryland, Bureau of Governmental Research, 1965, 116 pp.), analyzes the status of county chief executives in Maryland, with particular emphasis on their relationships to the county governing boards. (*See* Organization – Governing Boards: Maryland).

North Carolina

A section of a chapter in William H. Cape's monograph, THE EMERGING PATTERNS OF COUNTY EXECUTIVES (Lawrence: University of Kansas, Governmental Research Center, 1967, 123 pp., Governmental Research Series No. 35), is concerned with the three varieties of county executives in North Carolina: the county manager plan in eighteen counties; full-time chairmen of the governing boards in seven counties; and appointive administrators in two counties. Particular emphasis is given to the legislation which permits these forms.

ORGANIZATION

Chief Executives, Appointed

United States

Two chapters in William H. Cape's THE EMERGING PATTERNS OF COUNTY EXECUTIVES (Lawrence: University of

Kansas, Governmental Research Center, 1967, Governmental Research Series No. 35), are devoted to county managers. The first chapter is a general discussion of the county manager plan, while the following chapter evaluates its success. The author examines the requirement of the county manager plan that the chief executive established under it be termed a "true" county manager rather than an appointed chief administrator with lesser powers. There follows an exploration of the extensiveness of the adoption of county manager government, particularly counties recognized by the International City Managers' Association as "true" manager localities. The general characteristics of the county manager plan are described and variations in the plan are analyzed through the use of examples from particular states. Emphasis is given to the powers of the managers in budgeting, appointment, and general supervision of county operations. Also given particular attention is the restructuring of county government that has taken place upon the institution of the plan. The relationships between the manager and the county board and other county elected and appointed officials and boards are also given consideration.

In evaluating the success of the plan, a chapter stresses fiscal control over and coordination of county activities. The views of both proponents and opponents of the plan are presented. The results of studies that have analyzed the effects of the plan in particular counties are summarized: many stressed the reduction of various kinds of administrative costs of county government. The presentation and analysis of the views of certain county managers with regard to their positions are included.

"MORE ELECTED THAN APPOINTED COUNTY HEADS," *American County Government,* 30 (July 1965) 48, discusses responses to a questionnaire concerning county chief executives. The article discusses the statutory or charter-prescribed structure of those counties having chief executives. It then goes on to examine their salary ranges. A final section lists their titles, salary levels, and the size of population they serve. The questionnaire was distributed to officials of all county governments in the United States; the response rate was only slightly above 50 per cent.

California

In APPOINTED EXECUTIVE LOCAL GOVERNMENT: THE CALIFORNIA EXPERIENCE (Los Angeles: Haynes Foundation, 1952, 233 pp.), John C. Bollens considers managers and chief administrative officers in both counties and cities. He examines their personal characteristics, job duties, internal relations, and contacts with the community. He also presents various case studies illustrating attempts to adopt the two systems. The work concludes with an examination of two criticisms of appointed executive local government: low tenure of such executives and lack of sufficient elective political leadership.

A section of a chapter in William H. Cape's monograph, THE EMERGING PATTERNS OF COUNTY EXECUTIVES (Lawrence: University of Kansas, Governmental Research Center, 1967, 123 pp., Governmental Research Series No. 35), examines the appointed chief executive system in California. The author discusses on an individual basis each of California's three county manager counties—Santa Clara, San Mateo, and Sacramento. He collectively considers the other thirty-seven counties that have various forms of the appointed county administrative officer concept.

Earl R. Strathman makes some interesting points in his paper, "THE ACTUAL ADMINISTRATION OF CALIFORNIA COUNTY GOVERNMENT—COUNTY MANAGER COUNTIES, COUNTY ADMINISTRATIVE OFFICER COUNTIES AND OPERATIONS WITHOUT ADMINISTRATIVE HELP," in County Supervisors Association of California, *County Government, 1959: Proceedings, 4th Biennial County Government Institute* (Sacramento: 1959, pp. 52-55). The scope of this paper is not as all-encompassing as the title indicates. The author discusses the three general functions of county administrative officers—communication, coordination and control—and lists the control functions of a county administrative officer. The paper is one of several presented at the County Government Institute and published in the Proceedings of the Institute. The author based his paper on personal experience; at the time of this publication, he was County Administrator for Alameda County.

Virginia

William H. Cape devotes a relatively large section of a chapter in his monograph, THE EMERGING PATTERNS OF COUNTY EXECUTIVES (Lawrence: University of Kansas, Governmental Research Center, 1967, 123 pp., Governmental Research Series No. 35), to an examination of the system of county chief executives in Virginia. The section describes the operation of the county manager plan in four counties—Albemarle, Henrico, Fairfax, and Arlington. Although the plan is discussed generally, specific attention is given to the operation of the plan in Henrico County. In addition, there is extensive consideration of the county executive secretary plan which operates in thirteen Virginia counties. This office is a variation of the appointed administrative officer concept. Throughout the section, attention is given to the statutory provisions underpinning the two plans.

ALSO TO BE NOTED—FOR ORGANIZATION: CHIEF EXECUTIVES, APPOINTED:

General

C. B. Kinnison, "Administrative Responsibility in County Government," *Governmental Research Newsletter,* 1 (February, 1961), 1-3.

Alastair McArthur, "Research Briefs," *The County Officer,* 27 (March, 1962), 134.

National Association of Counties Research Foundation, *A Profile of Fifty County Administrators and Their Counties,* Information and Education Service Report No. 27 (Washington: 1963, 6 pp.).

Individual States

Alva W. Stewart, *The County Manager Plan in North Carolina,* County Study Report No. 7 (Washington: National Association of Counties Research Foundation, 1963, 4 pp.).

______, "Well-Managed Counties: Long and Successful North Carolina Experience Leads to Forecast of Manager Plan's General Use," *National Civic Review,* 54 (November, 1965), 540-545, 569.

Alan Raga, *The Executive Secretary Plan for Virginia Counties,* County Study Report No. 1 (Washington: National Association of Counties Research Foundation, 1963, 4 pp.).

ORGANIZATION

Chief Executives, Elected

United States

One chapter in William H. Cape's monograph, THE EMERGING PATTERNS OF COUNTY EXECUTIVES (Lawrence: University of Kansas, Governmental Research Center, 1967, 123 pp., Governmental Research Series No. 35), deals with elected county chief executives. The author begins his analysis of these officers by describing the major characteristics and variations of elected chief executive plans. He concentrates on the methods of election, general administrative and executive powers, and relationships between the executive and the county governing board. In this connection, the author discusses extensively a National Association of Counties survey of 253 counties which have some type of elected chief executive, including chairmen of the county governing boards, county judges, county clerks and auditors, and other elected officers officially designated as chief executives, as well as officers specifically elected as chief executives.

Attention is then focused on county chief executives who are specifically elected as chief executives. The author examines individually the twelve counties where such officers have been established by charter provisions: St. Louis County, Missouri; Nassau, Westchester, Suffolk, Erie, Onondaga, and Oneida counties, New York; De Kalb County, Georgia; Jefferson Parish, Louisiana; and Milwaukee County, Wisconsin. The remainder of the chapter presents and analyzes the views of these elected chief executives about their positions. Particular emphasis is given to the problems of leadership, responsibility, and accountability.

New York

William H. Cape deals with the elected chief executive system in six New York counties in his monograph, THE EMERGING

PATTERNS OF COUNTY EXECUTIVES (Lawrence: University of Kansas, Governmental Research Center, 1967, 123 pp., Governmental Research Series No. 35). The author is concerned specifically with Oneida, Monroe, and Onondaga counties. Throughout his discussion, he emphasizes the powers and responsibilities of the executives under the respective charters.

ALSO TO BE NOTED—FOR ORGANIZATION: CHIEF EXECUTIVES, ELECTED:

Bernard F. Hillenbrand, "A County Mayor," *The County Officer,* 24 (December, 1959), 363.

Alastair McArthur, "Research Briefs," *The County Officer,* 27 (January, 1962), 36, 42.

Thomas D. Wilson, "Elected County Chiefs: As Suburban Areas Grow, Pressures Increase to Provide 'Citified' Services," *National Civic Review,* 55 (November, 1966), 561-568.

Individual States

"The Chief Executive of an Organized Borough," *Alaska Local Government,* 1 (September, 1961), 1-5.

ORGANIZATION

Governing Boards

United States

The Cleveland Bureau of Governmental Research has made a short study of the various methods of selecting county governing boards in THE LEGISLATIVE BODY IN COUNTY GOVERNMENT, Governmental Facts About Greater Cleveland No. 38 (Cleveland: 1959, 8 pp.). The methods of selection studied are: all members elected at-large; all members elected by single-member districts; some members elected at-large and some by districts;

plural-member districts; nomination by districts with election-at-large; and representation from governmental units. The report explains and gives examples of each type and lists the arguments for and against each kind. It was prepared by the Bureau for the use of the Cuyahoga County Charter Commission.

An editorial by Bernard F. Hillenbrand, "REAPPORTIONMENT AND SALARIES OR FULL TIME–FULL PAY," *The County Officer,* 29 (December, 1964), 510, discusses governing boards in the United States. There is a description of the general nature of legislative bodies in the United States, with emphasis on the relationship between members' duties and salaries. Reapportionment is brought into the discussion, since this process makes county governing boards more publicly responsible, and greater responsiveness requires them to devote more time to their offices. There is also an analysis of the relationship between the level of salaries and the caliber of candidates for county offices. Finally, the author examines the duties of county officers in relation to their salaries.

GOVERNING BOARDS OF COUNTY GOVERNMENTS: 1965 (Washington: State and Local Government Special Studies No. 49, April, 1965, 46 pp.), prepared by the United States Bureau of the Census, consists primarily of a series of tables on size and types of governing bodies of the 3,049 counties in the United States.

The report begins with an extended definition of county governing boards. Membership, scope of responsibility, and limitations on freedom of action of the various boards throughout the nation are discussed. Concise descriptions are given of various types of governing boards: boards of commissioners or supervisors, boards of township supervisors, judges and justices of the peace boards, judge and commissioner boards, and miscellaneous (which includes forty-five different counties). Next the reasons for the frequent use of the different titles are explained and the number of counties adopting each title listed. Brief explanations are given of the different types of presiding officers and the varying sizes of the boards. An explanation is given of the different methods of selecting members, and specific examples are cited. Finally, the report distinguishes between county government and county areas where no distinctive county government exists. A breakdown of all the various types of county areas is given.

The majority of the report is devoted to five tables on governing boards: summary of number of county governments and county governing board members, by states, 1965; number of county governments, by method of selection of county governing board members, by states, 1965; number of members of county governing boards, by method of selection, by states, 1965; name of governing board and title of presiding officer, by method of selection, for county governments, by states, 1965; and number of members of county governing boards, by method of selection, for county governments, by states, 1965. The last two tables show individual counties.

This report is a very useful reference on governing bodies. The method of arranging the data parallels most common needs; thus, the tables are easy and time-saving references.

Indiana

In his article on "INDIANA COUNTY COMMISSIONERS AS POLICY MAKERS," in *Indiana Public Affairs Notes* (Bloomington: Indiana University, Bureau of Government Research, May-June 1962, 6 pp.), John E. Stoner concentrates on the highway function in analyzing the policy-making role of the county commissioners.

The author opens by explaining how county powers and functions have changed. He discusses why the increased volume and more complex nature of these duties require boards of county commissioners to become more deliberative. He points out, however, that many boards have not kept pace and are still mainly administrative. He then discusses the problems resulting from this rigidity.

The body of the article is devoted to an analysis of the changes that must be made in the operation of the board of commissioners and of the highway department. Professor Stoner first explains the new relation he believes must be fostered between the board and the county council (a financial body). Then he discusses ways in which the board of commissioners itself can be strengthened. Third, he suggests increased use and development of policy-making aids for the commissioners. Fourth, he explains why it is necessary to secure adequate executive talent for road administration and how this process can be improved to insure the services of better executives. Finally, Professor Stoner examines problems which should be solved and improvements which should be made in the internal management of the highway department.

Even though the author has limited his analysis to highway work, his findings and suggestions have a wider relevance, since the need for change and reform is appearing in all phases of county activity. By linking the currently used practices of the past with the needs of the future, he has presented worthwhile and practical steps of action for immediate application. Also, the complete nature of the data and the careful analysis on which he bases his conclusions make the steps very acceptable. At the time of this publication, Professor Stoner was a member of the Department of Government, Indiana University.

Maryland

Jean E. Spencer makes an extensive examination of the roles of and the interrelationships between the county governing board and chief executives in CONTEMPORARY LOCAL GOVERNMENT IN MARYLAND (College Park: University of Maryland, Bureau of Governmental Research, 1965, 116 pp.). The author begins with a discussion of the general status of the governing board within the broad setting of county government. This discussion leads to a description of the number, method of selection, and salaries of board members. The manner in which the boards actually operate is then described.

An analysis of the effects on the role of the county board of various kinds of county chief executives is presented. Various chief executive officers are examined: specifically noted are managers, elected executives, chairmen of the boards, county clerks, and administrative officers. The functions, powers, and relationships to the board of each type of chief executive officer is considered.

Michigan

Despite its title, the greater portion of THE COUNTY BOARD OF SUPERVISORS (East Lansing: 1959, 152 pp.) by the Bureau of Social and Political Research of Michigan State University is not devoted to the county board of supervisors in Michigan. However, certain early pages (6-26) are devoted to a study of the constitutional and statutory provisions pertaining to the board. The basis of representation on the board is described, the legal limitations placed on its members explained, and the organization of the board laid out. The committee system under which the board operates is presented in detail, with particular emphasis on the status of the finance committee. The method of selection, powers, and functions of this committee are delineated. The annual meeting of the board of supervisors is discussed at length, and other board meetings are mentioned. In addition, the meeting procedures and rules are given consideration; special attention is given to records of meetings.

There is detailed examination of expense remuneration and compensation of supervisors. There follows a lengthy discussion of the general powers of Michigan counties as related to the board of supervisors. In this connection, there is specific treatment of the legislative powers of the board, along with processes involved in its exercise of those powers. Much detail is given about the board's powers in relation to townships.

Ohio

Chapter 23 in Francis R. Aumann and Harvey Walker's THE GOVERNMENT AND ADMINISTRATION OF OHIO (New York: Thomas Y. Crowell, 1956, 489 pp.) is devoted to the county and contains a good description of the composition and functions of the board of county commissioners.

A discussion of the composition of the board and methods of transacting business during meetings opens the section. An inclusive list of all duties performed by the board follows. The section of the state code which allows the county to enter into contracts with other district or municipal authorities is included, and the actual procedure is explained. The quasi-municipal powers delegated to the county in planning and zoning are discussed, and the reasons this authority was sought are given. Then the specific powers granted are listed. The work of the county department of welfare, which is appointed by the county board of commissioners, is explained. The administration of a county hospital by a group composed of the commissioners, a board of hospital trustees, and judicial officers is discussed. The authority of the board of commissioners to establish sanitation districts and construct a veterans' memorial building is briefly discussed. The section concludes with a list of other important board functions.

Oklahoma

Bertil L. Hanson, in "COUNTY COMMISSIONERS OF OKLAHOMA," an article in the *Midwest Journal of Political Science,* IX (November, 1965), 388-400, states that his purpose is to examine some inadequately investigated but commonly accepted assumptions regarding local politicians. The subjects of this examination are the county commissioners of Oklahoma.

First, Professor Hanson investigates why the office of commissioner is sought after. He analyzes its ability to satisfy a need for political activity and its function as a source of material reward. Next, he analyzes the effectiveness and ability of the commissioners. He explains why application of technical standards proves their performance to be inadequate in highway and finance work. Following this indictment, the author analyzes the attitude of the commissioners and the manner in which they perform their duties. He emphasizes the personal and subjective atmosphere in which official work is handled. In the last section of the paper, Dr. Hanson examines the effect the commissioners have on state politics. He explores two vehicles they might use in exerting influence: personal contributions of effort, money, or patronage; or lobbying the state government through their professional organization, the County Commissioners' Association. In both cases he concludes that the commissioners try to be influential only when they feel a personal stake is involved.

This article is a scathing indictment of the caliber of commissioners in Oklahoma counties. Hanson's conclusions seem very credible; they are based on interviews with and stated opinions of the commissioners and on investigation of the concrete results of their activity. But, as the author emphasizes so clearly throughout this article, the potential, either good or bad, possessed by these officials indicates that this area should be given additional attention. At the time of this publication, the author was a faculty member at Oklahoma State University.

Tennessee

The chapter devoted to county government in Lee S. Greene and Robert S. Avery's GOVERNMENT IN TENNESSEE (Knoxville: The University of Tennessee Press, 1966, 2nd ed., 371 pp.) contains a good discussion of the organization and operation of the county governing board.

The article of the constitution which prescribes the composition of the court (governing body) is analyzed. The qualifications for office and the relation of the board vis-à-vis the state are mentioned. The committee procedure which is used to conduct most business is described. A complete list of functions of the board is given.

Criticisms which have been leveled against the court are described. The main ones considered are size, representation, lack of continuity and leadership. Particular emphasis is given to the lack of a county executive. The example of Washington County which elects its chairman directly to the position is discussed. A contrasting example is given of Knox County where executive power is scattered, and executive authority must be shared.

Virginia

An article by Carrol Quenzel, "MAN ON THE SPOT," *The County Officer,* 27 (March 1962), 119, 138-139, discusses the role of the "tie breaker" on Virginia county governing boards. There is first a discussion of the relatively few county governing boards in the United States with an even number of members. Then Virginia legislation about tie breakers is discussed. The article is based on a questionnaire sent to these officials in Virginia counties. At the time it was written the author was Professor of History at Mary Washington College, University of Virginia.

ALSO TO BE NOTED—FOR ORGANIZATION: GOVERNING BOARDS:

Dave Miller, "Unique Police Jury System in Louisiana," *The County Officer,* 29 (October, 1964), 455, 460.

ORGANIZATION

Home Rule

United States

DIGEST OF COUNTY MANAGER CHARTERS AND LAWS (New York: National Municipal League, 10th edition, 1967) is primarily useful as a source book on county charters in the United States and on the constitutions and statutes that authorize them. The book is divided into four sections. The first is a state-by-state listing of the state constitutions permitting county manager governments. Second comes a brief summary of the model county charter which was prepared by the National Municipal League and a presentation of the text of suggested state legislation for optional forms of county government, issued by the Council of State Governments.

The main portion of the book is devoted to separate digests of the constitutional provisions, laws, and charters in the following states: California, Florida, Georgia, Louisiana, Maryland, Minnesota, Missouri, Montana, Nevada, New York, North Carolina,

North Dakota, Ohio, Oregon, Tennessee, Texas, Virginia, and Washington. These summaries contain data on the structure of government used in the charter counties of these states. The final section is a review of other counties which have appointive executives but do not have other governmental features which are necessary in order that the county can be considered as operating under the county manager plan.

This book is a compilation of data and very useful as a reference. It does not contain any explanation or analysis of the effectiveness or quality of the various charters.

MODEL COUNTY CHARTER (New York: National Municipal League, 1956, 71 pp.) is divided into two main sections: (1) an introduction by John E. Bebout, then Assistant Director, the National Municipal League, and (2) the text of the model county charter itself.

The extensive introduction performs two functions. First, Mr. Bebout describes the history of the county; then he reviews and analyzes its present position and its future against this background. He points out the change and development in functions performed and the county's past and present position in the scheme of intergovernmental relations, after which he describes the weaknesses and problems of county government. This description leads into his discussion of the purpose of the model charter. He explains that it is intended as an aid to reconstruction of county government. He analyzes the main features of the charter and points out where it may need to be qualified and where caution may be needed in adapting it to a specific county.

Each of the ten main sections in the charter itself relates to one of the following considerations: the powers of the county; the county council; county manager; administrative departments, offices and agencies, and advisors; financial procedures; county planning; nominations and elections; initiative and referendum; general provisions which cover bonding of officers, personal financial interest, right to attend county council meetings, prohibitions, amendments to the charter, and separability; and transitional provisions which explain how to handle the period during which the new charter is being instituted.

The model charter can be of great use to all people interested in the betterment of county government, both practitioners and scholars alike. In itself, the charter is very clear and well-written. Mr. Bebout's introduction additionally increases its usefulness by pointing out clearly how the model charter can be utilized to greatest benefit.

"HOME RULE CHARTER COUNTIES" in *American County Government,* 33 (April, 1968), 15-18, 59-60, written by Allen H. Moore and Susan Torrence, is the county-oriented corollary to their article, "State Action for County Home Rule," which appears in the same issue of this magazine and approaches the problem from the state level. (See following entry in this bibliography.) In this article on home rule counties, the authors investigate the charters which have been adopted, rather than the state provisions that authorize the use of charters.

They discuss the provisions in various charters which relate to legislative bodies, executive leadership, and the transition to the new charter government. In this explanation, they focus on descriptions of particular county charters. A useful table is included which lists the counties, their form of government, and the year of charter adoption.

This analytical summary of charter provisions provides a good outline and guide for those seeking adoption of a charter. The article points out the necessity for considering local conditions and adapting any plan to local circumstances. At the time of this publication, Mr. Moore was Assistant Director of Research at the National Association of Counties, and Susan Torrence was a NACO research associate.

"STATE ACTION FOR COUNTY HOME RULE," an article by Allen H. Moore and Susan Torrence in *American County Government,* 33 (April, 1968), 10-14, 59, is a look at home rule for counties from the perspective of the state's role in this plan.

In the beginning of the article, the authors point out the benefits which would accrue to the states from adoption of home rule for counties. Then they describe the legal provisions in force in the thirteen states which qualify as home rule states under Charles R. Adrian's definition of home rule: "the power granted to local units of government to frame, adopt, and amend charters for their government and to exercise powers of local self-government, subject to the constitution and general laws of the state." They consider the special laws used in five states authorizing home rule only for specific counties. They explain the procedure followed in most states for drafting and adopting a charter and conducting charter elections; they cite many examples. The authors compare the legal provisions in the various states which pertain to the structure of government in charter counties. They set forth what they believe to be the essential elements regarding organizing the government to be incorporated in a charter. Following this discussion, the authors turn to an explanation of modified home rule states. They compare the alternative forms which are provided in the different constitutions.

The article is a very good explanation and comparison of the different provisions for county home rule used in the states. At the time of this publication, Mr. Moore was Assistant Director of Research, National Association of Counties, and Susan Torrence was a NACO research associate.

Louisiana

The chapter on local government in Louisiana Legislative Council, THE GOVERNMENT OF LOUISIANA (Baton Rouge: 1951, 405 pp.), contains a very detailed section on home rule. The discussion opens with a brief description of the two possible types of home rule. Then the principal problems encountered in granting home rule to parishes and municipalities are explained.

Detailed descriptions are given of the amendments which granted home rule to Jefferson Parish and East Baton Rouge Parish. The discussions are concerned solely with the provisions of the amendments and do not describe how home rule has actually worked.

Michigan

A REPORT TO THE SPECIAL COUNTY GOVERNMENT STUDY COMMITTEE (Pontiac: 1958, 15 pp.) by Civic Research Incorporated describes and presents the texts of four defeated county home rule constitutional amendment proposals in

Michigan. Additionally, very brief mention is given of why the amendments were defeated. This publication is almost entirely descriptive and is based on primary sources.

New York

LOCAL GOVERNMENT: A BRIEF SUMMARY OF LOCAL GOVERNMENT STRUCTURE, ORGANIZATIONS AND FUNCTIONS IN NEW YORK STATE (Albany: June 1964, 13 pp.) is a publication of the New York State Office for Local Government. It deals primarily with home rule authorizations and other state enactments which affect local government.

First, a brief overview of the structure and functions of county government is presented. Then the report describes the provisions of the 1963 home rule amendment to the state constitution and the subsequent implementing legislation. The powers guaranteed to the counties by the bill of rights embodied in the amendment are listed and explained. A concise summary of the county charters in New York is included. The report also explains the constitutional tax and debt limits placed on the fifty-seven up-state counties.

In general, this study is a good summary of the legal limits within which New York State counties must operate. However, it is technical, and very little commentary and analysis are included.

Oregon

Orval Etter's article, "COUNTY HOME RULE IN OREGON," in the *Oregon Law Review,* 46 (April, 1967), 251-285, presents a very inclusive picture of home rule for Oregon counties. In addition to giving a general explanation, Mr. Etter cites specific county examples and draws comparisons with other states to substantiate his explanation.

The author begins by sketching the scope and facets of home rule in Oregon today. Then he describes the historical background of its development, emphasizing the relevant constitutional amendments and statutes. The next section focuses on the 1958 amendment authorizing counties to assume home rule. He then singles out for specific explanation various aspects of this amendment. First he explains the non-self-executing authorization and the resulting county home-rule enabling act. Next, Mr. Etter elaborates on the particular sentence in the amendment which gives counties authority over matters of county concern. He then describes the general grant of powers incorporated in the typical charter. He clarifies the distinction between matters of county, state, and city concern and describes how conflicts between two governments in the same territory—a home-rule county and a city—are resolved. He then explains the legal and political relations between a home rule county and cities within it. He points out and explains the extent of county authority over the structure of a home rule county and, in comparison, its lack of power to avoid functions prescribed by the state. Three final aspects of home rule discussed by Mr. Etter are judicial personnel and district attorneys, initiative and referendum, and local improvements. He concludes by describing the number of home rule charters that have been adopted in Oregon.

The main emphasis of this article is to explain the legal technicalities and aspects of county home rule. The author clarifies the various phases of the authorizations and then analyzes the effect they have on the operations of county government. Few general sources on home rule are listed and most of the citations are from the revised state statutes, the state constitution, and various county charters. Mr. Etter is an attorney and has been a consultant to seven county charter committees.

ALSO TO BE NOTED—FOR ORGANIZATION: HOME RULE:

General

County Supervisors Association of California, "National Association of County Officials' Policy Statement on County Home Rule," *The County Officer,* 27 (February, 1962), 67.

Leslie A. Glick, "County Home Rule Charters: How Much Interest?" *American County Government,* 31 (November, 1966), 10-12, 61.

Luther Gulick, "Home Rule and the Urban County," *The County Officer,* 23 (June, 1958), 114-115.

Bernard F. Hillenbrand, "County Home Rule—Absolutely Imperative!" *The County Officer,* 23 (April, 1958), 81.

"Home Rule is Reviewed and Its Problems Outlined by Speakers," *The County Officer,* 28 (September, 1963), 327-328.

Raymond Lathop, "County Home Rule: Our County Governments Must be Given More Authority to Act," *The County Officer,* 23 (April, 1958), 80, 93.

National Association of Counties, *The American County Action Program for Home Rule* (Washington: 1962, 102 pp.).

Kenneth Verburg, *Home Rule—What Is It: Pro and Con Arguments* (East Lansing: Michigan State University, Institute for Community Development, 1961, 9 pp.).

Individual States

Stanley Scott, *Home Rule for California's General Law Counties* (Berkeley: University of California, Bureau of Public Administration, 1958, 7 pp.).

ORGANIZATION

Officers and Special Boards

United States

Chapter 3 of Herbert S. Duncombe's COUNTY GOVERNMENT IN AMERICA (Washington, D.C.: National Association of Counties, Research Foundation, 1966, 288 pp.) considers county officers.

First, the author investigates three broad types of official governing bodies in use: county commissioner, township supervisor, and others. He points out the areas of the nation in which each is found. Then he describes the apportionment of county governing bodies in general and their organization, meetings, and compensation.

He describes the various types of powers granted to most counties: ordinance-making, fiscal, licensing and regulation, appointment, supervision and review of administration, and day-to-day administrative responsibilities.

Next, he discusses the independently elected "row" officers, listing them and pointing out trends in their assimilation into the government structure. In discussing elected or appointed executives, he describes the use of the county manager, county administrative officer, and county executive. He points out their differences and gives examples of where they are used. He gives a brief description of the conditions under which county employees work and describes associations of county officials.

Charts are included on the annual salary of county board members, the frequency of use of the independently-elected county offices, a comparison between the responsibility of the board and manager in four areas, and a list of counties of 250,000 or more population having a county administrator or executive.

Kentucky

DUTIES OF ELECTED COUNTY OFFICIALS (Frankfort: Legislative Research Commission, June 1966, 83 pp.), prepared by Minnie Sue Ripy and Sue Wheeler of the Legislative Research Commission staff, is primarily a source book on the statutory duties of the elected county officials. It includes a brief introduction, descriptions of twelve offices, and a discussion of the proposed constitution as it relates to county officials.

The introduction presents a general explanation of the constitutional and statutory provisions which pertain to the source of officials' power; required county officials; terms and qualifications; the legislature's power to add qualifications; bond and residence requirements; prohibitions against misfeasance, malfeasance, and nonfeasance; concurrent holding of state and federal offices; vacancies; and compensation. Focusing on these characteristics and emphasizing powers and duties, the body of the report describes various offices: county judge, justice of the peace, county attorney, county court clerk, county tax commissioner, sheriff, jailer, coroner, constable, surveyor, circuit court clerk, and commonwealth's attorney.

This report is a straightforward listing and description of these twelve elective offices. No analysis or prescription for change is included. As stated in the foreword, this report stems from numerous requests by local officials for information concerning their powers and duties. The report fulfills its purpose very well.

Maryland

The kinds of county officers and boards in Maryland are the subject of a chapter in a book by Jean E. Spencer, CONTEMPORARY LOCAL GOVERNMENT IN MARYLAND (College Park: University of Maryland, Bureau of Governmental Research, 1965, 116 pp.). The chapter begins with a discussion of the changing structure of county government, brought about by modification of existing county offices and creation of new ones. This discussion is followed by a general examination of the relationship of the county governing board and the various county officials and boards. In this connection, the author presents an organizational chart of the traditional form of county government in Maryland. This structure is discussed in terms of the three patterns of relationships of county officials and boards to the county governing board.

The author then turns to an examination of the roles of the various county officers and boards. There is a discussion and analysis of the powers, functions, and method of selection of each. The elective officers discussed at length are the sheriff, treasurer, and surveyor. The three methods of appointment of county officers and boards are explained, and the officers and boards selected by each method are considered. The first method, direct appointment by the governing board, involves the county attorney, clerk to the county commissioners, and auditor. Extensive examination is made of the variations in the role of the clerk from county to county. In addition to these traditional officials who are appointed by the governing board, there is a general exploration of the role of board-appointed, program-oriented officials and boards which vary in number and kinds from county to county. There follows a consideration of a second method – the county officers and boards which are appointed by the governor: the boards of education; elections boards; boards of license commissioners (for liquor licenses); county library boards; and directors of county civil defense programs. Finally, the book discusses officials and boards appointed jointly by state agencies and the county governing body. This method includes county health officers; county welfare boards; county welfare directors; and county supervisor of assessments.

Missouri

In Chapter XI on local government in his book, GOVERNMENT, POLITICS AND ADMINISTRATION IN MISSOURI (St. Louis: Educational Publishers, Inc., 1949, 261 pp.), Carl McCandless concisely describes the functions of all officers and boards serving in some or all counties in the state.

The following elective officers are found in all counties: clerk of county court, sheriff, clerk of circuit court, recorder of deeds, treasurer, assessor, collector of revenue, prosecuting attorney, superintendent of public schools, county surveyor, highway engineer, coroner, and public administrator. The author points out which offices may be combined in certain classes of counties and covers the method of selection, salary, and duties of each one.

Conversely, the following officers and boards are not found in all classes of counties and are appointive: county auditor, county counselor, board of equalization, county planning commission, board of park commissioners, superintendent of public welfare, and county highway commission. The author points out in which class of counties or in how many counties these officers are found. He covers the method of selection and duties of each office. Brief discussions are also included in this section on the organization and functions of county health units and on the procedure for supporting and managing county hospitals.

Washington

Stephen R. Mitchell has made a study of the political and social characteristics of certain county officials in the state of Washington in WASHINGTON COUNTY OFFICIALS, A POLITICAL PROFILE (Pullman: Washington State University, Division of Governmental Studies and Services, 1967, 12 pp.). The county officials included are: assessors, auditors, clerks, commissioners, coroners, prosecutors, sheriffs, school superintendents, superior court judges, and treasurers. The author presents and analyzes data on the following matters: level of education, age, occupation, religion, union affiliation, rating by officials of several factors contributing to political success, activities engaged in during general election campaigns, political party preference of parents and reasons for it. All this information is classified by party preference. The data were gained from a 1963 survey questionnaire sent to Washington county officials. Throughout the study the author engages in astute analysis of the data and pays particular attention to their political consequences. At the time of this publication, the author was Associate Professor of Political Science, University of Calgary.

ALSO TO BE NOTED—FOR ORGANIZATION: OFFICERS AND SPECIAL BOARDS:

General

"Community Relations Commissions," *American County Government,* 31 (March, 1966), 14.

"The County Official: A Composite Picture," *The County Officer,* 26 (March, 1961), 68-69.

Lindsay Cowen, "The Need for County Legal Departments," *American County Government,* 31 (April, 1966), 42-43.

"The Selection of an Assessor," *The County Officer,* 27 (June, 1962), 303-304.

United States Bureau of the Census, *Census of Governments, 1967: Popularly Elected Officials of State and Local Governments,* Vol. 6, No. 1 (Washington: 1968, 216 pp.).

Individual States

Colorado Legislative Council, *County Superintendents of Schools* (Denver: 1962, 36 pp.).

University of Indiana, Bureau of Government Research, *1959 Survey of Indiana Elected County Officials* (Bloomington: 1960, 31 pp.).

University of North Carolina, Institute of Government, *Calendar of Duties for County Officials* [in North Carolina] (Chapel Hill: 1966, 13 pp.).

University of Oklahoma, Bureau of Government Research, *Duties and Powers of County Officers in Oklahoma* (Norman: 1952, 52 pp.).

"Assessors Ask Appointive Status [in Oregon]," *OAC Bulletin,* 6 (June 12, 1964), 1, 4.

Claude J. Davis, *The County Assessor in West Virginia* (Morgantown: University of West Virginia, Bureau for Government Research, 1965, 42 pp.).

ORGANIZATION

Optional Forms

Ohio

"ALTERNATIVE FORMS OF COUNTY GOVERNMENT," in *Newsletter on County Government,* II (Cincinnati: Hamilton County Research Foundation, September, 1961, n. p.), is based on an analysis of Ohio's Optional Forms of County Government Law passed in 1961.

It explains the procedure to be followed in placing one of the options on the ballot and describes the alternative forms of structure allowed and the powers which the government may exercise. The report then points out the two major improvements the optional forms offer over the traditional form of county government. Next, the report outlines types of county manager government used in other states and compares them with the system allowed under the Ohio optional laws. The conclusion is that this optional forms statute does nothing to reduce the basic weaknesses in county government.

This article is a penetrating description and analysis of Ohio's system of optional forms of county government. It points out specifically both the strengths and weaknesses of the plan.

Virginia

New forms of county government which may be established in Virginia as a result of the Optional Forms Act of 1961 is the subject of a section of Frank K. Gibson and Edward S. Overman's COUNTY GOVERNMENT IN VIRGINIA (Charlottesville: League of Virginia Counties and University of Virginia, Bureau of Public Administration, 1961, 38 pp.). This section of the monograph discusses the structure of the four optional forms of county government established under the Act as amended. The principal options examined are the county manager and the county executive forms. The county board form and the urban county form are also mentioned.

ALSO TO BE NOTED—FOR ORGANIZATION: OPTIONAL FORMS:

University of Oklahoma, Bureau of Government Research, *Optional Forms of County Government* (Norman: 1955, 12 pp.).

POLITICS

General

United States

AMERICAN STATE POLITICS: READINGS FOR COMPARATIVE ANALYSIS (New York: Thomas Y. Crowell, 1966, 489 pp.), edited by Frank Munger, is an anthology of thirty-one articles. Four contain material relevant to the county. They are: Hugh D. Price, "The Negro and Florida Politics, 1944-1954," 26-45 (*see* Politics—Elections: Florida); Frank J. Sorauf, "State Patronage in a Rural County," 130-140; Frank Munger, "Community Power and Metropolitan Decision-Making," 187-211; and V. O. Key, Jr., "Partisanship and County Office: The Case of Ohio," 274-289 (*see* Politics—Political Parties: Ohio). The Munger and Sorauf articles do not appear separately in this bibliography as they deal with individual counties.

As Professor Munger states in the preface, this volume is an attempt to collect some of the writings and studies of state and local politics in order to impose a pattern upon them. He has grouped the articles in five sections, four being regional divisions and one on comparative state politics.

Border States

John H. Fenton in his book, POLITICS IN THE BORDER STATES (New Orleans: The Hauser Press, 1957, 230 pp.), discusses political organization and political change in Maryland, West Virginia, Kentucky, and Missouri. His coverage of the county in all four states is good, and his descriptions of county activity in Kentucky and West Virginia are particularly useful and will be discussed in detail in separate headings under those two states. (*See* Politics – General: Kentucky; West Virginia.)

When discussing Missouri, the author explains the dominance of city machines in the state. However, he notes that agricultural interests dominate in the counties and discusses how they exert influence.

In the chapters on Maryland, Professor Fenton explains why some counties are dominated by the Republicans. He points out the influence of political party patronage in the control of a county, explains how the system of representation in the legislature affects the counties, and points out the influence of the statewide organization in these units. In a footnote he describes and explains the effects of the state's county unit law on the primaries.

When analyzing the political organization in these states, the author often uses case studies of particular counties or cities. He tells who the powerful people in the county are and why they have their power, and he explains the relation between the county political leaders and the state administration and organization, particularly in his discussions of Kentucky and West Virginia. Conscious effort is made throughout the book to show universals which apply to the entire region, and the organization and activity of the four states are often compared and contrasted.

This is a very well-written, interesting book, both descriptive and analytical. The author has combined the formal and informal aspects of politics to provide a very complete picture. References to the county are always clear and explicit.

The author states in his bibliography that the bulk of the data for the book came from interviews with political, farm, labor and business leaders in the four states. He later wrote a similar book,

Midwest Politics, which is included later in this commentary. (*See* Politics—General: Midwest.) At the time of this publication, the author was Assistant Professor of Political Science, Michigan State University.

New England

In his book, NEW ENGLAND STATE POLITICS (Princeton: Princeton University Press, 1959, 348 pp.), Duane Lockard examines Vermont, New Hampshire, Maine, Massachusetts, Rhode Island, and Connecticut. Because of the relative unimportance of the county in New England, very little coverage is given to it in this book. Also, since the author is more interested in politics at the state level, only a limited amount of information is given about the towns.

Professor Lockard includes a brief explanation of the town system in New England at the beginning of the book, noting the practice of according representation to each town in the state legislatures and the fact that the towns have powers usually allotted to counties in other states.

Throughout the book the author draws comparisons among these New England states themselves as well as between them and the politics in the southern states as discussed by V. O. Key. Factors considered in Lockard's discussions of all six states are localism in the legislature and the influence of friends and neighbors in elections.

The author discusses the strength or weakness of local party organizations in each of the New England states. In discussing Vermont, he points out areas of local strength of the Proctor machine. He contrasts the strong Republican organizations in the towns with the Democratic Party's lack of effort to reach down to this level. Maps are included which show county strengths of the two parties. Town representation in the legislature is considered. The discussion of Maine also emphasizes the "friends and neighbors" influence. The author also briefly discusses the use and importance of local organizations to Republican candidates and points out the activity and vitality of these party groups. This liveliness of the Republican local organizations is contrasted with the atrophy of local Democratic organizations. The author examines the weakness of party organizations in Massachusetts, emphasizing the lack of contacts between state and local units in the Democratic Party. He mentions the Republican practice of collecting money statewide and passing it on to town committees. In Massachusetts there is little local legislation. In discussing Rhode Island, Professor Lockard describes the strength of local party organizations in the state Republican Party, and emphasizes that the party is well-integrated from top to bottom. The Democratic organization is even more highly integrated and powerful. Lockard discusses sanctions the state can use against local units. He points out the dominance of small town members of the legislature. He discusses why rural overrepresentation and local legislation are particularly large problems in Connecticut.

Although a very interesting, well-written book, *New England State Politics* does not provide much information on either the county or the town. For all states, brief mention is usually given to whether local party units are weak or strong, but too often the author does not distinguish between city, town, or county units. Also a common feature discussed about all states is the influence of friends and neighbors in elections; another is town representation in the legislature, which usually leads to rural overrepresentation. Dr. Lockard used V. O. Key's *American State Politics* and *Southern Politics* (the latter included in this bibliography) as references and base points of comparison. He seems to have relied, too, for much of his information, on his own experience as a member of the Connecticut Senate and on interviews with people active in New England politics. At the time of this publication, the author was a political science faculty member at Connecticut College.

Midwest

John H. Fenton's MIDWEST POLITICS (New York: Holt, Rinehart and Winston, 1966, 244 pp.) is an inquiry into the politics of six midwest states: Michigan, Wisconsin, Minnesota, Ohio, Indiana, and Illinois. The author divides these states into two groups:

the issue-oriented parties states – Michigan, Wisconsin, and Minnesota; the traditional or job-oriented parties states – Ohio, Indiana, and Illinois.

Although none of the sections on the individual states includes an extensive description of county politics, they all contain extremely interesting incidents and illustrations derived from county activity. Voting patterns and changes are presented by counties. The material for each of these states is outlined in separate entries under the states themselves in this bibliography. (*See* Politics – General: Illinois, Indiana, Michigan, Minnesota, Ohio, and Wisconsin.)

The author has done an excellent job of describing and analyzing politics in these states. Much of the information came from interviews and discussions with people possessing first-hand knowledge of politics. Also much of his data on Ohio, Indiana, Wisconsin, and Minnesota was supplied by Louis Harris and Associates. At the time of this publication, the author was Professor of Government, University of Massachusetts.

South

V. O. Key, Jr., in his book, SOUTHERN POLITICS IN STATE AND NATION (New York: Random House, 1962, 675 pp.), presents very clearly the position and role of the county in the party machinery and organization of the South. The book is divided into two sections. The first deals with each state individually and the second with certain aspects common to politics in the South, such as factionalism, election machinery, and party organization. The county is considered in both sections.

In the second section of the book, Professor Key begins with a discussion of the Republican Party in the South. He compares the different geographic areas in which Republican strength is concentrated and discusses the scattered local control possessed by the party. When discussing one-party factionalism, he points out the strength that control of a county can give a would-be leader, emphasizing Georgia's county-unit system. He describes the social and economic characteristics of counties, which determine which party dominates and the extent of its control.

The author describes why, in the South, the party organization usually becomes merely a framework for intraparty factional and personal competition. He points out that when the Republican Party is active in a county, this activity usually spurs greater Democratic activity. He compares the advantages accruing from control of local party machinery in the various states, explaining the variance of control according to the functions assigned to the party. He explains why at the lower level, Democratic committees display the widest variance in favoritism toward candidates. He analyzes the differences in competition for party posts, emphasizing the importance of the control or lack of control that patronage makes. He then compares and contrasts the organization and government of the party in these states and explains why they often become one-man shows. He shows how campaigns are organized in the counties. When discussing nominations, he compares the primary and the convention systems and points out the effect of either on county activity.

Professor Key considers the control over and management of elections by the party officials in six southern states. He discusses the decentralization of election administration by the parties and explains why state appointment of election officials in general elections results in Democratic control even in Republican counties. He illustrates the discussion with appropriate examples from the various states.

The author describes the suffrage restrictions in effect in the South. He points out which county officials have responsibility for enforcing these restrictions in the various states. He explains how county boards of registration and elections use their powers against the Negro. He emphasizes the informal nature of the entire registration process, discusses collection of poll taxes in the counties, and analyzes the factors associated with high poll taxes in the counties.

Professor Key presents particularly interesting descriptions of the county's role in the following states: Virginia, Alabama, Tennessee, Georgia, Arkansas, and Florida. These states are considered in separate entries. (*See* Politics—General: Alabama, Arkansas, Florida, Georgia, Tennessee, and Virginia.)

When he discusses South Carolina, Professor Key emphasizes the influence of localism, or "friends and neighbors." Then he discusses the power exercised by the county legislative delegation in the state legislature itself and at the county level. He points out the inordinate influence in local affairs exercised by the senator from the county. In his discussion of Louisiana, Key explains the prominent position of the parish sheriff in local politics. Regarding North Carolina, Professor Key points out the effect Republican strength has on increasing the activity of the Democratic organization in counties. He mentions the sectional alignment of counties. He explains the importance of and competition for the sheriff's office in Mississippi counties. He points out the decentralization of county politics and its usual divorce from state politics. He explains why the machinery is often built around persons other than local officials. In his discussion of Texas, he points out the importance of county demagogues to the statewide factional organizations. He emphasizes the effect of the bloc votes in these counties for statewide races.

This book gives an excellent description and penetrating analysis of county politics in the South. Professor Key emphasizes the informal, actual operations over the formal structure and machinery. He frequently turns to quoted remarks from various local leaders to explain the operation. Specific examples from different counties are often given. Also, Key frequently points out the connection between the party and the government structure; he identifies the important persons and offices in the counties. Professor Key seems to rely mainly on primary sources for his information. Much of his data were collected through interviews with party workers and politically knowledgeable people. He often cites newspaper articles regarding specific incidents. At the time of this publication, the author was Professor of Government, Harvard University.

West

WESTERN POLITICS (Salt Lake City: University of Utah Press, 1961, 401 pp.), edited by Frank H. Jonas, contains chapters on thirteen western states, each written by an authority on the particular state. The states covered are: Alaska, Arizona, California, Colorado, Hawaii, Idaho, Montana, Nevada, New Mexico, Oregon, Utah, Washington, and Wyoming. These sections vary in value, but all of them contain some material on the county. Most of the material pertinent to the county is on parties, elections, and the legislature. Because of the limited amount of relevant material, separate entries have not been made in this bibliography.

The section on Alaska was written by Herman Slotnick. The author discusses the problems of local government in Alaska which he emphasizes still await solution. He explains the constitutional provisions for local government and the reasons why the framers chose the borough instead of the county, emphasizing their desire not to bind local government by traditional organization and to make it more flexible and innovative. He lists questions to be considered in setting up a local government system. He outlines the warning by W. Brooke Graves to Alaskans against establishing a large number of boroughs. The author analyzes the sources of resistance to establishment of boroughs and explains the establishment and responsibilities of the Local Affairs Agency in the governor's office.

Professor Ross R. Rice wrote the section on Arizona. He lists the different school districts in the state and points out that counties may operate junior colleges. Election procedure is outlined, the importance of patronage in the state noted, and efforts by state and county employees to establish a statewide merit system emphasized. He discusses the effect of the rise of the Better Government Association in Maricopa County on the decline in dispensation of patronage by elected Democratic officeholders in the county. He describes the control over the county government wielded by the BGA and its progress in reforming the government. He also mentions the role of pressure groups, such as a taxpayers association, in Maricopa County. He explains the system of apportionment of legislative seats; and includes a map of counties and congressional districts. In general, this section is primarily descriptive and concerned with formal structural characteristics. However, Professor Rice does provide analytical material in his discussion of Maricopa County.

Professor Totton J. Anderson prepared the section on California. He points out the limitations on party activity in the state and explains the composition of county committees. He shows that in counties with urban populations permanent offices are usually maintained and lists their functions. He notes the relative inactivity of other county committees and suggests that activity may be increased by recently instituted election-law changes. He discusses the effect of the apportionment of the legislature on the counties and includes a map of counties and congressional districts. The material relating to the county in this section is limited and concerned primarily with structure and formal characteristics. However, the author's discussion of the effects of election-law changes on the activity of county committees is analytical.

The section on Colorado is the work of Curtis Martin. It contains only a limited amount of material relevant to counties. Professor Martin describes the organization of parties at the county level and explains the nominating procedure for county office. He points out the detailed and specific statutory regulations regarding nomination and election of county officials. He describes the method of choosing county central committees and points out their independence. He discusses what effect the change to a four-year term for county and state officials may have on citizen interest. A chart of party organization in the state is included. He notes the benefit gained by rural counties under the system of apportionment. In general, Professor Martin describes formal, structural characteristics of county politics. Little attention is given to the informal and personal aspects.

Norman Meller and Daniel W. Tuttle, Jr., prepared the section on Hawaii. They present a very good description of the island geography of the counties and point out the effect of areal factors on the distinctive character of the City and County of Honolulu. They describe the centralized manner of conducting elections in Hawaii, emphasizing the more limited role played by the county here than in other states. They outline the organizational hierarchy of the parties and emphasize and explain the importance of legislative politics in local government. The effect of the apportionment system on the county is described. They mention the use of the initiative and referendum in the City and County of Honolulu. A map of the counties and congressional districts is included. As with most of the other sections in this book, the authors use primarily a descriptive approach and limit themselves to structural and formal characteristics of county government and politics.

Thomas Payne, author of the section on Montana, explains the decentralized character of election administration, emphasizing that the election machinery is largely operated by each county's board of commissioners and clerk. He lists the election duties of each of these offices. The author explains the method of selection and functions of the county committee and contrasts the actual activity of this body with that prescribed in theory. He explains the undue representation accorded to counties with small populations in the legislature, particularly in the senate. A map of counties and congressional districts is included. Although only limited material is included on the county, mainly a description of structure, the author has injected analysis in his discussion of the party organization.

The section on New Mexico is by Frederick C. Irion and contains only one item of relevance to the county – apportionment. The author explains the constitutional amendment on apportionment adopted in 1949 and its effect on county representation. A map of counties and congressional districts is included.

The section dealing with Nevada was prepared by Don W. Driggs. It presents very little material about counties. It gives a quite detailed description of the apportionment system and how it greatly overrepresents the rural counties. A map of Nevada counties and congressional districts is included.

Boyd A. Martin, author of the section on Idaho, gives only limited attention to the county. He identifies the county election officials, the method of their selection, and their functions. He outlines the formal party organization at the county level, points out the effect of apportionment of the legislature on the county, and indicates the importance of friendship rather than party label in these county legislative elections. A map of counties and congressional districts is included. The material on the county in this section is entirely descriptive and devoted to structural, legal characteristics of county politics.

John M. Swarthout is the author of the section on Oregon. He outlines the party structure of the state, pointing out the position of the county committee. He explains the system of apportionment in the legislature and the representation enjoyed by the counties. A map of counties and congressional districts is included. This section is of limited value to a study of counties. The material is of a descriptive nature and concerned wholly with structure and formal characteristics.

Frank H. Jonas wrote the section on Utah. The poor relations between the county and state committees are described, and the great influence exercised by the Salt Lake County organization is pointed out. A map of counties and congressional districts is included. Although the amount of material relevant to the county is extremely limited, the author's discussion and analysis of the relations between the county and state organizations are very useful.

Hugh A. Bone prepared the section on Washington. His discussion of party organization at the county level is complete. He points out the primary functions of the county chairmen and describes the method of selection of the county committees and county representation in the state committee. He describes the use of county commissioner districts as political subdivisions in some of the larger counties and emphasizes the partisan election of commissioners and the patronage they have to dispense. He discusses the widely varying uses of the county committees throughout the state. A map of counties and congressional districts is included. Most of the material on the county centers on structural and legal descriptions, but coverage of the connection between the party and the commissioners is analytical and extremely useful.

In his section on Wyoming, Charles P. Beall explains the difficulties the county political organizations encounter in trying to fill the ticket of county offices, particularly in securing candidates for the office of coroner. He describes the long and arduous process engaged in by certain counties in this quest. He lists the election duties of the board of county commissioners, emphasizing its contacts with party committees in performing these duties, and describes the organization of the county committees and lists their functions and primary methods of raising money. A chart of the political party structure in Wyoming is included. He points out the strength enjoyed by rural counties because of their overrepresentation in the legislature. A map of counties and congressional districts and another showing the Democratic and Republican counties are included. The author's discussion of the party activity is analytical, particularly when concerned with nominating candidates for county office. His description of the connection between the county governing body and the party in the election process is very worthwhile.

It is difficult to give a general commentary on this book, since each section was written by a different author. Usually the articles are quite descriptive, and many of them are at least somewhat analytical. Since each article was written by an individual familiar with the politics of his state, much of the material is obviously based on the writer's personal knowledge. Each author submitted a bibliography, primarily of journal and magazine articles. In the preface, Professor Jonas acknowledges the information supplied to the authors by politicians, public officials, and other knowledgeable people.

Alabama

In his discussion of Alabama in SOUTHERN POLITICS IN STATE AND NATION (New York: Random House, 1962, 675 pp.), V. O. Key, Jr., analyzes the position of the county leadership in politics. He describes the importance of the "friends and neighbors" pull and analyzes the consequent role of local support in building statewide followings. He describes the voter confusion at the county level as a result of this transient, fluid character of politics. He goes on to describe the more independent role of county machines. He discusses the key position of the probate judge, who is usually the leader of the dominant faction in the county and often the patriarch of the county. He explains why the judge's support is eagerly sought by candidates. Professor Key analyzes the decision process followed by the probate judge in deciding which candidate to back for governor and the importance, both to the county and to the personal status of the county judge, of backing the winner. He analyzes the middle position of county organizations in Alabama as compared to other southern states and explains why county groups are or are not powerful.

Arkansas

Arkansas is one of the southern states discussed by V. O. Key, Jr., in SOUTHERN POLITICS IN STATE AND NATION (New York: Random House, 1962, 675 pp.).

Professor Key discusses how the formation of statewide factions becomes to a large degree a matter of winning the support of local leaders because of the absence of broad and continuing issues and dominating personalities around which factions might coalesce. Thus, local potentates loom larger in Arkansas than in most southern states.

The author discusses the inner machinations and processes of machine counties, distinguishing between those which choose only a favorite candidate and use their influence to get him elected and those which manipulate the election count and returns for a consideration. He explains why the machines of the delta counties depend fundamentally on the relation of economic dependence between landlord and tenant and identifies other machine counties in the state. He explains how these deliverable counties sometimes trade off among themselves for reciprocal support of candidates.

The author documents the attempt of returning veterans after World War II to gain control of Garland County. He explains how the established machine insured that beneficiaries of its organization were held in line by using control of road and drainage work to keep the big planters in its camp. He discusses how in one county the organization leader, a county judge, and the Democratic county chairman announced that GI's would be excluded from the primary and how this led to action by the state committee to discredit barring of participation.

Colorado

COLORADO POLITICS (Denver: Big Mountain Press, 1960, 87 pp.), written by Crutis Martin, contains scattered references to counties. Particular attention is given to the role of county central committees in primary elections. At the time of this publication, the author was Professor of Political Science, University of Colorado.

Delaware

Chapter 3 of Paul Dolan's book, THE GOVERNMENT AND ADMINISTRATION OF DELAWARE (New York: Thomas Y. Crowell, 1956, 396 pp.), contains a detailed discussion of the county's political organization and activity. First, Professor Dolan outlines the effect of "countyism" on party control. He then discusses the party organization at the local level, including separate descriptions of the Republican and Democratic county committees. To complete his treatment of the party organization he analyzes the role of the county in the state committee. He describes the primary and convention systems of nomination, focusing on the inordinately strong role of the county in these procedures. The chapter also includes a detailed description of the registration and election machinery.

Florida

V. O. Key, Jr., makes some interesting comments on the county in his section on Florida in SOUTHERN POLITICS IN STATE AND NATION (New York: Random House, 1962, 675 pp.). He explains why the atomization of politics in this state means that each candidate for county office usually runs without collaboration with other local candidates. He also points out that few politicians exert real influence beyond their own county, and that those who can deliver their home county are few.

The author describes why the potency of the "courthouse ring" in state races is usually greatly exaggerated, emphasizing that normally there seems to be no "courthouse ring." He points out that it is each official for himself and that no single official tends to dominate county politics, as does the probate judge in many Alabama counties. He emphasizes that the local political structure provides no effective base for construction of a state factional organization composed of local rings and points out the exceptions to this general trend.

Georgia

Joseph L. Bernd, in GRASS ROOTS POLITICS IN GEORGIA (Atlanta: Emory University, Research Committee, 1960, 172 pp.), discusses, among other topics, elections, the impact of the county unit system (later abolished), county political leadership, interest group activity, and campaigning. Only a small portion of the book is devoted to counties, but the pertinent sections are quite good. Socio-economic factors and their influence on politics are discussed, and the number, geographical area, and population of counties are related to politics in the state. The monograph also discusses the conformance of political leaders in the state to community mores.

Chapter 4 on the political process in Georgia in Cullen B. Gosnell and C. David Anderson's book, THE GOVERNMENT AND ADMINISTRATION OF GEORGIA (New York: Thomas Y. Crowell, 1956, 403 pp.), deserves attention. In the discussion of the organization of the Democratic Party, the authors describe the representation of the county at the state Democratic convention and on the state executive committee and congressional district committees. Brief descriptions of the composition and functions of the county executive committees are also included. In the very limited space devoted to Republican politics, the authors discuss the county convention.

The importance of the political discussion in the book, however, derives from the emphasis given to the county unit system which was abolished after the writing of this book. The authors describe the historical development of the system, its operation, and effect on the nomination procedure. Mention is given to the chief arguments regarding its use. The steps in the fight to abolish the system by its opponents are described.

The discussion of Georgia in V. O. Key, Jr.'s SOUTHERN POLITICS IN STATE AND NATION (New York: Random House, 1962, 675 pp.) contains useful information on the county. In fact, one of the most interesting aspects of Georgia's politics is rural county hegemony. Professor Key explains how the Talmadge and anti-Talmadge cleavage divides the counties with large cities from those completely rural or having only small towns. He explains the advantage enjoyed by counties of small population under the county-unit system and how it is exploited by state factional politicians. He traces the historical reasons for this rural *vs.* populous county antagonism. He points out the influence the county unit system gives rural counties in the choice of governor.

Professor Key describes how the county-unit system operates

and its legal basis, analyzes the degree of deflation of the popular vote it causes in populous counties, and explains the effect of the system on methods of campaign organization and management. He discusses why it inflates the importance of the county organization and officeholders who can deliver votes in rural counties. He describes the methods used by the state organization in dealing with leaders in critical counties, emphasizing the importance in this process of "Atlanta" money. This, he explains, leads to a feeling in Georgia of the dominant hold of county machines. Another important factor he mentions in winning elections in the county is control of the election machinery by some local leaders. A chart is included that compares unit vote with population.

Illinois

Illinois is one of the six states described and analyzed by John H. Fenton in his book, MIDWEST POLITICS (New York: Holt, Rinehart and Winston, 1966, 244 pp.). He briefly analyzes the unique character of the Chicago-Cook County Democratic Party organization. He explains the importance of patronage in the politics of the rest of the state's counties. He analyzes the tendency of voters in low-income counties to vote for organization candidates and compares this with the situation in Kentucky. A map of the Democratic and Republican counties in the presidential elections, 1932-1960, is included. Also there is a graph comparing the voting patterns in Cook County, suburban Cook County, Chicago, downstate, and statewide.

Austin Ranney, in ILLINOIS POLITICS (New York: New York University Press, 1960, 64 pp.), makes only scattered references to county involvement in political parties and elections. Also much of the information has to do with the county as a geographic unit for political party organization, rather than with county politics. There is a discussion of how Cook County differs in political party organization and "politics" from the "downstate" counties. The author lays out a complex organizational chart of the political party, showing the institutional relations of the county organization to the rest of the state party organization. Attention is given to county administration of elections; the roles of various county officers in election administration are spelled out. The author discusses the role of the county party chairman in the dispensing of patronage. The methods of selecting county committeemen and county delegations to the state party conventions are also mentioned. In addition, a map showing the voting records of county voters in the presidential and gubernatorial elections from 1948 to 1956 is presented.

Professor Ranney largely describes the formal aspects of political party organization and elections. There is no analysis of political behavior of county voters or county officers. The relationship of county governmental officers to the county political party organization of their respective parties is not mentioned. The monograph makes use of many primary sources, particularly statutes and voting data, but secondary sources are also used. At the time he wrote this work, the author was Professor of Political Science, University of Illinois.

Indiana

The discussion of county politics in Indiana in John H. Fenton's MIDWEST POLITICS (New York: Holt, Rinehart and Winston, 1966, 244 pp.) contains information both on voting patterns and on party organization. Three maps of the state use county breakdowns: Democratic and Republican counties in presidential elections, 1932-1960; metropolitan counties and counties won by Republican and Democratic candidates in 1960; and Democratic gains in 1958, 1960, and 1962. A graph compares metropolitan counties, nonmetropolitan counties, and the total state voting patterns. In the text, the voting strength of the two parties is analyzed on a county basis.

Professor Fenton explains the Democratic Party procedure of letting the franchises for sale of license plates to county Democratic organizations as a method of fund-raising. He also explains the state organization's assessment of county groups and discusses why the county groups usually paid these assessments. He discusses the organization of the Republican Party, outlining its hierarchy, and explains the power of the people who hold party positions at all levels.

Kentucky

John H. Fenton's book, POLITICS IN THE BORDER STATES (New Orleans: The Hauser Press, 1957, 230 pp.), contains a very good discussion of the role and importance of the county in Kentucky political activity. Professor Fenton describes the five broad classes of people who are active in day-to-day politics at the county level, and also explains the influence of interest groups at this level. He utilizes case studies of three different counties to discuss the activity of the professional politician and those interested in offices and contracts. He explains how party bosses at the county level secure and maintain their influence, and he gives particular emphasis to the use of government patronage and to private business power. He discusses the post of administration man, the representative of the statewide political organization, in the county. He analyzes the power of this man, especially as a dispenser of patronage and favors.

Professor Fenton analyzes the importance of family in county politics and the power and importance of the position of county judge. The importance of maintaining close ties with business, labor, and state government leaders is emphasized. One of the case studies points out the political power at the county level which can accrue from economic power. In general, the author very completely explains the existence and influence of the organization at the county level. The connection between the political organization and the government is constantly defined. The three case studies are of Nelson, Harlan, and Trigg counties.

Maine

The sections of David B. Walker's A MAINE PROFILE; SOME CONDITIONS OF HER POLITICAL SYSTEM (Brunswick: Bowdoin College, Bureau for Research in Municipal Government, 1964, 55 pp.) that are relevant to counties start with a view of county government structure and emphasize elected officials. Discussions follow of parties, patronage, representation, and campaigning. The section on representation is the most extensive and is concerned with reapportionment and its effects on county government. At the time of this publication, the author was Assistant Professor of Government, Bowdoin College.

Massachusetts

MASSACHUSETTS POLITICS (Medford: The Tufts Civic Education Center, Tufts University, 1960, 85 pp.), by Earl Latham and George Goodwin, Jr., is a well-written and interesting picture of politics in that state. However, only two very brief references are made to the county. House seats are apportioned among the counties, and county officials are nominated in the state primary in September. The text, which was an outgrowth of courses given by the authors at Tufts University, contains no source citations. However, the authors do include a list of selected readings on Massachusetts government, politics, and politicians at the end of the book.

Michigan

Michigan is one of the six states described and analyzed by John H. Fenton in his book, MIDWEST POLITICS (New York: Holt, Rinehart and Winston, 1966, 244 pp.). Two useful maps that show a county-by-county breakdown of voting patterns are included. The first shows how Michigan geographically remained Republican even while Democrats were winning gubernatorial elections, 1948-1962. The second presents a county-by-county picture of Michigan becoming a two-party state via these gubernatorial elections, 1946-1962.

In discussing Democratic politics in the state, Professor Fenton explains how and why labor became active in county politics, particularly in Wayne County, and points out how control of the Wayne County delegation can influence statewide politics. He points out the importance of patronage in rural counties and discusses the conflict between the rural and urban counties. He analyzes the electoral strength of the Republicans by county. He explains that although the population trends bode ill for continued Democratic gains, the strong organization of the Democratic Party at the county level may offset this Republican edge.

Stephen B. and Vera H. Sarasohn, in POLITICAL PARTY PATTERNS IN MICHIGAN (Detroit: Wayne State University Press, 1957, 76 pp.), react against a persistent tradition of formalism in the study of political parties. They present a personal, dynamic view of the alliances, leadership, and adaptive processes of parties in Michigan, although they do consider the more formal aspects in order to insure a balanced treatment.

The narrative presentation does not call for separate chapters on the formal operation of the party at the various levels; thus, there is no separate chapter on the county. However, the county's importance and central position in the struggle for control of party cause it to be discussed often and extensively throughout the text.

Instead of relying on a formal, structural approach to political organization in laying out the book, the authors have used an historical scheme. They describe the task of factions and the role of the large counties in their creation, and analyze the big-county dominance of the three or four largest counties in state convention politics. After this introduction, they dissect and analyze the more important pre-depression factional county-based organizations in the Republican Party which were based on patronage. They point out the effect of the Depression on politics.

Then the authors describe the new politics of the Republicans after the Depression. They analyze the recurrence of the large county domination, the methods by which the factional leaders assured themselves control of the county delegations, and the importance of governmental contacts at all levels to insure this control. They describe and analyze at length the role of the automobile companies in these county delegations.

A similar analysis follows of the Democrats and their new politics. The authors describe how the first Democratic leader after the Depression built up his organization around control of the county highway commissions. They describe the battle for control of the Wayne County delegation and analyze the build-up and expansion of labor dominance in this fight. They constantly reiterate the benefits derived from labor cooperation in maintaining control. In general, the main theme of the book centers around the how and why of the growth and decline of the various county-based factions in the two parties in Michigan.

This book provides a fascinating insight into the actual operation of party organization. A discussion of what should happen is discarded in favor of an analysis of what actually does happen. The importance of the leaders in tying together the government and the party is constantly stressed. By combining complete analysis with a historical development, the authors have pointed out many problems and conditions of party organization.

Stephen B. and Vera H. Sarasohn were connected with the Department of Political Science, Wayne State University, when they wrote this study. Some of the material was obtained through private interviews, but the study is based to a great extent upon the political news in Michigan newspapers, particularly Detroit daily publications.

Minnesota

Minnesota is one of the six states discussed in John H. Fenton's MIDWEST POLITICS (New York: Holt, Rinehart and Winston, 1966, 244 pp.). Two interesting maps of the state are included. One shows Minnesota's native Protestant counties and the second shows the Republican counties in gubernatorial elections, 1946-1962. A graph charts voting trends in metropolitan and nonmetropolitan counties and in the entire state. The author discusses the Minnesota Commission of Public Safety established in 1918 as a campaign arm of the governor and points out that it had agencies in every county. He notes the trends in county voting in the 1948 and 1958 elections.

G. Theodore Mitau's book, POLITICS IN MINNESOTA (Minneapolis: University of Minnesota Press, 1960, 140 pp.), is an interesting and worthwhile study on Minnesota politics in general. However, it does not deal directly with the county's role in Minnesota's politics and consequently there is little material on the county itself. The most interesting section of the book relating to counties is on the organization and activities of farm lobbies. The author explains and analyzes the central role of the county in the organization of the Farm Bureau and the Minnesota Farmers Union.

The structural and legal aspects of county election activity are presented briefly. Also, Professor Mitau discusses the structural features of county political organization and the primary party functions performed at the county level. He combines description and analysis very well in this book on Minnesota politics. Although he does not cite any sources in the text, he has included an extensive bibliography, mainly secondary references, at the end of the volume. At the time of this publication, the author was Professor of Political Science, Macalester College.

New York

NEW YORK POLITICS (New York: New York University Press, 1960, 80 pp.) by Frank J. Munger and Ralph A. Straetz is a brief monograph published under the auspices of the Citizenship Clearing House. The study is concerned almost equally with New York City and upstate New York in general. No one section is devoted to the county specifically, but its importance as a unit of political organization both in New York City and in rural areas of the state is brought out throughout the work.

The discussion of New York City politics centers around Tammany Hall, the New York County organization of Carmen DeSapio. The authors describe and analyze the power held and wielded by this organization locally as well as in state and national politics. Comparisons are drawn between the power of DeSapio and the New York County organization and that of other county leaders in New York City and upstate. The role of patronage in the activity and strength of the county organizations is pointed out. The authors also discuss the problems and weaknesses of the Republican county organizations in New York City.

When discussing upstate politics, the authors analyze the unbeatable power of the Republicans in controlling county governments because of their great political strength in the counties. A map is included showing the party strength in the upstate counties.

The authors also describe the legal and structural organization of the party committees and point out the representation of the county in the state committee. They emphasize the power held by the county leaders, because of the use of the convention system, in the selection of nominees for governor and other statewide offices.

In this interesting and worthwhile study, the authors have described the operation of political activity in New York, presenting penetrating and insightful analysis of the informal and extra-legal aspects of politics. Particularly commendable is their portrayal of the connection between the party organization and the government itself.

Very few sources are cited in the text of the study, but the authors have included a brief list of selected readings on New York politics in the appendix. At the time of this publication, Munger was connected with Syracuse University and Straetz with New York University.

Ohio

One of the better coverages of county activity in John H. Fenton's MIDWEST POLITICS (New York: Holt, Rinehart and Winston, 1966, 244 pp.) occurs in the discussion of Ohio politics.

Four maps of voting patterns are included: Republican counties, 1940-1960; Republican voters, Civil War Republicans, farmers, and Germans; Democratic counties, presidential elections, 1932-1960; and Democratic voters, foreign-born and Civil War Democrats. A graph compares the voting patterns of metropolitan counties and of the state. This section contains a county analysis of Democratic and Republican strength up to 1960.

Professor Fenton describes the party organizations thoroughly. He discusses the tightly-knit organization set up in the Republican Party and emphasizes the centralized control exercised over the county parties. He points out that the Republican Party controls many county and courthouse jobs from which it obtains "voluntary contributions." He explains the connection between the Hamilton County machine and the business community and the leverage the machine's control of resources has given it over other county chairmen. He also emphasizes the machine's control over nominations.

The author also analyzes and explains the disorganized, loosely-knit Democratic organization. County and city organizations have their own sources of patronage and are not dependent on statewide groups.

A map shows a county-by-county breakdown of Republican organization strength, 1932-1962.

Oklahoma

Oliver Benson et al., in OKLAHOMA VOTES, 1907-1962 (Norman: University of Oklahoma, Bureau of Government Research, 1964, 147 pp.), discuss parties and voting in the state. The sections pertaining to the county are those on urbanization and political party strength on a county basis. The discussion interrelates these two topics. The authors start by discussing regional differentiation and relate it to support of one party or another. Then they discuss the relationship between urbanization and party strength. Various socio-economic variables are discussed in relation to party identification. Also presented is a history of geographic representation by party. At the time of this publication, the authors were on the staff of the Bureau of Government Research, University of Oklahoma.

Pennsylvania

In their book, PENNSYLVANIA POLITICS (New York: Holt, Rinehart and Winston, Inc., 1965, 153 pp.), Edward F. Cooke and Edward G. Janosik present a very good discussion of politics at the county level in Pennsylvania. In addition to the chapter on local party organization, the authors have included in other parts of the text a limited amount of material relevant to county politics.

The first reference to the county is at the beginning of the book when the authors point out that representation in the general assembly is based upon population. They then mention the importance of the state payroll to maintenance of many county party organizations, briefly explain the representation of the county on the state committee, and point out the activity of interest groups in all levels of party activity.

The county level is active in many political and electoral functions. The authors describe the work of the county registration commission, the nominating procedure in a county, the responsibility of the county committee (particularly the chairman in the conduct of campaigns and fund-raising), and the work of the county board of elections. They present a brief analysis of the role of patronage in motivating party activity.

In the chapter on local party organization, the authors begin by showing the range of size in county committees throughout the state. They describe the method of selection of county committee officers and analyze the power of the chairman, citing the specific example of Elk County. They describe the method of selection and the rationale for creation and uses of a county executive committee. They present a very complete description and analysis of the powers of the county chairman, describing his activities in securing candidates, organizing registration, preparing for elections, conducting social and fund-raising activities, replacing party officials, acting as spokesman in political controversies, dispensing patronage, and securing recognition by higher political authorities. They explain the relations between different levels of the local party organization. An interesting discussion of the connection between the county governing board and the political parties is presented, especially the practice of representation of the minority party on the board.

This book is simply written and descriptive. Its main value lies in its presentation of the informal, personal nature of Pennsylvania politics. The authors concentrate on what the county chairman and other party members actually do, rather than on the organizational structure. The inclusion of discussions of the relation between the party and the county government is particularly helpful. No sources are cited; however, in the preface, the authors refer to discussions with public officials and party leaders and their own observations of activities as being particularly useful. At the time of this publication, Edward Cooke was affiliated with the University of Pittsburgh and Edward Janosik with the University of Pennsylvania.

In his book, PARTY AND REPRESENTATION: LEGISLATIVE POLITICS IN PENNSYLVANIA (New York: Atherton Press, 1963, 178 pp.), Frank J. Sorauf devotes much attention to the county. He gives a background sketch of the counties, explaining their urban-rural, religious, and voting characteristics. He gives a complete description of the apportionment of seats in the legislature among the counties, citing much statistical data about certain ones, and refutes the justification of a guaranteed seat in the legislature for each county. When discussing the organization of parties at the county level, he analyzes the role of the county party, particularly of the chairman, in dominating legislative politics. He points out the intrusion of county courthouse officials into the power of the party hierarchies and explains the procedures and methods of operation followed in conducting party business.

Since the county is the basis of representation for legislators, Professor Sorauf discusses the influence of county residency on the selection and action of candidates. Recruitment is discussed at length, with attention focused on the methods of control over the candidate exercised by the local organization. The author analyzes the effect of the constituency on the legislative role and vote of the incumbent. He discusses localism in the legislature and the power of the constituencies.

This book is an excellent study of the power exercised by the county and the political party at the county level over government and governmental officials, particularly state legislatures. More explanation of the use of patronage would have been valuable. The volume is both descriptive and analytical in its coverage of the party organization and will be of interest to the lay reader as well as to the scholar. Much of the author's data comes from field interviews in the state capital and in many counties. At the time of this publication, Sorauf was a political science faculty member at Pennsylvania State University.

Tennessee

Tennessee is one of the southern states discussed by V. O. Key, Jr. in SOUTHERN POLITICS IN STATE AND NATION (New York: Random House, 1962, 675 pp.).

Professor Key shows how E. H. Crump, the boss of Shelby County, dominated state politics for more than fifteen years. He explains the factional divisions found in most counties and their ties with state candidates. He emphasizes the power gained from control of Shelby County and concentrates on the strength of the Crump organization. He analyzes the peculiar importance of legislative control as a means of rewarding and punishing local political leaders, citing as a main reason the large amount of local legislation required to operate county government. He discusses how the organization can use control in the legislature to control local leaders. Another source of control over county factions used by an organization is money sent into the county during campaigns; Crump's organization, in particular, employed this technique.

The author describes how Republican dominance in some eastern counties has caused the Democratic faction there to be tied very closely to state organizations. He discusses the political gossip which contends that the Democrats in these counties make no earnest fight for county and district offices.

Virginia

In his discussion of Virginia in SOUTHERN POLITICS IN STATE AND NATION (New York: Random House, 1962, 675 pp.), V. O. Key, Jr. explains the oligarchical organization of parties. He considers the leadership exercised by the state organization over counties and describes the different sanctions and control mechanisms used by the state leadership to discipline county leaders. He discusses the chief actors in the county machine: commonwealth's attorney, treasurer, commissioner of revenue, clerk of circuit court, and sheriff. He analyzes the power of the circuit judge in the county and his tie with the state organization. He describes why local officials affiliated with the organization usually stay in office for long periods and explains when and if the state organization will come to the aid of local officials. He analyzes the methods used to tie the county leaders to the state organization, emphasizing the use of patronage, and points out the disorganization which is characteristic of opposition groups in counties.

West Virginia

John H. Fenton, in POLITICS IN THE BORDER STATES (New Orleans: The Hauser Press, 1957, 230 pp.), gives a very complete picture of political organization and activity in West

Virginia counties. He considers the position of the statehouse man, the representative of the statewide political organization in the county who is the equivalent of the administration man in Kentucky counties. He explains the qualities considered in appointment of the statehouse man and the sources of his power. He discusses the position of the statehouse group in the county and the categories of people who work for it. He explains why this group in its competition with other factions in the party is strongest in Republican counties, where it does not control county patronage. He describes the support of the statehouse group by the mine workers.

Fenton contrasts the organization in Republican counties with that in the Democratic-controlled counties and provides a case study of a Republican county leader. In a case study of Hancock County, the author explains and analyzes the actual practice of the political organization and describes how certain personalities controlled the county.

Wisconsin

Leon D. Epstein, in POLITICS IN WISCONSIN (Madison: University of Wisconsin Press, 1958, 218 pp.), presents an interesting view of political institutions and practices in the state. A section of the book presents the formal process of county elections, which is then related to party organization and political campaigning. Comparisons are made between counties that are politically competitive and those dominated by one party and between urban and rural counties. The book makes use of interviews and has numerous graphs and charts that statistically describe the subject matter. At the time of this publication, the author was Professor of Political Science, University of Wisconsin.

Wisconsin is one of the six states discussed in John H. Fenton's MIDWEST POLITICS (New York: Holt, Rinehart and Winston, 1966, 244 pp.). The author chronicles the Democratic strength in Catholic counties and points out the influence of personalities in county control. He explains that the Republican strength in the state is based on the party's control of almost all local offices. He mentions the success of a recent Democratic chairman in developing party organization in each of the seventy-two counties.

Five interesting maps show information by counties: the La Follette counties in the 1946 Republican senatorial primary; Wisconsin Democratic counties in the 1962 gubernatorial election; Wisconsin's Yankee Protestant and Scandinavian counties; and Wisconsin's Republican counties, 1884. An interesting graph portrays voting trends by middle-urban, least-urban, and most-urban counties as contrasted with the total state.

POLITICS

Elections

Florida

In his article, "THE NEGRO AND FLORIDA POLITICS, 1944-1954," which appears in Frank Munger (ed.), *American State Politics* (1966), Hugh D. Price makes two points of usefulness to the study of county government. He mentions the extent to which Negroes are usually excluded from participation in the organization of the Democratic party. He explains that one of the areas in which Negro voting participation has been highest is in support of municipal and county officials regarded as favorable in their treatment of Negroes. The sources used are mainly court cases, registration figures, and censuses.

Illinois

The September, 1959, issue of *Illinois Government* (Urbana: University of Illinois, Institute of Government and Public Affairs, September, 1959), pp. 1-4, is devoted to an article by Samuel K. Gove, "THE 1958 COUNTY ELECTIONS." It is an analysis of the elections in 1958 for the county positions of judge, clerk, treasurer, sheriff, and superintendent of schools in the 102 Illinois counties.

Since election of these officers, with the exception of the superintendent of schools, is partisan, the effect of partisanship on county elections is examined in detail. In this connection, the relationship between the party vote for state officers and that for these county officers is explored. A chart and two maps illustrate this relationship. The maps also delineate the geographic patterns of partisanship in county elections in the state. The extent of competition for county offices and the relation of the nature of this competition to partisanship are discussed. Particular emphasis is given to the effects of incumbency on competition and to the nature of competition for the offices of sheriff and treasurer. The author reaches various conclusions and presents a number of hypotheses for further testing suggested by the data.

This excellent article contains findings relative to partisan county elections in Illinois which may be applicable to other states having similar partisan contests. While admitting the limitations of using data from only one election year and thus stressing the tentativeness of the conclusions to be drawn, the author utilizes the 1958 county elections in Illinois as his sole source. Extensive use is made of tables and maps. The approach to county elections and politics is unique and carried out in a very interesting, readable manner. At the time of this publication, the author was a staff member of the Institute of Government and Public Affairs, University of Illinois.

Thomas Kitsos in his article, "THE 1966 COUNTY ELECTIONS," in *Illinois Government* (Urbana: University of Illinois, Institute of Government and Public Affairs, April, 1968), 1-4, presents a well-documented analysis of the competition for various county offices in the 1966 elections in Illinois.

After a short introductory description of the two steps involved in the election of candidates, the author tackles the question of the degree to which candidates compete for these county offices. He establishes the criteria for deciding whether or not a race is competitive; using these measures, he determines which offices are the most competitive. He analyzes both competitive and noncompetitive races and points out factors which may have influenced the degree of competition. He gives special attention to the possible effect of the partisan composition of the counties on the races. The author then sets out the criteria for calling either a primary or general election competitive. On the basis of these measures he determines the number of intra- and interparty competitive races. Combining these two categories, he devises three categories into which he places all the races: no competition, partial competition, and full competition.

Kitsos' conclusions resulting from this analysis are very informative and striking. He finds that primaries are mainly used to ratify decisions made elsewhere and that the general elections also are not usually very competitive. As he states at the end of his paper, "the emerging picture of county elections seems to be one of electoral inertia rather than effective competitiveness." This conclusion seems warranted in light of the detailed and rigorous analysis he has applied in investigating these contests. He has included tables which present the data on which this analysis is based.

POLITICS

Political Parties

California

Dean R. Cresap's book, PARTY POLITICS IN THE GOLDEN STATE (Los Angeles: Haynes Foundation, 1954, 126 pp.), is a systematic study of party organization and activity in California. As Professor Cresap admits in the preface, he is not completely unbiased in his treatment. He has a thesis: "a more responsive two-party system is conducive to improved popular government." To this end, he traces the development of the present lack of harmony, disunity, and decentralization back to the reform era of progressivism at the beginning of the century.

In a chapter devoted to the county central committee, he explains why the county committees vary in effectiveness from county to county, and why any degree of effectiveness a particular committee may possess is a function of local conditions, not of the formal organizational set-up and prescribed duties. In this chapter, and in a later one entitled "The Campaign," the author analyzes the principal campaign-oriented activities of the county committee. However, he also emphasizes and explains the larger role of the more effective county committees.

Throughout the book, Professor Cresap investigates the differences in outlook between the county committees and the state committee. He explains their different bases of support and how their conceptions of the duties of the party organization differ.

The author suggests that the different levels should be made more responsive to the party electorate and that all levels should be formally coordinated and made to work together more harmoniously. This study has little information on the connection between the party organization and the government.

The book is well-written and insightful. The author substantiates most of his suggestions and conclusions with citations from various primary sources, such as interviews, questionnaire results, and newspaper articles. At the time of this publication, Professor Cresap was on the political science faculty of San Jose State College.

University of California, Seminar on Political Party Organization CALIFORNIA POLITICAL PARTY ORGANIZATION (Berkeley: 1960, 4 pp.) includes information on the method of selecting members, functions, and responsibilities of county central committees of political parties in California.

Michigan

A study of the statutory provisions for political party organization in Michigan by Orval Etter, SYNOPSIS OF MICHIGAN LAW ON POLITICAL PARTY STRUCTURE (Berkeley: University of California, Bureau of Public Administration, 1959, 6 pp.), includes an examination of the statutory provisions for county political party organization in that state. The paper discusses the selection and functions of the county committee and the county convention. Although the paper concerns statutory provisions, it is not written in a legalistic style but uses simple, easily-read language. At the time of this publication, the author was a staff member of the Bureau of Public Administration, University of California, Berkeley.

Missouri

In Chapter IX of his book, GOVERNMENT, POLITICS AND ADMINISTRATION IN MISSOURI (St. Louis: Educational Publishers, Inc., 1949, 261 pp.), Carl A. McCandless includes an interesting and complete discussion of political party organization and activity at the county level. He presents the general criteria for determining composition of county committees and explains the differences in committee size between large and small counties. Special features of St. Louis County organization are pointed out. He mentions the meeting place and type and method of selection of all committee officers, emphasizing the primacy of the chairman who conducts most of the business of the county group. He explains the varying amount of representation and importance enjoyed by the different counties, depending on their size, in congressional and senate district committees.

A very interesting, although too brief, section considers the existence of county party machines and their links with county governmental officials. The author explains the allocation of delegates from the counties to the Democratic and Republican conventions. He analyzes the amount of campaign expenditure allowed for candidates for county offices.

Ohio

V. O. Key, Jr. is the author of "PARTISANSHIP AND COUNTY OFFICE: THE CASE OF OHIO," which appears (pp. 274-282) in *American State Politics* (New York: Thomas Y. Crowell, 1966), edited by Frank Munger. The author investigates political patterns and suggests their importance to the structure of government, pointing out how they frustrate reformers and contribute to the unmalleable quality of rural government.

Professor Key explains that while the trend in party control of county government moves with the presidential trend, local candidates of both parties can, to a considerable extent, withstand the tides of the presidential ticket. He analyzes the sources and capacities of this survival ability and power of self-perpetuation of local party structures. He analyzes why this apparent durability of community structures may be at the bottom of the frustrations of reformers as well as being a factor in the unchanging quality of rural governmental institutions.

This analysis provides clues which could be pursued in an intensive study of individual counties. As the author states, the article suggests that comparative statistical analysis might be a means of elevating the case study to a position of usefulness in the general study of the political process and thereby enlarge the existing meager store of systematic knowledge of local politics.

Washington

WASHINGTON POLITICS, by Daniel M. Ogden, Jr. and Hugh A. Bone (New York: New York University Press, 1960, 77 pp.), is of some use in the study of counties. The authors begin by discussing the extent of office competition and the independence of voters in the various counties and point out the impact volunteer organizations may have on county committees. They touch on the registration procedure. The organization and operation of the county committee are discussed, its key role in state politics pointed out, and its most important functions listed. Special procedures followed in the urban counties are noted, and mention is made of the role of the executive committees and the chairmen. The authors consider the representation of the county on state and district party committees and analyze the decentralization of the party organization, emphasizing the dominant position of the county and the effect of patronage on securing this dominance. The representation of the county and method of selection of county delegates to the party conventions are described. The authors also describe the role of the county party in slate-making and organization of campaign committees and briefly discuss the conduct of elections.

When discussing party activities, Professors Ogden and Bone

focus on the role of the county in raising funds. They also mention the procedure followed in dispensing patronage and point out when the county political leader, or alternatively, a government official, will be the most influential figure. They explain the influence of various good-government leagues on local government.

Although the authors do not provide much detail or extensive analysis of the political role of the county, they do indicate certain areas to be considered and in general provide a good outline. Due to the shortness of the book and the breadth of the subject, not much more could be expected. Although the authors have tried to combine both formal and informal aspects, more attention is given to the former. At the time of this publication, Professor Ogden was associated with Washington State University and Professor Bone with the University of Washington.

REFORM

General

United States

In Chapter 26 of AMERICAN LOCAL GOVERNMENT (New York: Harper & Row, 1964, 619 pp.), George S. Blair considers two principal ways in which the county may perform a major role in the governing of heavily populated areas. He examines the transfer of functions to the county on either a mandatory or contractual basis. He also considers the consolidation of other governments with the county, thereby creating an areawide unit.

Arthur W. Bromage's AMERICAN COUNTY GOVERNMENT (New York: Holston House, Sears Publishing, 1933, 306 pp.) is a plea for reform of county government along the lines of the "good government" movement prominent in the first third of this century.

The author discusses the need for reform of county government because of inadequate area and antiquated structure. He points out the obstacles confronting reorganization and gives a concise history of the county, emphasizing the power of the past. He describes the forms of rural government: the New England town, the township-supervisor system, and the commissioner type. He then considers the changes and reforms that have taken place in municipal government and the possible influence these may have on county government.

A discussion of county-state relations follows. Professor Bromage describes constitutional limitations on the county as well as optional laws and county home rule. He compares the latter two, gives examples of home rule proposals from Ohio and Michigan, discusses the suggestions of "A Model State Constitution," and describes the advantages of local option.

Professor Bromage turns to a lengthy discussion of the county manager plan. He describes the comparability of city and county manager plans and analyzes obstacles and objections to county managers and the arguments for them. He describes "The Model County Manager Law" and its provisions – as well as various other proposals – for a county manager. He tells about county manager experience in Georgia, Montana, North Carolina, and Virginia. He shows how the gulf is narrowing between theory and practice in county management.

County administration is the author's next concern. He gives brief descriptions of the offices of sheriff, prosecuting attorney, treasurer, coroner, and auditor. He depicts how certain county functions such as health are administered and criticizes the lack of sufficient coordination of county functions. Again he cites the suggestions of the "Model County Manager Law." He describes the Montana and Virginia systems of departments, and reorganization proposals in Alabama and Michigan. He gives a detailed description of law enforcement in the county and the possibilities of reorganization. He discusses the need for instituting administrative standards in county operations. He describes the different methods followed for state control of county finances. Throughout the discussion he emphasizes the imperative nature of administrative reorganization.

The author then discusses county consolidation. He mentions the areal inadequacies of present units but stresses the difficulties in instituting widespread county consolidation. He describes various consolidation proposals, particularly those suggested in New York State. He lists the practical hindrances which beset county consolidation and counters these obstacles with a discussion of the financial savings and other benefits that would occur. He discusses other possible means of overcoming some of the objections, giving specific examples of the benefits resulting from consolidation. He then describes the possibilities of functional consolidation and the likelihood that it might lead to thoroughgoing consolidation. Finally, he considers the idea of replacing blocs of pauper counties with one state district. Professor Bromage describes the role of the township in a system of rural local government and analyzes the effect that elimination of township government would have upon the remaining units, the county and villages. At the conclusion, all the factors to be considered in any attempt to reconstruct local government are summarized and the prospects for sweeping changes are appraised.

The book's treatment of county government centers on Professor Bromage's desire to see that unit reformed and reorganized. His analysis of the possibilities and ramifications of change is very complete. In general, he has presented an extensive description of the historical background of the county, its structural design, the constitutional and political obstacles to reform, and some proposals for improvement.

A selected bibliography on county government reform is included at the end of the book. At the time of this publication, the author was Associate Professor of Political Science, University of Michigan.

The main thesis of the Committee for Economic Development report, MODERNIZING LOCAL GOVERNMENT TO SECURE A BALANCED FEDERALISM: A STATEMENT BY THE RESEARCH AND POLICY COMMITTEE OF THE COMMITTEE FOR ECONOMIC DEVELOPMENT (New York: 1966, 77 pp.), is that local government, including the county, is hopelessly archaic and therefore unable to function effectively and fulfill its proper role in the federal system.

After a brief introduction to the present character of intergovernmental relations, which emphasizes the dominance of the national level, the report sets forth and assesses the current weaknesses of local government. Then it suggests three alternative courses of action available to modernize it. The report explains why it is CED's opinion that the alternative of strengthening and revamping the local level itself rather than increasing reliance on either the national or state level should be followed. After this judgment is made, the study sets forth the minimum qualifications it believes local government must meet to be effective: political unity, sufficient size, adequate powers, and a rational structure. Nine guidelines for instituting these broad objectives are presented.

The report analyzes the present condition of county government and explains what changes should be made to revitalize it. The recommendations center on boundary change, use of the county as an areawide government, authority for the county to cooperate with other units across state lines, extended use of county home rule, which includes reconstituting the structure of county government, and adoption of executive government.

Building on its stated desire to see a more active role for the county in the federal system, the CED has presented a plan for reforming county government and thereby increasing its vitality. The report has been careful to point out the causes of the weaknesses of the present county system and has analyzed the effects and changes the Committee believes will result from the implementation of its suggestions. However, the report is largely prescriptive; there is little footnoting or mention of resource materials.

"A NEWS ANALYSIS: COUNTIES RIDING THE WAVE OF THE FUTURE, ACIR DIRECTOR TELLS KANSANS," *The County Officer,* 30 (April, 1965) 22, 52, is an article which reports on a speech by William G. Colman, Executive Director of the Advisory Commission on Intergovernmental Relations. Mr. Colman tells of the potentiality of the county government as an areawide unit. He also summarizes ACIR's recommendations which would make counties stronger governments for the performance of areawide functions.

The last chapter of Herbert S. Duncombe's COUNTY GOVERNMENT IN AMERICA (Washington, D. C.: National Association of Counties, Research Foundation, 1966, 288 pp.) deals with the future of county government and reform.

Professor Duncombe begins with an exposition of past trends in county government and then looks at metropolitan problems, which he sees as a challenge and opportunity for counties, and different solutions that have been tried. Nonmetropolitan counties are also discussed. In this section, problems of area, organization, and powers are considered. The author points out the legal and fiscal roadblocks in the way of improvement and change and examines the concept of county home rule as a reform movement to free counties from state restrictions.

The author discusses trends that he believes will affect the future of counties: continued population increase, reapportionment of county governing bodies, greater federal and state involvement in metropolitan and urban problems, expansion of local intergovernmental relations, and the increasing use and growth of the urban county. He explains at length why he believes the last-named development holds the most promise for the future of county government.

Even though H. S. Gilbertson's THE COUNTY: THE "DARK CONTINENT" OF AMERICAN POLITICS (New York: The National Short Ballot Organization, 1917, 297 pp.) was published over fifty years ago, it still retains much value for the study of counties since it was the first book dealing exclusively with this subject. The author wrote this volume because of lack of material on the county, and in the hope that it would stimulate further investigation—as it did.

As in the case of many writers of more recent years, Mr. Gilbertson opens his book with a discussion of the history and development of the county, in both England and the United States. He lays particular emphasis on the office of sheriff.

Reflecting the sponsorship of his work by the National Short Ballot Organization, the author explains why the American tradition of fear of a strong executive and the resultant use of the long ballot meant irresponsible government for the county. He explains why the development of "bossism" must be traced to the long ballot idea. He goes on to explain why "Without a doubt, the urban, and particularly the metropolitan county, is the county at its worst." After discussing these and other shortcomings of the county, he describes the past and possible future effects of the reform movement of that period on the county.

Mr. Gilbertson explains how a change in state-county relations may improve the county. He points out the areas of county government in which state intervention and direction will be useful. One of his main arguments is that the present personnel system is inefficient and corrupt and that a merit civil service system should be introduced.

Possible reorganization proposals are discussed. The two main ideas explored are county home rule and city-county consolidation, followed by attention to internal reform proposals. Mr. Gilbertson explains why the long ballot and the principle of separation of powers must be eliminated and gives examples of the use of the county manager plan. He calls for scientific administration, explaining at length the desirability and means of implementing new budgeting and accounting procedures. He concludes the book by explaining why he believes the county in the future will be found only in rural and semi-rural areas and by pointing out the innovations which will be made. In general, this book is a call for reform of the county along the lines of the "good government" movement of the period.

To lay the groundwork for his prescriptions, the author gives a very colorful description of the inadequacies of the existing system of county government. The appendix includes the texts of many proposals for county charters and home rule laws. Both the index and bibliography are very complete. In the preface the author acknowledges his debt to Professor John A. Fairlie for much of the historical material. At the time of this publication, the author was Assistant Secretary, National Short Ballot Organization.

An editorial by Bernard F. Hillenbrand, "GREAT-GRANDFATHER'S FIRM HAND ON COUNTY GOVERNMENT," *American County Government,* 31 (August, 1966), 6, laments the restrictions of nineteenth-century legislation and constitutional provisions on the structure of county government. The author is particularly disturbed over these restrictions because of the many functional responsibilities being placed on counties. He mentions some of the problems that outdated structure creates for county officials. Finally, there is a call for the support of citizens and county officials to reform antiquated county structure.

Basing his position on the belief that county government should assume a predominant role in the renovation of local government,

Alan F. Kiepper, in his article "COUNTY MODERNIZATION SHOULD BE PRESSED WITH SPECIAL VIGOR . . ." in *American County Government,* 32 (March, 1967), 36-37, 49, calls for its immediate major reform.

The author discusses weaknesses and offers suggestions for improvement in three areas. First, he explains that county organization is poorly structured and should be modernized. Second, he discusses how counties could benefit from the adoption of modern procedures for conduct of public business. Third, he points out that personnel practices are antiquated and explains how they could be updated.

This article is a concise and logically-presented call for reform. At the time of this publication, the author, who had been County Manager, Fulton County, Georgia, was about to assume the city managership of Richmond, Virginia.

Throughout the entire book, GOVERNMENT IN RURAL AMERICA, 2nd edition (New York: D. Van Nostrand, 1952, 375 pp.), Lane W. Lancaster advocates and explains the need for reform of rural local government. Chapter 15, near the end of the volume, is a summary of the problems he pointed out earlier and a discussion of suggestions for change and improvement.

The author discusses the possibility of consolidation of local areas, especially counties, and notes the main obstacles to this movement. Since such consolidation has not made much headway, he examines types of cooperation among local units and analyzes why this approach may meet with more success. He then moves on to internal reorganization, beginning with plans for centralizing responsibility in a county executive. He presents both the pros and cons of this plan and demonstrates how it might affect state-local relations. The last method he considers is reallocation of functions; here he examines which ones might be turned over to the state and which might best be left to the counties.

Professor Lancaster concludes by discussing the environment of reform. He analyzes the social, economic, and political prerequisites for reform and suggests which local interests might provide the necessary leadership.

Duane Lockard, in his book, THE POLITICS OF STATE

AND LOCAL GOVERNMENT (New York: Macmillan, 1963, 566 pp.), discusses the role of the county in the governing of metropolitan areas. He examines the pros and cons of using the county as a governmental instrument to transcend the parochialism of local governments and describes the difficulties encountered in attempting to transform the county into a metropolitan government. Then he cites and explains examples of cases where the county has been successfully used in this way. Extensive analysis is devoted to the "Lakewood Plan" in California and to the Dade County experiment; the latter is compared with the Toronto plan.

Arthur C. Millspaugh, in LOCAL DEMOCRACY AND CRIME CONTROL (Washington: Brookings Institution, 1936, 263 pp.), seeks to clarify the problems surrounding reorganization of local government. He wants to centralize many local functions in the state government. His main thesis is that many traditional concepts of local government and the attitude toward reform must be reassessed. Many ideas in the book that seemed innovative at the time have had considerable discussion since. Also, a point of clarification should be made concerning the title. Although the author devotes more time to crime control than to any other area, he by no means devotes the entire book to this problem. (*See* Services—Law Enforcement: United States.)

First, the author presents an overview of the traditional role of the county, its internal organization, and the activity of its more important law enforcement officers—sheriff, county police, and prosecuting attorney. He then traces the development of state-local relationships, particularly the use of state aid and shared functions. He discusses the trend toward closer state-local relations and functional integration, emphasizing direct statutory controls and legislative control of county officers. He describes state-county relations in the field of law enforcement and points out a modifying movement toward the greater use of local option and home rule.

The discussion proceeds to the pros and cons of local self-government and the factors to be considered in establishing the optimum local unit. Mr. Millspaugh analyzes the values of local self-government and possible tests of its vitality and financial responsibility. He describes the conditions that must be in evidence if a local unit is to be reinvigorated; in brief, there should be a partnership between local community life and governmental functioning.

Regional readjustment is considered. The author analyzes the status and future of county consolidation and discusses its ability to solve many problems facing local governments, such as areal adjustment, financial equalization, and savings. He points out the obstacles to consolidation, analyzes the problems of city-county overlapping, and discusses the three methods that have been tried: separation of the municipality from the county; county-city consolidation; and reallocation of functions. He analyzes the effect of urban readjustment on the rural county problem and explains at length locally-controlled functional cooperation and districting, pointing out both the advantages and disadvantages of the movement. He mentions the possibility of abolishing local units other than counties and municipalities.

The author considers internal reorganization as a possible solution to the problems of local government. He discusses centralization of functions into fewer offices, separation of legislative and administrative powers, and general administrative unification in a county executive. He compares county unification with functional integration.

Another possible solution discussed at length is functional reallocation, which would involve transferring some functions to the state. The author analyzes different methods of dividing the functions between the state and local unit, discussing criteria that might be used in establishing the division, and analyzing the effect on particular functions. He lists five procedures for effecting this reallocation. He analyzes the effects it would have on the local unit, on state-county relations, and on federal-state relations.

Mr. Millspaugh considers the problem of integrating crime control. He discusses the county reorganization needed in the light of functional reallocation and the changes that would occur in the offices of sheriff and prosecuting attorney and in county departments of justice. He concludes with a discussion of the procedures to be followed and the research needed in considering local reorganization.

This book is eminently applicable to the study of county government, particularly in analyzing reorganization at this level. The county is the unit of local government with which the author is most concerned, and most of his proposals center on a discussion of their effect on and applicability to the county. In presenting his thesis, the author does not devote much space to a description of the formal, structural characteristics of county government. Rather, he analyzes the effects of arrangements being practiced, the possibilities and capabilities of change, and the differences in operation that might occur if changes were effected. His prescriptions are presented in detail.

The final section of Clyde F. Snider's LOCAL GOVERNMENT IN RURAL AMERICA (New York: Appleton-Century-Crofts, 1957, 584 pp.) deals with reorganization of local government. Professor Snider states that problems of local reorganization fall into the categories of area, internal organization, allocation of functions, finance, and state-local relations.

Professor Snider begins by discussing the problems of area facing local governments, concluding that geographic consolidation of some type is a possible remedy. He describes and analyzes county consolidation, school consolidation, city-county consolidation, township abolition, and local deorganization on either a voluntary or compulsory basis.

The possibility of transfer of functions, particularly from the smallest units to the county and from the county to the state, is explored. The author describes functional consolidation and discusses why it might be used in rural as well as urban areas.

The other aspects of reorganization do not receive similar attention. The author considers the problems of internal organization and cites many examples. He discusses reallocation of functions, pointing out the trend to transfer functions from smaller to larger units. Problems of finance and state-local relations are also discussed. The section concludes with a look at what may lie ahead. The author lists six ideas deserving consideration in any program of readjustment of local government.

California

TRANSCRIPT OF PROCEEDINGS, MODERNIZATION OF COUNTY GOVERNMENT: SPECIAL DISTRICTS (Sacramento: June 15, 1960, 164 pp.) contains the testimony of county officials, academicians, representatives of special districts, and others before the California Assembly Interim Committee on Municipal and County Government on various matters relating to reorganization of county government and county relations with special districts. These matters include: the need for and opposition to legislation granting California general-law counties the power to establish a strong office of county administrative officer; the merits of consolidating certain county offices and making the consolidated office appointive; the merits of legislation to refer such consolidation and appointment to the voters of a county; the merits of granting greater home rule powers to general-law counties; approval and disapproval of legislation requiring counties to separate municipal, county, and special district taxes on tax bills; and a number of topics concerned with changing special district-county relations.

The testimony is particularly valuable because it demonstrates the attitudes of the public, state legislators, and various kinds of county officials toward reorganization of county government. It demonstrates graphically why county reorganization efforts have had difficulty in the state legislatures of many progressive states.

In the chapter on the county in CALIFORNIA GOVERNMENT AND POLITICS (Englewood Cliffs: Prentice-Hall, Inc., 1967, 4th ed., 318 pp.) by Winston W. Crouch, John C. Bollens, Stanley Scott, and Dean E. McHenry, the authors discuss the problems and progress of reform and reorganization in California counties. They begin by tracing the development of the county home rule movement and discuss the constitutional grant and specific charters adopted under it. They describe another approach to organizational reform which was spurred in part by the success of the home rule charters: the attempt to appoint rather than elect county officials. They point out the problems of administration that lend support to the adoption of this proposal. The manifestation of this tendency in California is the administrative officer trend. The authors describe this office and explain the reasons for its rapid growth.

Another reform undertaken in California which is discussed relates to certain assessment practices. A major scandal which came to light in 1965 and a sweeping property tax assessment reform bill which became state law in the following year are presented.

County reapportionment receives consideration as a third area of change. The authors explain the serious inequalities of representation which existed on many county boards of supervisors and describe the success in changing this situation. They discuss court decisions of the early 1960's and legislation requiring redistricting.

Colorado

The study by the Governor's Local Affairs Study Commission, "COUNTY GOVERNMENT IN COLORADO," in *Interim Reports on Local Government* (Denver: Government Report No. 1, 1964) contains an overview of the structure and functions of county government in Colorado, an investigation of outstanding problem areas, and recommendations for change in procedure.

The report begins with a history and discussion of the legal status of the county. It describes the organization and structure of county government and explains the structure and state legal requirements for the board of county commissioners. Brief descriptions are provided of each of the following offices: county clerk, treasurer, assessor, sheriff, coroner, superintendent of schools, surveyor, and attorney. A descriptive list then follows of the primary functions performed by the county. The activities covered are: roads and highways, welfare, health and sanitation, planning and zoning, licensing, agriculture and soil conservation, and creation of special districts. The extent of the policy-making and discretionary powers of the board of commissioners is discussed.

The Commission then presents its findings on certain problem areas of county government: lack of local self-determination, administrative inflexibility, inability to provide urban services, and insufficient legal authority to perform authorized functions. Recommendations, based on these findings, for change in county government are made. Permission to allow nonurban counties to adopt home rule charters is recommended. Specific provisions and details to be incorporated in the procedure are presented. The Commission also recommends measures which would grant emergency powers to the county. It makes suggestions for legislation in the areas of county government control of special district formation, licensing and bonding of road excavators, and control of speed laws.

This report is well-ordered and straightforward. The recommendations for change are adequately supported by the results of the investigation of the problem areas.

Illinois

The Illinois County Problems Commission, created as a permanent legislative agency in 1957, issues an annual report of its findings and recommendations based on its studies of county government in Illinois during the given year. Its publication of this type for 1967, REPORT TO GOVERNOR OTTO KERNER AND TO THE 75TH GENERAL ASSEMBLY OF ILLINOIS (Springfield: 1967, 37 pp.), contains a brief summary of the structure and functions of Illinois county government and presents findings and recommendations on county revenues, fiscal management, and apportionment of county boards.

Iowa

Iowa Legislative Research Bureau, in SOME POSSIBILITIES FOR CONSOLIDATION OF OFFICES OR FUNCTIONS WITHIN COUNTIES (Des Moines: 1959, 29 pp.), discusses functions and general administration. It considers the county's accounting function in terms of money collection, recordkeeping, and central purchasing. Welfare departments, the county board of supervisors, intergovernmental relations, and governmental reform are discussed, and interstate comparisons are made.

Missouri

Fred J. Culver, the author of "COUNTY GOVERNMENT IN RURAL MISSOURI," in *Public Affairs Newsletter* (Columbia: University of Missouri, August 1, 1966, 5 pp.), states that the article is an attempt to begin "an objective appraisal of the problems and potentials of rural government in Missouri." In tackling this project, he first describes and analyzes the weaknesses and problems of county government and then offers suggestions for reform and improvement.

The author begins by providing statistics on the size and population of the third- and fourth-class counties in Missouri, which are the subject of this paper. He starts his examination of the problems of these counties by analyzing their legal limitations which are evident in archaic structure and restricted taxing powers. Then he describes the problem these counties face in attempting to provide adequate services. He concentrates on their inability to provide necessary revenue, a situation resulting primarily from low tax bases and low income levels.

After this overview of the problems confronting these counties, Mr. Culver presents and explains five suggestions for improvement: consolidation; cooperation for administering joint or common services, including contractual agreements with municipalities; adopting alternative forms of county government; transferring responsibility to the state government; and providing additional revenue, including raising the property tax limit, instituting other taxes, or taking subsidies from the state. At the end of this discussion, Mr. Culver emphasizes that his suggestions are not necessarily all-inclusive. He hopes only that they will point the way for further research and improvement. This paper is a useful addition to a sorely neglected area, rural county government, which has too often been passed over in favor of the study of urban areas. Five useful sets of figures are provided on the following subjects: county expenditures per capita for selected purposes, per cent of county expenditures for selected purposes, four population groups for all Missouri counties, valuation of all real and personal property per capita, and median family income. Mr. Culver was formerly President of the Missouri Judges' Association and at the time of this publication was serving as Community Development Agent, University of Missouri.

Montana

At the conclusion of the chapter dealing with county government in THE GOVERNMENT AND ADMINISTRATION OF MONTANA (New York: Thomas Y. Crowell, 1958, 508 pp.), Roland R. Renne presents an interesting and analytical picture of reorganization of county government. He begins by listing the four major weaknesses of the present system. Then he explains the improvement programs provided for in the constitution. He describes three optional plans which he believes may provide responsible and sound organization—county manager plan, county-executive plan, and the commission form—and points out how they differ. Petroleum County is the only county that has adopted the manager plan, and the author describes and analyzes at length how it operates there and the success it has enjoyed. Two interesting figures for comparison are presented: one is of the organizational structure of regular county government; the other is of the commission-manager plan in Petroleum County.

New York

Bernard F. Hillenbrand, in his article "STRENGTHENING COUNTIES IN THE EMPIRE STATE," *Metropolitan Viewpoints,* 3 (Albany: State University of New York, Graduate School of Public Affairs, February, 1968), 1-4, argues that the county should be the focal point of local government for solving both urban and rural problems. He asserts that counties have five virtues that make them the most suitable local governments for this role: a broad tax base, areawide jurisdiction; economy of scale; closer ties with the state and national governments; and areawide political accountability.

The author then presents a number of reforms to strengthen counties for this proposed role. Although his remarks are directed specifically to New York State, he believes that such renovation is needed throughout the nation. First, he contends that counties should have home-rule residual powers—those not specifically denied to them by the state constitution, general laws, or local charter. Second, constitutional debt limitations should be removed, in part because they have produced special authorities that perform functions general governments, such as counties, should handle. Third, counties should be allowed to create subordinate taxing areas so that they may provide services at different levels in various portions of their jurisdictions and have tax rates that reflect varying service levels. Fourth, counties should be given maximum flexibility in making interlocal agreements, particularly contract services. Fifth, township supervisors no longer should be members of county boards, and counties should have single executive heads, preferably elected. Sixth, county planning powers should be strengthened, particularly as a coordinating agency for local planning and control. Seventh, provision should be made in state constitutions to facilitate the establishment of metropolitan councils of government in multicounty metropolitan areas. The author is Executive Director of the National Association of Counties.

South Dakota

A brief but interesting discussion of county structural reorganization and intercounty consolidation is found in an article by W. O. Farber, "IMPROVING COUNTY GOVERNMENT: REORGANIZATION AND CONSOLIDATION," *Public Affairs* (Vermillion: University of South Dakota, Governmental Research Bureau, August 15, 1963), 1-6. Although this article focuses upon a proposed South Dakota constitutional amendment (subsequently passed) for the consolidation of county elective offices, the author draws on the experience of other states to assess the South Dakota situation.

As a preface to the major topics of discussion, Professor Farber examines the geographic size of counties throughout the United States and compares average size and variations in size among states. He then turns to an analysis of trends in county population size and relates county population size to per capita costs of county government. He further relates geographic size and population size to two ways of reducing county per capita costs—reorganization of county government through consolidation of elective county offices, and intercounty governmental consolidation. In relation to office consolidations, he presents an interesting chart showing the variations in per capita cost of elective offices according to population size.

The author discusses the above-mentioned South Dakota constitutional amendment. He presents and analyzes the results of a survey questionnaire of the reactions of South Dakota county commissioners to the amendment proposal. The questions asked were: "Do you favor the constitutional amendment?"; "What combinations do you feel most worthy of consideration?"; "Do you believe there is a use for the amendment in your county?"

Intercounty consolidation is discussed. The author analyzes the political difficulties involved in bringing about such reform and describes the legal procedure to be followed in South Dakota. As alternatives to consolidation, he briefly mentions intercounty consolidation of particular county offices and intercounty contracts for the performance of certain functions.

This is a very readable article which places the issues involved in a general perspective. Farber uses census data and state documents as primary sources of information; however, he also mentions secondary sources that he used for the article. At the time of this publication, the author was Professor of Political Science, University of South Dakota.

Virginia

Chester W. Bain, in his book, "THE BODY INCORPORATE," THE EVOLUTION OF CITY-COUNTY SEPARATION IN VIRGINIA (Charlottesville: University of Virginia Press, 1967, 142 pp.), examines the history of municipal government, particularly the development of city-county separation in that state. Several chapters in part or in their entirety are valuable to the study of county government. A brief section of the first chapter, which deals with the colonial period, discusses the establishment of counties by the colonial General Assembly in 1634. Chapter Three discusses the historical and legal sources of city-county separation, analyzes the general nature of this device, and compares its use in Virginia and other states. The historical development of the practice is then considered in Chapter Four. A section of Chapter Five, which describes in detail the methods of municipal incorporation and their use, scrutinizes the consolidation of two or more cities or counties into a single municipality. The conversion of Warwick County into a city by a special legislative act is briefly treated in another section of the chapter. The effects of separation on municipalities are the subject of Chapter Six, which has as a continuing theme the assumption of county functions by separated municipalities.

Chapter Seven evaluates the practice of separation and examines the major causes of towns separating from counties to become independent municipalities. Some causes with which the author deals at length are: poor relations between town and county officials; advocacy of local control of the school system separate from the county; the desire of town officials to assess the value of property in the town without county interference; the objective of eliminating dual taxation (by both the town and the county); and the belief in separating urban from rural territory to make local governments, both city and county, more representative of constituents and responsive to their needs.

In the remainder of the chapter, the author levels some criticisms at city-county separation and points out some strengths. Of particular interest are his criticisms that separation ignores the declining distinction between counties and cities as units of local government and that it has greatly complicated city-county relations. Finally, he makes recommendations for reform which are aimed at producing a more judicious use of the separation device.

Professor Bain has presented a scholarly, thorough treatment of the subject. He has used both primary and secondary sources, including numerous historical documents. At the time of this publication, he was Professor of Political Science, University of South Carolina.

ALSO TO BE NOTED—FOR REFORM:

General

Bernard F. Hillenbrand, "Are There Too Many Counties?" *The County Officer,* 24 (July, 1959), 191.

______, "The Decade of the Three R's—Reapportionment, Reorganization, and Revitalization," *American County Government,* 30 (September, 1965), 9.

Mark O. Hatfield, "Developing Society," *American County Government,* 30 (September, 1965), 33, 88.

National Association of Counties, Washington, *County Reorganization Service,* No. 1 (September, 1967).

Henry Reining, "Are Counties Meeting Their Responsibilities?" *The County Officer,* 22 (November, 1957), 252-253.

Estal E. Sparlin, "The County Arrives," *The County Officer,* 27 (August, 1962), 350.

Alva W. Stewart, "Changes Proposed in Counties' Role: C. E. D. Sees Potential as Most Vital Unit," *National Civic Review*, 55 (October, 1966), 527-530.

John Stoner, "County Government–Grave Stone or Corner Stone?" *The County Officer,* 21 (December, 1956), 286-289.

United States Congress, House Committee on Government Operations, Subcommittee on Intergovernmental Relations, *Unshackling Local Government, a Survey of Proposals by the Advisory Commission on Intergovernmental Relations* (Washington: 1966, 47 pp.).

Individual States

California Legislature, Assembly Interim Committee on Municipal and County Government, *Functional Consolidation of Local Government: Final Report* (Sacramento: 1959, 27 pp.).

Jack Durrance and Howard Weston, "County Government in Florida; Present Deficiencies and Proposed Reforms," *Governmental Research Bullet n* (Tallahassee: Florida State University, Institute of Government Research), 3 (May, 1966), 1-4.

Florida Local Government Study Commission, *Recommendations Relative to Local Government in Florida* (Tallahassee: Florida Legislative Council, 1967, 9 pp.).

Association County Commissioners of Georgia, *How Practical Is Merging of County Services Across County Lines?* (Atlanta: 1953, v.p.).

"County Reorganization Gets Under Way in Iowa," *National Civic Review,* 48 (July, 1959), 367-368.

Nebraska Legislative Council, *Report of the Committee on County Government Reorganization* (Lincoln: 1966, 34 pp.).

State of New Jersey, County and Municipal Government Study Commission, *Creative Localism: A Prospectus,* Interim Report (Trenton: March 11, 1968, 104 pp.).

George S. Blair, "Modernizing County Government in Pennsylvania," *The County Officer,* 25 (January, 1960), 6-7.

Weldon Cooper, "Updating Local Government in Virginia: the Post War Period and Beyond," *The University of Virginia Newsletter,* 43 (December 15, 1966), 13-16.

REFORM

Abolition of Counties

Connecticut

Merle W. DeWees, in "COUNTY GOVERNMENT OBSOLETE," *Your State and Local Government, News and Views*, No. 68 (April 7, 1959), presents the views of the Connecticut Public Expenditure Council regarding the abolition of county government in the state. He sees such abolition as an important step toward the establishment of a sounder and more efficient system of state and local government. The chief function of counties at the time of publication was the operation of the jails. Among the arguments cited in favor of change is that the town should remain the basic unit of local government. At the time of this publication, the author was Executive Director, Connecticut Public Expenditure Council.

The bulk of Rosaline Levenson's book, COUNTY GOVERNMENT IN CONNECTICUT – ITS HISTORY AND DEMISE (Storrs: University of Connecticut, Continuing Education Service, Institute of Public Service, 1966, 237 pp.), is devoted to the circumstances surrounding the abolition of county government in Connecticut and its aftermath. There are six chapters which deal with this subject. The first looks at the only function of county government in Connecticut which was of current importance – the maintenance of jails. The author examines the administration and operation of county jails by the county high sheriff; and she reviews the findings and recommendations of several committees and commissions which had studied county administration of the jails. The author asserts that the laxities of county jail administration combined with jail disturbances in the early 1950's were among the reasons for abolition of the counties.

Chapter Two analyzes the history of county child welfare functions which were terminated in 1955, when county homes for neglected children were abolished and county child welfare functions were transferred to the state. The author emphasizes the criticisms which were made of county operation of the children's homes by such organizations as the Connecticut Legislative Council, the Child Welfare League of America, and others. Included is an astute analysis of the political maneuvers that finally resulted in the transfer of county child welfare functions to the state.

The third chapter, which examines the political environment and the political strategies involved in the abolition of county government, is extremely interesting and is perhaps the most important in the book. The author states that she is seeking to relate why, given the weakened state of county government by 1931, it took so long for counties to be abolished. She finds the answer in the nature of partisan politics in the state and in the spoils system connected with county government. The chapter ends with an analysis of the abolition bill itself. This analysis also probes into the politics behind the bill which permitted the retention of the elected county high sheriff with continued, though substantially reduced, responsibilities for jail administration.

Chapter Four describes the process of the distribution of county functions to various state departments and agencies. It deals specifically with the following problems: the assumption of funds held in trust by the counties; the assumption of county debt; the ownership of equipment which had been used jointly by the counties and other local governments; the restructuring of the revenue system to finance state operation of county functions; and the transfer of county employees to state service. The many ramifications of these problems are presented in great detail. Particular emphasis is given to the problems involved when the state took over the county jails.

In another chapter, the author analyzes why the abolition of counties in Connecticut had practically no effect on either the citizens or the government of the state. In the process of this analysis, she lists five factors that brought about abolition of county government. The administrative weaknesses of the counties are explored, and the author explains that the counties lacked imagination, leadership and innovation. This discussion evolves into an analysis of the political basis for the longevity and eventual downfall of the counties. The chapter concludes with a lengthy consideration of the economies and improvements in operations which have resulted from the transfer of county functions to the state.

The final chapter examines whether a need exists for a metropolitan unit. The author states that the removal of counties left no void because they did so little, but, nevertheless, a need may exist for a metropolitan government. She discusses the many metropolitan and municipal-type functions performed by the state and makes an analysis of the emergence of planning regions as a possible intermediate or metropolitan level of government.

REFORM

Reapportionment

United States

"EQUAL PROTECTION EXTENDED IN SCOPE," *National Civic Review,* 57 (May, 1968), 261-262, reports on the *Avery v. Midland County* decision of the United States Supreme Court. This decision applies the equal protection clause of the 14th Amendment to the governing boards of counties, towns, and cities. The article examines the manner in which the court used the equal representation or "one man, one vote" principle, which it had laid out in *Reynolds v. Sims.* In addition, it describes some details of the *Midland County* case itself and discusses the majority opinion of the court.

Daniel R. Grant and Robert E. McArthur, in their article, "'ONE MAN–ONE VOTE' AND COUNTY GOVERNMENT: RURAL, URBAN AND METROPOLITAN IMPLICATIONS," *George Washington Law Review,* 36 (May 1968), 760-777, seek to predict the effects of reapportionment on a population basis on county governing boards. Their assessment begins with a brief exposition of some laxities of county government, particularly the extent and effects of malapportionment of their governing boards. This is followed by a review of court decisions which made the redistricting of a majority of counties on an equal population basis seem imminent.

The authors analyze the administrative and political changes that reapportionment will probably bring to counties. Administrative changes relate to modernization of governmental form and processes. Political changes involve new kinds of policies and programs resulting from increased representation of urban interests and improved access by certain groups to decision makers. Attention is given to the political effects of redistricting on rural populations. The authors present a case study of the consequences of reapportionment in Nashville-Davidson County, Tennessee. A lengthy section is devoted to analyzing the impact of county reapportionment on government in the metropolis. Specific evaluation is made of its probable consequences for city-county cooperation, city-county consolidation, functional consolidation, the county as a provider of municipal services, annexation, metropolitan councils of government, and proposals for multicounty metropolitan governments. At the time of this publication, Grant was Professor of Political Science, Vanderbilt University, and McArthur was Assistant Professor of Political Science, Vassar College.

"HIGH COURT RULE ROCKS LOCAL BOAT," *National Civic Review,* 57 (June, 1968), 318-320, seeks to assess the future effects of the United States Supreme Court's *Avery v. Midland County* decision, which applies the "one man, one vote" principle to the governing boards of general local governments. A sampling of the editorial reaction of newspapers throughout the nation is presented. The article also reports the present status of action on local, particularly county, reapportionment in the following states: Alabama, Connectucut, Georgia, Illinois, Kentucky, Maryland, Massachusetts, New York, Ohio, Oregon, Pennsylvania, and Tennessee.

Virginia

Philip L. Martin's article, "VIRGINIANS REAPPORTION OWN COUNTIES" in *American County Government,* 32 (October, 1967), 55, is a notation of the fact that Virginia's state code provides for reapportionment by a citizens' commission and therefore does not require a judicial command. The author explains the procedure to be followed and the historical origins of this provision. He analyzes what he believes to be the chief defect of the system—the circuit judge's participation in the selection of the citizens' commission.

This article is a clear, informative explanation of the procedure followed in one state for handling an important matter. At the time of this publication, the author was Associate Professor of Political Science, Virginia Polytechnic Institute.

ALSO TO BE NOTED—FOR REFORM: REAPPORTIONMENT:

General

Citizens Research Council of Michigan, *Apportionment of County Boards of Supervisors, Michigan and Other States,* Memorandum No. 212 (Detroit: 1965, 21 pp.).

Robert G. Dixon, "New Constitutional Forms for Metropolis; Reapportioned County Boards; Local Councils of Governments," *Law and Contemporary Problems*, 30 (Winter, 1965), 57-75.

Bernard F. Hillenbrand, "Is Reapportionment a Threat to Counties?" *The County Officer,* 29 (November, 1964), 471.

______, "Reapportionment and Home Rule," *The County Officer,* 29 (August, 1964), 335.

Jack B. Weinstein, *The Impact of the Supreme Court on Reapportionment of County Government* (New York: National Municipal League, National Conference, 1964, 21 pp.).

Individual States

John F. Gallagher, *Apportionment in California Counties: The Impacts of Judicial Decisions* (Davis: University of California, Institute of Governmental Affairs, 1964).

William W. Siegal, "Court Orders Redistricting of Counties in California," *The County Officer,* 29 (July, 1964), 314.

Richard A. Atkins, *Reapportionment and Local Government,* Pamphlet Series No. 1 (Albany: New York, Executive Department, Office for Local Government, 1965, 9 pp.).

New York Executive Department, Office for Local Government, *Proceedings of the Conference on Reapportionment of Local Government Legislative Bodies* (Albany: 1965, 85 pp.).

______, *Reapportionment—Local Government Legislative Bodies,* No. 1 (January 31, 1966)—No. 10 (November 30, 1967).

Joseph S. Ferrell, "Area Representation in North Carolina Counties," *Popular Government,* 33 (September, 1966), 18-25.

John M. Hunger, *Equal Representation on Wisconsin County Boards* (Madison: University of Wisconsin, Bureau of Government, 1963, 33 pp.).

Richard L. Stauber, *County Apportionment Plans and Problems of Equality* (Madison: University of Wisconsin, University Extension, Institute of Government Affairs, 1965, 24 pp.).

SERVICES

General

United States

In Chapter 4 of COUNTY GOVERNMENT IN AMERICA (Washington: National Association of Counties, Research Foundation, 1966, 288 pp.), Herbert S. Duncombe discusses county services. He reports the results of different surveys undertaken to determine the number and types of services provided by counties throughout the nation. He points out the extent of optional services and the amount of joint provision of them. He analyzes why counties are providing urban services and how activity in this area grows.

Professor Duncombe provides brief descriptions of a number of general governmental services: assessment and collection of property taxes, election administration, judicial administration, recording of legal documents, other general government functions, agriculture, education and libraries, and health and welfare. He distinguishes the different types of health and welfare activities and describes some of the institutions maintained by the county. He gives a good explanation of the expansion of county activity in providing parks and recreational facilities.

The author's coverage of physical planning and development in the county is quite extensive. He discusses the different methods of organization of planning activity and explains the uses of zoning and subdivision regulation. He discusses how and why the county participates in urban renewal, points out the growing number of counties which are using building codes, housing codes, and public housing to aid their residents, and explains the measures being used by counties to encourage industrial development.

Public safety, including law enforcement, fire protection, and civil defense, is described. Professor Duncombe discusses the growing cooperation among local units in this field. The final area of county services the author investigates is public works and transportation. He explains the conditions which cause increased public works activity by the county and discusses the problems of providing adequate highways and the reasons for transfer of this function to the state level. He describes the additional problems experienced by metropolitan counties, discussing their increased involvement in mass transportation, the extent of their ownership of airports, and the problems encountered in providing water, sewage, and refuse facilities.

An extensive table is included on the percentage of counties furnishing selected services. A second table shows the percentage of reporting counties of various population classes that provide services by themselves or jointly with another governmental unit. Tables are included on the public school systems in the United States and on the number of public library systems by major source of support.

Alabama

Chapter III of James D. Thomas' monograph, A MANUAL FOR ALABAMA COUNTY COMMISSIONERS (University: University of Alabama, Bureau of Public Administration, 1963, 96 pp.), discusses county highway administration, and Chapter V examines other county functions and services. The former chapter describes the powers of the governing board in the establishment of road and highway systems within the counties and examines variations among the counties in the administration of the highway function. Many aspects of the office of county engineer are explored. The nature of county road contracts with independent, private firms is explained. The sources of funds for county highway construction and maintenance are described, a lengthy treatment of state aid is presented, and state-county highway relations are analyzed.

Chapter V examines county administration of elections. Included are analyses of statutes about election districts, voting machines, and election costs. There is a short section on the nature of county agricultural extension services. A lengthy section is devoted to county planning and zoning activities: it describes county powers to engage in general planning and to participate in regional planning activities. The content and adoption of a county or regional master plan are discussed, and actual county activities in planning are briefly scrutinized. County powers to adopt zoning and subdivision regulations are also mentioned. An interesting county practice explained in this chapter is the use of public building authorities to provide county buildings in order to avoid issuing general obligation bonds. The chapter also analyzes statutes which relate to county provision of the following municipal-type services: public utilities, airports, hospitals, water conservation and irrigation, forest protection, recreation, and public housing.

California

The County Supervisors Association of California has published data on the number of county-city functional consolidations in each California county for the years 1956, 1960, and 1964. These data are contained in charts which give the total number of consolidations in each county for various functions: assessing, tax collection, personnel services, public health services, library services, dog control, election services, prisoner care, law enforcement communication, civil defense, ambulance service, maps, road laboratory service, building inspection, planning, airports, flood control, recreation, and miscellaneous functions. The title of the charts is COUNTY-CITY FUNCTIONAL CONSOLIDATION IN CALIFORNIA (Sacramento: 1964, 4 pp.). A comparison of the charts for the three years illustrates trends in county-city functional consolidation.

Hawaii

One section of the Public Administration Service report, STATE AND LOCAL GOVERNMENT RELATIONSHIPS

IN THE STATE OF HAWAII (Chicago: 1962, 234 pp.), examines the services of Hawaii counties generally, a later section looks at specific services. The general section begins with an analysis of state-assigned services that counties must perform. This is followed by a discussion of the municipal-type services of counties: fire and police; public works; parks and recreation; hospitals; planning, zoning, subdivision control, and building inspection; regulatory and inspectional services, such as air pollution control, motor vehicle registration, and sanitation services; water supply and distribution; and civil defense. The section outlines county responsibilities in these services and describes their administration and financing.

A later section looks at county involvement in services that are essentially county-state shared functions: education, health and welfare, and public works and transportation. With regard to education, the report explains the manner in which counties provide a large proportion of the finances for education but in which the state exercises control over most educational policy-making and strictly supervises the administration of the schools. There is also a description of the division of health and welfare responsibilities between the state and the counties, with the latter having a relatively small role. The division of responsibility in public works and transportation is also outlined. Considerable emphasis is given to the major role of counties in the construction and maintenance of highways. The efficiency of Hawaii counties in providing highways is compared with that of counties in the other states, and a number of criticisms are leveled against the former. Several tables present figures on county highway finance. The functions of county departments of public works are outlined. Finally, some conflicts that have developed between the counties and the state in the field of public works and transportation are identified.

Maryland

A very large section of Jean E. Spencer's CONTEMPORARY LOCAL GOVERNMENT IN MARYLAND (College Park: University of Maryland, Bureau of Governmental Research, 1965, 116 pp.) deals with the functions of county government. Particular emphasis is given to the variations among Maryland counties in the kinds of services provided and in the means through which counties furnish them. The intergovernmental aspects of providing services is also given attention.

The status of local governments as "local program agents and participants" is first examined. Then the following functions performed by counties largely as state agents are considered: education, welfare, health, roads and highways, and liquor control.

The discussion moves to the role of the county as a provider of urban, municipal-type services, and the increasing viability of Maryland counties as urban and metropolitan governments is explored. Specific urban services of counties in Maryland—fire protection, police protection, sewerage systems, water supply, refuse collection and disposal, planning and zoning, and others—are considered in detail.

Massachusetts

The Massachusetts Legislative Research Council has made a detailed study of the services of county government in Massachusetts in its report, COUNTY GOVERNMENT IN MASSACHUSETTS (Boston: 1962, 167 pp.). The introductory chapter presents an overview of county services. It details the services which Massachusetts counties provide and describes the variations among the counties in the extent to which they provide these services, as well as discussing the annual expenditures for each. Among the services considered in the report are: courts; health and hospitals; public works, including public building maintenance, highways, airports, waterways and dams; planning; county sheriffs' activities and the operation of jails; activities of the district attorneys, medical examiners, registries of deeds, law libraries, masters in chancery, public administrators and registries of probate; education (agriculture and training schools); agricultural aid; parks and recreation; civil defense; and fire fighting.

Later chapters treat each service separately and cover the responsibilities of the various county officers and boards for their operation. The division of responsibility for these services and the relations between the state and the counties are also explored. The exact nature of the services is explained, with emphasis upon the limited nature of county operations. Many past proposals for change in county administration are examined.

At the Tenth Massachusetts Governor's Conference, Leo Nourse, then Commissioner of Plymouth County, Massachusetts, delivered a paper that briefly outlines the functions of county government in Massachusetts. It is deceivingly titled "LOCAL INTERGOVERNMENTAL RELATIONS THROUGH THE COUNTY" and is contained in *The Proceedings of the Tenth Governor's Conference* (Amherst: University of Massachusetts, Bureau of Governmental Research, 1958, pp. 19-21). The general topic of the Conference was intergovernmental relations in Massachusetts. The paper is largely a descriptive listing of functions and contains little analysis.

New Jersey

James M. Collier's COUNTY GOVERNMENT IN NEW JERSEY (New Brunswick: Rutgers University, Bureau of Government Research, 1952, 64 pp.) includes much material on county services. A section of Chapter 3 considers county law enforcement; it describes county activities in the apprehension of lawbreakers, prosecution of suspects and those convicted for short terms, and probation. The author analyzes the powers and duties of the following county officers, employees, and departments having law enforcement responsibilities: sheriffs, police, detectives, investigators, coroners and medical examiners, prosecutors, probation officers, and probation departments.

Chapter 4 scrutinizes other county functions. The nature of the county welfare board is explored and its functions listed. Each county welfare program – including old age assistance, almshouses and welfare houses, disability assistance, foster home care, aid to dependent children, child welfare services, aid to the handicapped, and aid to crippled children – is scrutinized.

County health activities are considered. The functions of the county health departments are described, and the level of their actual services analyzed, and the means of establishing such departments discussed. The functions of the six kinds of county hospitals and the extent of county operation of them are discussed, and other county health activities—health clinics, mosquito extermination, and sewage disposal—are explained.

The author deals with county activities in education. The functions of the county superintendent of schools are described, and the educational activities of the county agricultural and home demonstration agents are laid out. The extent and characteristics of county vocational education programs and the selection and functions of the county boards of education are discussed. A briefer section notes the extent of as well as means of administration of county activities in parks and recreation.

An examination of county powers and responsibilities in the construction and maintainance of roads and highways follows. Here, the author discusses the administration of the county highway system through the county highway department, which is headed by a supervisor of roads. The nature of state grants-in-aid for highways is considered. The selection, powers, and responsibilities of the county planning board are described; the manner in which counties administer the conduct of elections explained; and the responsibilities of the county clerk, county superintendent of elections, and the county board of elections in election administration examined. Also, county depository or recordkeeping activities are explored, and, in this connection, the functions of the county clerk, surrogate, and register of deeds and mortgages are noted.

North Carolina

Clyde L. Ball's study, THE AUTHORITY OF THE GENERAL ASSEMBLY TO VEST POWER IN, AND TO IMPOSE DUTIES UPON, COUNTIES AND CITIES (Chapel Hill: University of North Carolina, Institute of Government, July 1960, 21 pp.), deals in part with state-local constitutional and statutory relations in North Carolina. The focus of the study is on how judicial decisions have shaped these relations and have resulted in new activities for county government.

The author first examines the constitutional limitations placed on the county and the duties concerning the county imposed on the state. He then analyzes court cases which affect the ability of the legislature to delegate powers to the county. He describes how many of these court decisions have resulted in the county's being charged with many new functions and sharing others originally considered to be strictly municipal. The author's conclusions regarding the future functions of the county are very interesting. His findings are well-documented, principally with citations to court cases.

ALSO TO BE NOTED—FOR SERVICES:

General

Carson Bain, "County Government and City People," *The County Officer,* 25 (October, 1960), 356-357, 368.

Russell M. Ross, "Twentieth Century Functions: The Ultimate Salvation of the County," *The County Officer,* 21 (April, 1956), 64-65.

Individual States

C. J. Hein, "Kansas Counties: Basic Administrative Areas for Many Services," *The County Officer,* 20 (October, 1955), 214-216.

SERVICES

Agriculture and Conservation

United States

Chapter 18 of Clyde F. Snider's LOCAL GOVERNMENT IN RURAL AMERICA (New York: Appleton-Century-Crofts, 1957, 584 pp.) encompasses a very informative and detailed discussion of agriculture and conservation activities of local government. The chapter begins with a description and discussion of the purposes of agricultural extension. The author explains the county's role in administration of this program, describes in detail the work of the county and home demonstration agents, and points out the activity of the farm bureau in rural areas. He discusses the county's activities in weed control, control of predators, soil erosion, public land management, and operation of parks and forests. He discusses at length the extent and uses of rural zoning, giving many examples, particularly from the Midwest.[2]

ALSO TO BE NOTED—FOR SERVICES: AGRICULTURE AND CONSERVATION

General

National Association of Counties Research Foundation, *Community Action Program for Air Pollution Control,* Nos. 1-8 (Washington: 1966-1967, v.p.).

______, *Community Action Program for Water Pollution Control,* Revised edition (Washington: 1967, 182 pp.).

Individual States

"Mid-Valley Counties [in Oregon] Attack Air Pollution," *OAC Bulletin,* 7 (July, 1965), 1, 3.

SERVICES

Law Enforcement

United States

Russell J. Arend's article, "INDEPENDENT COUNTY POLICE AGENCIES," *American County Government,* 32 (May, 1967), 38-40, is a brief description of an emerging type of law enforcement agency in counties—a police system independent of the sheriff's office. The article is based on the data obtained from responses to a 1966 questionnaire survey conducted jointly by the National Association of Counties and the Automotive Safety Foundation.

The author points out the geographic locations in which these

2. From this point on in the bibliographical commentary, the entries are limited in number and are simply illustrative of many more that could be presented. Many of these entries have been derived from general items discussed earlier in this commentary.

new forces are being used and outlines the general functions for which such a police organization is responsible. He uses specific examples to point out the variations in type and extent of service rendered and of personnel strength in different counties. He concludes the article by describing the type of equipment generally employed by these agencies and the salary and work-week range for the officers.

An excellent chart provides data on the counties that have these independent police forces and on the organization of these agencies. In general, this article is a straightforward presentation of the basic data on this new type of service in counties. At the time of the publication of this article, Mr. Arend was associated with the Safety Division of the Automotive Safety Foundation.

In his monograph, TRAFFIC INVESTIGATION RESPONSIBILITIES OF COUNTY LAW ENFORCEMENT AGENCIES (Washington: Automotive Safety Foundation, 1967, 71 pp.), Russell J. Arend examines the nature, extent, and regional variations of traffic investigation responsibilities of county law-enforcement agencies and how certain characteristics of existing county programs differ from those of a model he constructs. The basic data for his study are questionnaire responses from more than 1,000 county sheriffs' departments and independent county law enforcement units.

After a brief introduction, the author explains his methodology and describes the ideal model to which he later compares actual county accident investigation practices. He then presents a review of the literature on accident investigation, including material on the development of the county as a police unit. A chapter follows on the extent to which counties have responsibilities in accident investigation. Variations are reported regionally and by county population size; sheriffs' departments and independent police agencies are analyzed separately. This chapter also gives information on the types of roads over which county law-enforcement agencies exercise jurisdiction.

The author then compares county practices with the ideal model which he developed earlier. The four basic elements of comparison are: the sufficiency of accident-investigation training for recruits, the adequacy of such training on a regular in-service basis, the extent of filing of police traffic accident reports and the use of accident-location spot maps, and the existence of the practice of forwarding copies of accident-investigation reports to the state accident records agency. The author found that many county sheriffs' departments and other law-enforcement organizations fell below the standards of the model on each dimension. The monograph also includes appendixes which contain the questionnaire as well as detailed tabulations of the data.

The author has made an excellent empirical study of this specialized but important subject. The monograph is a condensed version of the author's master of science thesis at Michigan State University.

Although Arthur C. Millspaugh, in LOCAL DEMOCRACY AND CRIME CONTROL (Washington: The Brookings Institution, 1936, 263 pp.), is not as concerned with crime control as the title might indicate, a preponderant amount of the specifics of the analysis refer to this function.

Early in the book, when the traditional operation of county government is being described, the author presents detailed descriptions of the functions of the sheriff, the county police, and the prosecuting attorney. He emphasizes the areas in which the traditional organization of these functions is weakest. He describes state-county relations in the crime control field, analyzes the amount of transfer of this activity to the state level accomplished in spite of the entrenched position of these local officers, and compares the per capita expenses of crime control in urban and rural counties. When concentrating on internal reorganization of counties, he considers the possible effect of administrative unification on crime control.

Chapter VIII is concerned exclusively with crime control integration. The author discusses the impediments to reorganization and describes steps needed in state reorganization of this function before the local-state allocation of responsibility can be altered. Then he analyzes the reorganization that must be effected at the county level before functions can be reallocated, including changes to be made in the organization and operation of the offices of sheriff and prosecuting attorney. Throughout the entire discussion, he emphasizes the need to have local policing and local prosecution separated before and during reorganization.

SERVICES
Planning

United States

Robert M. Anderson and Bruce B. Roswig have compiled the state statutory provisions for county planning, zoning, and subdivision in their book, PLANNING, ZONING AND SUBDIVISION: A SUMMARY OF STATUTORY LAW IN THE 50 STATES (Albany: New York State Federation of Official Planning Organizations, 1966, 231 pp.). This volume includes state-by-state summaries of state-enabling legislation for county planning and zoning commissions, planning departments or planning staffs, various types of zoning adjustment boards, subdivision controls, official maps, zoning ordinances, and other county agencies and legal devices related to county planning, zoning and subdivision.

California

Based on his experience as a member of the Butte County (California) Planning Commission, Lew Oliver made a rather impressionistic analysis of the county planning function in a speech before the 5th Biennial County Government Institute for New County Supervisors. In this speech, "THE ROLE OF PLANNING IN MODERN COUNTY GOVERNMENT" (Sacramento: County Supervisors Association of California, 1961, 15 pp.), Professor Oliver is prescriptive and discusses at length what he calls "The Ten Commandments for the County Planning Commission and Board of Supervisors." He presents an interesting analysis of the roles of the planning commission and the board of supervisors and of the relations between them. He also includes an enlightening examination of the use of consultants by rural counties. These bits of analysis are, however, caught in a rambling prescriptive discourse. At the time of this publication, the author was on the faculty of Chico State College.

Delaware

In Chapter 22 of his book, THE GOVERNMENT AND ADMINISTRATION OF DELAWARE (New York: Thomas Y. Crowell, 1956, 396 pp.), Paul Dolan takes a comprehensive look at the county's role in planning and development in Delaware, focusing mainly on the work in New Castle County. Professor Dolan traces the development of the Regional Planning Commission of New Castle County since its formation in 1931 and describes its organization and activity. He considers the composition of county park and recreation commissions and cites specific examples from New Castle County. He discusses the importance of zoning as a factor in planning and development, citing the work of the New Castle Zoning Commission. Throughout the discussion, the author is careful to explain the connection of the levy court, which is the governing body of the county, with these efforts.

Georgia

Hal A. Davis, in "SPECIFIC PROGRAMS FOR PARTICULAR NEEDS," *Georgia County Government Magazine* (May, 1965), 20-23, discusses intercounty planning in Georgia. The article centers on the role of the Coastal Plains Area Planning and Development Commission in the economic and physical development of nine counties in the state. Cooperative programs for planning and development and plans for recreation and transportation are discussed. The article is descriptive, using primary sources. At the time of this publication, the author was Executive Director, Coastal Plains Area Planning and Development Commission.

In "NINE RURAL GEORGIA COUNTIES ORGANIZE REGIONAL DEVELOPMENT," *American County Government,* 30 (October, 1965), 18-19, Max Harral discusses economic development in the state. The article describes area planning commissions in Georgia, indicating whether they are located in rural or urban areas. The organization, membership, and functions (including economic development activities) of a nine-county planning commission are considered. At the time of this publication, the author was Executive Director, Slash Pine Area Planning and Development Commission.

Carroll C. Underwood, in "AREA COUNTY PLANNING IN GEORGIA," *Georgia County Government Magazine,* 16 (January, 1965), 8-9, discusses planning and development in thirteen counties of the state. The discussion centers around the role of the Southwest Georgia Planning Development Commission. County planning in the past and the probable effects of the commission are considered, and planning cooperation is discussed. At the time of this publication, the author was Executive Director, Southwest Georgia Area Planning and Development Commission.

ALSO TO BE NOTED—FOR SERVICES: PLANNING:

General

American Society of Planning Officials, Chicago, *ASPO Newsletter.*

Norman Beckman, "County Planning and HUD Goals," *American County Government,* 32 (September, 1967), 77-78.

Karl Bessler, "The County and Community Aesthetics," *American County Government,* 31 (March, 1966), 48-49.

"Bridges and Building Blocks," *American County Government,* 31 (September, 1966), 55, 63.

William K. Brussat, *The County's Role in Planning for Regional Problems* (Washington: United States Bureau of the Budget, 1966, 12 pp.).

Thomas Haga, "The County Chameleon," *American County Government,* 32 (November, 1967), 16-18.

Alastair McArthur, "The Urban County and its Role in Metropolitan Planning," in Drew University, Institute for Research on Government, *Metropolitan Problems* (Madison, N.J.: 1963, pp. 75-82).

Frank E. Moss, "Local-Federal Partnership in Meeting Human Problems," *American County Government,* 30 (September, 1965), 32, 81.

National Association of Counties, *The County Planning Congress: Proceedings of the 28th Annual Conference of the National Association of Counties* (Washington: 1963, 72 pp.).

———, *Federal Aid Guide for Local Governments,* Information and Education Service Report No. 18 (Washington: 1962, n.p.).

National Association of County Engineers, *County Development—Volume I: Comprehensive Planning* (Washington: 1964, 46 pp.).

United States Senate, Committee on Government Operations, Subcommittee on Intergovernmental Relations, *The Effectiveness of Metropolitan Planning* (Washington: 1964, 209 pp.).

______, *1964 Survey of Metropolitan Planning* (Washington: 1965, 121 pp.).

Individual States

Chancellor's Committee on Regional Planning, *Proceedings, Third Annual Institute on Regional Planning—the Role of the County in Regional Planning* (Davis: University of California Extension, University of California, Davis, 1964, 80 pp.).

Elizabeth F. Goodwin and John C. Buechner, *Federal Aids Available for County Planning in Colorado* (Boulder: University of Colorado, Bureau of Governmental Research and Service, 1966, 53 pp.).

Thera H. Righter and Pauline D. Palmer, *Area Planning and Development in Georgia* (Atlanta: Georgia Department of Industry and Trade, Planning Division, 1965, 61 pp.).

Minnesota Department of Business Development, Division of Community Planning, *Planning for Minnesota Communities* (St. Paul: 1965, 24 pp.).

"Planning in New Jersey," *ASPO Newsletter,* 28 (May, 1962), 47-53.

New Jersey Department of Conservation and Economic Development, Division of State and Regional Planning, *The Setting for Regional Planning in New Jersey* (Trenton: 1961, 100 pp.).

Anthony W. Wiles, "Planning to Channel Growth [in New Jersey]," *American County Government,* 31 (February, 1966), 36-37.

New York Department of Commerce, *Local Planning and Zoning* (Albany: 1966, 129 pp.).

"County Planning Grows in Oregon," *AOC Bulletin,* 7 (May, 1965), 4.

James G. Coke and Thomas Anton, *Planning in the Penjerdel Region* (Philadelphia: Pennsylvania-New Jersey-Delaware Metropolitan Project, 1962, 38 pp.).

"Planning in Philadelphia and the Delaware Valley," *ASPO Newsletter,* 32 (March, 1966), 26-32.

SERVICES

Poverty Program

United States

"THE WAR IS ON POVERTY," *American County Government,* 31 (September, 1966), 22-24, 50, is an abridged version of a speech given by Sargent Shriver, then Director of the national

Office of Economic Opportunity. The article begins with a description of the organization of the Office of Economic Opportunity and advisory committees to it. The goals of the OEO are examined, and the relationship of county government to local poverty programs is discussed.

ALSO TO BE NOTED—FOR SERVICES: POVERTY PROGRAM:

United States Office of Economic Opportunity, *County Government in the Nation's War on Poverty* (Washington: 1966, 2 pp.).

SERVICES

Public Health

California

H. D. Chope presents an extensive discussion of the county public health function in his paper, "COUNTY HEALTH DEPARTMENT OPERATIONS," in County Supervisors Association of California, *County Government, 1959: Proceedings, 4th Biennial County Government Institute* (Sacramento: 1959, pp. 91-98). The author examines the extent to which California counties have undertaken public health activities and presents an outline delineating county public health responsibilities in environmental sanitation, communicable disease control, maternal and child health, human accounting, public health laboratory service, and health education. Much of the discussion is devoted to county mental health activities under the Short-Doyle Act. The paper is a descriptive presentation; the author does not seek to analyze or prescribe. At the time of this publication, the author was Director, San Mateo County Department of Public Health.

Michigan

The constitutional and statutory provisions for the county public health functions are examined in Michigan State University, Bureau of Social and Political Research, THE COUNTY BOARD OF SUPERVISORS (East Lansing: 1959, 152 pp.). The establishment by the board of supervisors of a county public health department under a county board of health is discussed. The method of instituting an intercounty public health district or city-county health department is also explored, and the apportionment of expenses of the district among participating counties or between city and county is examined. State regulation over county health functions and employees is considered. The selection, qualifications, and duties of public health nurses are explained. County health functions and pertinent statutory regulations are set forth; particular emphasis is given to the role of the board of supervisors. Consideration is given to the financing, construction, and maintenance of county hospitals. The method of selection and functions of the county board of hospital trustees are detailed. County tuberculosis sanitariums are briefly mentioned. In the remainder of the section on public health, the office of county coroner is discussed, specifically, the method of selection, means of abolishing the office, and use of trained medical examiners.

An interesting study of the pattern of intergovernmental relations in the Michigan public health program – which has developed as a result of federal aid to public health activities – is contained in a chapter of a report by the Public Administration Service to the United States Commission on Intergovernmental Relations. The report is THE FEDERAL GRANT-IN-AID SYSTEM – ITS IMPACT IN THE STATE OF MICHIGAN (Chicago: May, 1954, 163 pp.). Since counties are eligible for federal aid channeled through the state along with other local governments, the county role in intergovernmental relationships stimulated by federal aid is only indirectly considered.

The report discusses a number of topics concerning local government in relation to federal public health grants to the state. Those considered include state agencies which channel federal aid for public health purposes to local governments; method of allocation of state and federal aid funds to local government; individual federal public health grant programs, such as venereal disease control, heart disease control, and Hill-Burton hospitals; local accounting for federal aid; effects of federal regulations on the quality of local public health personnel; the effects of federal aid on local public health programs; and effects of federal aid on state-local relationships in public health programs.

Minnesota

Mike Gorman, in "THE ROLE OF THE COUNTY IN HELPING OUR MENTALLY ILL," *American County Government,* 31 (May, 1966), 13-14, presents statistics and national legislation on mental health and discusses mental health programs in Minnesota. The organization and activities of such programs in Minnesota are considered and their effects on county efforts in this field examined. At the time of this publication, the author was Executive Director, National Committee Against Mental Illness.

SERVICES

Public Welfare

Kansas

The chapter on public welfare in James W. Drury and Associates, THE GOVERNMENT OF KANSAS (Lawrence: University of Kansas Press, 1961, 393 pp.) deserves attention because of its extensive coverage and analysis of the county's welfare activities. The authors begin with a historical development of the county's responsibility for welfare services and then cover the county's role in public assistance administration, child welfare, services to the blind, services for the aging. They explain how the boards of county commissioners serve as county boards of social welfare and discuss the composition of the welfare staff, focusing on the role of the welfare director. They explain the assessment of a property tax for support of county welfare services and describe the preparation and use of county welfare budgets. In a discussion of trends and future developments, they consider the effect of inadequate financing at local levels, the areas of discretion and influence enjoyed by county boards, and the increasing demands on the county to participate in institutional programs.

Michigan

A discussion of the constitutional and statutory provisions concerning county welfare functions is contained in Michigan State University, Bureau of Social and Political Research, THE COUNTY BOARD OF SUPERVISORS (East Lansing: 1959, 152 pp.). The first topic of discussion is state supervision of county welfare functions. An examination of county welfare activities then follows. The role of the state welfare commission as the dispenser of state and federal aid to counties is mentioned, and the powers of the county social welfare board and the supervisor of the county bureau of social aid are presented in detail. The status and interrelationships of the county welfare department and the bureau of social aid are explained. Intercounty district departments of social welfare are also considered. The method of selection and the powers and duties of the county director of social welfare are set forth, and the functions of the county welfare department are laid out in detail. County medical aid facilities for the indigent are mentioned, and the child welfare work done by the probation officer under the direction of the juvenile division of the probate court is discussed. Brief examination is made of the financing of county welfare functions.

An interesting study of the pattern of intergovernmental relations in the public welfare program in Michigan is contained in a chapter of a report by the Public Administration Service to the United States Commission on Intergovernmental Relations, THE FEDERAL GRANT-IN-AID SYSTEM—ITS IMPACT IN THE STATE OF MICHIGAN (Chicago: May 1954, 163 pp.). Since the county is the unit of government in Michigan which locally administers the public welfare program, any study of the impact of federal aid on the public welfare program in Michigan necessarily involves county government. Among the topics concerning the impact of federal aid on county welfare functions are: a brief history of the evolution of the county welfare program since the Federal Emergency Relief and Reconstruction Act of 1932, particularly the change in the county's relationship to the state in the welfare field; analysis of the present relationship between the county and the state in welfare programs and the effects of federal aid upon the relationship; county organization for performance of welfare activities; a general discussion of the child welfare program, especially its intergovernmental aspects; the effects of the federal welfare program's categorical structure and federal requirements on county administration of the welfare program; and the state welfare plan.

Montana

In the chapter on public welfare in his book, THE GOVERNMENT AND ADMINISTRATION OF MONTANA (New York: Thomas Y. Crowell, 1958, 508 pp.), Roland R. Renne gives a description of the county's role in this field. He describes the organization of the county welfare board and discusses its duties. He considers its organization and position vis-a-vis the board of the county welfare department whose personnel is originally selected by the county governing board. He outlines the supervision exercised by the state Department of Public Welfare over the activities of the department. When he explains the operations of the county departments, he shows at what point the county board and state board participate. The actual administration of service to recipients is described in detail.

The author describes the taxes that the county board of commissioners is authorized to levy for public welfare, discusses state supervision of the preparation of the county welfare budget, and mentions the operation of a county poor farm and the letting of contracts by the county board for the care of the poor.

Included in coverage of administration and financing of various welfare programs is discussion of old-age assistance, child welfare, care of the needy blind, care of the permanently and totally disabled, and general relief. The section concludes with a discussion of the need for and methods of improving the public welfare program.

North Carolina

Chapter 15 of Robert S. Rankin's THE GOVERNMENT AND ADMINISTRATION OF NORTH CAROLINA (New York: Thomas Y. Crowell, 1955, 429 pp.) is devoted to a discussion of public welfare in the state. The author presents a detailed picture of the relation between state and local units and their cooperative efforts in administering welfare programs. He lists the duties of the various divisions of the State Board of Public Welfare which relate to local administration, points out the administrative aspects of children's services handled by the county, and notes state-county relations in this field. The inspection activities engaged in by state agencies of county institutions are explained. The general liaison between the state department and county welfare boards is discussed.

The author explains the extent of administration carried on at the local level and discusses the duties, especially the financial ones, of the county welfare board. He lists and explains the duties of the county superintendent and gives attention to the work of the Veterans' Commission and to the provision of juvenile detention facilities.

SERVICES

Public Works

United States

An article by Bernard F. Hillenbrand, "CAN OUR COUNTIES CUT BACK ON CAPITAL PROJECT SPENDING?" *American County Government,* 31 (June, 1966), 6, treats the subject of capital project expenditures. The first section describes the need for the counties to finance various kinds of capital projects. An examination is then made of what the counties and the national government can do in order to economize and cut back on county capital expenditures in times of inflation and war. At the time of this publication, the author was Executive Director, National Association of Counties.

California

Victor W. Sauer has written an extensive paper on the county public works function in California, "ADMINISTRATION OF COUNTY HIGHWAYS AND PUBLIC WORKS," in County Supervisors Association of California, *County Government, 1959: Proceedings, 4th Biennial County Government Institute* (Sacramento: 1959, pp. 139-151).

The paper begins with an examination of the functions and duties of county public works officials. The author presents a chart showing the different kinds of county public works officials established by statute and their required qualifications. To illustrate the variations in the patterns of public works administrative arrangements, the author cites examples from several counties. The office of county road commissioner is discussed, and the relationship between this commissioner, or a county engineer who performs his duties, and the county board of supervisors is explained. The use of management consultants to review county public works operations is examined.

The paper is largely descriptive, although both analysis and prescriptions are included. The author uses both primary and secondary sources, the former including statutory law and personal experience. At the time of this publication, the author was Public Works Director, Contra Costa County.

Louisiana

In its book, THE GOVERNMENT OF LOUISIANA (Baton Rouge: 1951, 405 pp.), the Louisiana Legislative Council emphasizes that highway administration is one of the principal duties of the parish government. In the chapter on the major functions of government, the authors describe at length the activities of the parish in highway administration. Only brief mention is given to the ward system of administration which receives merely limited use; however, the operation of the unit system is described more fully. The three-part classification of roads in the state and the extent of the parish road system are explained.

Michigan

Michigan State University, Bureau of Social and Political Research, THE COUNTY BOARD OF SUPERVISORS (East Lansing: 1959, 152 pp.), devotes a section (pp. 77-86) of this publication to an examination of the constitutional and statutory provisions for the public works functions of Michigan counties. A description is given of the powers and responsibilities of the board of supervisors for public roads and highways, and the process of adoption of a county road system is explained. There follows a general discussion of the board of county road commissioners, including the method of their selection, term of office, powers, and responsibilities. The establishment of intercounty highway systems and intercounty road commissions is discussed. Considerable attention is given to the financing of county road and highway construction and maintenance. The powers of the board of supervisors to establish and operate a port district within the county are examined.

The election, compensation, term of office, powers and functions of the county drain commissioner are examined, and the operation of county and intercounty drainage districts is explored. The formation of intercounty water management districts and commissions is also considered.

Certain Michigan counties may establish departments of public works. The method of establishing such an agency and the composition, method of selection, and powers of the county board of public works are explained. The public works functions of water supply, sewage disposal, rubbish collection, and water pollution abatement are discussed, with particular attention to financing and intergovernmental contracts.

ALSO TO BE NOTED—FOR SERVICES: PUBLIC WORKS:

General

National Association of Counties Research Foundation, *Highway Planning on the County Level,* Information and Education Service Report No. 12 (Washington: 1961, 10 pp.)

National Association of County Engineers, *County Road Management Actions* (Washington: 1958, 20 pp.).

Philip Warren, "Counties in Midst of Greatest Public Works Building Program in History, NACO Survey Shows," *The County Officer,* 28 (October, 1963), 364-365.

Individual States

"County Road Study Shows $621 Million Needs [in Oregon]," *AOC Bulletin,* 6 (May, 1964), 1, 6-7.

Will Wilson, "Importance of County to Local Self-Government is Stressed [in Texas]," *County Progress,* 31 (July, 1954), 5-6, 18, 20.

SERVICES

Recreation

United States

Morton Grodzins in Chapter 5 of THE AMERICAN SYSTEM (Chicago: Rand McNally, 1966, 404 pp.), edited by Daniel J. Elazar, discusses county recreation activities. Examples are given of county forests and county parks. The many types of federal grants that directly and indirectly aid county recreation are described, and the vast variations in state assistance presented.

ALSO TO BE NOTED—FOR SERVICES: RECREATION:

General

National Association of Counties, *County Action for Outdoor Recreation* (Washington: 1964, 48 pp.).

National Association of Counties Research Foundation, *Outdoor Recreation, Community Action Program for Public Officials,* Nos. 1-10 (Washington: 1967-1968, v.p.).

Joseph Prendergast, "The County's Role in Public Recreation," *The County Officer,* 26 (May, 1961), 140-141, 156.

Individual States

North Carolina Recreation Commission, *County Recreation in North Carolina* (Raleigh: 1966, 10 pp.).

"Counties Act to Qualify for Park Funds [in Oregon]," *AOC Bulletin,* 8 (February, 1966), 1, 4.

Robert E. Stipe, "The Trends Toward County Control [in North Carolina]," *American County Government,* 31 (August, 1966), 40-41.

ALSO TO BE NOTED—FOR SERVICES: OTHER SERVICES:

General

"County Civil Defense Activities Take Many Forms, Stress Ideas," *The County Officer,* 29 (November, 1964), 482.

National Association of Counties, *The County Official's Community Relations Manual* (Washington: n.d., v.p.).

Paul E. Pierce, "Why Keep It Secret? Counties Are Big Business," *American County Government,* 31 (April, 1966), 41 [Public Information].

Individual States

Leslie J. Pryde, "The Uniform County Systems Plan in EDP [in California]," *American County Government,* 31 (August, 1966), 16-17, 22.

"Counties Act in Christmas Floods [in Oregon]," *OAC Bulletin,* 7 (January, 1965), 1, 3-4 [Civil Defense].

"County Library Standards [in Oregon]," *AOC Bulletin,* 6 (May, 1964), 7.

"Total Resource Development Charts Path for Economic Growth of Wisconsin Counties," *The County Officer,* 29 (December, 1964), 514-515.

INDEX OF AUTHORS

INDEX OF TITLES